Learning Vocabulary in Another Language

THE CAMBRIDGE APPLIED LINGUISTICS SERIES

Series editors: Michael H. Long and Jack C. Richards

This series presents the findings of work in applied linguistics which are of direct relevance to language teaching and learning and of particular interest to applied linguists, researchers, language teachers, and teacher trainers.

Recent publications in this series:

Learning Vocabulary in Another Language

I. S. P. Nation
Victoria University of Wellington

CAMBRIDGE
UNIVERSITY PRESS

PUBLISHED BY THE PRESS SYNDICATE OF THE UNIVERSITY OF CAMBRIDGE
The Pitt Building, Trumpington Street, Cambridge, United Kingdom

CAMBRIDGE UNIVERSITY PRESS
The Edinburgh Building, Cambridge CB2 2RU, UK
40 West 20th Street, New York, NY 10011–4211, USA
477 Williamstown Road, Port Melbourne, VIC 3207, Australia
Ruiz de Alarcón 13, 28014 Madrid, Spain
Dock House, The Waterfront, Cape Town 8001, South Africa

http://www.cambridge.org

First published 2001
Fifth printing 2004

Printed in the United Kingdom at the University Press, Cambridge

Typeface Sabon 10.5/12 pt.   *System* QuarkXPress™ [SE]

A catalogue record for this book is available from the British Library

ISBN 0 521 800927 hardback
ISBN 0 521 804981 paperback

Contents

course has been learned?   375
How can we measure how well learners have control of
the important vocabulary learning strategies?   378

11 Designing the vocabulary component of a language course 380
    Goals   380
    Needs analysis   381
    Environment analysis   383
    Principles of vocabulary teaching   384
    Content and sequencing   385
    Format and presentation   388
    Monitoring and assessment   389
    Evaluation   391
    Autonomy and vocabulary learning   394

    Appendixes
    1. Headwords of the *Academic Word List*   407
    2. 1,000 word level tests   412
    3. A Vocabulary Levels Test: Test B   416
    4. Productive Levels Test: Version C   425
    5. Vocabulary Levels Dictation Test   429
    6. Function words   430

    References   432

    Subject index   464
    Author index   470

Series editors' preface

There was a time when teaching and learning a foreign or second language was viewed primarily as a matter of controlling its grammar. 'Methods' as different as ALM and Grammar Translation had mastery of structures as their main goal, and vocabulary development was approached as some kind of auxiliary activity, often through memorising decontextualised word lists. The relatively minor importance attached to the lexicon was also visible in the scant attention paid to it by second language acquisition researchers until the last decade.

Fortunately, not everyone held this view, and a handful of pioneers in Nottingham, Swansea, Amsterdam, Haifa and elsewhere set out to rectify the situation through what were initially rather isolated research programmes. Among the first was Paul Nation, now recognised as one of the world's leading authorities on L2 vocabulary. He and a small group of colleagues, plus a succession of fine graduate students, have made Victoria University of Wellington a leading centre for almost every aspect of research on the lexicon, including a great deal of widely respected corpus-based work.

Nation's latest book, *Learning Vocabulary in Another Language*, makes a substantive contribution to an area now recognised as of central importance for grammarians, acquisition specialists, language teachers and language learners alike. Writing in an engagingly direct style, the author provides a comprehensive overview of what research findings show it means to 'know' a word; how best to teach words and collocations; vocabulary in L2 listening, speaking and writing; specialised lexicons; vocabulary learning strategies, and strategies for inferring the meaning of unknown words in context; chunking and collocation; vocabulary testing; and course design for vocabulary development. The bibliography is extensive and up to date, and will be a valuable resource for graduate students embarking on theses and dissertations. The volume constitutes a welcome addition to the field and to the Cambridge Applied Linguistics Series.

Michael H. Long
Jack C. Richards

Acknowledgements

Parts of chapter 4 appeared in Joe, A., Nation, P. and Newton, J. (1996) 'Speaking activities and vocabulary learning', *English Teaching Forum* 34, 1: 2–7. Parts of chapter 5 appeared in Nation, I. S. P. (1997) 'The language learning benefits of extensive reading', *The Language Teacher* 21, 5: 13–16. Parts of chapter 11 appeared in Nation, I. S. P. (1998) 'Helping learners take control of their vocabulary learning', *GRETA* 6, 1: 9–18. Parts of chapter 8 appeared in Nation, I. S. P. (1982) 'Beginning to learn foreign vocabulary: a review of the research', *RELC Journal* 13, 1: 14–36. *Animal Farm* by George Orwell (Copyright © George Orwell 1945) reproduced by permission of A M Heath & Co. Ltd on behalf of Bill Hamilton as the Literary Executor of the Estate of the Late Sonia Brownell Orwell and Martin Secker & Warburg Ltd. I am grateful for permission to use these references.

Introduction

This book is about the teaching and learning of vocabulary, but the teaching and learning of vocabulary is only part of a language development programme. It is thus important that vocabulary teaching and learning is placed in its proper perspective.

Learning goals

Vocabulary learning is only one sub-goal of a range of goals that are important in the language classroom. The mnemonic LIST is a useful way of remembering these goals, which are outlined in the table below. L = Language, which includes vocabulary, I = Ideas, which covers content and subject matter knowledge as well as cultural knowledge, S = Skills, and T = Text or discourse, which covers the way sentences fit together to form larger units of a language.

Table. *Goals for language learning*

General goals	Specific goals
Language items	pronunciation vocabulary grammatical constructions
Ideas (content)	subject matter knowledge cultural knowledge
Skills	accuracy fluency strategies process skills or subskills
Text (discourse)	conversational discourse rules text schemata or topic type scales

Although this book focuses on the vocabulary sub-goal of language, the other goals are not ignored. However, they are approached from the viewpoint of vocabulary. There are chapters on vocabulary and the skills of listening, speaking, reading and writing including vocabulary and discourse; and pronunciation, spelling, and grammar are looked at in relation to vocabulary knowledge in chapter 2.

The four strands

The approach taken in this book rests on the idea that a balanced language course should consist of four major strands. These strands may appear in many different forms, but they should all be present in a well-designed course.

Firstly there is learning from comprehensible meaning-focused input. This means that learners should have the opportunity to learn new language items through listening and reading activities where the main focus is on the information in what they are listening to or reading. As we shall see in the following chapter, learning from meaning-focused input can best occur if learners are familiar with at least 95% of the running words in the input they are focusing on. In other words, learning from meaning-focused input cannot occur if there are lots of unknown words.

The second strand is one that has been subject to a lot of debate. This is language-focused learning, sometimes called form-focused instruction (Ellis, 1990). There is growing evidence (Long, 1988; Ellis, 1990) that language learning benefits if there is an appropriate amount of usefully-focused deliberate teaching and learning of language items. From a vocabulary perspective, this means that a course should involve the direct teaching of vocabulary and the direct learning and study of vocabulary. As we shall see, there is a very large amount of research stretching back to the late 19th century which shows that the gradual cumulative process of learning a word can be given a strong boost by the direct study of certain features of the word.

The third strand is meaning-focused output. Learners should have the chance to develop their knowledge of the language through speaking and writing activities where their main attention is focused on the information they are trying to convey. Speaking and writing are useful means of vocabulary development because they make learners focus on words in ways they do not have to while listening and reading. Having to speak and write encourages learners to listen like a speaker and read like a writer. This different kind of attention is not the only contribution that speaking and writing activities can make to language development. From a vocabulary perspective, these productive activities can strengthen knowledge of previously met vocabulary.

The fourth strand in a balanced course is fluency development. In activities which put this strand into action learners do not work with new language; instead, they become more fluent in using items they already know. A striking example of this can be found in the use of numbers. Usually, learners quickly learn numbers in a foreign language. But if they go into a post office and the clerk tells them how much the stamps they need are going to cost, they might not understand because the numbers have been said too quickly for them. By doing a small amount of regular fluency practice with numbers (the teacher says the numbers, the learners write the figures) learners will find that they can understand one digit numbers said quickly (1, 7, 6, 9) although they have trouble with two digit numbers said quickly (26, 89, 63, 42) or three digit numbers (126, 749, 537, 628). Further practice will make these longer numbers fluently available for comprehension. If a course does not have a strong fluency element, then the learning done in the other three strands will not be readily available for normal use.

In a language course, the four strands should get roughly the same amount of time. This means that no more than 25% of the learning time in and out of class should be given to the direct study of language items; no less than 25% of the class time should be given to fluency development. If these strands are not equally represented, then the design of the course needs to be looked at again.

These four strands need to be kept in mind while reading this book. Where recommendations are made for direct vocabulary learning, these should be seen as fitting into that 25% of the course which is devoted to language-focused learning. Seventy-five per cent of the vocabulary development program should involve the three meaning-focused strands of learning from input, learning from output and fluency development.

In this book we will look at how vocabulary fits into all four strands. It is worth stressing that meaning-focused input and output are only effective if learners have sufficient vocabulary to make these strands *truly* meaning-focused. If activities which are supposed to be meaning-focused involve large amounts of unknown vocabulary, then they become language-focused because much of the learners' attention is diverted from the message to the unknown vocabulary. Similarly, fluency development activities need to involve little or no unknown vocabulary or other language items, otherwise they become part of the meaning input and output strands, or language-focused learning.

Main themes

A small number of major themes run through this book but are first dealt with in chapters 1, 2 and 3. Firstly, there is the cost/benefit idea based on the results of word frequency studies. Its most important application is in the distinction between high-frequency and low-frequency vocabulary and the different ways in which teachers should deal with these two categories of vocabulary. The cost/benefit idea also applies to individual words in that the amount of attention given to an item should be roughly proportional to the chances of it being met again, that is, its frequency.

Secondly, there is the idea that learning a word is a cumulative process involving a range of aspects of knowledge. Learners need many different kinds of meetings with words in order to learn them fully. There is still little research on how vocabulary knowledge grows and how different kinds of encounters with words contribute to vocabulary knowledge. In this book knowing a word is taken to include not only knowing the formal aspects of the word and knowing its meaning, but also being able to use the word.

Thirdly, it is suggested that teachers and learners should give careful consideration to how vocabulary is learned; in particular, the psychological conditions that are most likely to lead to effective learning. Because these conditions are influenced by the design of learning tasks, quite a lot of attention is given to the analysis and design of vocabulary learning activities.

The audience for this book

This book is intended to be used by second and foreign language teachers. Although it is largely written from the viewpoint of a teacher of English, it could be used by teachers of other languages.

This book is called *Learning Vocabulary in Another Language* partly in order to indicate that most of the suggestions apply to both second and foreign language learning. Generally the term *second language* will be used to apply to both second and foreign language learning. In the few places where a contrast is intended, this will be clear from the context.

Tasks which help clarify important ideas, which encourage teachers to apply the ideas to their own teaching and suggestions for research can be found at the following web address: www.cambridge.org/elt. Many of these could easily be the starting point for graduate research projects and theses.

This book builds on my earlier *Teaching and Learning Vocabulary* (1990). Although the present work does not assume much previous linguistic and applied linguistics knowledge, readers may gain an introduction to this book by reading the earlier one. Since 1990, I have become aware of early overlooked research and there has been an enormous increase in the amount of research and writing about vocabulary. There is now an international community of vocabulary researchers and I am grateful to them for the knowledge, support and encouragement that they have given me in the preparation of this book.

1   *The goals of vocabulary learning*

How much vocabulary do learners need to know?

Whether designing a language course or planning our own course of study, it is useful to be able to set learning goals that will allow us to use the language in the ways we want to. When we plan the vocabulary goals of a long-term course of study, we can look at three kinds of information to help decide how much vocabulary needs to be learned: the number of words in the language, the number of words known by native speakers and the number of words needed to use the language.

How many words are there in the language?

The most ambitious goal is to know all of the language. However, even native speakers do not know all the vocabulary of the language. There are numerous specialist vocabularies, such as those of nuclear physics or computational linguistics, which are known only by the small groups who specialise in those areas. Still, it is interesting to have some idea of how many words there are in the language. This is not an easy question to resolve because there are numerous other questions which affect the way we answer it, including the following.

What do we count as a word? Do we count *book* and *books* as the same word? Do we count *green* (the colour) and *green* (a large grassed area) as the same word? Do we count people's names? Do we count the names of products like *Fab*, *Pepsi*, *Vegemite*, *Chevrolet*? The few brave or foolish attempts to answer these questions and the major question 'How many words are there in English?' have counted the number of words in very large dictionaries. *Webster's Third New International Dictionary* is the largest non-historical dictionary of English. It contains around 114,000 word families excluding proper names (Goulden, Nation and Read, 1990). This is a very large number and is well beyond the goals of most first and second language learners.

There are several ways of deciding what words will be counted.

Tokens

One way is simply to count every word form in a spoken or written text and if the same word form occurs more than once, then each occurrence of it is counted. So the sentence 'It is not easy to say it correctly' would contain eight words, even though two of them are the same word form, *it*. Words which are counted in this way are called 'tokens', and sometimes 'running words'. If we try to answer questions like 'How many words are there on a page or in a line?' 'How long is this book?' 'How fast can you read?' 'How many words does the average person speak per minute?' then our unit of counting will be the token.

Types

We can count the words in the sentence 'It is not easy to say it correctly' another way. If we see the same word again, we do not count it again. So the sentence of eight tokens consists of seven different words or 'types'. We count words in this way if we want to answer questions like 'How large was Shakespeare's vocabulary?' 'How many words do you need to know to read this book?' 'How many words does this dictionary contain?'

Lemmas

A lemma consists of a headword and some of its inflected and reduced (*n't*) forms. Usually, all the items included under a lemma are the same part of speech (Francis and Kučera, 1982: 461). The English inflections consist of plural, third person singular present tense, past tense, past participle, *-ing*, comparative, superlative and possessive (Bauer and Nation, 1993). The Thorndike and Lorge (1944) frequency count used lemmas as the basis for counting, and the more recent computerised count on the *Brown Corpus* (Francis and Kučera, 1982) has produced a lemmatised list. In the Brown count the comparative and superlative forms are not included in the lemma, and the same form used as a different part of speech (*walk* as a noun, *walk* as a verb) are not in the same lemma. Variant spellings (*favor, favour*) are usually included as part of the same lemma when they are the same part of speech.

Lying behind the use of lemmas as the unit of counting is the idea of learning burden (Swenson and West, 1934). The learning burden of an item is the amount of effort required to learn it. Once learners can use the inflectional system, the learning burden of for example *mends*, if the learner already knows *mend*, is negligible. One problem in forming lemmas is to decide what will be done with irregular forms such as *mice, is, brought, beaten* and *best*. The learning burden of these is clearly heavier than the learning burden of regular forms like *books, runs, talked, washed* and *fastest*. Should the irregular forms be counted as a part of the same lemma as their base word or should they be put into separate lemmas? Lemmas also separate closely related items such as the adjective and noun uses of words like *original*, and the noun and verb uses of words like *display*. An additional problem with lemmas is what is the headword – the base form or the most frequent form? (Sinclair, 1991: 41-42).

Using the lemma as the unit of counting greatly reduces the number of units in a corpus. Bauer and Nation (1993) calculate that the 61,805 tagged types (or 45,957 untagged types) in the *Brown Corpus* become 37,617 lemmas which is a reduction of almost 40% (or 18% for untagged types). Nagy and Anderson (1984) estimated that 19,105 of the 86,741 types in the Carroll, Davies and Richman (1971) corpus were regular inflections.

Word families

Lemmas are a step in the right direction when trying to represent learning burden in the counting of words. However, there are clearly other affixes which are used systematically and which greatly reduce the learning burden of derived words containing known base forms. These include affixes like *-ly, -ness* and *un-*. A word family consists of a headword, its inflected forms, and its closely related derived forms.

The major problem in counting using word families as the unit is to decide what should be included in a word family and what should not. Learners' knowledge of the prefixes and suffixes develops as they gain more experience of the language. What might be a sensible word family for one learner may be beyond another learner's present level of proficiency. This means that it is usually necessary to set up a scale of word families, starting with the most elementary and transparent members and moving on to less obvious possibilities.

How many words do native speakers know?

A less ambitious way of setting vocabulary learning goals is to look at what native speakers of the language know. Unfortunately, research on measuring vocabulary size has generally been poorly done (Nation, 1993c), and the results of the studies stretching back to the late nineteenth century are often wildly incorrect. We will look at the reasons for this later in this book.

Recent reliable studies (Goulden, Nation and Read, 1990; Zechmeister, Chronis, Cull, D'Anna and Healy, 1995) suggest that educated native speakers of English know around 20,000 word families. These estimates are rather low because the counting unit is word families which have several derived family members and proper nouns are not included in the count. A very rough rule of thumb would be that for each year of their early life, native speakers add on average 1,000 word families a year to their vocabulary. These goals are manageable for non-native speakers of English, especially those learning English as a second rather than foreign language, but they are way beyond what most learners of English as another language can realistically hope to achieve.

How much vocabulary do you need to use another language?

Studies of native speakers' vocabulary seem to suggest that second language learners need to know very large numbers of words. While this may be useful in the long term, it is not an essential short-term goal. This is because studies of native speakers' vocabulary growth see all words as being of equal value to the learner. Frequency based studies show very strikingly that this is not so, and that some words are much more useful than others.

Table 1.1 shows part of the results of a frequency count of just under 500 running words of the Ladybird version of *The Three Little Pigs*. It contains 124 different word types.

Note the large proportion of words occurring only once, and the very high frequency of the few most frequent words. When we look at texts our learners may have to read and conversations that are like ones that they may be involved in, we find that a relatively small amount of well-chosen vocabulary can allow learners to do a lot. To see this, let us look at an academic reading text and examine the different kinds of vocabulary it contains. The text is from Neville Peat's (1987) *Forever the Forest. A West Coast Story* (Hodder and Stoughton, Auckland).

Sustained-*yield* management ought to be long-term government **policy** in *indigenous* forests *zoned* for production. The adoption of such a **policy** would represent a *breakthrough* – the boundary between a *pioneering*, **extractive phase** and an *era* in which the *timber* industry **adjusted** to living with the forests in *perpetuity*. A forest **sustained** is a forest in which harvesting and *mortality* combined do not **exceed** *regeneration*. Naturally enough, faster-growing forests produce more *timber*, which is why attention

Table 1.1. *An example of the results of a frequency count*

the	41	met	3	come	1
little	25	myself	3	door	1
pig	22	not	3	down	1
house	17	on	3	fell	1
a	16	pigs	3	go	1
and	16	please	3	grew	1
said	14	pleased	3	had	1
he	12	shall	3	hair	1
I	10	soon	3	here	1
me	10	stronger	3	him	1
some	9	that	3	houses	1
wolf	9	they	3	huff	1
build	8	three	3	knocked	1
't	8	want	3	live	1
third	8	who	3	long	1
was	8	with	3	mother	1
of	7	won	3	must	1
straw	7	yes	3	my	1
to	7	yours	3	next	1
you	7	big	2	off	1
man	6	by	2	once	1
second	6	care	2	one	1
catch	5	chin	2	puff	1
first	5	day	2	road	1
for	5	does	2	set	1
will	5	huffed	2	so	1
bricks	4	let	2	their	1
built	4	'm	2	them	1
himself	4	no	2	there	1
now	4	puffed	2	took	1
sticks	4	strong	2	up	1
than	4	take	2	upon	1
very	4	then	2	us	1
asked	3	time	2	walked	1
carrying	3	too	2	we	1
eat	3	along	1	went	1
gave	3	are	1	were	1
give	3	ate	1	which	1
his	3	blow	1	your	1
in	3	but	1	yourselves	1
it	3	came	1		
'll	3	chinny	1		

would tend to swing from *podocarps* to *beech* forests regardless of the state of the *podocarp* **resource**. The colonists cannot be blamed for *plunging* in without thought to whether the **resource** had limits. They brought from *Britain* little experience or understanding of how to **maintain** forest **structure** and a *timber* supply for all time. Under *German* management it might have been different here. The *Germans* have practised the **sustained approach** since the seventeenth century when they faced a *timber* shortage as a result of a **series** of wars. In *New Zealand* in the latter part of the twentieth century, an **anticipated** shortage of the most valuable native *timber*, *rimu*, prompts a **similar response** – no more **contraction** of the *indigenous* forest and a balancing of yield with *increment* in **selected areas**.

This is not to say the idea is being *aired* here for the first time. Over a century ago the first *Conservator* of Forests proposed **sustained** harvesting. He was cried down. There were far too many trees left to bother about it. And yet in the *pastoral* **context** the dangers of *overgrazing* were **appreciated** early in the piece. *New Zealand geography* students are taught to this day how *overgrazing* causes the *degradation* of the soil and hillsides to slide away, and that with them can go the *viability* of hill-country sheep and cattle farming. That a forest could be *overgrazed* as easily was not widely accepted until much later – so late, in fact, that the *counter* to it, **sustained**-*yield* management, would be forced upon the industry and come as a shock to it. It is a simple enough **concept** on paper: balance harvest with growth and you have a natural *renewable* **resource**; forest products forever. **Plus** the social and **economic benefits** of regular work and **income**, a regular *timber* supply and relatively **stable** markets. **Plus** the **environmental benefits** that *accrue* from **minimising** the **impact** on soil and water qualities and wildlife.

In practice, however, **sustainability** depends on how well the **dynamics** of the forest are understood. And these **vary** from **area** to **area** according to forest make-up, soil *profile*, *altitude*, *climate* and **factors** which forest science may yet discover. *Ecology* is deep-felt.

We can distinguish four kinds of vocabulary in the text: high-frequency words (unmarked in the text), academic words (in bold), and technical and low-frequency words (in italics).

High-frequency words

In the example text, these words are not marked at all and include function words: *in, for, the, of, a*, etc. Appendix 6 contains a complete list of function words. The high-frequency words also include many content words: *government, forests, production, adoption, represent, boundary*. The classic list of high-frequency words is Michael West's (1953a) *A General Service List of English Words* which contains around 2,000 word families. Almost 80% of the running words in the text are high-frequency words.

Academic words

The text is from an academic textbook and contains many words that are common in different kinds of academic texts: *policy, phase, adjusted, sustained*. Typically these words make up about 9% of the running words in the text. The best list of these is the *Academic Word List* (Coxhead, 1998). Appendix 1 contains the 570 headwords of this list. This small list of words is very important for anyone using English for academic purposes (see chapter 6).

Technical words

The text contains some words that are very closely related to the topic and subject area of the text. These words include *indigenous, regeneration, podocarp, beech, rimu* (a New Zealand tree) and *timber*. These words are reasonably common in this topic area but not so common elsewhere. As soon as we see them we know what topic is being dealt with. Technical words like these typically cover about 5% of the running words in a text. They differ from subject area to subject area. If we look at technical dictionaries, such as dictionaries of economics, geography or electronics, we usually find about 1,000 entries in each dictionary.

Low-frequency words

The fourth group is the low-frequency words. Here, this group includes words like *zoned, pioneering, perpetuity, aired* and *pastoral*. They make up over 5% of the words in an academic text. There are thousands of them in the language, by far the biggest group of words. They include all the words that are not high-frequency words, not academic words and not technical words for a particular subject. They consist of technical words for other subject areas, proper nouns, words that almost got into the high-frequency list, and words that we rarely meet in our use of the language.

Let us now look at a longer text and a large collection of texts.

Sutarsyah, Nation and Kennedy (1994) looked at a single economics textbook to see what vocabulary would be needed to read the text. The textbook was 295,294 words long. Table 1.2 shows the results. The academic word list used in the study was the *University Word List* (Xue and Nation, 1984).

What should be clear from this example and from the text looked at earlier is that a reasonably small number of words covers a lot of text.

Table 1.2. *Text coverage by the different kinds of vocabulary in an economics textbook*

Type of vocabulary	Number of words	Text coverage
1st 2000 word families	1,577	82.5%
Academic vocabulary	636	8.7%
Other vocabulary	3,225	8.8%
Total	5,438	100.0%

Table 1.3. *The coverage by the different kinds of vocabulary in an academic corpus*

Type of vocabulary	% coverage
1st 1000 words	71.4%
2nd 1000 words	4.7%
Academic Word List (570 words)	10.0%
Others	13.9%
Total	100.0%

Coxhead (1998) used an academic corpus made up of a balance of science, arts, commerce and law texts totalling 3,500,000 running words. Table 1.3 gives the coverage figures for this corpus.

Figure 1.1 presents the proportions in a diagrammatic form. The size of each of the sections of the right-hand box indicates the proportion of the text taken up by each type of vocabulary.

Table 1.4 gives the typical figures for a collection of texts consisting of five million running words.

Some very important generalisations can be drawn from Table 1.4 and the other information that we have looked at. We will look at these generalisations and at questions that they raise. Brief answers to the questions will be given here but will be examined much more closely in later chapters.

High-frequency words

There is a small group of high-frequency words which are very important because these words cover a very large proportion of the running words in spoken and written texts and occur in all kinds of uses of the language.

Sustained-*yield* management ought to be long-term government **policy** in *indigenous* forests *zoned* for production. The adoption of such a **policy** would represent a *breakthrough* – the boundary between a *pioneering*, **extractive phase** and an *era* in which the *timber* industry **adjusted** to living with the forests in *perpetuity*. A forest **sustained** is a forest in which harvesting and *mortality* combined do not **exceed** *regeneration*. Naturally enough, faster-growing forests produce more *timber*, which is why attention would tend to swing from *podocarps* to *beech* forests regardless of the state of the *podocarp* **resource**. The colonists cannot be blamed for *plunging* in without thought to whether the **resource** had limits. They brought from *Britain* little experience or understanding of how to **maintain** forest **structure** and a *timber* supply for all time. Under *German* management it might have been different here. The *Germans* have practised the **sustained approach** since the seventeenth century when they faced a *timber* shortage as a result of a **series** of wars. In *New Zealand* in the latter part of the twentieth century, an **anticipated** shortage of the most valuable native *timber*, *rimu*, prompts a **similar response** – no more **contraction** of the *indigenous* forest and a balancing of yield with *increment* in **selected areas**.

This is not to say the idea is being *aired* here for the first time. Over a century ago the first *Conservator* of Forests proposed **sustained** harvesting. He was cried down. There were far too many trees left to bother about it. And yet in the *pastoral* **context** the dangers of *overgrazing* were **appreciated** early in the piece. *New Zealand geography* students are taught to this day how *overgrazing* causes the *degradation* of the soil and hillsides to slide away, and that with them can go the *viability* of hill-country sheep and cattle farming. That a forest could be *overgrazed* as easily was not widely accepted until much later – so late, in fact, that the *counter* to it, **sustained**-*yield* management, would be forced upon the industry and come as a shock to it.

High-frequency vocabulary
2000 words 80% or more text coverage a, equal, places, *behaves*, *educate*
Academic vocabulary
Technical vocabulary
Low-frequency vocabulary

Figure 1.1 Vocabulary type and coverage in an academic text

How large is this group of words? The usual way of deciding how many words should be considered as high-frequency words is to look at the text coverage provided by successive frequency-ranked groups of words. The teacher or course designer then has to decide where the coverage gained by spending teaching time on these words is no longer worthwhile. Table 1.5 shows coverage figures for each successive 1,000 lemmas from the *Brown Corpus* – a collection of various 2,000-word texts of American English totalling just over one million tokens.

Usually the 2,000-word level has been set as the most suitable limit for high-frequency words. Nation and Hwang (1995) present

Table 1.4. *Vocabulary size and coverage (Carroll, Davies and Richman (1971))*

Number of words	% text coverage
86,741	100
43,831	99
12,448	95
5,000	89.4
4,000	87.6
3,000	85.2
2,000	81.3
1,000	74.1
100	49
10	23.7

Table 1.5. *The percentage text coverage of each successive 1000 lemmas in the Brown Corpus*

1000 word (lemma) level	% coverage of text (tokens)
1000	72
2000	79.7
3000	84
4000	86.7
5000	88.6
6000	89.9

evidence that counting the 2,000 most frequent words of English as the high-frequency words is still the best decision for learners going on to academic study.

What are the words in this group? As has been noted, the classic list of high-frequency words is Michael West's *General Service List* which contains 2,000 word families. About 165 word families in this list are function words such as *a, some, two, because* and *to* (see appendix 6). The rest are content words, that is nouns, verbs, adjectives and adverbs. Older series of graded readers are based on this list.

How stable are the high-frequency words? In other words, does one properly researched list of high-frequency words differ greatly from another? Frequency lists may disagree with each other about the frequency rank order of particular words but if the research is based on a well-designed corpus there is generally about 80% agreement about

Table 1.6. *Ways of learning and teaching high-frequency words*

Direct teaching	Teacher explanation
	Peer teaching
Direct learning	Study from word cards
	Dictionary use
Incidental learning	Guessing from context in extensive reading
	Use in communication activities
Planned encounters	Graded reading
	Vocabulary exercises

what particular words should be included. Nation and Hwang's (1995) research on the *General Service List* showed quite large overlap between it and more recent frequency counts. Replacing some of the words in the *General Service List* with other words resulted in only a 1% increase in coverage. It is important to remember that the 2,000 high-frequency words of English consist of some words that have *very* high frequencies and some words that are only slightly more frequent than others not in the list. The first 1,000 words cover about 77% and the second 1,000 about 5% of the running words in academic texts. When making a list of high-frequency words, both frequency and range must be considered. Range is measured by seeing how many different texts or subcorpora each particular word occurs in. A word with wide range occurs in many different texts or subcorpora.

How should teachers and learners deal with these words? The high-frequency words of the language are clearly so important that considerable time should be spent on them by teachers and learners. The words are a small enough group to enable most of them to get attention over the span of a long-term English programme. This attention can be in the form of direct teaching, direct learning, incidental learning, and planned meetings with the words. The time spent on them is well justified by their frequency, coverage and range. Table 1.6 lists some of the teaching and learning possibilities that will be explored in more detail in later chapters of this book.

In general, high-frequency words are so important that anything that teachers and learners can do to make sure they are learned is worth doing.

Table 1.7. *Text type and text coverage by the most frequent 2000 words of English and an academic word list in four different kinds of texts*

Levels	Conversation	Fiction	Newspapers	Academic text
1st 1000	84.3%	82.3%	75.6%	73.5%
2nd 1000	6%	5.1%	4.7%	4.6%
Academic	1.9%	1.7%	3.9%	8.5%
Other	7.8%	10.9%	15.7%	13.3%

Specialised vocabulary

It is possible to make specialised vocabularies which provide good coverage for certain kinds of texts. These are a way of extending the high-frequency words for special purposes.

What special vocabularies are there? Special vocabularies are made by systematically restricting the range of topics or language uses investigated. It is thus possible to have special vocabularies for speaking, for reading academic texts, for reading newspapers, for reading children's stories, or for letter writing. Technical vocabularies are also specialised vocabularies. Some specialised vocabularies are made by doing frequency counts using a specialised corpus, others are made by experts in the field gathering what they consider to be relevant vocabulary.

There is a very important specialised vocabulary for second language learners intending to do academic study in English. This is the *Academic Word List* (Coxhead, 1998; see appendix 1). It consists of 570 word families that are not in the most frequent 2,000 words of English but which occur reasonably frequently over a very wide range of academic texts; the list is not restricted to a specific discipline. That means that the words are useful for learners studying humanities, law, science or commerce. Academic vocabulary has sometimes been called sub-technical vocabulary because it does not contain technical words but rather formal vocabulary.

The importance of this vocabulary can be seen in the coverage it provides for various kinds of texts (Table 1.7).

Adding the academic vocabulary from the *UWL* to the high-frequency words changes the coverage of academic text from 78.1% to 86.6%. Expressed another way, with a vocabulary of 2,000 words, approximately one word in every five will be unknown. With a vocabulary of 2,000 words plus the *Academic Word List*, approximately one word in every ten will be unknown. This is a very significant change. If, instead of learning the vocabulary of the *Academic Word List*, the learner had moved on to the third 1,000 most frequent words, instead of an additional 10% coverage there would only have been 4.3% extra coverage.

What kinds of words do they contain? The *Academic Word List* is in appendix 1. Much research remains to be done on this list to explain why the same group of words frequently occur across a very wide range of academic texts. Sometimes a few of them are closely related to the topic, but most probably occur because they allow academic writers to do the things that academic writers do. That is, they allow writers to refer to others' work (*assume, establish, indicate, conclude, maintain*); and they allow writers to work with data in academic ways (*analyse, assess, concept, definition, establish, categories, seek*). We consider this issue again in chapter 6.

Technical words contain a variety of types which range from words that do not usually occur in other subject areas (*cabotage, amortisation*) to those that are formally like high-frequency words but which have specialised meanings (*demand, supply, cost* as used in economics). Chapter 6 looks more fully at technical words.

How large are they? There has been no survey done of the size of technical vocabularies and little research on finding a consistently applied operational definition of what words are technical words. A rough guess from looking at dictionaries of technical vocabulary, such as those for geography, biology and applied linguistics, is that they each contain less than a thousand words.

How can you make a special vocabulary? The *Academic Word List* was made by deciding on the high-frequency words of English and then examining a range of academic texts to find what words were not among the high-frequency words but had wide range and reasonable frequency of occurrence. Range was important because academic vocabulary is intended for general academic purposes. Making a technical vocabulary is a little more problematic. One of the problem areas is that some technical vocabulary occurs in the high-frequency words and the *Academic Word List*. *Wall* in biology, and *price, cost, demand* in economics are all high-frequency words which have particular technical uses. Sutarsyah, Nation and Kennedy (1994) found that 33 content words made up over 10% of the running words of an economics text, but accounted for less than 1% of the running words in a similar sized set of mixed academic texts. One way of making a technical vocabulary is to compare the frequency of words in a specialised text with their frequency in a general corpus.

What should teachers and learners do about specialised vocabulary? Where possible, specialised vocabulary should be treated like high-frequency vocabulary. That is, it should be taught and studied in a variety of complementary ways. Where technical vocabulary is also high-frequency vocabulary, learners should be helped to see the connections and differences between the high-frequency meanings and the technical uses. For example, what is similar between a cell *wall* and other less specialised uses of *wall*? Where technical vocabulary requires specialist knowledge of the field, teachers should train learners in strategies which will help them understand and remember the words. Much technical vocabulary will only make sense in the context of learning the specialised subject matter. Learning the meaning of the technical term *morpheme* needs to be done as a part of the study of linguistics, not before the linguistics course begins.

Low-frequency words

There is a very large group of words that occur very infrequently and cover only a small proportion of any text.

What kinds of words are they?

1. Some low-frequency words are words of moderate frequency that did not manage to get into the high-frequency list. It is important to remember that the boundary between high-frequency and low-frequency vocabulary is an arbitrary one. Any of several thousand low-frequency words could be candidates for inclusion within the high-frequency list simply because their position on a rank frequency list which takes account of range is dependent on the nature of the corpus the list is based on. A different corpus would lead to a different ranking particularly among words on the boundary. This, however, should not be seen as a justification for large amounts of teaching time being spent on low-frequency words at the third or fourth thousand word level. Here are some words that in the *Brown Corpus* fall just outside the high-frequency boundary: *curious, wing, arm* (vb), *gate, approximately.*

2. Many low-frequency words are proper names. Approximately 4% of the running words in the *Brown Corpus* are words like *Carl, Johnson* and *Ohio.* In some texts, such as novels and newspapers, proper nouns are like technical words – they are of high-frequency in particular texts but not in others, their meaning is closely related to the message of the text, and they could not be

sensibly pre-taught because their use in the text reveals their meaning. Before you read a novel, you do not need to learn the characters' names.

3. 'One person's technical vocabulary is another person's low-frequency word.' This ancient vocabulary proverb makes the point that, beyond the high-frequency words of the language, people's vocabulary grows partly as a result of their jobs, interests and specialisations. The technical vocabulary of our personal interests is important to us. To others, however, it is not important and from their point of view is just a collection of low-frequency words.

4. Some low-frequency words are simply low-frequency words. That is, they are words that almost every language user rarely uses, for example: *eponymous, gibbous, bifurcate, plummet, ploy*. They may represent a rarely expressed idea; they may be similar in meaning to a much more frequent word or phrase; they may be marked as being old-fashioned, very formal, belonging to a particular dialect, or vulgar, or they may be foreign words.

How many low-frequency words are there and how many do learners need to know? A critical issue in answering this question is to decide what will be counted as a word. For the purpose of providing a brief answer to the question of desirable vocabulary size, word families will be used as the unit of counting. Webster's *Third New International Dictionary* (Gove, 1963) contains 267,000 entries of which 113,161 can be counted as base words including base proper words, base compound words, and homographs with unrelated meanings (Goulden, Nation and Read, 1990: 351). Calculations from *The American Heritage Word Frequency Book* (Carroll, Davies and Richman, 1971) suggest that in printed school English there are 88,533 distinct word families (Nagy and Anderson, 1984: 315). Although not all these words need to be known to be a very successful language user, it is very important that learners continue to increase their vocabulary size. To read with minimal disturbance from unknown vocabulary, language users probably need a vocabulary of 15,000 to 20,000 words.

How should teachers and learners deal with low-frequency vocabulary? Teachers' and learners' aims differ with low-frequency vocabulary. The teacher's aim is to train learners in the use of strategies to deal with such vocabulary. These strategies include guessing from context clues, using word parts to help remember words, using vocabulary cards and dictionaries. When teachers spend time on low-frequency

Table 1.8. *The differing focus of teachers' and learners' attention to high- and low-frequency words*

	High-frequency words	Low-frequency words
Attention to each word	Teacher and learners	Learners
Attention to strategies	Teacher and learners	Teacher and learners

words in class, they should be using the words as an excuse for working on the strategies. The learners' aim is to continue to increase their vocabulary. The strategies provide a means of doing this.

As Table 1.8 shows, learners should begin training in the strategies for dealing with vocabulary while they are learning the high-frequency words of the language. When learners know the high frequency vocabulary and move to the study of low-frequency words, the teacher does not spend substantial amounts of class time explaining and giving practice with vocabulary, but instead concentrates on expanding and refining the learners' control of vocabulary learning and coping strategies. Learners however should continue to learn new words.

Testing vocabulary knowledge

In this chapter, a very important distinction has been made between high-frequency words and low-frequency words. This distinction has been made on the basis of the frequency, coverage and quantity of these words. The distinction is important because teachers need to deal with these two kinds of words in quite different ways, and teachers and learners need to ensure that the high-frequency words of the language are well known.

It is therefore important that teachers and learners know whether the high-frequency words have been learned. Appendix 3 of this book contains a vocabulary test that can be used to measure whether the high-frequency words have been learned, and the progress of the learner in the learning of low-frequency vocabulary. *The Vocabulary Levels Test* exists in two different versions. There are also productive versions of the test (Laufer and Nation, 1995; Laufer and Nation, 1999) (see appendix 4). See Schmitt, Schmitt and Clapham (in press) for some research on this test.

The test is designed to be quick to take, easy to mark and easy to interpret. It gives credit for partial knowledge of words. Its main purpose is to let teachers quickly find out whether learners need to be working on high-frequency or low-frequency words, and roughly how much work needs to be done on these words.

There is much more to vocabulary testing than simply testing if a learner can choose an appropriate meaning for a given word form, and we will look closely at testing in a later chapter. However, for the purpose of helping a teacher decide what kind of vocabulary work learners need to do, the levels test is reliable, valid and very practical.

2 *Knowing a word*

Words are not isolated units of language, but fit into many interlocking systems and levels. Because of this, there are many things to know about any particular word and there are many degrees of knowing. One of the major ideas explored in this chapter is the relationship and boundaries between learning individual items and learning systems of knowledge. For example, it is possible to learn to recognise the form of a word simply by memorising it. It is also possible to learn to recognise the form of a regularly spelled word by learning the systematic sound–spelling correspondences involved in the language. Recognition of the word then involves the application of some of the spelling rules. The relationship between item knowledge and system knowledge is complex and there has been enormous debate about certain aspects of it; for example, as it affects young native speakers of English learning to read. For each of the aspects of what it means to know a word, we will look at the item–system possibilities. A second major idea explored in this chapter is the receptive/productive scale of knowledge and how it applies to each aspect of vocabulary knowledge.

The aims of this chapter are: to examine what could be known about a word, to evaluate the relative importance of the various kinds of knowledge, to see how they are related to each other, and to broadly suggest how learners might gain this knowledge. The chapter also looks at what needs to be learned for each word and what is predictable from previous knowledge.

Learning burden

The 'learning burden' of a word is the amount of effort required to learn it. Different words have different learning burdens for learners with different language backgrounds and each of the aspects of what it means to know a word can contribute to its learning burden. The general principle of learning burden (Nation, 1990) is that the more a word represents patterns and knowledge that learners are already familiar with, the lighter its learning burden. These patterns and this knowledge can be from the first language, from knowledge of other languages, and from previous knowledge of the second language. So, if a word uses sounds that are in the first language, follows regular spelling patterns, is a loan word in the first language with roughly the same meaning, fits into roughly similar grammatical patterns as in the first language and has similar collocations and constraints, then the learning burden will be very light and the word will not be difficult to learn. For learners whose first language is closely related to the second language, the learning burden of most words will be light. For learners whose first language is not related to the second language, the learning burden will be heavy.

Teachers can help reduce the learning burden of words by drawing attention to systematic patterns and analogies within the second language, and by pointing out connections between the second language and the first.

Teachers should be able to estimate the learning burden of words for each of the aspects of what is involved in knowing a word, so that they can direct their teaching towards aspects that will need attention and towards aspects that will reveal underlying patterns so that later learning is easier.

The receptive/productive distinction

The validity of the receptive/productive distinction as a way of distinguishing types of knowledge in most cases depends on its resemblance to the distinction between the 'receptive' skills of listening and reading and the 'productive' skills of speaking and writing (Palmer, 1921: 118; West, 1938; Crow, 1986). Receptive carries the idea that we receive language input from others through listening or reading and try to comprehend it, productive that we produce language forms by speaking and writing to convey messages to others. Like most terminology receptive and productive are not completely suitable because there are productive features in the receptive skills – when listening and reading we produce meaning. The terms 'passive' (for listening and reading) and 'active' (for speaking and writing) are sometimes used as synonyms for receptive and productive (Meara, 1990a; Corson, 1995; Laufer, 1998) but some object to these terms as they do not see listening and reading as having some of the other characteristics which can be attached to the term passive. Here the two sets of terms will be used interchangeably to reflect the use of the particular writer being discussed.

Essentially, receptive vocabulary use involves perceiving the form of a word while listening or reading and retrieving its meaning. Productive vocabulary use involves wanting to express a meaning through speaking or writing and retrieving and producing the appropriate spoken or written word form. Melka Teichroew (1982) shows the inconsistent use of the terms receptive and productive in relation to test items and degrees of knowing a word and considers that the distinction is arbitrary and would be more usefully treated as a scale of knowledge.

Although reception and production can be seen as being on a continuum, this is by no means the only way of viewing the distinction. Meara (1990a) sees the distinction between active and passive vocabulary as being the result of different types of association between words. Active vocabulary can be activated by other words, because it has many incoming and outgoing links with other words. Passive vocabulary consists of items which can only be activated by external stimuli. That is, they are activated by hearing or seeing their forms, but not through associational links to other words. Meara thus sees active and passive as not being on a cline but representing different kinds of associational knowledge. One criticism of this view might be that language use is not only associationally driven, but, more basically, is meaning driven. Being able to actively name an object using a second language (L2) word can be externally stimulated by seeing the object without necessarily arousing links to other L2 words.

Corson (1995: 44–45) uses the terms active and passive to refer to productive and receptive vocabularies. Passive vocabulary, according to Corson, includes the active vocabulary and three other kinds of vocabulary – words that are only partly known, low-frequency words not readily available for use and words that are avoided in active use. These three kinds of vocabulary overlap to some degree. Corson's description of active and passive vocabulary is strongly based on the idea of use and not solely on degrees of knowledge. Some passive vocabulary may be very well known but never used and therefore never active. Some people may be able to curse and swear but never do. From Corson's viewpoint, the terms active and passive are more suitable than receptive and productive. He occasionally uses the term unmotivated to refer to some of the passive vocabulary.

Corson (*ibid.*: 179–180) argues that for some people the Graeco-Latin vocabulary of English may be passive for several reasons. Firstly, Graeco-Latin words are generally low-frequency words and thus require more mental activation for use. Secondly, the morphological structure of Graeco-Latin words may be opaque for some learners, thus reducing the number of nodes or points of activation for each of these words. Thirdly, some learners because of their social background get little opportunity to become familiar with the rules of use of the words. Corson's idea of the lexical bar (barrier) is thus important for the receptive/productive distinction.

What the lexical bar represents is a gulf between the everyday meaning systems and the high status meaning systems created by the introduction of an academic culture of literacy. This is a barrier that everyone has to cross at some stage in their lives, if they are to become 'successful candidates' in conventional forms of education. (*ibid.*: 180–181)

In short, the barrier is the result of lack of access to the academic meaning systems strongly reinforced by the morphological strangeness of Graeco-Latin words. For some learners much vocabulary remains at best receptive because of the lexical bar.

The scope of the receptive/productive distinction

The terms receptive and productive apply to a variety of kinds of language knowledge and use. When they are applied to vocabulary, these terms cover all the aspects of what is involved in knowing a word. Table 2.1 lists these aspects using a model which emphasises the parts. It is also possible to show the aspects of what is involved in knowing a word using a process model, which emphasises the relations between the parts. At the most general level, knowing a word involves form, meaning and use.

From the point of view of receptive knowledge and use, knowing the word, for example, *underdeveloped* involves:

- being able to recognise the word when it is heard
- being familiar with its written form so that it is recognised when it is met in reading
- recognising that it is made up of the parts *under-*, *-develop-* and *-ed* and being able to relate these parts to its meaning
- knowing that *underdeveloped* signals a particular meaning
- knowing what the word means in the particular context in which it has just occurred
- knowing the concept behind the word which will allow understanding in a variety of contexts
- knowing that there are related words like *overdeveloped*, *backward* and *challenged*
- being able to recognise that *underdeveloped* has been used correctly in the sentence in which it occurs
- being able to recognise that words such as *territories* and *areas* are typical collocations

Table 2.1. *What is involved in knowing a word*

Form	spoken	R	What does the word sound like?
		P	How is the word pronounced?
	written	R	What does the word look like?
		P	How is the word written and spelled?
	word parts	R	What parts are recognisable in this word?
		P	What word parts are needed to express the meaning?
Meaning	form and meaning	R	What meaning does this word form signal?
		P	What word form can be used to express this meaning?
	concept and referents	R	What is included in the concept?
		P	What items can the concept refer to?
	associations	R	What other words does this make us think of?
		P	What other words could we use instead of this one?
Use	grammatical functions	R	In what patterns does the word occur?
		P	In what patterns must we use this word?
	collocations	R	What words or types of words occur with this one?
		P	What words or types of words must we use with this one?
	constraints on use (register, frequency ...)	R	Where, when, and how often would we expect to meet this word?
		P	Where, when, and how often can we use this word?

Note: In column 3, R = receptive knowledge, P = productive knowledge.

- knowing that *underdeveloped* is not an uncommon word and is not a pejorative word

From the point of view of productive knowledge and use, knowing the word *underdeveloped* involves:

- being able to say it with correct pronunciation including stress
- being able to write it with correct spelling
- being able to construct it using the right word parts in their appropriate forms
- being able to produce the word to express the meaning 'underdeveloped'
- being able to produce the word in different contexts to express the range of meanings of *underdeveloped*
- being able to produce synonyms and opposites for *underdeveloped*
- being able to use the word correctly in an original sentence
- being able to produce words that commonly occur with it
- being able to decide to use or not use the word to suit the degree of formality of the situation (At present *developing* is more acceptable than *underdeveloped* which carries a slightly negative meaning.)

Table 2.1 and the accompanying example *underdeveloped* give an indication of the range of aspects of receptive and productive knowledge and use. It should be clear from this that if we say a particular word is part of someone's receptive vocabulary, we are making a very general statement that includes many aspects of knowledge and use, and we are combining the skills of listening and reading. In general, it seems that receptive learning and use is easier than productive learning and use, but it is not clear *why* receptive use should be less difficult than productive use. There are several possible explanations which are probably complementary rather than competing (see Ellis and Beaton, 1993: 548–549).

1. The 'amount of knowledge' explanation. Productive learning is more difficult because it requires extra learning of new spoken or written output patterns (see Crow, 1986, for a similar argument). This will be particularly noticeable for languages which use different writing systems from the first language and which use some different sounds or sound combinations. For receptive use, learners may only need to know a few distinctive features of the form of an item. For productive purposes their knowledge of the word form has to be more precise. This is clearly seen in young children who can display good receptive knowledge of a word such as *spaghetti*, but can only very roughly approximate its spoken form productively as *'stigli'* or *'parsghetti'*.

The form of items is more likely to influence difficulty than meaning, because there is much more shared knowledge of meaning between two distinct languages than there is shared form. Words in two languages might not have precisely the same meaning but in most cases the overlap is much greater than the distinctions. Initially, this knowledge of the word form is more likely to be the factor affecting difficulty than knowledge of meaning, and more precise knowledge of the word form is required for productive use, thus making productive learning more difficult than receptive learning.

2. The 'practice' explanation. In normal language learning conditions, receptive use generally gets more practice than productive use, and this may be an important factor in accounting for differences in receptive and productive vocabulary size, particularly in measures of total vocabulary size. There is some evidence that both receptive learning and productive learning require particular practice to be properly learned (DeKeyser and Sokalski, 1996). This argument goes against the one which maintains that productive knowledge includes all the knowledge necessary for receptive use. This degree of practice factor is easily controlled in experimental studies.

3. The 'access' explanation. Ellis and Beaton (1993: 548–549) suggest that a new foreign language word in the early stages of learning has only one simple link to its first language (L1) translation (the receptive direction).

The receptive direction

Foreign word	$\longrightarrow$	L1 translation
kaki	$\longrightarrow$	*leg*

The L1 word however has many competing associations (the productive direction) and thus productive recall is more difficult than receptive because there are many competing paths to choose from, and the ones within the L1 lexical system are likely to be stronger.

The productive direction

L1 word	$\longrightarrow$	Foreign word
leg	$\longrightarrow$	*kaki*

‐ ‐ ‐ ‐ ‐ ‐ ‐ ‐ ‐ ‐ ‐ ‐ ‐ ‐ ‐ ‐ ‐ ‐ ‐ ‐

(inside the L1 lexical system)

$\longrightarrow$	collocates of *leg*
$\longrightarrow$	synonyms of *leg*
$\longrightarrow$	opposites of *leg*
$\longrightarrow$	etc.

The tip of the tongue experiments (Brown and McNeill, 1966) provide some evidence of this.

4. The 'motivation' explanation. Learners are not motivated, for a variety of reasons including socio-cultural background, to use certain kinds of knowledge productively (Corson, 1995). Although some vocabulary may be well known and could be used productively, it is not used and remains in the learners' passive vocabulary. Note that from this point of view, for some words the receptive/productive distinction is not a knowledge continuum but a distinction between motivated and unmotivated vocabulary. If a learner knows a word well enough to use it productively but never uses it productively, is it a part of that learner's productive vocabulary?

To truly compare the relative difficulty of receptive and productive learning, it is necessary to use test item types that are equivalent in all significant features affecting difficulty except the receptive/productive distinction. It also seems important, if the receptive/productive distinction is seen as a knowledge scale, that there be one scale for oral use (listening and speaking) and one for written use (reading and writing).

Experimental comparisons of receptive and productive vocabulary

When comparing receptive and productive learning, the two test items (one to measure receptive learning and one to measure productive learning) should be both recognition items or both recall items. Some studies use a recognition item for measuring receptive knowledge,

kaki   a. book
           b. leg
           c. face
           d. fruit

and a recall item for measuring productive knowledge, e.g.
Translate this word into Indonesian (the second language):
leg   _____

It is then impossible to tell how much the difference in scores is a result of the productive/receptive distinction or the recognition/recall distinction. Other confounding differences in test items may be the presence and absence of sentence context, oral and written presentation, and integration in and separation from a communicative task. Some studies however have avoided this problem of confounding variables.

Table 2.2. *Average scores for receptive and productive learning and testing of French vocabulary*

	Receptive test (French–English)	Productive test (English–French)	Total
Receptive learning (French–English) Group A	15.1	6.0	21.1
Productive learning (English–French) Group B	13.1	8.0	21.1
Total	28.2	14.0	

Stoddard (1929) was one of the earliest foreign vocabulary learning studies to directly compare receptive and productive learning and to test with equivalent test formats. Half of Stoddard's 328 school-age subjects learned 50 French–English word pairs (receptive learning). The other half learned the same items as English–French word pairs (productive learning). Both groups sat the same recall test with half of the items tested receptively (see the French word, write the English translation) and half of the items tested productively (see the English word, write the French translation). Table 2.2 gives Stoddard's results.

The conclusions to be drawn from Stoddard's data are:

1. Receptive tests are easier than productive tests. The score for the receptive test (28.2) was twice as high as that for the productive test (14.0).
2. The type of test favours the type of learning. Those who learned receptively got higher scores on the receptive test than those who learned productively (15.1 and 13.1). Those who learned productively got higher scores on the productive test than those who learned receptively (8.0 and 6.0).
3. The effect of the type of test is greater than the effect of the type of learning. Learners had similar scores (21.1) for both kinds of learning, and the receptive learners' score on the receptive test (15.1) was much higher than the productive learners' score on the productive test (8.0).

Stoddard's study used simple comparison of raw scores, did not control for an order effect in testing (the receptive test always preceded the productive), and did not exercise deliberate control over the direction of learning to ensure that the receptive learning was indeed in the direction of French to English and that the productive learning was indeed in the other direction.

Waring (1997a) performed an experiment somewhat similar to Stoddard's but with the same learners being tested on the same items receptively first and then productively. Waring also tested retention on the same day, the next day, one week after the learning and a month after the learning. The results, especially with delayed recall, were remarkably similar to Stoddard's, with the same three conclusions being confirmed. Waring also found that receptive learning took less time than productive learning, and that scores on productive tests were consistently at lower levels over time than scores on receptive tests, with very little being scored on the productive tests after three months. Waring also found extremely large individual differences in learning rate and amount recalled, with a very low correlation (0.29) between receptive and productive learning times, indicating that many learners are not proficient at both receptive and productive learning.

These two experiments show the importance of the receptive/productive distinction especially with test types. With test items that differ only on the receptive/productive dimension, receptive tests are much easier than productive tests. There is a relationship between the way something is learned and the way it is tested but this is not nearly as strong as the effect of test type. If we make a very large and partly justified mental jump and equate testing with language use, then these experiments suggest the following.

1. More time and repeated effort is needed to learn vocabulary for speaking and writing than is needed for listening and reading. All things being equal, receptive learning is easier than productive learning.
2. Generally it is more efficient to do receptive learning for receptive use, and productive learning for productive use.
3. If productive use is needed, there must be productive learning. This goes against the comprehensible input hypothesis in that it says that receptive learning is not always sufficient as a basis for productive use. It is still not clear if readiness for productive use can be reached by receptive 'over-learning', for example large quantities of reading or listening, or whether there must be 'pushed' output with learners being made to speak or write (Swain, 1985).
4. Learners will differ greatly in their skill at learning vocabulary and in their skill at learning vocabulary for different purposes. It is thus worthwhile checking the receptive and productive learning of learners, and providing training to help those who need it.

Griffin (1992) conducted a series of experiments on vocabulary learning focusing mainly on list learning and learning with a context sentence. Griffin's studies show that there are numerous factors such as proficiency, perceived goal and materials that can affect learning. Learning from lists is a complex activity and care needs to be taken in interpreting the results of such studies. Griffin found that: receptive learning is easier than productive learning, learners score higher when the testing format matches the learning format, and that the associations formed are bi-directional (receptive learning can result in productive knowledge and vice versa). Griffin also found that most forgetting seems to occur soon after learning. Griffin tentatively concluded that if learning is only to be done in one direction, then learning L1→L2 pairs (productive learning) may be more effective than L2→L1 (receptive learning). A major strength of Griffin's work is that he brings a strong background in psychology and in his review and discussion draws on areas of research not often considered in second language vocabulary learning.

Ellis and Beaton (1993) investigated the productive learning of German vocabulary (English–German) under keyword and other conditions. The testing involved firstly receptive testing (see and hear the German word, type in the English translation) and subsequently productive testing (see the English word, type in the German translation). Receptive testing (German–English) gave significantly more correct responses (68%) than did English–German productive testing (53%) both by subjects and by words (Ellis and Beaton, 1993: 541). This superiority for receptive testing occurred even though the experiment confounded direction of testing and order of tests (receptive was always tested before productive) which could have boosted the productive scores (*ibid.*: 548).

Aspects of knowing a word

The distinctions made in Table 2.1 (see p. 27) are not just arbitrary conveniences. For example, drawing heavily on research in experimental psychology and language acquisition, N. Ellis (1994: 212) distinguishes the form learning aspects of vocabulary learning (Ellis calls them Input/Output aspects) and the meaning aspects of vocabulary. This distinction is based primarily on the kind of learning best suited to the various aspects.

Ellis (*ibid.*: 212; 1995) argues for a dissociation between explicit and implicit learning where formal recognition and production rely on implicit learning but the meaning and linking aspects rely on explicit, conscious processes.

Implicit learning involves attention to the stimulus but does not involve other conscious operations. It is strongly affected by repetition. Explicit learning is more conscious. The learner makes and tests hypotheses in a search for structure (Ellis, 1994: 214). Explicit learning can involve a search for rules, or applying given rules. It is strongly affected by the quality of the mental processing. What Ellis calls the 'mediational' aspect is the mapping or linking of knowledge of the word form to knowledge of the meaning of the word.

What this means is that, especially for high-frequency words, teachers should explain the meaning of words, and learners should do exercises, look up in dictionaries, and think about the meanings. After brief attention to spelling and pronunciation however, experience in meeting and producing the word form should be left to encounters in meaning focused use.

Aitchison (1994: Chapter 15) sees children acquiring their first language vocabulary as performing three connected but different tasks: a labelling task, a packaging task and a network building task (*ibid.*: 170). These correspond to the three divisions in the Meaning section of Table 2.1: form and meaning, concept and associations.

Table 2.3 provides a broad overview of the different kinds of knowledge and the most effective kinds of learning. It is important to note however that it is possible and helpful to approach the learning of word forms, for example, through explicit learning, but that essentially the most effective knowledge for this aspect of vocabulary is implicit and there must be suitable repeated opportunities for this kind of learning to occur.

The grammar and collocation aspects of use involve pattern recognition and production and thus are most effectively the goal of implicit learning (Ellis and Sinclair, 1996: 236–238). The constraints on vocabulary use are more closely related to meaning and would benefit more from explicit learning. That is, the teacher and learner should discuss where and when certain words should not be used.

Robinson (1989) argues for a 'rich' approach to vocabulary teaching and uses Canale and Swain's (1980) division of communicative competence into grammatical, sociolinguistic, discourse and strategic competence as a checklist for ensuring that all the dimensions of vocabulary knowledge and skill are covered. Robinson stresses the importance of ensuring learners have the skill of negotiating the meaning of words.

Levelt's process model of language use

Table 2.1 (see p. 27) lists the various aspects of what is involved in knowing a word without considering how these aspects are related to

Table 2.3. *Kinds of vocabulary knowledge and the most effective kinds of learning*

Kinds of knowledge		Kinds of learning	Activities
Form		implicit learning involving noticing	repeated meetings as in repeated reading
Meaning		strong explicit learning	depth of processing through the use of images, elaboration, deliberate inferencing
Use	grammar collocation	implicit learning	repetition
	constraints on use	explicit learning	explicit guidance and feedback

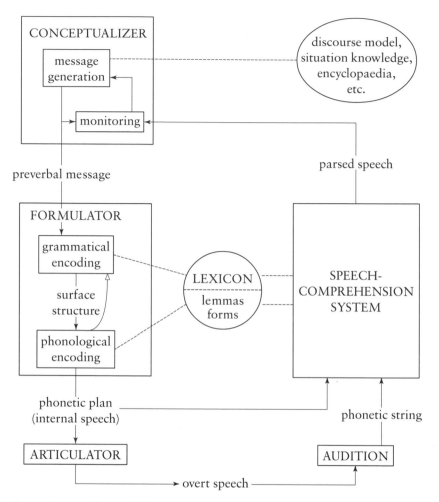

Figure 2.1 Levelt's model (1989: 9) of speech production

each other and how they are involved in normal language use. It is also of value for making decisions about the teaching and learning of vocabulary to see how the aspects of vocabulary knowledge fit into the process of language use. In order to see this we will look at Levelt's (1989; 1992) model of language use and its adaptations (Bierwisch and Schreuder, 1992; de Bot, 1992).

In this model we are most interested in the lexicon and so a brief description will be enough to outline the other parts of the model.

The square boxes represent processing components which make use of procedural knowledge. The two rounded components represent knowledge stores of declarative knowledge. Procedural knowledge is not accessible through introspection. Declarative knowledge is largely examinable through conscious thought and reflection. This is a very important distinction, because models of language acquisition (for example, R. Ellis, 1990) see quite different roles for procedural and declarative knowledge in the development of second language proficiency.

The conceptualizer is where the spoken message begins. The sub-processes involve: intending to say something, choosing the necessary information, putting it in a roughly suitable order, and checking that it fits with what has been said before. The message fragments output of the conceptualizer is input for the formulator which changes the pre-verbal message into a phonetic plan. This change involves grammatically encoding the message and then phonologically encoding the message. In the grammatical encoding, information in the lemma part of the lexicon is accessed by procedures in the grammatical encoder. The most striking feature of this is that these procedures are 'lexically driven' (Levelt, 1989: 181), that is, the grammar, morphology and phonology are determined by the particular words that are chosen. Levelt (*ibid.*: 181) calls this the 'lexical hypothesis'. This idea fits very well with Sinclair's (1987) 'idiom principle' (see chapter 9). In the phonological encoding, the form part of the lexicon is accessed by procedures in the phonological encoder. The output of the formulator is a phonetic plan. The articulator changes this plan into actual speaking. The rest of the model is involved in self-monitoring. That is, listening to what is being produced, comprehending it, and using it to adjust further production. De Bot, Paribakht and Wesche (1997) present an adaptation of Levelt's model to include both language production and language reception.

Let us now look more closely at the lexicon component in Levelt's model. We have already noted two very important points about it. Firstly, that the knowledge it contains is declarative. That is, it is consciously known and can be built up through both incidental learning and formal study. Secondly, it is the choice of particular words that determines the grammar and phonology of sentences, and so grammar and other aspects are important components of what it means to know a word and this knowledge must be closely related to each particular word. This underlines the importance of meeting words in use as a way of developing vocabulary knowledge. It also shows how the decontextualised learning of vocabulary is not sufficient, although it may be useful, for 'knowing a word'.

Levelt (1989: 9, 188) divides the lexicon into two parts, one that contains lemmas and one that contains forms. The lemmas each consist of semantic and grammatical knowledge – that is, knowledge of the meaning components of a word, and knowledge of the syntactic category (part of speech) of a word, its grammatical functions and some other grammatical restrictions and marking that determine its use, including person, number and tense. It is possible that, in addition to meaning components, each lemma contains information about appropriateness, style and other constraints that make it fit particular contexts well (*ibid.*: 183). The information about the lemma is linked by what Levelt calls a 'pointer' to the morpho-phonological form of the word. This simply means that meaning and form are linked in the lexical store.

The various bits of information about any particular word in the lexicon are related to each other not only because they are about the same word but also in a more organised way that relates to the processes of producing or receiving the word. Here is a typical speaking production sequence.

1. The conceptualizer produces a preverbal message consisting of information the speaker wishes to convey.
2. The formulator accesses the lexicon to find the lemma with the appropriate meaning components.
3. Some of these meaning components will be directly connected to particular grammatical features. Other grammatical components that are part of the lemma will be activated.
4. The meaning and grammar components of the lemma are linked to the morphological and phonological features of the word.
5. The appropriate morphological form is chosen or produced for the word to encode the meaning and grammatical function of the word.
6. The phonological features of the word are produced to match the morphological form of the word.
7. The articulator produces the word.

The steps crudely outlined above are very closely related to each other in a series of cause–effect sequences. For example, the link between steps 2 and 3 in the case of the word *painter* is that the meaning of 'someone who paints' is related to a singular countable noun 'expressing the agentive of the action expressed by the verb stem' (Levelt, *ibid.*: 183). Step 4 links this explicitly to the form *painter*. At step 5 the morphological form *paint* + *er* is chosen because the suffix *-er* connects to the agentive function of the word and is an affix producing a noun. At step 6 the appropriate stress pattern can be chosen. The suffix *-er* does not alter the phonological form of the root *paint*.

All of the aspects of knowing a word described here are present in

Table 2.1. The difference is however that in this process based description using Levelt's model, the aspects are shown to be influencing each other.

Levelt (*ibid*.: 183) distinguishes between item relations *within* entries in the lexicon (the types of cause–effect relations for a single word we have just been looking at) and item relations *between* entries (different words). He also considers that inflections are items belonging to the same lexical entry. That is, they are related *within* an entry. Derivations, however, are different lexical entries.

Levelt divides relations *between* entries into two kinds: intrinsic and associative. Intrinsic relationships are based on the four features of meaning, grammar, morphology and phonology. Thus, words can be related because they enter into semantic relations of antonymy, synonymy, etc., or through being members of the same lexical set such as days of the week or parts of the body. Words may be related because they are the same part of speech or fulfil the same grammatical function. Words can be morphologically related to each other through derivation by being members of the same word family. Words may also be related to each other because of their phonological form; for example, they share the same initial or final sounds.

It is generally true to say that when sets of words are being learned, the relations between these new entries in the lexicon can be a source of interference making the learning task more difficult: learning opposites, morphologically similar words, or phonologically similar words together can make learning much more difficult. When words are not learned in sets, the relations by analogy between new and known words can make learning easier. That is, if you already know several words with a certain consonant cluster, then learning a new one with the same initial cluster will be easier. Similarly, already knowing the word for 'a male relative older than your parents' will make the learning of the word for 'a male relative younger than your parents' easier.

Associative relations (Levelt, *ibid*.: 184) depend mainly on frequent collocations rather than on aspects of meaning. Examples include *green* and *grass*, *heat* and *light*, *thunder* and *lightning*. Associative and intrinsic relationships may overlap if intrinsically related items also often occur together. Associative relations carried over from the first language may help deepen the level of processing in the learning of second language words.

Schmitt and Meara (1997) suggest that morphology and associations are related in that when more members are included within a word family because of increasing control of the morphological system, there will be a greater range of potential associations, as each affixed form will tend to bring different associations.

Let us now look at the nine aspects of what is involved in knowing a word as shown in Table 2.1 to see what each aspect includes. Because some of these aspects – word parts, word meaning and collocations – are covered in later chapters, they will be dealt with only briefly here.

Spoken form

Knowing the spoken form of a word includes being able to recognise the word when it is heard and, at the other end of the receptive–productive scale, being able to produce the spoken form in order to express a meaning. Knowledge of the spoken form can be broken down into many parts and research on the 'tip of the tongue' phenomenon (Brown and McNeill, 1966) has revealed some of this knowledge. The tip of the tongue phenomenon occurs when you cannot recall a known word and you search your brain for it. By looking at what information is produced such as the number of syllables in the word, its stress pattern and its initial letter, we can get some idea of how words are classified and stored in the brain. The formal similarities that occur between the target word form and the forms that the search tosses up include number of syllables, initial letter, final letter, syllabic stress, and suffix.

Producing the spoken form of an English word includes being able to pronounce the sounds in the word as well as the degrees of stress of the appropriate syllables of the word if it contains more than one syllable. Research on vocabulary difficulty indicates that an important factor affecting learning is the pronounceability of a word (Rodgers, 1969; Higa, 1965; Ellis and Beaton, 1993). Pronounceability depends on the similarity between individual sounds and suprasegmentals like stress and tone in the first language and second languages, the ways in which these sounds combine with each other, called 'phonotactic grammaticality' (Scholes, 1966), and the relationship between the spelling and sound systems. Numerous contrastive analysis studies have shown that predicting the pronunciation difficulty of individual sounds is not a simple process (see, for example, Hammerly, 1982). Second language sounds that are only slightly different from first language sounds may be more difficult than learning some sounds that do not occur at all in the first language.

Each language allows certain combinations of sounds and does not allow others. The implicit learning of these patterns allows young native speakers of English to reliably distinguish between words which are permitted English words according to the patterns and those which are not. Treiman (1994) in a study based on word games presents evidence that native speakers regard consonant clusters, particularly initial consonant clusters, as units and are reluctant to split them up when playing word games. Final consonant clusters may also be regarded as units rather than a string of phonemes but the rules underlying their structure are more complex. The learning of these patterns however is one way in which the learning of a system makes the learning of individual words easier. This may account for the greater ease in vocabulary learning as learners' proficiency in the second language develops.

Research by Gathercole and Baddeley (1989) indicates that an important factor influencing vocabulary learning is the ability of learners to hold a word in their phonological short-term memory. A variable influencing this for second language learners must be the learners' ability to 'chunk' the spoken form of a word into meaningful segments which in turn depends on L1 and L2 similarity and the learners' level of proficiency in L2. Papagno, Valentine and Baddeley (1991), in a series of experiments, compared several conditions for learning word pairs. Essentially three conditions were examined.

1. Learners associate word forms that are already familiar to them. For example, English speakers had to learn to associate words in pairs, like *roof artist*. In this kind of learning the learners do not have to learn new forms; they simply have to associate known forms. Deliberately interfering with phonological memory did not have serious effects on this kind of learning, probably because the learners were using meaning based associations to remember the pairs.

2. Learners associate word forms that consist of a known first language word and a foreign language word, where the foreign language word resembles some other first language word, for example *throat garlo*, where the Russian word *garlo* has some formal similarities with the English word *gargle*. Because the foreign words were 'meaningful' for the learners, deliberately interfering with phonological short-term memory did not have serious effects on this kind of learning, largely because the learners were using meaning cues rather than phonological rehearsal to remember the new foreign language forms.

3. The learners associate word forms that consist of a known first language word and a foreign language word, where the form of the foreign language word does not readily give rise to associations with known forms, for example *oak sumu* (a Finnish

word). Interfering with phonological short-term memory had serious effects on this kind of learning. This was probably because the learners needed to use phonological rehearsal to learn the new forms (the Finnish words) because they were not readily able to create meaningful associations with the new forms.

Papagno, Valentine and Baddeley's piece of research is very important because it shows that learners need not be limited by the capacity of their short-term phonological memory. In previous research with native speakers (Gathercole and Baddeley, 1989), the size of individuals' short-term phonological memory was found to be a good predictor of their first language vocabulary learning. Service (1992), looking at foreign language vocabulary learning, found that young Finnish learners' skill at repeating nonsense words was the best predictor of their achievement in English in the following two years (Papagno, Valentine and Baddeley, 1991: 332).

Papagno, Valentine and Baddeley's research indicates that foreign language learners can overcome limitations on phonological memory and limitations created by foreign languages whose word forms are very different from those of the learners' first language, by developing meaning based association learning techniques such as the 'keyword' technique. In this, instead of solely relying on phonological repetition to make the form of a foreign word stick in the mind, learners should be making connections between the shape of the foreign word and the shape of already known words either in their first language, the foreign language, or other languages they know. This idea fits neatly within the levels of processing hypothesis where the quantity of learning depends on the quality of the mental processing that occurs when the learning takes place. It also underlines the importance of helping learners to see that the shape of the foreign words they have to learn is not random but is patterned on implicit rules. That is, there is a phonotactic grammaticality underlying the spoken forms of the words.

The influence of phonological short-term memory must not be underestimated. In a well conducted experiment with second language learners, Ellis and Beaton (1993) looked at receptive and productive knowledge of foreign language (German)/first language (English) word pairs learned in various conditions, including keyword and repetition conditions. For productive learning (L1→L2) the similarity between the phonological patterns of the two languages was very important. The more pronounceable the foreign words were, the easier they were to learn. Pronounceability was not found to be so

Table 2.4. *Age and the correlation of the non-word repetition test with vocabulary size for young native speakers (Gathercole and Baddeley, 1993)*

Age	Correlation
4	0.559
5	0.524
6	0.562
8	0.284

important for receptive learning (L2→L1). Learning using the keyword technique is most effective when the foreign word form is very easy to learn or when the form of the keyword closely resembles the form of the foreign word. When either of these two conditions does not apply, then repetition of the foreign word form to establish a secure memory for its form is a very important part of vocabulary learning.

There seem to be different effects for phonologically based and mnemonically based strategies on long-term retention. Wang and Thomas (1992) found that although mnemonic keyword learning took less time and gave better results for immediate recall, on a long-term measure (one week later) rote repetition was superior. Part of the explanation for this is that learners using the mnemonic strategy did not choose their own keywords. Nevertheless it is clear that repetition of new word forms is a useful strategy, and sustained follow-up of initial learning is essential for long-term memory.

Research (Gathercole and Baddeley, 1993: 49) also shows that for native speakers the size of phonological short-term memory plays a less important role in vocabulary learning as learners get older.

The decreasing size of the correlations suggests that the more words you know, the easier it is to learn new words because of the phonological features that the new words share with already known words. Research by Service (1992) with young Finnish learners of English shows that it is not age that is the likely cause of the reduction of the importance of phonological short-term memory but previous learning. The contribution of phonological short-term memory is probably most important when beginning to learn another language because there is often little other relevant knowledge to relate new forms to (Gathercole and Baddeley, 1993: 56).

Cheung (1996) found that for 12-year-old second language learners the capacity of their phonological short-term memory was a significant factor in learning for those with lower second language proficiency. Learners with higher proficiency may have been drawing more on long-term knowledge of the second language to support their learning (see also Hulme, Maughan and Brown, 1991).

It is thus very important in vocabulary learning that learners rapidly develop knowledge and strategies that increase the efficiency of, and reduce dependence on, short-term phonological memory. Learners differ in the size of their short-term phonological memories and this can have marked effects on their long-term learning. The more they can use meaning based techniques of learning word forms such as the keyword approach, and the more they can support their short-term phonological memory through analogy with known words and familiarity with the underlying phonotactic patterns, the less their learning will be restricted by the size of their short-term phonological memory. Familiarity with underlying patterns can be achieved in several complementary ways. Firstly, and most importantly, learners should quickly become familiar with a large number of words. Secondly, learners' attention can be deliberately drawn to the patterning of sounds in the second language. This can be done by grouping regularly spelled, similarly patterned words together, and by asking learners to distinguish real words from nonsense words which do not follow permissible sound combinations. Thirdly, words containing infrequent or unusual sequences of sound can be deliberately avoided in the early stages of language learning. Words which have a similar form to first language words will have a lighter learning burden than words containing unfamiliar sounds and unfamiliar combinations of sounds.

Written form

One aspect of gaining familiarity with the written form of words is spelling. As Brown and Ellis (1994) point out in the introduction to their excellent collection of articles about spelling, this has been a growth area for research. What is striking about the research on spelling is the way that it reflects the issues involved in other aspects of vocabulary and language knowledge; that is, the same questions arise. What are the roles of system knowledge and stored wholes? How do these different kinds of knowledge interact in the development of the skill? What are the roles of language use and direct study of language in the development of the spelling skill? How do the different aspects of vocabulary knowledge – spoken form, word building, grammar, collocations, meaning – affect each other?

The ability to spell is most strongly influenced by the way learners represent the phonological structure of the language. Studies of native speakers of English have shown strong effects on spelling from training in categorising words according to their sounds and matching these to letters and combinations of letters (Bradley and Huxford, 1994). The training in one of the studies involved 40 ten minute training sessions but the positive effects persisted for years. Early training helps create a system that improves later learning and storage. Playing with rhymes can help in this awareness of phonological units and is an effective categorisation activity.

Comparison of the spelling of English speakers with speakers of other languages shows that irregularity in the English spelling system creates difficulty for learners of English as a first language (Moseley, 1994). Poor spelling can affect learners' writing in that they use strategies to hide their poor spelling. These include using limited vocabularies, favouring regularly spelled words and avoiding words that are hard to spell. Although there is no strong relationship between spelling and intelligence, readers may interpret poor spelling as a sign of lack of knowledge. There is a strong link between spelling and reading. Some models suggest that changes in spelling strategy are related to changes in reading strategy. Skill at reading can influence skill at spelling and there is evidence that literacy can affect phonological representations.

Learners can represent the spoken forms of words in their memory in a variety of ways: as whole words, as onsets (the initial letter or letters) and rimes (the final part of a syllable), as letter names, and as phonemes. One way of representing a model of spelling is to see it as consisting of two routes. One accesses stored representations of whole words and the other constructs written forms from sound–spelling correspondences. However, it is generally considered that this model is too simplistic, that the two routes influence each other and the choice of routes depends on the type of processing demands.

The learning burden of the written form of words will be strongly affected by first and second language parallels (Does the first language use the same writing system as the second language?), by the regularity of the second language writing system, and by the learners' knowledge of the spoken form of the second language vocabulary.

A training programme to improve spelling should involve:

1. Opportunities for substantial amounts of extensive reading at levels where fluency can improve, that is, with texts containing virtually no unknown vocabulary.
2. Practice in categorising and analysing words according to their spoken form. This can involve rhyming activities where learners put rhyming words into groups, think of rhymes for given words, listen to rhymes, and make simple poems.
3. Relating spoken forms to written forms at a variety of levels: the word level, the rime level, the syllable level and the phoneme level. Most attention should be given to regular patterns. It may be helpful to make mnemonic links using analogy, and to match motor movements (writing in the air, tracing, writing) to sound.
4. Spaced repeated retrieval. The programme should involve short lessons, preferably three or four times a week, involving recall of previously practised words and patterns of sound–spelling correspondence.
5. Monitoring and feedback. Teachers should check that learners are making progress and should inform learners of their progress. Regular checks could involve dictation, classifying words according to sound patterns and spelling patterns, and monitoring free written work.
6. Learners being trained in the use of learning strategies and the goals of those strategies and being encouraged to become independent in the application of the strategies. Strategies may include: finding analogies, cover and recall, focusing on difficult parts and setting regular learning goals. Learners should also apply the strategies to words that they see as important and problematical for them.

Schmitt (2000) has a useful discussion of the importance of speed in word form recognition.

Word parts

The learning burden of words will be light if they consist of known parts, that is, affixes and stems that are already known from the first language or from other second language words. Some affixes and stems change their form when they are joined together, for example, *in-* + *legal* = *illegal*.

Knowing a word can involve knowing it is made up of affixes and a stem that can occur in other words. There is evidence that, for first language users of English, many low-frequency, regularly formed, complex words are rebuilt each time they are used. That is, a word like *unpleasantness* is not stored as a whole unanalysed item, but is reformed from *un*, *pleasant* and *ness* each time it is used. This does not necessarily mean that the word is learned in this way. It may be that for some words their whole unanalysed form is learned initially, and it is later seen as fitting into a regular pattern and is then stored differently.

This way of dealing with complex words suggests that there are reasonably regular predictable patterns of word building. Bauer and Nation (1993) have attempted to organise these into a series of stages based on the criteria of frequency, regularity of form, regularity of meaning and productivity. Lying behind this series of stages is the idea that learners' knowledge of word parts and word building changes as their proficiency develops.

It is thus also possible to argue that knowing a word involves knowing the members of its word family, and what are considered members of the word family will increase as proficiency develops. For example, knowing the word *mend* can also involve knowing its forms, meanings and uses: *mends*, *mended* and *mending*. At a later stage of proficiency, knowing *mend* may also involve knowing *mender*, *mendable* and *unmendable*. There is research evidence to support the idea that word families are psychologically real, and that when we talk about knowing a word, we should really be talking about knowing a word family. Nagy, Anderson, Schommer, Scott and Stallman (1989) found that for native speakers the speed of recognition of a word was more predictable from the total frequency of its word family than from the frequency of the particular word form itself.

There is value in explicitly drawing learners' attention to word parts. In particular, an important vocabulary learning strategy is using word parts to help remember the meaning of a word. This strategy requires learners to know the most frequent and regular affixes well, to be able to recognise them in words, and to be able to re-express the meaning of the word using the meanings of its word parts. The learning burden of a word will depend on the degree to which it consists of already known word parts and the regularity with which these fit together.

We will look at word parts much more closely in chapter 8.

Connecting form and meaning

Typically, learners think of knowing a word as knowing what the word sounds like (its spoken form) or looks like (its written form) and its meaning. But learners not only need to know the form of a word and its meaning, they need to be able to connect the two. For example, a learner of English might be aware of the form *brunch*. The learner might also know that there is a concept for a single meal which takes the place of breakfast and lunch. The learner might also know that the form *brunch* is the appropriate form to communicate the concept of a meal combining breakfast and lunch. It is possible to know the form *brunch* and have no concept of its meaning. It is also possible to be familiar with the form, to have the appropriate concept but not to connect the two.

The strength of the connection between the form and its meaning will determine how readily the learner can retrieve the meaning when seeing or hearing the word form, or retrieve the word form when wishing to express the meaning. Baddeley (1990) suggests that each successful retrieval of the form or meaning strengthens the link between the two. It is thus very important that the learners not only see the form and meaning together initially, but have plenty of spaced repeated opportunities to make retrievals. This is looked at more closely in chapter 8, which includes a section on the use of word cards.

Making the form–meaning connection is easier if roughly the same form in the first language relates to roughly the same meaning. That is, the learning burden of making the form–meaning connection is light if the word being learned is a cognate or a loan word shared by the first language and the second language. For some languages, the presence of loan words makes learning much easier.

Daulton (1998) notes the enormous number of English loan words in Japanese: up to 38% of the 2000 most frequent words of English, and 26% within the *University Word List* (Xue and Nation, 1984). Daulton's study and other studies on Japanese indicate that the existence of loan words helps the learning of English even in cases (the majority) where the learners need to extend the limited meaning that the loan word has in Japanese. Some examples of loan words in Japanese are: *paatii* (party), *piano* (piano), *booru* (bell), W*aarudo Shiriizu* (World Series).

Another way of making the form–meaning connection easier is to put a first language link between the second language word form and the meaning. This is the basis of the keyword technique which is described more fully in chapter 8.

The form–meaning connection is easier to make if the sound or shape of the word form has a clear connection to the meaning. In New Zealand sign language some signs are to some degree iconic, that is, their shape and movement clearly relate to the meaning. The sign for *minute* (a period of time) is represented by a minute hand moving around a clock face. The *Dictionary of New Zealand Sign Language*

(Kennedy, 1997) includes short hints in many of its entries to draw readers' attention to these connections to make learning easier.

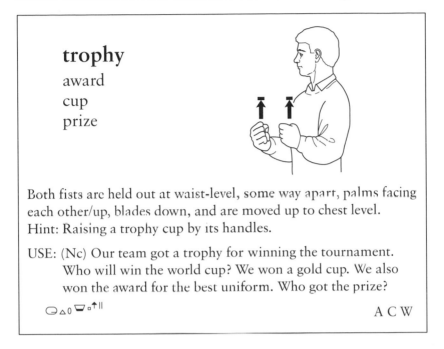

trophy

award
cup
prize

Both fists arc held out at waist-level, some way apart, palms facing each other/up, blades down, and are moved up to chest level.
Hint: Raising a trophy cup by its handles.

USE: (Nc) Our team got a trophy for winning the tournament. Who will win the world cup? We won a gold cup. We also won the award for the best uniform. Who got the prize?

A C W

Concept and referents

A feature of words that is especially striking when they are looked up in a dictionary is that they have a lot of different meanings. This is particularly so for high-frequency words. The entry for a very high-frequency word may cover a page or more of a standard dictionary. When we look at the range of meanings which may be included for a single word, we may notice that some are quite different from each other. For example, for the word *bank*, we may find *the bank of a river* and *the national bank*. In this case, words which share the same form and part of speech are derived from different sources, old Norse and Latin. Words which have the same form but have completely unrelated meanings are called **homonyms**; a term which also includes **homographs** (words with identical written forms) and **homophones** (words with identical spoken forms). Homonyms should be counted and learned as different words, preferably at different times.

Some of the meanings for a particular word will show a clear relationship with each other. For example, *bear a heavy physical load* and *bear emotional distress*; *a person's head* and *the head of a school*.

Should these related uses be treated as the same word or as different words? Nagy (1997) points out that there are two ways in which language users can deal with related meanings, and both ways are essential to normal language use.

1. The language user may have a permanent internal representation of each related meaning. This means that when the word form is met, the user has to select the appropriate sense of the word from those stored in the brain. This process can be called '**sense selection**'.

2. The language user has an underlying concept for a word that is appropriate for the range of meanings with which the word is used. For example, the word *fork* is best represented by a two pronged shape which covers its range of uses: the fork you can eat with, a fork in the road, forked lightning, etc. When the learner meets the word in use, the learner has to work out during the comprehension process what particular real world items the word is referring to. This process is called '**reference specification**'. For example, *John* is a name used by males. If someone tells us, 'John will be here at 6pm,' we have to decide which particular *John* is being referred to.

Both of these processes, sense selection and reference specification, are normal features of language use. The interesting question is which process is the one that accounts for most of the allocation of meaning to a word? From a teaching and learning point of view, do learners have to learn and store multiple meanings for a word or do they need to have an underlying meaning which they use to work out particular meanings for a word when they use language? Should teachers be trying to show the meaning underlying different uses of a word or should the teacher treat the different uses as different items to learn? Dictionaries try to distinguish several meanings of a word rather than show the common features running through various uses. For example, *root* is given the meanings: part of a plant which is normally in the soil; part of a hair, tooth, tongue, etc. which is like a root in position or function; that from which something grows; form of a word; (arith.) quantity which multiplied by itself . . .

For learning, words can be defined with reference to learners' first language or to English. For example, from the point of view of an Indonesian the word *fork* is several words: *garpu* (the fork we eat with), *pertigaan* or *simpang jalan* (the fork in the road), *cabang* (the fork in a tree, the same word as *branch*). However, from the point of view of the English language, *fork* is one word. It is possible to describe the meaning of *fork* so that this meaning includes most uses of the word. Defining a word by looking for the concept that runs through all its uses reduces the number of words to learn. Instead of having to learn three words represented by the form *fork*, by learning the underlying concept of *fork* the learners have only one item to learn. There are other reasons for approaching vocabulary learning from this point of view. One of the educational values of learning a foreign language is seeing how the foreign language divides up experience in a different way from the first language. From an Indonesian point of view, *fork* is defined mainly by its function – something to push food on to your spoon. From an English point of view, *fork* is defined by its shape. Treating meaning in English as if it was just a mirror of the first language hides this difference. Another reason for drawing attention to the underlying concept is that every occurrence of the word will act as a repetition of what was taught instead of as a different item. That is, each occurrence of the word will contain known features and will build on previous learning.

To decide if you are dealing with one word or more than one word, see if extra learning is required. Can *branch* (of a tree) be taught in such a way that *branch* (of a bank or business) requires no additional learning?

Ruhl (1989) argues that rather than follow dictionaries in seeing words as having multiple meanings we should assume that each word has a single inherent lexical meaning. There are two major sources of meaning when we comprehend a word in context: (1) its inherent lexical meaning (what it means as an isolated word), and (2) the inferential meaning which we infer from other words in the immediate context, and from our knowledge of the world. The lexical meaning may be very abstract. Where a word has more than one sense, we should assume that these senses are related to each other by general rules that apply to other words. These rules include the idea that words can have a range of senses from concrete to abstract and these differences in concreteness and abstractness are inferred from the context. Similarly, whether an object is viewed as being animate or inanimate need not be part of the lexical meaning but may be inferred from context and our world knowledge.

Ruhl produces evidence to support his position by examining many examples of use and shows that apparent variations in meaning can be accounted for by inferential meaning, and that a stable though abstract meaning can be seen which runs through all senses of a word.

There is often a cultural dimension to the meaning and use of vocabulary, and teachers should help learners explore this. Some of the most striking cultural differences relate to food, family relationships and politeness behaviour. Spinelli and Siskin (1992: 313) suggest some useful guidelines.

1. Present and practise vocabulary within culturally authentic semantic fields and networks of relationships.
2. Present and practise vocabulary in ways that distinguish the native and target culture.
3. Use authentic visuals where native culture/target culture referents differ in form.
4. Present and practise a word's denotation and connotation (what we have termed concept and associations).
5. Present and practise vocabulary in ways that will reinforce appropriate behaviour in the target culture.

When working with lexical sets and associational links, care needs to be taken that related items do not interfere with each other through the wrong links being made.

Kellerman (1985) reports cases where Dutch learners of German initially accept correct Dutch-like idioms in German, then reject them, and then eventually accept them. Kellerman sees L1 playing an important role at stage 1 and stage 2. At stage 1, where the Dutch-like idiom in German is accepted, L1 is a source of support for learning. In stage 2, learners are developing awareness of differences between L1 and L2 and thus tend to be suspicious of similarities. At stage 3, as the Dutch learners have a more native-speakerlike command of German, L1 has a diminished effect and the idioms are accepted as German idioms. Levenston's (1990) data on advanced English learners' lack of acceptance of abstract uses of words like *cement* in *cement a relationship* may be a result of similar behaviour with the learners being at stage 2.

Associations

In a fascinating paper, Miller and Fellbaum (1991) describe the semantic relationships between a very large number of English words. They show that it is necessary to distinguish between parts of speech to describe the organisational structure of the lexicon. The most pervasive and important relationship is synonymy, but nouns, adjectives and verbs each use preferred semantic relations and have their own kind of organisation. Understanding these relations is useful for explaining the meanings of words and for creating activities to enrich learners' understanding of words. Understanding how the lexicon might be organised is also useful for the creation of limited vocabularies for defining words and for the simplification of text. Miller and Fellbaum's goal is to model how the lexicon is organised so that we can better understand the nature of language, language knowledge and language use.

Nouns

Nouns can be organised into hierarchies represented by tree diagrams and these hierarchies can involve many levels. Here is one strand of a hierarchy.

animal
vertebrate
mammal
herbivore
perissodactyl
equid
horse
pony

Miller and Fellbaum (*ibid*.: 204–205) say that 26 unique beginning points are sufficient to begin tree diagrams that include every English noun. These beginning points are:

act, action, activity	natural object
animal, fauna	natural phenomenon
artefact	person, human being
attribute, property	plant, flora
body, corpus	possession, property
cognition, ideation	process
communication	quantity, amount
event, happening	relation
feeling, emotion	shape
food	society
group, collection	state, condition
location, place	substance
motive	time

The relationship between items in a hierarchy is called hyponymy (*tree* is the hypernym, *beech* is the hyponym). *Hypo*- means 'under' as in *hypodermic* – an injection *under* the skin. Three additional kinds of information are needed to distinguish between nouns: parts, attributes and functions. House is a hyponym of *building* and it has certain parts (bedrooms, kitchen) and a certain function (for people to live in). The whole–part relationship (house–kitchen) is called meronymy (*kitchen* is a meronym of the holonym *house*).

Adjectives

Predicative adjectives need to be distinguished from non-predicative adjectives. This is one of many instances of the connection between lexical organisation and syntactic behaviour. Non-predicative adjectives cannot be used after the verb *to be* as the predicate of a sentence (*'The leader is former'), are not gradable (*'very previous'), and cannot be made into nouns. Non-predicative adjectives are organised like nouns in hyponymic relationships. Predicative adjectives are basically organised into opposites (antonymy) (see also Deese, 1965). There is meaning-based antonymy (*hot/cold*), and word form-based antonymy (*healthy/unhealthy*). Adverbs are organised like adjectives.

Verbs

A basic distinction needs to be made between verbs representing an event and those representing a state (a distinction which is also important in the grammatical behaviour of verbs). Verbs representing an event can be organised into shallow hierarchies. Miller and Fellbaum (1991: 215) suggest that there are fourteen semantically distinct groups.

bodily care	contact
bodily functions	creation
change	motion
cognition	perception
communication	possession
competition	social interaction
consumption	weather

There tend to be many items at one particular level of these shallow hierarchies. So the category of *motion* can include *move* (make a movement) and *move* (travel, displace). This last category includes walk which is the superordinate of about 65 words including *march*, *strut*, *traipse* and *amble*. The hierarchical relationship for verbs is different from that for nouns. Miller and Fellbaum term it 'troponymy', and it expresses the idea that something is done in a particular manner. So, *to stroll* is 'to walk in a particular manner'. There is a variety of other relationships that Miller and Fellbaum call 'entailment', which means that engaging in one action involves engaging in the other. So, *snore* entails *sleep*, *win* entails *play*, and *stagger* entails *walk*. Antonymy can exist between co-troponyms.

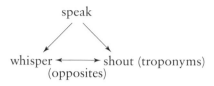

Cruse (1986) provides an exhaustive treatment of lexical relations.

The relationships described here (synonymy, hyponymy, meronymy, antonymy, troponymy, entailment) are useful starting points for devising classification activities with words that learners already know. Classification activities can involve distinguishing and grouping similar items in various ways, justifying the distinguishing and grouping by explaining relationships, and using the relationships to produce or change text, such as suggesting cause–effect chains, expressing the opposite of a statement, making a generalisation from a particular piece of evidence, or restating something in a precise way (see Sokmen, 1992, for some examples). The grouping and distinguishing of items can make use of schematic aids like tree diagrams, Venn diagrams, flow diagrams and matrices.

Learners can be helped in explaining relationships by the teacher providing descriptive phrases to use including: *x is a part of y*; *x is a kind of y*; *x is y done in a certain way*; *x is the opposite of y*; *x is like y*; and *x involves y*.

Care needs to be taken in reading first language research because various meanings are given to terms like 'contextual' and 'association'. For Stahl and Fairbanks (1986: 74) 'contextual knowledge' is knowledge of a core concept and how it is realised in different contexts – what we have called knowing its referents. Stahl and Fairbanks (*ibid.*: 75) also include 'associations' within knowing the meaning of a word but use it to refer to the link between a word form and its meaning.

Yavuz (1963) and Yavuz and Bousfield (1969) found that even when a partly learned word had been forgotten, the connotative aspects of its translation were still retained.

Grammatical functions

In order to use a word it is necessary to know what part of speech it is and what grammatical patterns it can fit into. Many linguists now consider the lexicon to play an important, if not central, role in grammar.

Sinclair's (1987) corpus based research suggests that lexical choice, particularly of verbs, largely determines the grammatical construction of the rest of the sentence. Levelt's (1989) description of speech production looked at earlier in this chapter sees aspects of grammatical knowledge being included in the lexicon.

The grammatical learning burden of items depends on parallels between the second language and the first language, and the parallels in grammatical behaviour between words of related meaning. If a second language word takes the same grammatical patterns as its rough equivalent in the first language, then the learning burden will be light. If words of related meaning like *hate* and *like* take similar patterns then the learning burden of one of them will be lighter because the previous learning of the other will act as a guide.

Collocations

Knowing a word involves knowing what words it typically occurs with. Is it more usual, for example, to say that we ate some *speedy food*, *quick food*, or *fast food*? Pawley and Syder (1983) argue that the reason we can speak our first language fluently and choose word sequences that make us sound like native speakers is because we have stored large numbers of memorised sequences in our brain. Instead of constructing these each time we need to say something, we frequently draw on these ready made sequences.

Collocations differ greatly in size (the number of words involved in the sequence), in type (function words collocating with content words (*look* with *at*), content words collocating with content words (*united* with *states*)), in closeness of collocates (*expressed* their own honest *opinion*), and in the possible range of collocates (*commit* with *murder*, *a crime, hara kiri, suicide* . . .). We will look at these features and many other aspects in chapter 9.

The availability of large corpora, cheap effective software and powerful computers has helped research on collocation considerably. However, the research can only be done to a certain point by computer and then researcher judgement and analysis must be used. Studies of collocation which have relied solely on computing procedures have yielded results which are not very useful. Research on collocations shows that there are patterns. An awareness of these patterns can reduce the learning burden of certain words. Where collocations are similar between the first and second language, the learning burden will be lighter.

Collocation is only one of a wide range of relationships that relate to the appropriate interpretation and productive use of vocabulary.

Miller (1999) shows that a very important aspect of knowing a word is having a cognitive representation of the set of contexts in which a given form can be used to express a given meaning. This contextual knowledge can involve situational context, topical context and local context. Collocation is largely local context information provided by words in the immediate neighbourhood of a word. Topical context information comes from knowledge of the topic that is being written or spoken about. Thus understanding the meaning of *ball* could at least partly depend on what topic is being dealt with, *dancing*, *football*, *golf* or *partying*. Situational information involves general knowledge and knowledge of the particular situation in which the communication occurs.

Constraints on use

Most words are not constrained in their use by sociolinguistic factors. Where there are constraints, the clues for constraints on use can come from the way the word is translated into the first language or from the context in which the word is used. In some languages there are very severe constraints on the terms used to refer to people, particularly in showing the relationship of the speaker to the person being referred to. Learners may anticipate this and be cautious in this area when using a second language.

There are several factors that limit where and when certain words can be used. Failure to observe these can result in inappropriate use. One way of seeing the range of constraints on the use of words in general and of gaining information about constraints on particular words is to look at the 'style values' or usage labels used in dictionaries (Cassidy, 1972; Hartmann, 1981). Hartmann notes the difficulty in consistently assigning words to the various categories. Cassidy observes that the labels 'low', 'barbarous' and 'corrupt' are no longer used, and suggests a set of scales which include: *extent* (international–national–regional–local–individual), *quantity* (frequency), *currency* (out of use–going out of use–in present stable use–of uncertain stability), *recency*, *restrictedness*, *level* (cultivated–general–uncultivated), *register* (formal–informal–familiar), *figuration* (literal–ametaphoric–extremely metaphoric).

The typical frequency of a word acts as a constraint on its use. If a teacher spends a lot of time on a word and overuses it, this affects the learners' use of the word. Overusing low-frequency words has a comical effect ('Salamanca Road bifurcates at the Terrace'). If time is given to words according to their usefulness in English then this can be avoided. Learners may have difficulty with low-frequency words in knowing whether to use them productively or to prefer a more frequent word.

Constraints on use may differ across cultures. In Thai, names like *pig*, *fatty*, *shrimp* and *mouse* are common nicknames. They are less acceptable in English. Adjectives like *fat* and *old* have to be used with care in English when describing someone who is present; in some cultures to say someone is fat is a compliment indicating that they are well off and well cared for. To say someone is old carries with it ideas of wisdom and respect.

Most constraints on use are best dealt with by discussion and explicit cross-cultural comparison. The frequency constraint is best dealt with by familiarity with the language, although in the early stages of learning direct information about whether a word is commonly used or not is useful. Some dictionaries (*COBUILD* and the *Longman Dictionary of Contemporary English*) include frequency information.

Item knowledge and system knowledge

In several of the aspects of what it means to know a word we have seen the choice that exists between attention given to the systems which lie behind vocabulary (the affixation system, the sound system, the spelling system, collocation, the grammatical system, lexical sets) and the unique behaviour of each word. This choice gives rise to several important questions.

What systematic aspects of vocabulary deserve explicit attention? N. Ellis (1994, 1995) argues for less explicit attention to formal features and more to meaning, relying largely on experience to build up knowledge of word forms. Ellis does not rule out the value of explicit attention to sound, spelling and grammar rules, but sees experience as being a strong essential component of learning. The cautious position adopted in this book is that both kinds of learning are useful. The teacher's skill lies in balancing the kinds of attention across the four strands of a course. Explicit attention to form and system should never occupy more than 25% of class time, but it should not be absent.

When should this attention to the systematic aspects of vocabulary knowledge be given, when the individual items are first met, or after they have been at least partly learned? That is, should words be first learned as unanalysed wholes without careful concern for the other words they relate to, and only later their place within word building systems, lexical fields, and grammatical patterns be explored? This would certainly parallel first language learning. Myles, Hooper and Mitchell (1998) present evidence to support this position in second language learning. There is no doubt that attention to form and rules must be supported and prepared for by experience with the items in use. In some cases this may involve memorisation of units that will later be analysed and in other cases may involve learning a rule or pattern that is then subsequently practised and used.

There is undoubtedly a relationship between frequency of occurrence of individual items and the role of system knowledge in their use; high-frequency items are used largely on the basis of particular experience with that item rather than on the application of rules. Very frequent derived forms like *impossible* and *beautiful* are stored and used as if they were base words rather than being reconstructed according to derivational rules each time they are used. We will look at this issue again in chapter 9.

3 Teaching and explaining vocabulary

This chapter looks at teaching and learning activities. It looks at the jobs that teaching activities need to perform, how teachers can communicate the meanings of words to learners and a wide range of activities for vocabulary teaching and learning.

Learning from teaching and learning activities

This section looks at the psychological conditions that need to occur in order for vocabulary learning to take place. It is organised around four questions that teachers should ask about any teaching or learning activity.

1. What is the learning goal of the activity?
2. What psychological conditions does the activity use to help reach the learning goal?
3. What are the observable signs that learning might occur?
4. What are the design features of the activity which set up the conditions for learning?

The section ends with a detailed look at repetition and vocabulary learning.

Let us first look at a vocabulary teaching technique to see how these questions might be used.

The 'What is it?' technique (Nation, 1978a) is a useful way of learning new vocabulary, in particular becoming familiar with the spoken form of the word and linking it to its meaning. The teacher gradually communicates the meaning of a word by using it in context. When the learners think they know what the word means, they raise their hands. After enough hands are raised, the teacher asks a learner for a translation or explanation of the meaning. The teacher's description might go like this. The word being taught is *precise*.

'Sometimes it is important to make a precise measurement. Sometimes it is not important to be precise. Doctors need a lot of information to find the precise nature of a disease. If you tell me your precise age, you will tell me how old you are in years, months, and days! When you give someone precise instructions, the instructions must be accurate and complete . . .'

When using this technique several things are important. First, not too much information is given about the word at the beginning, so that the learners have to listen attentively to the word in a range of contexts. Second, the teacher repeats the sentences saying each sentence at least twice when it is first used and going back over the previously said sentences. The teacher does not ask the first learners who raise their hands for the meaning of the word (a translation, a synonym, or a definition), but keeps on describing until most of the class have raised their hands. If this technique is used properly, the learners will have made a very good start to knowing the word *precise*. It is however easy to use the technique badly: by giving the meaning too quickly, by not repeating the sentences, by removing any challenge for attention. This is another way of saying that there are features in the effective use of the technique that encourage learning. These design features are the repetition of the word and its contexts, the presence of a variety of rich contexts, and the need to give careful attention to the word and its contexts in order to be able to complete the activity by working out its meaning.

These features set up conditions that research tells us are important for language acquisition. These conditions include having a positive attitude to the activity (helped by its puzzle-like nature), noticing the item several times and thoughtfully processing its meaning. These conditions help reach the vocabulary learning goal. It is therefore important that teachers are aware of the important features of techniques so that they know how to use them and what to look for when they are being used (see Loschky and Bley-Vroman, 1993: 165).

When the technique is being used the teacher should be looking for signs that it might be achieving its learning goal. These signs include: the learners are interested and paying attention; they are trying to find an answer, and they do find the answer but not too soon.

We will now look at each of the four questions in detail.

What is the learning goal of the activity?

As we have noted (see p. 1), a learning goal may be a language goal (vocabulary, grammar), ideas or content such as cultural knowledge or safety information, skills (accuracy, fluency), and text (discourse schemata, rhetorical devices, interaction routines). In this book we are interested in the vocabulary learning goal and when looking at

Table 3.1. *The learning goals of some vocabulary activities*

Activity	Learning goals
Guessing from context	Word meaning, collocates Learn a strategy
Keyword technique	Link form to meaning, word meaning Learn a strategy
Breaking words into parts	Link form to meaning, word meaning Learn a strategy
Split information tasks with annotated pictures	Bring receptive vocabulary into productive use
'It's my word . . .' Learners present words they have met	Teach word form, meaning and use Develop an awareness of what is involved in knowing a word

teaching and learning activities, we can answer this question in a very general way by saying a vocabulary learning goal. But we can also be more specific by considering all the aspects of what is involved in knowing a word (see Table 2.1) and deciding which of these is the learning goal of the activity. For example, is the learning goal to learn the spelling of some words, their pronunciation, or, more commonly, to recognise a word form and link it to its meaning? In general when looking at learning goals and analysing how a goal will be reached, it is simplest to consider only one learning goal at a time. Most activities however can achieve several learning goals. Let us look at some vocabulary activities to see what their specific vocabulary learning goal might be.

In order to reach a goal, the knowledge or information that makes up that goal needs to be available. Information about words, for example words' meanings, can come from textual input such as a reading or listening text, or the context provided on a worksheet; information can come from a reference source such as a teacher or a dictionary, or it can come from the learners in a group who already know something about the word. Newton's (forthcoming) study found that when learners discussed the meanings of words from a worksheet with each other, the vast majority of discussions resulted in useful and accurate information being provided about the words. This is not surprising. Vocabulary tests of learners who have roughly the same proficiency level usually show a remarkable diversity of knowledge (Saragi, Nation and Meister, 1978). All learners usually know the higher frequency words, and one or two learners know many of the other words appropriate to their level of proficiency. Newton (1993), for example, found that in his pre-test to the speaking tasks, 35% of the 111 tested words were known by all learners, 54% by one or more learners but not everyone, and 11% were not known by anyone. It was the 54% that were known by at least one person that could most usefully be discussed by the learners. In addition, the learners could use the context clues to work out the meanings of the words that nobody knew before the activity.

What psychological conditions does the activity use to help reach the learning goal?

There are three important general processes that may lead to a word being remembered. These comprise noticing (through formal instruction, negotiation, the need to comprehend or produce, awareness of inefficiencies), retrieval, and creative (generative) use. These processes can be viewed as three steps with the later steps including the earlier steps.

Noticing

The first process encouraging learning is noticing, that is giving attention to an item. This means that learners need to notice the word, and be aware of it as a useful language item (see Ellis, 1991; McLaughlin, 1990; Schmidt, 1990 for discussions of noticing). This noticing may be affected by several factors, including the salience of the word in the textual input or in the discussion of the text, previous contact that the learners have had with the word, and learners' realisation that the word fills a gap in their knowledge of the language (Schmidt and Frota, 1986; Ellis, 1990). Noticing also occurs when learners look up a word in a dictionary, deliberately study a word, guess from context, or have a word explained to them.

Motivation and interest are important enabling conditions for noticing. The choice of content can be a major factor stimulating interest. In his study of learning from listening, Elley (1989: 185) found quite different results from the same learners listening to two different stories. This seemed to have been due to the lack of involvement of the learners in one of the stories because of its strangeness, lack of humour, low levels of action and conflict and so on. Without the engagement and aroused attention of the learners, there can be little opportunity for other conditions favouring learning to take effect. Although there is no generally accepted theory of why interest is important and the factors that arouse interest, teachers need to watch their learners carefully and seek their opinions about what stories and topics they find interesting. There is some evidence (Bawcom, 1995) that teachers' views of what will be interesting do not match with what learners find interesting.

Interest can also be looked at from the word level. Elley (1989) asked teachers to rate vocabulary in a story according to its importance to the plot of the story that was read to the class. This is a kind of measure of interest in relation to the story. There was a moderate correlation (.42) between the ratings of importance to the plot and vocabulary learning. This indicates that if teachers chose to write up or define words that figured centrally in the plot, the chances of them being learned would be higher than with words not so important for the plot.

Noticing involves decontextualisation. Decontextualisation occurs when learners give attention to a language item as a part of the language rather than as a part of a message. This can occur in a variety of ways.

- While listening or reading, the learner notices that a word is new or thinks, 'I have seen that word before,' or thinks, 'That word is used differently from the ways I have seen it used before.'
- The teacher highlights a word while writing it on the blackboard.
- The learners negotiate the meaning of a word with each other or with the teacher.
- The teacher explains a word for the learners by giving a definition, a synonym, or a first language translation.

Notice that decontextualised does not mean that the word does not occur in a sentence context. All the examples given above can occur, for example, with words that are in a story that the teacher is reading aloud to the class. Decontextualisation means that the word is removed from its message context to be focused on as a language item. The focus can be very brief or can be for a long time. It may be that all language learning necessarily involves some degree of contextualisation. That is, in order to acquire the language, learners need to consciously see language items as parts of the language system rather than only as messages. The problem is in deciding how much of this kind of attention to give, what to direct it to, and when to give it. However, even if decontextualisation is not an essential element of language learning, there is evidence that it can certainly help learning. We will look at two kinds of decontextualisation, negotiation and defining.

Negotiation. There is a growing number of studies that show that vocabulary items that are negotiated are more likely to be learned than words that are not negotiated (Newton, 1995; Ellis, Tanaka and

Yamazaki, 1994). This is not a surprising finding, but care needs to be taken in interpreting it. Ellis, Tanaka and Yamazaki found that although negotiation helped learning, the negotiated task took much more time than the non-negotiated elaborated input task. In the Newton study, it was found that although negotiated items were more likely to be learned than non-negotiated items (75% to 57%), negotiation only accounted for about 20% of the vocabulary learning. This is probably because only a few items can be negotiated without interfering too much with the communication task. So, although negotiation really helps vocabulary learning, it is not the means by which most vocabulary is learned. It is thus important for teachers to draw on other complementary ways of decontextualising items to improve the quality of learning.

Negotiation studies have revealed another feature of learning through negotiation that is of significance to learning from input, namely learners observing negotiation learn vocabulary just as well as the learners who do the actual negotiation (Stahl and Vancil, 1986; Stahl and Clark, 1987; Newton, forthcoming; Ellis, Tanaka and Yamazaki, 1994; Ellis and Heimbach, 1997). This indicates that it is not the negotiation itself which is important but the learning conditions of noticing and gaining information that negotiation sets up. If learners are engaged in a task, then observing others negotiating is just as effective as doing the negotiation. This is good news for large class, teacher-centred activities where there is not an opportunity for every learner to negotiate.

Newton (forthcoming) found that all the instances of negotiation of meaning in the four tasks he studied involved negotiating items in the textual input. No vocabulary items that were introduced in the discussion and that were not in the textual input were negotiated. This indicates that teachers can have a major effect on determining what is noticed. We will look more closely at this in the vocabulary of speaking section in chapter 4.

Definition. Some studies (Elley, 1989; Brett, Rothlein and Hurley, 1996) show that vocabulary learning is increased if vocabulary items are briefly explained while learners are listening to a story. In Elley's study, such defining more than doubled the vocabulary gains. Some studies of reading similarly indicate that looking up words in a dictionary increases learning (Knight, 1994), although this finding is not consistently supported in other studies (Hulstijn, 1993).

This inconsistency may be at least partly explained by a finding by R. Ellis (1995) which indicated that simple definitions were the most effective. A simple definition is short and includes only a few defining characteristics of the word. This agrees with a study by Chaudron

(1982) which found that more elaborate definitions tended to be confusing rather than helpful. Several studies of learning from lists or word cards (Nation, 1982) have shown that for many learners learning is faster if the meaning of the word is conveyed by a first language translation. First language translations are probably the simplest kind of definition in that they are short and draw directly on familiar experience.

Like negotiation, defining while telling a story is a form of decontextualisation, that is, focusing attention on words as words rather than as parts of a message. In order to increase incidental vocabulary learning while listening to a story, teachers can put target words on the blackboard as they occur, point to them on the blackboard as they recur, translate them, define them simply, and encourage learners to negotiate their meaning with the teacher. Ellis and Heimbach (1997), working with young learners of English as a second language, found that a group negotiating with the teacher was more effective for vocabulary learning than when there was individual negotiation in one-to-one interaction with the teacher. A variant of story telling is for the teacher to read the story to a particular learner who is set up to negotiate with the teacher while the rest of class are eavesdroppers on the story telling and negotiation. Ellis and He (1999) found learner to learner negotiation more effective for older learners.

An argument against the decontextualisation of vocabulary is the teachability hypothesis (Pienemann, 1985) which argues that explicit teaching of language items will not be effective if the learners are not at the right stage of language development. It is likely that much vocabulary learning is not affected by developmental sequences and thus explicit teaching has the potential to directly contribute to implicit knowledge (Ellis, 1990). If this is true, then the temporary decontextualisation of vocabulary items during a message focused task like listening to a story is of major benefit to second language proficiency.

Teachers can have a direct influence on noticing in speaking and writing tasks by giving thought to where wanted vocabulary items are placed in the written input, and by some form of pre-teaching or 'consciousness-raising' of wanted items before the activity. Teachers can use a range of attention drawing techniques in listening and reading tasks to encourage noticing.

Retrieval

The second major process that may lead to a word being remembered is retrieval (Baddeley, 1990: 156). A word may be noticed and its meaning comprehended in the textual input to the task, through teacher explanation or dictionary use. If that word is subsequently retrieved during the task then the memory of that word will be strengthened. Retrieval may be receptive or productive. Receptive retrieval involves perceiving the form and having to retrieve its meaning when the word is met in listening or reading. Productive retrieval involves wishing to communicate the meaning of the word and having to retrieve its spoken or written form as in speaking or writing. Retrieval does not occur if the form and its meaning are presented simultaneously to the learner.

Several studies (Elley, 1989; Stahl and Fairbanks, 1986) have shown the importance of repetition as a factor in incidental vocabulary learning. As Baddeley (1990: 156) suggests, it is not simply repetition which is important but the repeated opportunity to retrieve the item which is to be learned. When learners hear or see the form of the word, they need to retrieve what they know of its meaning. This retrieval is likely to be retrieval of ideas stored from previous meetings and retrieval of content and information from the present meeting. Baddeley suggests that each retrieval of a word strengthens the path linking form and meaning and makes subsequent retrieval easier. It may be possible to calculate how much input, in terms of number of running words, a learner needs to get within a certain time in order for there to be an opportunity to meet a recently met word again before the memory of the previous meeting fades. If too much time has passed between the previous meeting and the present encounter with the word, then the present encounter is effectively not a repetition but is like a first encounter. If however a memory of the previous meeting with the word remains, then the present encounter can add to and strengthen that memory. There are two major factors involved in such a calculation: the learner's vocabulary size, and the length of time that the memory of a meeting with a word lasts.

The learner's vocabulary size. The more words a learner knows, the less frequently occurring are the next words he or she needs to learn. For example, if we use figures from the Francis and Kučera (1982) frequency count, a learner who knows 1,000 different words would have to read or listen to 10,000 running words in order for a word at the 1,000-word level to be repeated. If the learner knew 2,000 different words, she would have to read or listen to 20,000 running words, on average, for a word at the 2,000 level to be repeated. The larger the vocabulary size, the greater the quantity of language that needs to be processed in order to meet the words to be learned again.

The length of time that the memory of a meeting with a word lasts. A repetition can only be effective if the repetition is seen by the learner to be a repetition. That is, there must be some memory of the previous meeting with the word. A critical factor is the length of time that such a memory lasts. Delayed post-tests of vocabulary learning indicate that memory for words can last several weeks. Elley (1989) found the memory for the new words remained after three months. Elley's design however involved three repetitions of the stories and also incorporated some use of definitions. Brett, Rothlein and Hurley (1996) found that words were still remembered after six weeks. Their design used serialised stories with definitions. Ellis, Tanaka and Yamazaki (1994) used two post-tests – one two days after the treatment, and one about a month later. A more sensitive delayed post-test about two and a half months after the treatment was also used and showed that the learning was still retained. Bearing in mind that the treatments in the three studies allowed some repeated opportunities to meet the unknown words and also involved some deliberate focusing on the words through definition or negotiation, a conservative interpretation would be that we could reasonably expect learners to retain a memory for a meeting with a word at least a month later. This estimation of how long a memory for a word will remain must be very inexact as there are numerous factors affecting such a memory, including the quality of the meeting with a word. Research indicates that repetitions need to be increasingly spaced with a short gap between early meetings and much larger gaps between later meetings (Pimsleur, 1967; Baddeley, 1990: 156–158). Thus the number of previous meetings with the word will influence the length of time a memory remains.

However, with these cautions in mind, it is very useful to try to estimate how much listening and reading a learner would need to be doing per week in order for incidental receptive vocabulary learning to proceed in an effective way. This is looked at more closely in the section on simplification in chapter 5, but on average learners would need to listen to stories at least three times a week for about fifteen minutes each time. They would need to read about one graded reader every two weeks (Nation, 1997; Nation and Wang, 1999).

Creative or generative use

The third major process that may lead to a word being remembered is generation. There is now an increasing number of studies that show that generative processing is an important factor in first and second language vocabulary learning. Generative processing occurs when previously met words are subsequently met or used in ways that differ from the previous meeting with the word. At its most striking, the new meeting with the word forces learners to reconceptualise their knowledge of that word. For example, if a learner has met the word *cement* used as a verb as in 'We cemented the path' and then meets 'We cemented our relationship with a drink', the learner will need to rethink the meaning and uses of *cement* and this will help firmly establish the memory of this word. Generative use is not restricted to metaphorical extension of word meaning and can apply to a range of variations from inflection through collocation and grammatical context to reference and meaning. Joe (1995) found that quality of knowledge as measured by three different tests of each word was closely related to the degree of generative use of each word in a retelling task. R. Ellis (1995) found that a factor he called 'range' was significantly related to vocabulary learning in a negotiated listening task. The task involved second language learners listening to directions and having to place items on a picture. 'Range' referred to the number of separate directions that a word occurred in, and could be considered a kind of measure of generativeness. Stahl and Vancil (1986) found that discussion was a crucial factor in learning vocabulary from semantic mapping. The discussion presumably provided an opportunity for the new vocabulary to appear in differing forms and contexts. Elley (1989) found that pictorial context for a word in a story was a significant factor in vocabulary learning from listening to stories. Although it is stretching the idea of generative use to make a picture a generative use of a word, the accompaniment of a text by a picture, like generative use, can lead to a form of mental elaboration that deepens or enriches the level of processing of a word (Baddeley, 1990: 160–177) and thus enhances learning. Our knowledge of the nature of generative use and the classification of uses into different degrees of generativity is still sketchy. Negotiation improves learning not only through decontextualisation but possibly also through the opportunity for generative use. During negotiation a word is used in a variety of grammatical contexts, often in a variety of inflected or derived forms, and often with reference to a variety of instances.

Generation, or generative processing, can also be receptive or productive. In its receptive form it involves meeting a word which is used in new ways in listening or reading. In its productive form, it involves producing new ways of using the wanted vocabulary in new contexts (Wittrock, 1974; 1991). This means that a word is used generatively if it is used in speaking in a way which is different from its use in the textual input.

There are degrees of generation. Generation occurs, but is low, if the linguistic context for the word is only slightly different from the textual input. For example, *chronic pain* becomes *very chronic pain*.

Generation is high if the word is used in a substantially different way, perhaps indicating that the word has begun to be integrated into the learner's language system. For example, *chronic pain* becomes *chronic backache* or *chronic illness*.

Joe (1995) found that degree of generation was closely related to amount of learning in retelling tasks. Newton (1993) found that negotiation of the meaning of a word greatly increased its chances of being learned. Negotiation of the meaning of a word will usually involve generative use of that word during the negotiation. The most striking receptive generative uses of vocabulary are those where meeting the word in a new context forces learners to reconceptualise the meaning that they previously had for that word.

In a well-controlled experiment, Hall (1991; 1992) looked at the effect of split information tasks on the learning of the mathematics vocabulary *parallel, diagonal, vertical, perimeter*. The experiment involved a comparison of split information pairs, teacher-fronted learning and individual study. All groups made gains in vocabulary learning, but the split information group made significantly more than the other groups. An analysis of the transcripts showed that there was a low correlation (.36) between total exposure to the words and learning, but that there was a high correlation (.93) between learning and the number of uses of the words not closely dependent on input. This means that having to produce the words in ways which are not just repetitions of the written exercise material results in superior learning.

'Instantiation' (Anderson, Stevens, Shifrin and Osborn, 1978) may involve generation. Instantiation involves recalling or experiencing a particular instance or example of the meaning of a word. For example, we see an actual ball when we meet the word form *ball*. Notice that it is possible to learn vocabulary without instantiation. For example, when using word cards to make L2–L1 connections, it is possible to look at the L2 word and recall its L1 translation without thinking of a particular instance of the meaning. It may be that an important reason why using words in real life situations helps learning is that each use involves instantiation. That is, each use is connected with a particular meaningful example.

Stahl (1985, cited in Stahl and Fairbanks, 1986) suggests a three-point scale for describing depth of processing for vocabulary.

1. Association – learning a form-meaning connection.
2. Comprehension – recalling the meaning of a previously met item.
3. Generation – producing a novel response to an item such as restating a definition in different words or making an original sentence.

These levels roughly correspond to the levels of noticing, retrieving, and generating used here.

Table 3.2. *Tasks and amount of involvement for vocabulary learning*

Task	Need	Search	Evaluation
Reading with questions. Words glossed are not relevant to the task	–	–	–
Reading with questions. Words glossed are relevant to the task	+	–	–
Reading with questions. Needed words looked up	+	+	+
Read and fill in given words	+	–	+
Write sentences using given words	+	–	++
Writing a composition	++	++	++

Notes:
– – no involvement load, + = moderate involvement, ++ = strong involvement

Laufer and Hulstijn (in press) investigated the effect of what they called 'task involvement' on incidental vocabulary learning. They saw involvement as being affected by three features in tasks. Their description of these features can be seen as an attempt to operationalise levels of processing.

- Need. Need does not exist if the target vocabulary is not needed to complete the task. Need is moderate if the task requires the target vocabulary, and it is strong if the learner feels the need for the vocabulary. It is an attitudinal component of involvement.
- Search. Search does not exist if the word forms or their meanings are supplied as a part of the task. Search is moderate if learners have to search for the meaning of the item, and strong if learners have to search for the form to express a meaning. This parallels retrieval as described above, and can involve a mental search or search in a dictionary.
- Evaluation. Evaluation involves deciding if a word choice is appropriate or not. Evaluation is moderate if the context is provided and is strong if the learner has to create a context. Choosing between sub-entries in a dictionary entry involves evaluation.

Involvement is affected by each of these features and they can occur in combination. Laufer and Hulstijn's research shows that the greater the involvement load, the more effective the learning.

Table 3.2 contains some tasks with an analysis of their involvement load.

What are the observable signs that learning might occur?

Most conditions in action have some observable sign. Negotiation, repetition, generative use, involvement and successful completion of a task are among the most observable. Deep processing, focus on the meaning and the need to comprehend are less directly observable. Presence of the signs does not guarantee learning, but looking for them may help a teacher decide if an activity needs adapting. We have already seen earlier in this chapter how observers of negotiation seem to learn just as well as those who actively negotiate. If a teacher sees that learners are negotiating then this should be considered as a positive sign for both negotiators and those learners who observe the negotiation.

What are the design features of the activity which set up the conditions for learning?

Design features such as split information, shared information, types of outcomes, and the presence of unfamiliar items in written input, encourage the occurrence of learning conditions. Shared and split information tasks encourage the negotiation of meaning. Removal of written input may encourage retrieval of vocabulary.

It is useful for teachers to be aware that the design features that help a particular technique achieve a learning goal are also present in other techniques, and it is possible to create and adapt techniques that have those features.

Designing activities to encourage noticing

If words occur in important parts of the written input to a task they are likely to be noticed. The chances of a word being noticed can be increased by pre-teaching, highlighting the word in the text by using underlining, italics or bold letters, and glossing the word.

Designing activities to encourage retrieval

An effective way to get repeated retrieval is to read the same story several times. With younger children this is not difficult to do and is welcomed by them. Older learners may not be so receptive. A second option is to serialise a long story, that is, to read a chapter at a time. There is a tendency in continuous stories for vocabulary to be repeated. Teachers could maximise this by briefly retelling what happened previously in the story before continuing with the next instalment. Much research still needs to be done on the effect of a continuous story on repetition. Hwang and Nation (1989) looked at the effect on repetition of reading follow-up newspaper stories on the same topic. They found that follow-up stories provided better repetition of vocabulary than unrelated stories.

The repeated readings or the serial instalments should not be too far apart. Listening to a story two or three times a week is likely to be more beneficial than once a week. If the teacher notes target vocabulary on the board as it occurs in the story, it is best to put it up just after it is heard rather than before. This will encourage retrieval rather than recognition.

Teachers can design retrieval into speaking activities by making it necessary for learners to reuse words that occurred in the textual input. This can be done by making the task involve retelling of the textual input, by making the task involve a procedure whereby the same material has to be discussed or presented several times through a change in group membership as in the 'pyramid' procedure (Jordan, 1990), or by making the solution to the task involve considerable discussion of the information provided in the textual input, as in a problem solving discussion.

In a strip story activity (Gibson, 1975) the learners are each given a sentence to memorise from a paragraph. They then must tell their sentences to each other and decide whose sentence is first, second and so on. No writing is allowed. Because the learners must memorise their sentences, they then have to retrieve them each time they tell them to the rest of the group. Memorisation thus ensures a form of retrieval.

Designing activities to encourage generation

Teachers can try to affect the quality of the mental processing of vocabulary while learners listen to input in the following ways.

- Rather than read the same story several times, as in the Elley (1989) study, it may be better to use a longer story and present it part by part as a serial. As we have seen in the section on repeated retrieval, long texts provide an opportunity for the same vocabulary to recur. If this recurrence is in contexts which differ from those previously met in the story, then this generative use will contribute to learning. There have not been any studies examining the degree of generative use of vocabulary in long texts such as simplified readers.
- If the teacher is able to supplement the story telling with pictures, by using blackboard drawings, an OHP or a blown-up book, then this will contribute positively to vocabulary learning.

- If it is possible to provide simple contextual definitions of words, that is definitions using example sentences, then this could help learning if the example sentences are different from those that contain the word in the story. The contextual definition would then be a generative use of the word.
- Teachers can encourage productive generative use by requiring retelling of the written input from a different focus, by distributing the information in a way that encourages negotiation, and by requiring learners to reconstruct what was in the text rather than repeat it.

Table 3.3 is an attempt to relate the conditions favouring vocabulary learning to the signs that they are occurring and the features of the activities that encourage them. As our knowledge of vocabulary learning increases, it may be possible to develop a more detailed table where the various aspects of vocabulary knowledge are related to different learning conditions and the design features of activities.

In chapter 4 on vocabulary and listening and speaking, we will look more closely at design features for speaking tasks with a vocabulary learning goal.

Vocabulary in classrooms

There is a growing number of studies looking at what teachers do about vocabulary in classrooms. A common theme in many of the studies is that what happens in the classroom does not take account of the full range of options suggested by theory and research. This seems true of both first language (Blachowicz, 1987; Watts, 1995) and second language (Sanaoui, 1996) classrooms. Investigative procedures have included questionnaires for learners to answer, interviews with teachers and classroom observation. Scholfield and Gitsaki (1996) compared the treatment of vocabulary in private language schools and government schools, concluding that the difference was primarily one of quantity rather than quality.

Meara, Lightbown and Halter (1997) examined the vocabulary used in intensive second language classrooms in Canada. The corpus sizes were small, but indicated that the learners were exposed to plenty of unknown words.

Repetition and learning

Repetition is essential for vocabulary learning because there is so much to know about each word that one meeting with it is not sufficient to gain this information, and because vocabulary items must not

Table 3.3. *The conditions of learning, signs and features in activities with a vocabulary learning goal*

Psychological conditions encouraging learning	Signs that the conditions are likely to be occurring	Design features of the activity that promote the conditions
Noticing a word	The learner consults a glossary The learner pauses over the word The learner negotiates the word	Definition, glosses, highlighting Unknown words in salient positions
Retrieving a word	The learner pauses to recall a meaning The learner does not need to consult a dictionary or gloss The learner produces a previously unknown word	Retelling spoken or written input
Using the word generatively	The learner produces a word in a new sentence context The learners produce associations, causal links, etc.	Role play based on written input Retelling without the input text Brainstorming

only be known, they must be known well so that they can be fluently accessed. Repetition thus adds to the quality of knowledge and also to the quantity or strength of this knowledge.

There has been a great deal of research on how items should be repeated and much of this is relevant to learning vocabulary in another language.

The spacing of repetitions

A very robust finding in memory research in general (Baddeley, 1990) and second language vocabulary learning research in particular (Bloom and Shuell, 1981; Dempster, 1987) is that spaced repetition results in more secure learning than massed repetition. Massed repetition involves spending a continuous period of time, say fifteen minutes, giving repeated attention to a word. Spaced repetition involves spreading the repetitions across a long period of time, but not spending more time in total on the study of the words. For example, the words might be studied for three minutes now, another three minutes a few hours later, three minutes a day later, three minutes two days later and finally three minutes a week later. The total study time is fifteen minutes, but it is spread across ten or more days. This spaced repetition results in learning that will be remembered for a long period of time. The repetitions should be spaced at increasingly larger intervals.

Seibert (1927), Anderson and Jordan (1928) and Seibert (1930) investigated retention over periods of up to eight weeks. Their findings are all in agreement with Pimsleur's (1967) memory schedule. Most forgetting occurs immediately after initial learning and then, as time passes, the rate of forgetting becomes slower. Anderson and Jordan measured recall immediately after learning, after one week, after three weeks and after eight weeks. The percentages of material retained were 66%, 48%, 39% and 37% respectively. This indicates that the repetition of new items should occur very soon after they are first studied, before too much forgetting occurs. After this the repetitions can be spaced further apart. Griffin (1992) also found that most forgetting seems to occur soon after learning.

Bahrick (1984) and Bahrick and Phelps (1987) examined the recall of second language vocabulary items after very long periods of non-use, from 8 to 50 years. They found that the nature of the original learning influenced recall. Items which were initially easy to learn and which were given widely spaced practice (intervals of 30 days) were most likely to be retained over many years. The memory curves showed a decelerating drop for the first 3 to 6 years and then little change up to 25 to 30 years after which there was further decline. Bahrick and Phelps' research supports the well established finding of the superiority of spaced over massed practice.

Pimsleur (1967), in a very clear and useful article, proposes a memory schedule to act as a guide for the size of the spaces between the repetitions. Pimsleur's suggestion, based on research evidence, is that the space between each repetition should become larger, with the initial repetitions being closer together and the later repetitions much further apart. There is no particular reason why the spacing between the repetitions should be a matter of precise measurement, but it is interesting to look at Pimsleur's scale as a rough guide for the type of spacing suggested. The scale is exponential, so if the first interval was five seconds, then the next interval should be $5^2 = 25$ seconds, the next $5^3 = 125$ seconds, and the next $5^4 = 625$ seconds (about 10 minutes) and so on. Table 3.4 applies the calculation across 11 repetitions.

The general principle which lies behind the spacing is that the older a piece of learning is, the slower the forgetting. This means two things. Firstly, after a piece of learning, the forgetting is initially very fast and then slows down. Secondly, on the second repetition a piece of learning is older than it was on the first repetition and so the forgetting on the second repetition will be slower than it was. On the third repetition the forgetting will be even slower. The right probability of recall level is one where the learner has forgotten enough to feel that the repetition is worthwhile attending to and yet not forgotten too much so that there is still a good chance of recalling and thereby strengthening the form–meaning connection.

Baddeley (1990: 154–155) speculates that, because long-term learning depends on physical changes in the brain, spacing repetitions allows time for the regeneration of neuro-chemical substances that make these changes. Massed learning does not allow enough time for these substances to regenerate and thus they cannot continue to make the physical changes needed for learning. This explanation is still a matter for debate and investigation.

Mondria and Mondria-de Vries (1994) describe the 'hand computer' as a way of organising and focusing repetition. The hand computer is simply a box divided into five sections, with the second section larger than the first, the third larger than the second and so on. The words to be learned are put on cards and initially go into section 1. When a word is known it is put into section 2. When section 2 fills up the words in there are reviewed and those that are still known go into section 3 and those not recalled go back to section 1. The same procedure continues for sections 3, 4 and 5, with words not recalled going back to section 1. This procedure can be easily computerised.

Table 3.4. *Pimsleur's memory schedule*

Repetition	1	2	3	4	5	6	7	8	9	10	11
Time spacing before the next repetition	5 secs	25 secs	2 mins	10 mins	1 hour	5 hours	1 day	5 days	25 days	4 months	2 years

Types of repetition

Learning from repetition not only depends on the spacing of the repetitions but also on the nature of the repetition. If there is a delay between the presentation of a word form and its meaning, learners have an opportunity to make an effort to guess or recall the meaning, and presumably this extra effort will result in faster and longer retained learning. However, the guessing can only be successful if the foreign word form gives a good clue to its meaning, either because the foreign and native words are cognates, or because the word form and its translation have previously been seen together. Experimental evidence shows that simultaneous presentation of a word form and its meaning is best for the first encounter and, thereafter, delayed presentation is best because there is then the possibility of effort leading to successful recall.

In an experiment by Royer (1973) the learners saw each foreign word and its English translation simultaneously on the first trial and guessed by attempting to recall on subsequent trials. The group who were studying under the recalling procedure learned significantly more correct responses on a test given immediately after the learning sessions. Successful recall increases the chances that something will be remembered. Retrieving rather than simply seeing the item again seems to strengthen the retrieval route (Baddeley, 1990: 156).

Landauer and Bjork (1978: 631) suggest that retrieval may be more effective than simultaneously seeing the word and its meaning because retrieval involves greater effort, or because retrieval is more similar to the performance required during normal use.

The use of retrieval is a very important part of the strategy of using word cards (see chapter 8). It is the main justification for using cards instead of lists or notebooks. Learners need to know the importance of retrieval and how to make it a part of the whole range of their learning activities. Meeting words in listening and reading texts provides an opportunity for retrieval as does using words in speaking and writing. Teachers should tolerate and allow for delays in retrieving vocabulary in the strands of meaning-focused input and meaning-focused output because the retrievals are contributing to learning. The combination of spaced repetition with retrieval is the basis of a strategy that Baddeley considers is easy to use and widely applicable (1990: 158).

So far, we have been looking at repetition as being repetition of the same material. That is, the repetition contributes mainly to strength of knowledge. However, repetition can extend and enrich previous meetings. Table 3.5 outlines some of the possibilities.

There are many degrees of generation depending on the closeness of

Table 3.5. *Types of repetition of word meaning*

Type of processing	Type of repetition
Noticing	Seeing the same word form and simultaneously presented meaning again
Retrieval	Recalling the same meaning several times
Generation	Recalling the meaning in different contexts requiring a different instantiation of the meaning

the relationship of the meaning to be instantiated to the previously met concept or instantiation.

Learning from word cards will usually involve repetition of the same material because the cards themselves do not change from one repetition to another. However, learners can change the way they process the cards by thinking of new sentences containing the word, applying new mnemonic techniques, thinking of new instantiations of the word and imagining contexts of use.

When words are met in reading and listening or used in speaking and writing, the generativeness of the context will influence learning. That is, if the words occur in new sentence contexts in the reading text, learning will be helped. Similarly, having to use the word to say new things will add to learning (Joe, 1995).

The types of repetition are related to the goal of learning. McKeown, Beck, Omanson and Pople (1985: 533) found that if simple definitional learning was the goal then more repetitions were better than fewer, but fewer repetitions (four encounters) achieved respectable results. If making use of the newly learned word was the goal, then the previous vocabulary teaching had to allow the learners to meet the new word being used in several different ways so that the meaning of the word was enriched, not just repeated, by each meeting. This enrichment was even more critical when fluency of access was required.

Stahl and Fairbanks (1986: 97) in a meta-analysis of vocabulary studies found somewhat similar results with repetition of the same forms, meanings and contexts having strong effects on measures of meaning recall. It seemed however that more elaborative repetition such as extending the meaning of the word and meeting some of its collocations had stronger effects on passage comprehension measures than repetition of the same information.

The number of repetitions

Repetition is only one of a number of factors affecting vocabulary learning and the correlations between repetitions and learning generally are only moderate. For example, Saragi, Nation and Meister (1978) found a correlation of about .45 indicating that repetition accounted for around 20% of the factors involved in learning. It is thus not easy to fix on a particular number of repetitions needed for learning to occur.

Kachroo (1962) found that words repeated seven times or more in his coursebook were known by most learners. Crothers and Suppes (1967) found that most items in their vocabulary learning experiments were learned after six or seven repetitions. Tinkham (1993), like many other researchers, found that learners differed greatly in the time and number of repetitions required for learning. Most learners required five to seven repetitions for the learning of a group of six paired associates. A few required over twenty repetitions.

This section has looked at some of the important conditions that can lead to vocabulary learning. Teachers should develop the skill of examining the activities they use to determine why they are using the activity (the goals), if it is doing what it is supposed to be doing (the conditions and signs), and how it can be improved to better reach its goal (the features).

Communicating meaning

Direct communication of word meaning can occur in a variety of situations – during formal vocabulary teaching, as incidental defining in lectures, story telling or reading aloud to a class, during deliberate teaching of content in lectures and on-the-job instruction, and glossing or 'lexical familiarisation' in academic reading.

When considering what could be learned from the deliberate communication of information about a word, it is important to consider the following factors, which all relate to the idea that learning a word is a cumulative process (Swanborn and de Glopper, 1999). That is, except in the unusual circumstance where the various features of a second language word are very closely parallel to an equivalent item in the first language, we should expect knowledge of a word to be gradually built up as the result of numerous spaced meetings with the word. A word is not fully learned through one meeting with it, even if this meeting involves substantial deliberate teaching. There are three reasons for this.

1. There are numerous things to know about a word: its form (spoken, written, and component affixes and stem), its meaning (underlying concept, particular instantiations and associations), and its use (collocations, grammatical patterns and constraints on its use).
2. There are several strands through which knowledge of a word needs to develop: through meeting in meaning focused input, through direct study and teaching, through meaning focused production, and through fluency development activities.
3. As we shall see, learners seem to be capable of dealing with only a limited amount of information at a time; too much confuses.

Because of this, we should expect only limited learning from single meetings with a word and should bear this in mind when we plan or carry out those meetings. This means that a small positive step forward in knowledge, such as being told the translation of a word, should not be criticised as being a partial and inadequate representation of the word, but should be seen as a useful step in the cumulative process of learning that word.

The effectiveness of the communication and comprehension of word meaning will depend on three major sets of factors: the skill of the teacher, writer, or lecturer, the skill of the learner, and the features of the language involved. These three sets of factors are closely related to each other, but we will look at each separately.

The skill of the speaker or writer in communicating meaning

The way in which a word is defined can have a major effect on the learning that occurs. McKeown (1993) examined the effectiveness of dictionary definitions for young native speakers of English. She found that if definitions were revised to use simpler language, focused on the typical underlying meaning of the word and encouraged learners to consider the whole definition, then learners were more able to write typical sentences using the new word and to explain aspects of its meaning. Unhelpful definitions were too general or vague, consisted of disjointed parts, and used words whose typical meanings took learners off on the wrong track. The revised meanings that were more effective tended to be longer than the original dictionary definitions.

R. Ellis (1995) looked at the factors affecting vocabulary acquisition from oral input. In one treatment, the input was pre-modified, that is, definitions and explanations were built into the text. In the other treatment, the input was interactionally modified, that is, definitions and elaborations occurred as a result of student requests. In the interactionally modified input condition, it was found that the shorter the definition and the fewer defining characteristics it contained, the more likely acquisition was to occur. Ellis (*ibid.*: 426) interpreted this to mean that too much elaboration of word meaning results in capacity overload for learners with limited short-term memories. Short, direct definitions work the best in oral input. Ellis (*ibid.*: 429; 1994: 17) also suggests that too much information makes it difficult for a learner to identify what features are critical to the meaning of a word. This finding is supported by Chaudron's (1982) study of teachers' oral definitions. Chaudron suggests that over-elaborated definitions may make it difficult for learners to know if the same information is being repeated or if new information is being added. For example, in 'The Japanese have this tremendous output and this tremendous productivity,' the learner may be unsure if *output* and *productivity* are synonyms or different pieces of information. Chaudron presents a substantial list of structures and semantic–cognitive relationships that can be used to classify the kinds of elaborations that teachers use to help learners with vocabulary.

Studies with native speaking children (Miller and Gildea, 1987; Scott and Nagy, 1997) and non-native speakers (Nesi and Meara, 1994) have found that learners often misinterpret dictionary definitions by focusing on just one part of a definition. Nesi and Meara, for example, cite the definition, *intersect* = divide (sth) by going across it; and the learner sentence, **'We must intersect the river for arrive village.'*

Sometimes dictionary definitions encourage this.

There is no conflict between Ellis's (1995) and Chaudron's (1982) contentions that shorter definitions are best and that elaboration may cause confusion, and McKeown's (1993) finding that clearer definitions tend to be longer than their less revealing counterparts. In essence all three researchers are saying that good definitions need to be specific, direct, unambiguous, and simple. The 'Goldilocks principle' may apply here – not too much, not too little, but just right.

The skill of the learner in comprehending meaning

Learners may differ in the way they build up the concept of a word. Elshout-Mohr and van Daalen-Kapteijns (1987) distinguished two styles of building up a concept of a word through repeated meetings with the word in context. Some learners used a holistic model of the word meaning which often meant abandoning a concept if seemingly conflicting information occurred. More successful learners used a more analytic approach which involved developing a concept for a word which consisted of several separate meaning components. This analytic approach allowed the incorporation of new information and led to a more efficient building up of a concept. This is important because learners need to develop a reasonably unchanging concept of what a word means. This allows learners to comprehend the word in new contexts, and to enrich that meaning of the word cumulatively through new meetings.

Elshout-Mohr and van Daalen-Kapteijns suggest that it is possible to measure learners' control of the verbal comprehension skill in three major ways.

- We can look at what learners have already done in using their verbal comprehension skill. This can be done by using a classical vocabulary test. This tests how skilfully word meanings have been learned in the past (a product measure). Past learning is used to predict future performance. A disadvantage is that it does not distinguish skill from past effort and past opportunity.
- We can look at what learners could do. This can be measured by using an on-task guessing from context test. This tests the knowledge available and the quality of that knowledge (a skill-in-action measure). This is very useful diagnostically. Its main disadvantage is that it does not distinguish what learners can do from what they actually do.
- We can test what learners actually do. This can be tested by using an incidental learning measure. This tests degree of automaticity or fluency of control of the skill. The learners do one task (for example, read critically) but are tested on another (vocabulary learning). A disadvantage of this is that it does not recognise the purposeful variation of the application of a skill.

Each of these tests looks at the same skill under different conditions and they complement each other by triangulating information and by making up for the disadvantages of the other measures.

It is commonly suggested that for many words learning occurs as a cumulative process with aspects of word knowledge being strengthened and enriched through subsequent meetings with the word (Nagy, Herman and Anderson, 1985). Learners' skill at maintaining and adjusting word knowledge will have a major effect on the eventual amount of learning.

The nature of definition

We have looked at the teacher and the learner in communicating and comprehending meaning. The third major factor is the language, that is the words themselves and the nature of definition. This has been examined in spoken presentations such as university lectures (Flowerdew, 1992) and in written academic text (Bramki and Williams, 1984).

There are many ways of communicating word meanings:

- by performing actions
- by showing objects
- by showing pictures or diagrams
- by defining in the first language (translation)
- by defining in the second language
- by providing language context clues

The choice of way of communicating meaning of a word should be based on two considerations: the reason for explaining the meaning of the word, and the degree to which the way of explaining represents the wanted meaning for the word. Let us now look briefly at the various ways of communicating the meanings of words.

Using actions, objects, pictures or diagrams

Real objects, pictures, etc. are often seen as the most valid way of communicating the meaning of a word, but as Nation (1978b) points out, all ways of communicating meaning involve the changing of an idea into some observable form, are indirect, are likely to be misinterpreted, and may not convey the exact underlying concept of the word. An advantage of using actions, objects, pictures or diagrams is that learners see an instance of the meaning and this is likely to be remembered. If this way of communicating meaning is combined with a verbal definition then there is the chance that what Paivio calls 'dual encoding' will occur (Paivio and Desrochers, 1981). That is, the meaning is stored both linguistically and visually. Because objects and pictures often contain a lot of detail, it may be necessary to present several examples so that learners can determine the essential features of the concept or accompany the object or picture with focusing information. A picture is not necessarily worth a thousand words, but one which clearly represents the underlying concept of the word undoubtedly is.

Translating

Translation is often criticised as being indirect, taking time away from the second language, and encouraging the idea that there is an exact equivalence between words in the first and second languages. These criticisms are all true but they all apply to most other ways of communicating meaning. For example, there is no exact equivalence between a second language word and its second language definition. Similarly, a real object may contain many features that are not common to all instances of the word it exemplifies. Pictures and demonstrations take time away from the second language in the same way that using the first language to communicate word meaning takes time away from the second language. Translation has the advantages of being quick, simple, and easily understood. Its major disadvantage is that its use may encourage other use of the first language that seriously reduces the time available for use of the second language.

Defining in the second language

We will now look in greater detail at communicating meaning using the second language because this occurs very often in academic lectures and textbooks. Learners can benefit from practice in recognising and interpreting these definitions.

Flowerdew (1992) carried out a very careful analysis of the definitions used in sixteen biology and chemistry lectures to non-native speakers of English. On average, there was a definition every 1 minute 55 seconds or about 20 per lecture, showing that deliberate definition is a significant way of communicating meaning. The classic definition type, called a 'formal' definition, consists of a term (the word to be defined), the class it fits into and its defining characteristic(s). Here are some examples from Flowerdew (1992) and Bramki and Williams (1984). The parts of the first few are lettered to mark the (a) term, (b) class, and (c) defining characteristics.

1. (a) Consumer goods are those (b) commodities which (c) satisfy our wants directly.
2. (a) A middle zero is (b) a zero which (c) has no digits on each side.
3. Now, (b) a photo that (c) we take through a microscope we call (a) a micrograph.
4. A way of defining a metal is by saying that it is an element that readily forms a cation.
5. A fully planned economy is one in which all the important means of production are publicly owned.
6. An activity which helps to satisfy want is defined as production.
7. One major objective of science is to develop theories. These are termed general statements or unifying principles which describe or explain the relationship between things we observe in the world around us.

8. Remember, I said ultra-structure is the fine structure within the cell.

Note that the order of the parts is not always term + class + characteristic(s), that the class word may be a 'dummy', that is, a word that repeats the term (example 2) or a referential item (example 5), and that there are various formal signals of definition (bolding, italicising or quotation marks, indefinite noun groups, *which* or *that*, *define* and *call*, etc.). 'Semi-formal' definitions do not contain the class and so consist of only the term and the characteristic(s). Here are some examples.

9. You remember that we said that (a) compounds were (c) made from two or more different elements combined chemically.
10. So all living organisms were responding to stimuli; this we call responsiveness.
11. A stable electronic configuration is like the inert gases.

Flowerdew (1992) has a third major category of definition types called 'substitution' where a word, word part, phrase or phrases with a similar meaning is used to define the term. This can be done using a synonym, paraphrase or derivation.

12. by fuse I mean join together
13. opaque . . . you can't see through it
14. cytopharynx / cyto meaning cell . . . and so cytopharynx just means the pharynx of a cell

Flowerdew classifies the characteristic part of formal and semi-formal definitions according to the semantic categories of behaviour/process/function (example 4), composition/structure (example 9), location/occurrence (example 8), and attribute/property (example 2).

A fourth minor category of definition types is the use of objects, photographs or diagrams.

Definition has a wide variety of forms, and learners may have difficulty in recognising some of them. Flowerdew found that about half of his definitions were clearly signalled, most frequently by the use of *call* (as in *we call, is called, called*, etc.), and also by *mean(s), or, known as, that is, defined*. Research is needed on second language learners' recognition and comprehension of definitions, and the learning that occurs from various types of definitions.

Definitions can be classified into two main types according to the role they play in the discourse in which they occur. 'Embedded' definitions have the purpose of helping the listener or reader continue to comprehend the text; the words defined are generally not the focus of the information (Flowerdew, *ibid.*: 209) in the text. Most of these are likely to be in the form of synonym or paraphrase (see examples 12 and 13). Other definitions may play an important role in organising the discourse where a definition is used to introduce a subtopic that is then expanded on (understanding the technical terms is understanding the discipline).

Flick and Anderson (1980) compared native speakers' and non-native speakers' understanding of explicit and implicit definitions in academic reading material. They found that implicit definitions were more difficult to understand than explicit definitions. The difference in difficulty was similar for both native speakers and non-native speakers.

Bramki and Williams (1984) examined the first four chapters of an economics text. They noted the following features of the words that were intentionally defined in the text.

1. Almost all were nouns or nominal compounds.
2. Terms in titles, headings and sub-headings were often later defined.
3. Sometimes there were typographic clues that a word was being defined, such as the use of italics or quotation marks.
4. Most defining occurred early in the corpus.
5. The defining was often done by a combination of devices.

Bramki and Williams found 136 examples in 17,802 running words – a rate of about once every 130 running words or two to three times per page. Table 3.6 lists the various types of lexical familiarisation that they found.

Haynes and Baker (1993), in a comparison of native speakers and second language learners learning from lexical familiarisation, concluded that the major reason for second language learners' relatively poor performance was the presence of unknown vocabulary in the definitions provided in the text. Both native speakers and non-native speakers experienced some difficulty with familiar words that were used in narrower ways, mainly through not giving enough attention to the clues in the text.

Richards and Taylor (1992) looked at the strategies used by intermediate and advanced learners of English as a second language and adult native speakers of English to produce written definitions of words. They found that the part of speech of the word influenced the type of definition chosen, and intermediate learners experienced difficulty in finding classifying (class) terms for analytic definitions. Richards and Taylor's list of definition types and examples shows something of the range of possibilities available.

Table 3.6. Types and frequency of lexical familiarisation devices in an economics text

Category	Frequency (%)	Examples	Common signals
exemplification	44 (32%)	Durable consumer goods include such things as books, furniture, television sets, motor cars	such as, for example, is typified by
explanation	42 (31%)	Saving is the act of foregoing consumption	Frequently unmarked, i.e., means that
definition	35 (26%)	Economics is essentially a study of the ways in which man provides for his material well-being	X is a Y which . . .
stipulation	7 (5%)	'Land' in Economics is taken to mean . . . . (a type of definition limited to a given situation)	B uses X to describe Y
synonymy	5 (4%)	Working capital is sometimes called circulating capital	
non-verbal illustration	3 (2%)	A diagram	
	136 (100%)		

1. synonym   *beautiful* means *nice*
2. antonym   *young* means *not old*
3. analytic definition   An X is a Y which . . .
4. taxonomic definition   *autumn* is a *season*
5. definition by exemplification   *furniture* – something like a chair, sofa, etc.
6. definition by function   *pen* – use it to write
7. grammatical definition   *worse* – comparison form of *bad*
8. definition by association   *danger* – lives have not been protected
9. definition by classification   *family* – a group of people

Helping learners comprehend and learn from definitions

Having looked at the effects of the teacher or writer, the learner and the language in communicating and comprehending word meaning, it is possible to provide guidelines for teachers in helping learners benefit from definitions. This section tries to answer the question 'How should teachers (or writers) explain words?' Some of the guidelines presented here will go beyond the research reviewed in this chapter to draw on points made in other chapters of this book.

1. *Provide clear, simple, brief explanations of meaning.* The research evidence clearly shows that, particularly in the first meetings with a word, any explanation should not be complicated or elaborate. Learning a word is a cumulative process, so teachers need not be concerned about providing lots of information about a word when it is first met. What is important is to start the process of learning in a clear way without confusion. There are strong arguments for using the learners' first language if this will provide a clear, simple, and brief explanation (Lado, Baldwin and Lobo, 1967; Mishima, 1967; Laufer and Shmueli, 1997). The various aspects of knowing a word can be built up over a series of meetings with it. There is no need and clearly no advantage in trying to present these all at once. Elley's (1989) study of vocabulary learning from listening to stories showed that brief definitions had a strong effect on learning.
2. *Draw attention to the generalisable underlying meaning of a word.* If knowledge of a word accumulates over repeated meetings, then learners must be able to see how one meeting relates to the previous meetings. In providing an explanation of a word, the teacher should try to show what is common in the different uses of the word.

3. *Give repeated attention to words.* Knowledge of a word can only accumulate if learners meet the word many times. Repeated meetings can have the effects of strengthening and enriching previous knowledge. There is no need for a teacher to draw attention to a word every time it occurs but, particularly in the early stages of learning, drawing attention increases the chance that learners will notice it on later occasions. Teachers need to see the learning of particular words as a cumulative process. This means that they need to expect not to teach a word all in one meeting. They need to keep coming back to it to strengthen and enrich knowledge of the word.

4. *Help learners recognise definitions.* Definitions have certain forms (Bramki and Williams, 1984; Flowerdew, 1992) and may be signalled in various ways. Teachers can help learners by clearly signalling the definitions they provide, by testing learners to diagnose how well they can recognise and interpret definitions, and by providing training in recognising and interpreting definitions. A useful starting point for this is recognising definitions in written text. Bramki and Williams suggest that learners can be helped to develop skill in making use of lexical familiarisation by, firstly, seeing marked up text which indicates the word, the signal of lexical familiarisation and the definition; plenty of examples are needed at this stage. And, secondly, getting the student to then mark up some examples with the teacher gradually reducing the guidance given. Flowerdew (1992: 216) suggests that teachers and learners should discuss the various forms of definitions as they occur in context.

5. *Prioritise what should be explained about particular words.* There are many things to know about a word, and different aspects of word knowledge enable different word use skills (Nist and Olejnik, 1995). Some of these aspects of knowledge can be usefully taught, some are best left to be learned through experience, and some may already be known through transfer from the first language or through patterns learned from other English words. When deliberately drawing attention to a word, it is worth considering the learning burden of that word and then deciding what aspect of the word most deserves attention. Most often it will be the meaning of the word, but other useful aspects may include its spelling or pronunciation, its collocates, the grammatical patterning, or restrictions on its use through considerations of politeness, formality, dialect or medium.

6. *Help learners remember what is explained.* Understanding and remembering are related but different processes. The way in

which a teacher explains a word can affect understanding or it can affect understanding and remembering. In order to help remembering, information needs to be processed thoughtfully and deeply. The quality of mental processing affects the quantity of learning. Teachers can help remembering by showing how the word parts (affixes and stem) relate to the meaning of the word, by helping learners think of a mnemonic keyword that is like the form of the new word, by putting the word in a striking visualisable context, by encouraging learners to retrieve the word form or meaning from their memory while not looking at the text, and by relating the word to previous knowledge such as previous experience or spelling, grammatical, or collocational patterns met before.

7. *Avoid interference from related words.* Words which are similar in form (Laufer, 1989a) or meaning (Higa, 1963; Tinkham, 1993 and 1997; Waring, 1997b; Nation, 2000a) are more difficult to learn together than they are to learn separately. When explaining and defining words, it is not helpful to draw attention to other unfamiliar or poorly established words of similar form, or words which are opposites, synonyms, free associates or members of the same lexical set such as parts of the body, fruit or articles of clothing. The similarity between related items makes it difficult for the learner to remember which was which. Confusion rather than useful learning is often the result. In the early stages of learning it is not helpful to use the opportunity to teach a word as the opportunity to teach other related words.

Examples of quick explanations

- *head* 'the top or most important part, for example, head of your body, head of a match, head of the organisation'
  This explanation is given in the learners' first language. It is brief, is reinforced by examples, and focuses on the underlying meaning. Dictionaries have over twenty sub-entries for *head*. Most can be fitted into one underlying meaning.
- *comprehensive* 'includes all the necessary things together'
  This explanation tries to include the meaning of the prefix *com* (together) in the explanation. This definition should be related to the context in which the word occurred.
- *freight* 'goods carried'
  This explanation is very brief because this is a low-frequency word and does not deserve time. It could be given as a first

language translation. It is enough to satisfy the learners and to allow the class to move on quickly.

Spending time on words

Teachers should deal with vocabulary in systematic and principled ways to make sure that the learners get the most benefit from the time spent. There are two major decisions to be made for each unknown word when deciding how to communicate its meaning.

- *Should time be spent on it?*
- *How should the word be dealt with?*

It is worth spending time on a word if the goal of the lesson is vocabulary learning and if the word is a high-frequency word, a useful topic word or technical word, or contains useful word parts. It is also worth spending time on a word if it provides an opportunity to develop vocabulary strategies like guessing from context and using word parts.

Let us now look briefly at a range of ways for dealing with words, examining the reasons why each particular way might be chosen. We will assume that the words that we are considering giving attention to occur in a reading text.

1. *Preteach*. Preteaching usually needs to involve 'rich instruction' (see p. 94) and should only deal with a few words, probably five or six at the most. If too many words are focused on, they are likely to be forgotten or become confused with each other. Because preteaching takes quite a lot of time, it is best suited to high-frequency words, and words that are important for the message of the text.
2. *Replace the unknown word in the text before giving the text to the learners*. Some texts may need to be simplified before they are presented to learners. In general, low-frequency words that are not central to the meaning of the text need to be replaced. Replacing or omitting words means that the teacher does not spend class time dealing with items that at present are of little value to the learners.
3. *Put the unknown word in a glossary*. This is best done with words that the teacher cannot afford to spend time on, particularly high-frequency words, but glossing need not be limited to these. Long (Watanabe, 1997) argues that putting a word in a glossary gets repeated attention to the word if the learners look it up. That is, they see the word in the text, they see

it again in the glossary when they look it up, and then they see it again when they return to the text from the glossary. It could also be argued that between each of these three steps the word is being kept in short term memory. Glossing could thus be a useful way of bringing words to learners' attention. Glossing helps learning (Watanabe, 1997).

4. *Put the unknown word in an exercise after the text.* The words that are treated in this way need to be high-frequency words or words that have useful word parts. Exercises that come after a text take time to make and the learners spend time doing them. The words need to be useful for the learners to justify this effort.

5. *Quickly give the meaning.* This can be done by quickly giving a first language translation, a second language synonym or brief definition, or quickly drawing a picture, pointing to an object or making a gesture. This way of dealing with a word has the goal of avoiding spending time and moving on to more important items. It is best suited to low-frequency words that are important for the message of the text but which are unlikely to be needed again. Quick definitions help learning (Elley, 1989).

6. *Do* nothing about the word. This is suited to low-frequency words that are not important for the meaning of the text. It avoids drawing attention to items that because of their low-frequency do not deserve class time.

7. *Help the learners use context to guess, use a dictionary, or break the word into parts.* These ways of dealing with words are suited to high-frequency words because time is spent on them while using the strategies, but they are also suitable for low-frequency words that are easy to guess, have several meanings, or contain useful parts. The time spent is justified by the increase in skill in these very important strategies.

8. *Spend time looking at the range of meanings and collocations of the word.* This is a rich instruction approach and because of the time it takes needs to be directed towards high-frequency words and other useful words.

Rich instruction

Sometimes the reason for explaining a word is to remove a problem so that learners can continue with the main task of understanding a text or communicating a message. In these cases, a short clear explanation is needed. Often a translation, a quick definition in the form of a synonym, or a quickly drawn diagram will be enough. Sometimes however, because the word is important, it may be appropriate to provide what Beck, McKeown and Omanson (1987: 149) call 'rich instruction' and McWilliam (1998) 'rich scripting'. This involves giving elaborate attention to a word, going beyond the immediate demands of a particular context of occurrence. In general, rich instruction is appropriate for high-frequency words and words for which the learner has special needs. The best time to provide rich instruction is when learners have already met the word several times and may be ready to make it part of their usable vocabulary. The aim of rich instruction is to establish the word as an accessible vocabulary item. Rich instruction involves: spending time on the word; explicitly exploring several aspects of what is involved in knowing a word; and involving the learners in thoughtfully and actively processing the word. Rich instruction can be a teacher-led activity or it can be student-led particularly when students report on words they have met and explored; it can be done as group work or it can be done in individualised exercises.

Arguments against rich instruction

This chapter looks at how vocabulary can be taught, particularly through the use of classroom activities. Many of these activities can be done as individual work. Even when this happens, teachers may need to spend time devising the exercises and giving feedback on them. Many first language researchers question the value of spending teaching time on particular words, especially using rich instruction.

The arguments used against the direct teaching of vocabulary for first language learners include the following.

1. There are too many words to teach. Research on the vocabulary size of native speakers shows that, even by the most conservative estimates (D'Anna, Zechmeister and Hall, 1991; Nation, 1993c), native speakers know tens of thousands of word families. Direct teaching could only have a very trivial impact on such knowledge.
2. There is a lot to learn about each word (Nagy, 1997). Chapter 2 of this book outlines the various aspects of what is involved in knowing a word. Nagy challenges the idea of a word family, showing that for many complex and compound forms of words there is substantial extra learning required.
3. To have an immediate effect on vocabulary knowledge, substantial time has to be spent on teaching each word. McKeown, Beck, Omanson and Pople (1985) had to spend at

least 15 minutes per word to have a significant effect on language use. This means that not many words could be dealt with in this way in class time. However, McDaniel and Pressley (1989) found that with 30 seconds' concentrated learning time on each word, subsequent comprehension of a reading text was significantly improved.

4. There are other ways of increasing vocabulary size which require less teacher effort and less classroom time, and which have numerous other benefits. These involve the incidental learning of vocabulary through meeting the words in reading and listening, and in using the words in speaking and writing. Although incidental learning is not as effective as direct deliberate learning for any particular word, there is so much more opportunity for incidental learning that it accounts for most of first language vocabulary learning.

5. There are also arguments about the effectiveness of teaching. Although it is likely that aspects of vocabulary learning are affected by teaching in ways that grammatical learning is not, teaching is still an activity with very uncertain outcomes.

All of these arguments are true and suggest caution in the use of substantial direct vocabulary instruction with native speakers of a language. There are however some important differences between native speakers and second language learners which allow for a greater but still cautiously applied role for direct vocabulary instruction for learners of vocabulary in another language. The major differences are as follows.

• Native speakers of a language quickly learn the high-frequency words. By the age of five, it is likely that native speakers of English have a vocabulary of around 5,000 word families. Non-native speakers beginning their study of English generally know very few English words. Because the high-frequency words of the language are so important for language use and consist of a relatively small number of words (about 2,000), it is practical and feasible to directly teach a substantial number of them.

• Native speakers have enormous opportunities to learn from input and to produce output. Foreign language learners and some second language learners do not have the same rich opportunities. Language courses try to increase these opportunities but they will still be only a fraction of what native speakers have access to. In addition, while native speakers receive input adjusted to their level of proficiency, it is difficult for foreign language learners to find this outside the classroom. Direct vocabulary learning is a way of trying to bridge the gap between second language learners' present proficiency level and the proficiency level needed to learn from unsimplified input.

- Second language learners have less time for learning. They usually begin their study of the second language around the age of twelve and at the age of seventeen or eighteen may need to read unsimplified texts and compete with native speakers in an English-medium university. Direct vocabulary study is a way of speeding up the learning process.

There are three very important cautions which apply to the use of direct vocabulary instruction with learners of another language. Firstly, the instruction should be directed towards the high-frequency words of the language. Where learners are going on to academic study this would also include the *Academic Word List* vocabulary. The benefits of knowing high-frequency vocabulary compensate for the time and effort required for direct vocabulary instruction. Secondly, direct vocabulary instruction is only one part of one of the four strands of a balanced course. It should thus occupy only a small proportion of the course time. Thirdly, direct instruction can deal effectively with some aspects of word knowledge and not very effectively with others, which rely on quantity of experience and implicit rather than explicit knowledge.

Rich instruction, therefore, must be used only with appropriate vocabulary, in conjunction with the other strands of the course, and with an allocation of time that does not disadvantage the other strands.

Providing rich instruction

There are several ways of providing rich instruction.

1. Learners examine a range of contexts and uses. For example, contexts containing the word are analysed to provide a definition or translation of the word. Learners look at concordances or dictionary entries for collocations.
2. Learners do semantic mapping based on a text or around a theme. Variations of semantic mapping can include using a word to think of cause–effect relationships between that word and other words, and thinking of specific examples or components of a more general word (Sokmen, 1992).
3. Learners analyse the form and meaning of a word breaking it into

word parts, isolating parts of its meaning and extensions of its meaning. The etymology of the word can be examined (Ilson, 1983).
4. Several definition types are combined as in the 'What is it?' activity where learners listen to contextual definitions of a word and try to think of a second language synonym or a first language translation (Nation, 1990).
5. A new word is placed in a lexical set with known words. This can involve the use of classification activities where learners put newly met words and known words into groups and perhaps grade or scale them in some way.

In Table 3.7 these activities are classified according to the various aspects of what is involved in knowing a word. Rich instruction would involve giving attention to several of these aspects for the same word. Table 3.7 is followed by descriptions and examples of the activities.

Spoken form

Attention to the spoken form has the goals of getting learners to be able to recognise a word when they hear it, and to be able to pronounce a word correctly. Instruction is a useful way of beginning this process but, as N. Ellis (1995) argues, large amounts of meaning-focused use are necessary to develop fluency.

Pronounce the words

The teacher puts up words on the blackboard that the learners have met during the week. The teacher pronounces them and the learners repeat after the teacher. Then the learners take turns pronouncing the words without the teacher's model and get feedback on their attempts.

Read aloud

Learners read words aloud from a text and get feedback.

Written form

Although English has a very irregular spelling system, there are patterns and rules which can guide learning. Some learners may need to pay particular attention to writing the letter shapes if their first language uses a different writing system from English.

Table 3.7. *A range of activities for vocabulary learning*

Goal		Activities
Form	spoken form	Pronounce the words Read aloud
	written form	Word and sentence dictation Finding spelling rules
	word parts	Filling word part tables Cutting up complex words Building complex words Choosing a correct form
Meaning	form–meaning connection	Matching words and definitions Discussing the meanings of phrases Drawing and labelling pictures Peer teaching Riddles
	concept and reference	Finding common meanings Choosing the right meaning Semantic feature analysis Answering questions Word detectives
	associations	Finding substitutes Explaining connections Making word maps Classifying words Finding opposites Suggesting causes or effects Suggesting associations Finding examples
Use	grammar	Matching sentence halves Putting words in order to make sentences
	collocates	Matching collocates Finding collocates
	constraints on use	Identifying constraints Classifying constraints

Word and sentence dictation

Learners write words and sentences that the teacher dictates to them. This can be easily marked if one learner writes on the blackboard. The teacher corrects this and the other learners use it to correct their own work or their partner's work.

Finding spelling rules

Learners work in groups with a list of words to see if they can find spelling rules.

Word parts

In chapter 8, the section on word parts describes the goals and knowledge required for this aspect of vocabulary learning. Attention to word parts allows learners to make full use of the word families they know, and also contributes to remembering new complex words.

Filling word part tables

Learners work in pairs to complete tables like the following. Not all spaces can be filled. They check their work with another pair before the teacher provides the answers.

Noun	Verb	Adjective	Adverb
argument			
	evaluate		
		distinct	
			normally

Cutting up complex words

Learners are given a list of words that they divide into parts. They can be asked to give the meaning of some of the parts.

Building complex words

Learners are given word stems and make negatives from them, or make vague words (using *-ish, -y, -like*).

Choosing the correct form

Learners are given sentences containing a blank and a word stem in brackets. They have to change the stem to the appropriate inflected or derived form to complete the sentence.

I went to the doctor for a _____ (consult).

Strengthening the form–meaning connection

This aspect of knowing a word tries to separate recognising the form and knowing a meaning from being able to connect a particular form to a particular meaning. This aspect of knowledge was looked at more closely earlier in this chapter in the section on repetition. Strengthening the form–meaning connection involves having to recall a meaning when seeing or hearing a particular word, or having to recall a spoken or written form when wanting to express a meaning.

Matching words and definitions

Learners are given a list of definitions. Some could be in the form of synonyms and they must match them with a list of words they have met before. An alternative is to get the learners to find the words in a reading text to match the definitions.

Discussing the meaning of phrases

Learners are given a list of phrases containing words that they have met before and have to decide on the meaning of the phrase.

Drawing and labelling pictures

Learners read or listen to descriptions containing words they have recently met and draw or label pictures. Palmer (1982) describes a wide range of these information transfer activities.

Peer teaching

Learners work in pairs. One learner has to teach the vocabulary in his list to the other learner. The learner who is the teacher has the word and a picture illustrating its meaning. Feeny (1976) found that the learners who acted as teachers learned almost as well as those who were being taught.

Riddles

Riddles like the following can be used to help the meaning of a word be easy to remember (Sen, 1983; Kundu, 1988).

- When it is new it is full of holes. (*net*)
- It has a head but cannot think. (*match*)

- What is the longest word in the world? (*smiles* – because there is a mile between the first and last letters)

Concept and referents

This aspect of word knowledge involves having a clear idea of the underlying meaning of a word running through its related uses, and also involves being aware of the range of particular uses it has, that is, what it can refer to. It is this knowledge which contributes to being able to understand a word when it is used in a new situation, and being able to use a word in creative ways.

Finding common meanings

A useful technique for helping learners see the underlying concept or core meaning of a word is to see what is similar in different uses of the word.

- He was *expelled* from school.
- They were *expelled* from their villages.
- The breath was *expelled* from her body.

Visser (1989) describes an easily made activity which helps learners see the core meaning of a word and put the word to use. Here is an example. The learners work in pairs or small groups.

1	2	3
Your *environment* consists of all the influences and circumstances around you.	The *environment* is the natural world.	Say what the similar ideas are in columns 1 and 2.
What are the features of a stimulating *environment*?	Describe three factors polluting the *environment*.	

Note that there is a task for learners to perform for each of the two uses of the word. Visser found that learners are usually successful in group tasks at seeing the common features in the uses. This can be made more certain by getting different groups to compare the core meanings they decided on.

Choosing the right meaning

Learners are given a list of words in a reading text and have to choose the appropriate meaning from the dictionary. Instead of using a dictionary, the teacher can provide a set of possible meanings. All the meanings should be possible meanings for the word, but only one would fit in the context. For example, They were scrubbing the flags in front of the house. Here *flags* means flagstones.

Semantic feature analysis

Numerous writers (Channell, 1981; Stieglitz and Stieglitz, 1981; Rudzka, Channell, Putseys and Ostyn, 1981; Stieglitz, 1983) suggest that learners should fill in grids to refine their knowledge of related words. Here is an example from Rudzka *et al.* (*ibid.*: 65). The learners have to mark the boxes in the grid where the element of meaning relates to the particular word.

	because unexpected	because difficult to believe	so as to cause confusion	so as to leave one helpless to act or think
surprise	✓			
astonish		✓		
amaze			✓	
astound				✓
flabbergast				✓

This type of activity has the potential to cause interference between related items (Higa, 1963; Tinkham, 1993; Waring, 1997b; Nation, 2000a) and should only be used when learners are already familiar with most of the items being compared; it is thus used for revision.

Answering questions

The learners are given questions to answer which contain words that they have recently met. The questions help them instantiate and apply the words (Winn, 1996).

- When do you like to work with a *partner*?
- Who would you call *darling*?

Word detectives

Learners look for words they have already met in class and report back to the class about where they found them and the information they gathered about the word (Mhone, 1988). This activity is like McKeown, Beck, Omanson and Pople's (1985) 'extended rich instruction' where learners brought back evidence that they had seen or used a target word outside the classroom.

Associations

Knowing a range of associations for a word helps understand its full meaning and helps recall the word form or its meaning in appropriate contexts. To a large degree the associations of a word are a result of the various meaning systems that the word fits into. These include, for example, synonyms, opposites, family members of the same general headword, words in a part–whole relationship, and superordinate and subordinate words.

Finding substitutes

Learners choose words from a list to replace underlined words in a text.

Explaining connections

Learners work in pairs or small groups to explain the connections between a group of related words: *analyse – criteria – exclude – justify – classify*.

Making word maps

Learners work in groups or with the teacher to make a semantic map based on a target word.

Classifying words

The learners are given lists of words that they classify into groups according to certain criteria, for example, classifying words according to whether they have positive or negative connotations, or whether they are living or non-living. Dunbar (1992) suggests getting learners to classify the new vocabulary they are working on as a way of integrating vocabulary knowledge with subject-matter knowledge. Such an activity is likely to lead to generative processing, particularly when learners explain and justify their classification. The examples Dunbar provides are in the form of tree diagrams.

Finding opposites

Learners are given a list of words, or words from a text, and find opposites for them.

Suggesting causes or effects

Sokmen (1992), in an article rich in suggestions for vocabulary development, describes a useful activity where learners are given words or phrases which they have to see as causes or effects. They have to then think of causes for the effects or effects to go with the causes. So, a phrase like *medical consultation* could get learners to think of the causes *illness, pain, tiredness* and the effects *medicine, hospital,* and *reassurance*.

Suggesting associations

Learners are given four or five words. They work in small groups to list associates for those words. They then scramble the associated words and give them to another group who have to classify them under the same words. The two groups compare and discuss their classifications.

Finding examples

The teacher provides the learners with a list of categories like *food, household objects, numbers, jobs,* etc. Each learner chooses or is given one category. The learner then has to write as many words as possible under the category heading on a piece of paper. So, *food* should contain items like *bread, meat* etc. The learners should write known words, not look up unknown words. After a set time, a learner passes their paper to the next learner who then tries to add words not already listed. Then the paper is passed on until each learner regains their original sheet of paper. The learner has to check the spelling with a dictionary and then these sheets become a class dictionary that is added to as new words are met (Woodward, 1985).

Grammar

Knowing a word involves knowing how to use it in sentences. There is continuing debate (Sinclair, 1991) about the relative roles of vocabulary and grammar in determining how words are used.

Matching sentence halves

Learners are given sentence halves containing vocabulary they have met before and they have to match the halves to make sensible complete sentences.

Ordering words

Learners put words in order to make sentences. They may need to supply some of the function words.

Collocation

More information about collocation is becoming available with the development of large corpora and the means to get information from them. Knowing what words can occur with other words contributes to the fluency with which language can be used. Chapter 9 looks in detail at collocation.

Matching collocates

Learners are given lists of words to match. It may be possible to make several pairs with the same words (Brown, 1974).

Finding collocates

Learners look in dictionaries, draw on their experience and use parallels with their first language to list collocates for given words.

Constraints on use

Most words are not affected by constraints on use. That is, they are neutral regarding constraints like formal/informal, polite/impolite, child language/adult language, women's usage/men's usage, American/British, spoken/written. When these constraints do occur, it is usually important to be aware of them because they can affect the interpretation of the communication.

Identifying constraints

Woodward (1988) suggests using codes like F for formal, I for informal, N for neutral to put next to words to classify them when they are put up on vocabulary posters in class.

Classifying constraints

Learners are given lists of words that they must classify according to a given constraint on use, for example American usage vs. British usage.

Vocabulary teaching procedures

To conclude this discussion of rich instruction, we will look at a few vocabulary teaching procedures. A procedure is a series of clearly defined steps leading to a learning goal. Teachers apply procedures to make sure that learners cover what needs to be covered in a task. From a vocabulary learning perspective, procedures can be used to ensure that words are repeated and that various aspects of what is involved in knowing a word are covered. Here are some examples of such procedures.

Recycled words

Blake and Majors (1995) describe a five step procedure involving (1) preteaching of vocabulary, (2) oral reading of a text containing the vocabulary with discussion of the meaning of the text, (3) deliberate word study, (4) vocabulary puzzles, quizzes, or tests, and finally (5) writing making use of the vocabulary. This procedure moves from receptive use to productive use with a focus on deliberate learning.

The second-hand cloze

This activity involves three steps: (1) The learners read texts containing the target vocabulary, (2) they deliberately study the vocabulary. (3) learners are then given cloze passages which are summaries of the ones they originally read. In this step the learners are helped to recall the target words by being given a list of L1 equivalents of the target words that they have to translate into L2, and then use to fill the gaps in the cloze text. Laufer and Osimo (1991) tested the procedure experimentally and found superior learning for the words practised using the second-hand cloze procedure compared to the study of list translations. The second-hand cloze seems to have added a generative element to learning.

The vocabulary interview

The nine headings in Table 3.7 (see p. 99) can be used as a basis for learners to interview the teacher or each other about particular words. If learners interview each other, they should be aware of the nine aspects of knowing a word that the questions are based on and should have a chance to research their word. One of the goals of the interview procedure is to make learners aware of the aspects of knowing a word. Another goal is for them to learn new words.

Rich instruction involves knowing what the learning burden of a word is so that the variety of activities used can focus on useful aspects of knowledge.

Computer-assisted vocabulary learning

Computers provide a very effective way of putting many of the principles of good vocabulary learning into practice, particularly with regard to providing spaced repetition and opportunity for retrieval. They can also help fill many of the requirements for rich instruction. One way of looking systematically at software for computer-assisted vocabulary learning (CAVL) is to take a curriculum design perspective on it (see chapter 11). In part, this involves looking at the vocabulary content of the material (what words are focused on and what aspects of word knowledge are covered), the presentation of the material (which conditions for learning are set up) and the monitoring of learners' performance (what feedback and treatment of error is provided). It is also worth considering the flexibility of the program in adapting to student needs, adapting to environmental constraints like the amount of time available, and modifying the learning principles.

Vocabulary content

Some software chooses vocabulary to focus on based on usefulness. *Wordchip* (van Elsen, van Deun and Decoo, 1991) draws on information from several frequency-based vocabulary lists to ensure that the vocabulary occurring in its activities will be generally useful to learners. Burling (1983) suggests that basic information on frequency level should be provided to learners so that they can decide whether to spend time on a particular word or not. Well designed programs need to draw on frequency information and also need to have the flexibility for teachers and learners to play a part in choosing the vocabulary to focus on.

Programs can also focus on the various kinds of knowledge involved in knowing a word (see Table 2.1, p. 27). These include: knowledge of the written and spoken forms of the word, knowledge of word parts, inflectionally and derivationally related words, knowledge of grammar, collocations, restrictions on use and knowledge of meaning and associations.

Harrington (1994) describes a program, *CompLex*, that explicitly develops and monitors form-based and meaning-based links between words. For each word, the program can provide example sentences, related forms, a spoken form, synonyms, hyponyms (class–member), meronyms (part–whole), collocations, some grammatical information, and L1 and L2 meanings. The program keeps a record of the words a particular student knows and links are only made to other known items. The program is designed to complement courses and can be used in several ways. The learner can choose or supply words to go into the learner database and these are automatically checked against the program database. The learner can review and look up items. Harrington sees the strengths of *CompLex* as coming from the links it makes to many aspects of word knowledge, the restriction of these links to known vocabulary, and thus the opportunity for continual review through the activation of these links.

In a very simple form of CAVL, learners can use a hypercard database to record various aspects of word knowledge such as those listed above. The database can then make links between items listed in more than one place (Richardson, 1990).

The *Learning OS* developed by Edunomics (cass@gol.com) has a set of vocabulary learning programs which provide opportunity for spaced retrieval, which make use of associational learning and which can utilise the learners' first language. The software keeps detailed records of progress and provides useful feedback on the activities. A variety of exercise types allows for useful enrichment of the vocabulary items.

Presentation of material

Earlier in this chapter we looked at conditions for vocabulary learning, focusing on the conditions of noticing, retrieval and generative use. CAVL can set up these conditions very effectively. Noticing can be encouraged through the use of coloured, highlighted or flashing text. Retrieval can be encouraged through the use of delay and providing gradually increasing clues. Generative use is encouraged through meeting the vocabulary in a variety of contexts and in a variety of forms: spoken, written and pictorial.

Fox (1984) describes several programs that encourage retrieval of vocabulary with varying degrees of textual context. Those with little textual context involve finding opposites, collocations and analogies. Those with substantial textual context involve restoring previously seen text or predicting the items needed to complete or continue a given text.

We will look at the use of concordances later in this chapter.

Vocabulary learning can occur incidentally. Palmberg (1988a) found that text-based computer games were an effective source of vocabulary learning. Some of the vocabulary in such games may not have relevance to the daily use of the language (*pirate, treasure, cutlass*) so adaptation may be needed to ensure that useful vocabulary goals are being met. Such programs may require dictionary access and some experiments have looked at computerised dictionary access (Hulstijn, 1993).

Monitoring progress

The research on the spacing of repetitions (see pp. 76–78) indicates a useful role for computers in ensuring that learners' efforts are directed towards vocabulary that most needs it. Some studies have looked at the effect on learning of giving learners control of the opportunity to repeat vocabulary or giving this control to a computer. Atkinson (1972) compared four repetition strategies.

1. The vocabulary is repeatedly presented in a random order.
2. The learners determine what vocabulary will occur in each trial.
3. The computer assumes that all items are of equal difficulty and provides repetition according to the learner's previous performance.
4. The computer assumes that all items are not of equal difficulty and provides repetition according to the learner's previous performance.

The best results as measured by a delayed post-test came from condition 4, with 2 and 3 about equal and the random sequence the least effective. The differences in performance were large, with condition 4 resulting in twice as much learning as the random order condition. In a somewhat similar study, van Bussel (1994: 72) found that learning style preference interacted with the type of sequence control.

Atkinson's study did not look at spaced repetition. Mondria and Mondria-de Vries's (1994) spacing suggestions for vocabulary cards can easily be applied to CAVL and some programs have done this.

Using concordances

A concordance is a list of contexts exemplifying a word or word family.

1.	under another name. Suddenly, Ntsiki	whispered	a warning. Biko stopped writing
2.	here running in the hall. Excited voices	whispered.	A servant, partly dressed and
3.	hand touched my shoulder. 'Smee?'	whispered	a voice that I recognized at once
4.	Ntsiki. 'He was a great man, Ntsiki,' he	whispered.	'A man the world will always
5.	But there was no reply. 'Mark?' I	whispered	again. I had been wrong, then.
6.	'I've never seen so much money before,'	whispered	Aku-nna, staring at Chike's
7.	the white man's anger. After a lot of	whispering	among themselves,
8.	think we had better rescue these,' she	whispered.	And they both gasped with
9.	Then Wilson spoke, but no longer in a	whisper,	and I thought I heard my own
10.	Then he began to speak. He spoke in a	whisper,	and his voice filled me with
11.	about it. Now, I understood from the	whispers	around the table, that this was
12.	and went to the door. 'Steve,' he	whispered	as he opened the door. Biko

Several writers and researchers recommend the use of concordances as a way of promoting vocabulary learning. The advantages of examining concordances are seen as being:

- Learners meet vocabulary in real contexts. The information which these provide often differs from non-corpus-based descriptions.
- Multiple contexts provide rich information on a variety of aspects of knowing a word including collocates, grammatical patterns, word family members, related meanings and homonyms.
- The use of concordances involves discovery learning, where the learners are being challenged to actively construct generalisations and note patterns and exceptions.
- Learners control their learning and learn investigative strategies.

To work effectively, however, learners need training in how to use concordances, and the data obtained from the concordances needs to be comprehensible to the learner. One way of overcoming the comprehensibility issue is for prepared 'dictionaries' of concordances to be used (Descamps, 1992). These dictionaries may be already partly organised with the examples in a concordance for a particular word already grouped under headings.

Learners can perform a variety of activities with concordances: they can classify the items in a concordance into groups. Guidance, such as group headings, questions or a table to fill, may be already provided. They can make generalisations and rules based on the data. They can recall items when the contexts are presented with the concordance word deleted (Stevens, 1991). Thurstun and Candlin (1998) provide examples of exercises. Schmitt (2000) also suggests activities that make use of a corpus and a concordancer.

Most concordance programs allow the user to determine the amount of context provided; typical variations include: one line of context determined by what fills a line on a computer screen, a complete sentence, a complete paragraph, a set number of characters each side, or a set number of lines. Concordance programs may also allow sorting. This can be done by choosing the direction of the sort (to the left or to the right), or by sorting according to the way the user has tagged them. Concordance programs usually allow a limit to be placed on the number of contexts to be searched for.

Using concordances may initially require learners (and teachers) to understand how a concordance is made and where the information comes from (Stevens, 1991). If learners are searching for their own concordances, they need to understand how to use the wild card to search for members of the word family. Learners also need to understand that some items are highly frequent while others are much less frequent. This helps them understand that some of their searches yield little data and others too much.

In the only experimental test of the value of concordances for learning, Cobb (1997) reported on an innovative program called *PET 200* which presents learners with example sentences drawn from a corpus. With several of these example sentences present, the learners can (1) choose the meaning for the target word from a multiple-choice set of definitions, (2) identify a form to fit the example sentences where the target word has been replaced by a blank, (3) spell the target word after hearing its spoken form and seeing contexts with a blank for the word, (4) choose words from a list to fill blanks in texts, and (5) recall words to fill blanks in short contexts. The study involved pre- and post-testing with the *Vocabulary Levels Test* (see appendix 3) and weekly quizzes involving spelling and gap filling in a text. When learners used the concordance information, their scores on the subsequent quizzes were higher than when they learned without this information. Use of concordances seems to help learning, especially where use in context is required. A feature of all activities in the program is that the level of mental processing required is deep and thoughtful.

Research on CAVL

Hubbard, Coady, Graney, Mokhtari and Magoto (1986) looked at vocabulary learning through a CALL program which taught vocabulary using a short definition, an example sentence, and the opportunity to type in a keyword mnemonic. After a training session in using the program, the experimental group worked on the program independently for one hour a week in the computer laboratory. The results showed no correlation between vocabulary gains and gains on a reading test.

When they looked back on the ways the learners used the program, Hubbard *et al.* (1986) found that the CALL program was accounting for only marginally more gains than what was happening outside the program. They also found that the learners using the program were not using it effectively: they did not use the review lessons, they did not use the keyword mnemonic properly and they did not use the practice tests. This was probably the result of low motivation and inadequate learning. Clearly CALL is strongly dependent on the human element.

James (1996) compared the academic vocabulary and reading development of ESL learners who used a computerised vocabulary development program and those who practised reading. The academic vocabulary program involved the learners in seeing the word, seeing its definition (using *COBUILD* as the source), seeing a sentence containing the word, and seeing a short text containing the word. The vocabulary group learned more academic words than the reading group, but both groups remained equal on the reading measures. Small but significant correlations were found between vocabulary learning difficulty and part of speech, word length, and deceptive transparency (synforms).

A study by Chun and Plass (1996) of incidental vocabulary learning from a reading text found text and picture annotations of 'looked-up' words to give better short-term and delayed (two weeks) retention than text alone or text and video. The amount of incidental vocabulary learning was quite high compared with other studies that did not use multimedia.

This chapter has looked at activities and procedures for teaching and learning vocabulary including teaching techniques, ways of communicating meaning and computer-assisted vocabulary learning. These are all means of bringing conditions for learning into play but the quality of mental processing set up by those learning conditions is what really matters. Teachers need to be able to examine the techniques that they use and determine what goals they are trying to achieve, how they will achieve them and how they can adapt what they are doing if things are not going as planned.

4 Vocabulary and listening and speaking

This chapter looks at opportunities for vocabulary learning through the oral skills of listening and speaking. With careful thought and planning, listening and speaking can be important means of vocabulary growth.

What vocabulary knowledge is needed for listening?

Learning vocabulary through listening is one type of learning through meaning-focused input. Learners would need at least 95% coverage of the running words in the input in order to gain reasonable comprehension and to have reasonable success at guessing from context. A higher coverage of around 98% (one unknown word in every 50 words, or 2 to 3 unknown words per minute) would be better (Hu and Nation, in press). Studies of spoken language, especially colloquial spoken language used in informal situations, indicate that a vocabulary of around 2,000 word families can provide over 95% coverage (Schonell, Meddleton and Shaw, 1956). More formal academic spoken language would probably require knowledge of the *Academic Word List*, although this still remains to be investigated.

Cummins (1986) attempted to incorporate the skills of L2 face-to-face communication and performance on L2 cognitive/academic tasks into a construct of 'language proficiency', in order to account for the relationship between language proficiency and academic achievement. Cummins used two continua.

Informal speaking skills are in the top left section, usually being cognitively undemanding (dealing with familiar topics) and context embedded (related to here and now). Academic discourse is in the bottom right being cognitively demanding (having a high information load) and context reduced (constructing its own mental reality).

Bonk (in press) used four short tape recorded texts which were equated for total number of words, number of unique words, number of unique lexical words, number of syllables, and duration of record-

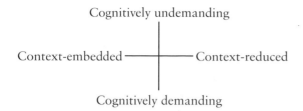

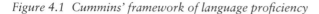

Figure 4.1 Cummins' framework of language proficiency

ing. They were all on similar topics of imaginary native customs. The texts deliberately differed from each other in the number of low-frequency words that each contained. Learners listened to all four texts and wrote a recall protocol using either L1 or L2 as they preferred. These were scored on a four point scale as a measure of comprehension of the texts. The same passages were then given as dictations with pauses between the phrases. The lexical words in the dictations were scored (minor spelling and grammatical errors were ignored) as a measure of the familiarity of the lexical items. That is, if a lexical word was adequately reproduced in the dictation by the learners it was considered to be known. If not, it was considered by the researcher as unknown. Bonk found a significant but moderate correlation of .446 between comprehension (L1 or L2 recall) and amount of familiar lexis (dictation score). There was a significant difference between lexical recognition scores associated with good text recall and those associated with poor text recall. There were however many examples of 100% lexical scores associated with inferior comprehension. There was no clear lexical cut off point for good comprehension, but lexical scores under 80% were unlikely to be matched with good comprehension.

A vocabulary correlate of the cognitively demanding/context-reduced tasks would be the *Academic Word List*, that is, the sub-technical academic vocabulary common to a wide range of academic disciplines (appendix 1). This contrasts with the pre-requisite high-frequency general service vocabulary which would serve most communication needs in cognitively undemanding/context-embedded tasks. Cummins (1986: 156–157) considers that it takes immigrant students two years to gain face-to-face L2 communication skills, but between five to seven years to approach grade norms in L2 academic skills. From a vocabulary perspective, this means about two years to gain control of the two thousand high-frequency general service words, and three to five years more to gain control of the academic vocabulary and other relevant low-frequency and technical words. It is thus important to look at learners' proposed language use when deciding what vocabulary will be needed.

The true/false test in appendix 2 can be used to test listening vocabulary. The learners need to be able to see the relevant pictures when they are required. There are two forms of the test and the test items were graded according to the frequency of the tested words in West (1953). Details of the construction of the test can be found in Nation (1983). A vocabulary based dictation test is described in Fountain and Nation (2000) and Nation (1990: 86–87). This test consists of five paragraphs with each successive paragraph containing words from a lower frequency level. Only the content words are scored when marking the test. There is a form of the test in appendix 5.

Providing vocabulary support for listening

There are several ways of supporting listening by providing written input that is directly related to the listening task. These ways are very useful where learners have quite a large reading vocabulary but have little opportunity to improve their listening skills.

Receptive information transfer

Receptive information transfer activities involve turning listening input into some diagrammatic form. Here is an example where learners have to fill in a timetable as they listen to two students talking to each other about their classes.

	Monday	Tuesday	Wednesday	Thursday	Friday
9–10			Mathematics		
10–11	Geography			English	
11–12					
1–2		Art	Sport		
2–3			Sport		

Note that some of the spaces are already filled in. This helps the learners check where they are on the task and provides helpful vocabulary that they will hear in the spoken description. Some of the words required to fill in the table may be provided under the table. Palmer (1982) has a wide range of suggestions for the content of information transfer activities. Here are some of his categories.

- Maps and plans: streets, tours, architects' plans, theatre seats, weather forecasts
- Grids and tables: passport details, polls, timetables, football results
- Diagrams and charts: family tree, climate, pie graphs, flow charts
- Diaries and calendars: office holidays, appointments, hotel bookings
- Lists, forms, coupons: radio programme, menus, diets, shopping list, car rental forms

Listening while reading

Learners can listen while they also see a written version of what they are listening to. Several graded readers are now accompanied by audio-tapes and these can provide useful work for the language laboratory.

Listening to stories

The teacher reads a story to the learners and writes important words on the blackboard as they occur. During a ten minute period about 20 to 30 words will be written on the board. While reading the story aloud the teacher should repeat sentences, and go at a speed that the learners can easily keep up with. This should be done two or three times a week for a few minutes each time in the same way as a serial occurs on television. Graded readers which are within the learners' vocabulary level are suitable. Hill's list of readers in Day and Bamford (1998) is a useful source of good titles. Learners can also listen to stories that they have already read.

Quizzes

Quiz competitions can be a useful means of vocabulary expansion. Learners can be divided into teams and points given for correct answers. Manzo (1970) suggests that extra points be given for a correct answer plus some extra detail. The teacher can prepare the questions so that useful vocabulary occurs in them.

Learning vocabulary from listening to stories

There is a growing body of evidence (Elley, 1989; Brett, Rothlein and Hurley, 1996) that learners can pick up new vocabulary as they are being read to. There are several conditions that make this learning more likely and in this section we will look at how teachers can make sure that these conditions occur when they read aloud to their learners. The main conditions are: interest in the content of the story, comprehension of the story, understanding of the unknown words and retrieval of the meaning of those not yet strongly established, decontextualisation of the target words, and thoughtful generative processing of the target vocabulary.

Interest

The most important condition to encourage learning relates to the choice of what is read, namely interest (Elley, 1989; Penno, Wilkinson and Moore, forthcoming). Learners need to be interested in what they are listening to. Elley (1989) explained the differing amounts of vocabulary learning from two stories by the lack of involvement of the learners with one of the stories. Similarly, the vocabulary most likely to be learned was strongly related to the main ideas of the story. Teachers can help arouse learners' interest by choosing stories that learners are likely to be interested in, by presenting a story in serial form so that interest increases episode by episode, and by involving learners in the story as in shared book reading where the teacher interacts with the learners about the story.

Comprehension

Learners need to be able to understand the story. There are several sources of difficulty in learning vocabulary from listening to stories: there is the vocabulary load of the story, that is the density of unknown words. On the other hand there is the support provided by background knowledge, pictures and definitions (Elley, 1989). And then there are difficulties with the forms and meanings of the words themselves.

There is still insufficient research on the effect of the ratio of unknown words to known words in a text aimed at incidental vocabulary learning. Hirsh and Nation (1992) looked at the relationship between vocabulary size and new word density in reading texts, but did not look at the effect on learning. Hu and Nation (in press) looked at the density of unknown words in a written fiction text and found that learners needed to know 98% of the running words in order for most of them to gain adequate comprehension. It is likely that for extensive listening the ratio of unknown words to known should be around 1 in 100. Teachers need to choose 'easy' books.

Difficulty also operates at the word level (Higa, 1965; R. Ellis, 1995). R. Ellis (1994) found that shorter words were easier to learn than longer words. This suggests that when reading aloud to a class, it may be useful to break longer words into parts, if they are complex words, so that their formally simpler stems and affixes can be seen.

Repeated retrieval

Repeated retrieval can be achieved by hearing the same story several times, by listening to a serialised story where the same vocabulary returns again and again, and by hearing several stories on the same topic. There is a tendency in continuous stories for vocabulary to be repeated. Teachers could maximise this by briefly retelling what happened previously in the story before continuing with the next instalment. Much research still needs to be done on the effect of a continuous story on repetition. Hwang and Nation (1989) looked at the effect on repetition of reading follow-up newspaper stories on the same topic. They found that follow-up stories provided better repetition of vocabulary than unrelated stories.

Decontextualisation

Learners need to focus on words not only as a part of the message but as words themselves. This can be helped by noting words on the blackboard, and by providing short definitions or translations of words. Elley (1989) and Brett, Rothlein and Hurley (1996) found that vocabulary learning is considerably increased if the teacher defines a word when it occurs in the story. This defining does two things. Firstly, it takes the word out of its message context and draws attention to it as a language item; that is, decontextualises it. Secondly, it provides a meaning for the word. The most effective definitions are likely to be clearly marked as definitions, and are short and clear, possibly involving a first language translation. There is as yet no research on the effect of first language translation on the learning of vocabulary through listening.

Penno, Wilkinson and Moore (forthcoming) examined vocabulary learning from listening to stories with a group of young, largely native speakers of English who heard each story three times with a week's gap between each retelling. Vocabulary learning was measured by pre- and post-vocabulary tests and an oral retelling task. Some words were explained during the listening. With each repetition of the story, learners used more of the previously unknown vocabulary, roughly one more word per repetition. Vocabulary that was explained during the story was learned better than that which was not explained. Higher ability students made greater vocabulary gains than lower ability students. Explanation of words in a story resulted in greater learning of non-explained words compared with listening to a story where no words were explained. That is, there was a generalisation effect for vocabulary explanation. There was a strong story effect in the study indicating that the choice of book to read to students is very important for learning.

In a series of experiments, Hulstijn (1992) compared incidental and intentional vocabulary learning, and compared inferring from context under several conditions with having meanings provided. In incidental learning, learners were not aware that they would be tested on the vocabulary they met, even though in some of Hulstijn's conditions synonyms or choices were provided, and for native speakers nonsense words were used. The incidental learning conditions resulted in very low learning scores, although it should be noted that Hulstijn's tests were quite demanding, involving receptive recall in one test and productive recall in another. Where learners were made aware that they would be tested on vocabulary knowledge, learning increased substantially and generally obliterated any differences between inferring and having meanings provided.

In the incidental learning conditions, having to infer the meaning of a word resulted in more learning than when the meaning was provided in a gloss. However, Hulstijn noted that wrong inferences often resulted even when the inference was partly guided by the presence of multiple-choice answers. This condition should not be interpreted as a reason for discouraging inferring from context, because most native speakers' vocabulary learning occurs in this way (Nagy, Herman and Anderson, 1985). It underlines the need for training learners in guessing from context and for complementing learning from context with more deliberate vocabulary focused learning.

Generative processing

Learners need to meet new words in differing contexts that stretch their knowledge of the words: in a range of linguistic contexts, in association with pictures (Elley, 1989), and in discussion and negotiation. Teachers can try to affect the quality of the mental processing of vocabulary while learners listen to stories in the following ways.

• Rather than read the same story several times, as in the Elley (1989) study, it may be better to use a longer story and present it part by part as a serial. As we have seen in the section on repeated retrieval, long texts provide an opportunity for the same vocabulary to recur. If this recurrence is in contexts which differ from those previously met in the story, then this generative use will contribute to learning. There have not been any studies examining the degree of generative use of vocabulary in long texts such as simplified readers.

- If the teacher is able to supplement story telling with pictures, by using blackboard drawings, an OHP or a blown-up book, then this will contribute positively to vocabulary learning.
- If it is possible to provide simple contextual definitions of words, that is definitions using example sentences, then this could help learning if the example sentences differ from those where the word occurs in the story. The contextual definition would then be a generative use of the word.

Learning vocabulary from spoken input is an effective means of vocabulary expansion. The Elley (1989) and Brett, Rothlein and Hurley (1996) studies both examined long-term retention (three months, and six weeks) and found that words were retained.

The five conditions considered here have been treated as separate, but they clearly interact: interest and comprehension are clearly related and we have seen how decontextualisation, repetition and deep processing affect each other. What is striking about the conditions is that they apply not only to incidental learning from spoken input but also to more deliberate language-focused learning.

It should also be clear that we should not accept processes like negotiation and definition at their face value but need to see what conditions for learning they are setting up. By doing this we can distinguish between useful and not so useful instances of negotiation or definition, and we can see if the same conditions can be set up in other processes that draw attention to vocabulary.

Table 4.1 lists the five conditions and features that have been mentioned here. Using a variant of this table, it would be possible to rate a teacher's performance in reading a story aloud to a class, by giving points for each of the features listed in the table. The table suggests that some features (using interesting material) deserve more points than others (involving the learners). Some features, such as serialisation, however, occur in several places on the table and this would need to be accounted for in an observation checklist. The assignment of features to useful, very good and excellent is partly supported by research but is largely intuitive. It makes the point that research is a very useful guide in shaping our teaching activities but our intuitions and feelings as experienced teachers must also be recognised.

Table 4.1. *Conditions and features enhancing vocabulary learning from listening to stories*

		Features	
Conditions	1 useful	2 very good	3 excellent
Interest	Involve the listeners	Serialise	Use interesting material
Comprehension	Choose easy words to focus on	Control the pace Simplify	Choose easy material Use pictures
Repeated retrieval	Don't note up too soon Don't wait too long between readings	Serialise a long story Use related texts	Reread/retell the same stories
Decontextualisation	Put words on the blackboard Point to a word on the blackboard	Encourage negotiation	Define simply Translate
Deep processing	Use contextual definitions	Use pictures	Serialise Retell differently

Learning vocabulary through negotiation

In several studies, Rod Ellis and his colleagues have looked at the role of unmodified input, premodified input and negotiation on vocabulary learning. The tasks used typically involved learners having to place small pictures of pieces of furniture or a utensil on a larger picture of an apartment or room. The different treatments usually involved the following kinds of input.

1. *Baseline directions.* Typical native speaker instructions were used based on native speakers communicating with native speakers.
2. *Premodified input.* Second language learners heard the baseline directions and negotiated the parts they did not understand with a native speaker. These interactions were recorded and used to prepare premodified directions. So when the task was performed there was no negotiation but the input had already been modified on the basis of negotiation with a different group of learners.
3. *Interactionally modified input.* The learners negotiated the baseline directions with the teacher as the task was being done. To help the learners, typical negotiating directions were put up on the blackboard, such as 'What is a _____ ?', and 'Could you say it again?'
4. *Negotiated output.* The learners performed the task in pairs so that they and not the teacher provided the input.

Ellis, Tanaka and Yamazaki (1994) found that there were very large differences in the amount of time taken to perform the tasks, with the group getting interactionally modified input taking four and a half times the amount of time taken by the premodified group. There was also much greater repetition of target items for the interactionally modified group. Premodified input resulted in vocabulary learning but not as much as the interactionally modified input. Rod Ellis (1995: 409) noted in an analysis of one of the studies reported in Ellis, Tanaka and Yamazaki that although more word meanings were learnt from the interactionally modified input than from the premodified input, the rate of acquisition (in words per minute) was faster with the premodified input. Ellis and He (1999) controlled for the factor of time spent on the task, comparing premodified input, interactionally modified input and negotiated output. Learning occurred in all three treatments. They found that although the interactionally modified input group consistently scored higher than the premodified group, the differences were not statistically significant. The negotiated output group scored significantly higher than the other two groups.

Ellis and He explain this better learning by learners working together in pairs in two complementary ways. Firstly, the learners had more chance to produce the new words and thus process them more deeply. Secondly, the quality of the negotiation between the non-native speaking learners was better than the negotiation between the teacher and the learners. This quality differed in the comprehensibility of the definitions provided (the learners used simpler words), the systematic approach to the task, and the one-to-one support provided by continual checking and feedback. Good negotiation works better than poor negotiation for vocabulary learning.

Newton (forthcoming) looked at vocabulary learning with learners working in groups of four on communication tasks. He found that negotiation of vocabulary made learning more certain, but it did not account for most of the learning, which seemed to occur simply by guessing from context. As the Ellis, Tanaka and Yamazaki studies showed, negotiation takes time and thus only a relatively small number of items can be negotiated when the goal is to get on and complete the communication task.

Ellis and Heimbach (1997) looked at young ESL children's negotiation and learning through negotiation. Children negotiated more when they were part of a group than when working one to one with a teacher. There was not a strong relationship between comprehension and acquisition of vocabulary. That is, vocabulary in sentences that were clearly understood was not necessarily learned.

There are important lessons from these studies that deserve repeating.

Firstly, premodified input and negotiation both lead to vocabulary learning. Secondly, it is likely that the amount of learning from both these kinds of input depends on the quality of the support for learning that each provides. That is, good simplification and glossing within a text is likely to lead to better learning than poor negotiation, and good negotiation will lead to better learning than poor simplification and glossing. Thirdly, premodification and negotiation are not in themselves conditions affecting learning, but they provide opportunities for conditions like retrieval, generative use and instantiation to occur.

Ellis and He's study did not control for repetition and generation, factors which have been shown to be important for vocabulary learning. It would be interesting to see how controlling for these factors would affect the premodified/negotiated comparison of effects.

Teachers can encourage negotiation by ensuring that learners have the capability, willingness and opportunity to negotiate. Ellis and colleagues ensured capability by providing learners with a list of sentences that are useful in negotiating. Learners can be given practice in negotiating by setting negotiating as a goal and then modelling and providing practice in doing it. Learners can be made more willing to negotiate by using grouping arrangements where they feel comfortable asking for help (Ellis and Heimbach, 1997). These arrangements are likely to be with other learners of a similar proficiency level. The opportunity to negotiate can be provided by using split information tasks, by deliberately designing vocabulary gaps into tasks as in Woodeson's (1982) communicative crosswords, and by ensuring the written input to the task has some vocabulary that is not in the written input of others in the group.

The vocabulary of speaking

Word frequency studies indicate that a much smaller vocabulary is needed for speaking than for writing. This difference however is probably as much a difference influenced by degree of formality and topic as it is by the spoken and written modes. We tend to write about more weighty matters than speak about them.

Pawley and Syder (1983) suggest that as well as vocabulary knowledge we need to have memorised large numbers of clauses and phrases which we can then easily retrieve and use. This allows us to speak in a fluent way sounding like native speakers because the words in the memorised chunks fit together well. This issue is looked at more deeply in the chapter on collocation.

Certainly, for the beginning stages of listening and speaking, it is important to work out a manageable list of items that should be learned to a high degree of fluency. Crabbe and Nation (1991) did this for learners who had the goal of being able to use another language for short periods of travel or residence in another country. This 'survival' vocabulary consisted of around 120 items and included greetings, politeness formulas, numbers, ways of requesting food, accommodation, help and directions, and ways of describing yourself, buying goods, and, where necessary, bargaining. The words and phrases needed to do a limited set of things like this do not take very long to learn, but they need to be practised until they reach a high degree of fluency. This is particularly true of numbers and greetings.

Items in a basic spoken fluency list need to be practised as single items with learners having to retrieve the spoken forms while seeing the first language translation or some other way of representing the meaning. Then they need to be practised in flexible dialogues where there is some element of unpredictability. This can be done in small simulations and role plays.

There are several vocabulary items which are mainly used in spoken language and are unlikely to occur performing the same functions in written texts. Here is a list from Stenstrom (1990: 144) from the *London-Lund Corpus.*

- Apologies: *pardon, sorry, excuse me, I'm sorry, I beg your pardon*
- Smooth-overs: *don't worry, never mind*
- Hedges: *kind of, sort of, sort of thing*
- Expletives: *damn, gosh, hell, fuck off, good heavens, the hell, for goodness sake, good heavens above, bloody hell*
- Greetings: *hi, hello, good evening, good morning, Happy New Year, how are you, how do you do*
- Initiators: *anyway, however, now*
- Negative: *no*
- Orders: *give over, go on, shut up*
- Politeness markers: *please*
- Question tags: *is it, isn't it*
- Responses: *ah, fine, good, uhuh, OK, quite, really, right, sure, all right, fair enough, I'm sure, I see, that's good, that's it, that's right, that's true, very good*
- Softeners: *I mean, mind you, you know, you see, as you know, do you see*
- Thanks: *thanks, thank you*
- Well: *well*
- Exemplifiers: *say*
- Positive: *mhm, yeah, yes, yup*

There are several ways of looking at whether learners have enough vocabulary to carry out speaking tasks. The *Vocabulary Levels Test* (appendix 3) is a useful starting point. If learners' receptive vocabulary is very small, their productive vocabulary is likely to be smaller. It would be useful to accompany this testing by doing the listening version of the 1000 word level test (see appendix 2) to make sure that the low score is the result of a small vocabulary and not a lack of reading skill.

Most tests of spoken English which involve rating scales contain a scale for rating the vocabulary component of speaking. This is useful as a way of increasing the reliability of a spoken test by increasing the number of points of assessment, but it would not be wise to try to isolate the vocabulary score from such a set of scales as a valid measure of vocabulary size.

A more focused way would be to do several small role plays based on 'survival' situations, then statements could be made about spoken vocabulary knowledge in terms of performance in certain situations, such as: 'Has the vocabulary to go shopping.'

Developing fluency with spoken vocabulary

The fluency development strand of a course is important at all stages of learning. Learners should become fluent with what they learn from the beginning, developing fluency with greetings, numbers, time, days of the week, time indicators like *today, yesterday, next week, last month*, some colours, and other items which could be used frequently.

This fluency practice is a first step. It is a listen-and-point activity and is best done with learners working in pairs with one learner acting as the teacher; but it can be done with the whole class as a teacher-led activity. In this description we will use numbers as the focus of fluency development and assume that the teacher is working with just one learner. The learner has the numbers from 1 to 10 on a sheet in front of him.

The teacher says a number, for example 'five', and the learner points to 5. If the learners are working in pairs, it may be necessary for the learner in the teaching role to have a list of the numbers written out in their full form. The teacher keeps saying numbers, gradually increasing the speed so that the learner is pushed to the limits of his fluency. If the learner points to the wrong number, the teacher says 'No' and says the number again. If the learner hesitates, the teacher waits until the learner points. The teacher can note which numbers are less fluently recognised by the learner and give these extra practice. Several minutes should be spent on this activity with the numbers being covered in a random order many times. This practises listening fluency.

The second step is for the learner to become the teacher so that speaking fluency is practised. The third step also practises speaking fluency: the teacher points to a number and the learner says it.

Learners should reach a high level of fluency at step 1 before moving on to step 2. Fluency practice on the same items should be done on several different days so that there is opportunity for spaced retrieval. For variety, and in a teacher-led activity with the whole class, the learners can write the numbers as they hear them instead of pointing. Because this fluency practice is being done with lexical sets, it is very important that the learners have plenty of opportunity to learn words separately before they do the fluency practice. If the words are not well established, fluency practice could cause confusion of the words and their meanings.

When the first language uses a different writing system from the

Table 4.2. *Examples of vocabulary focus and activities for fluency practice for beginners*

Vocabulary	Sequence of difficulty	Chart to point to
Numbers	Single digit numbers Double digit numbers, etc. Cardinal numbers Ordinal numbers	The numbers written as figures 1 2 3 4 5 6 7 . . .
Days of the week	Days Days plus date e.g. Monday the 3rd Days plus date plus month e.g. Monday the third of August	First language words in order or a week cut from a first language calendar
Months of the year	As for days of the week	First language words in order or a twelve month first language calendar
Time indicators: *today, tomorrow, last week, this month, next year*		A set of boxes with the middle one representing now, or a calendar

second language, it is important to do fluency practice with the letters of the second language and their sounds.

Suggestions for more advanced fluency practice can be found in chapter 9 (see p. 336).

Using teacher input to increase vocabulary knowledge

As we will see in the chapter on writing, it is not easy to bring learners' receptive vocabulary knowledge into productive use. The knowledge required for production is greater than the knowledge required for reception. An important way of helping learners gain control of this knowledge is for the teacher to enter into a dialogue with the learners, encouraging them to produce vocabulary that the teacher models. One way of doing this is through semantic mapping.

Semantic mapping

Semantic mapping involves the teacher and the learners working together to build up on the blackboard a visual framework of connections between ideas.

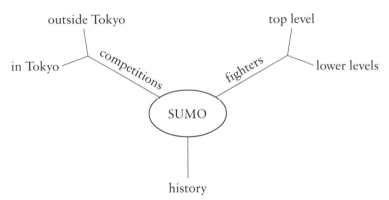

There can be several starting points for semantic mapping. It can involve the recall of a previously read story, a recent current event, a film, a unit of study, or simply learners' general knowledge of a topic. Stahl and Vancil (1986) point out in their study of native speakers of English that it is the discussion that occurs during the building up of the semantic map that makes the activity contribute to vocabulary learning. Skill is important in the way the teacher enters into a dialogue with the learners, encourages them and supports their participation in the dialogue.

In a semantic mapping activity aimed at increasing productive vocabulary, we would expect to see some of the following features.

1. The teacher encourages learners to produce vocabulary that can be put into the map. Rather than supplying word forms to the learners, the teacher gives the learners suggestions that will help them retrieve the word from their receptive vocabulary. These suggestions can include paraphrases or first language translations of wanted items, and formal clues like the initial letters or sounds of the word.

2. The teacher asks the learners to explain, justify and increase the connections between items in the semantic map. This has several learning goals. Firstly, it encourages repetition to help establish the vocabulary. Secondly, it encourages generative use by enriching associations with other items. Thirdly, it allows the teacher to help shape learners' production by rephrasing what they say. This helps them with grammatical and collocational aspects of the words. Fourthly, it helps learners explore the meaning of the relevant vocabulary.

3. The teacher goes back over what has already been put into the map, repeating important vocabulary and reinforcing the connections. The teacher can encourage learners to participate in this revision.

4. The map is not the final outcome of the activity. After it has been completed, it is then used as a basis for talks or writing.

Gibbons' (1998) study of classroom interaction highlights ways in which the teacher can contribute to learners' language development by making their thinking and reporting more explicit through recasting what they say. The basis for the recasts is a dialogue between the teacher and the learners. It is not unusual to see the vocabulary of the teacher's recasts coming through in the learners' later speech and written reports.

Making decisions

This activity described here is representative of a range of similar problem solving activities where the teacher can provide vocabulary input and encourage reuse of the vocabulary during the activity. It has four stages.

1. The teacher presents the topic which is expressed as an alternative question, for example, 'Should children continue to live with their

parents after they finish school or should they leave home?' The teacher gives an example reason for each of the alternatives: live with their parents because this saves money; leave home because this encourages independence.

2. The learners form groups of about four people. Each group has to list reasons to support *one* side of the question. While the learners do this, the teacher goes around the groups, providing needed vocabulary and suggesting reasons that include useful vocabulary. The teacher gets the learners to note down the vocabulary so that it will be used.

3. The groups of four now join together to make groups of eight. Each group of eight must comprise a group of four that prepared reasons for one side of the question and a group that prepared reasons for the other side. The learners must explain their reasons to each other and must reach a decision. They do not have to support their side of the question. They should try to use the vocabulary that the teacher provided for them during the activity.

4. The groups of eight now report their decisions and reasons to the rest of the class, once again using the provided vocabulary.

Using labelled diagrams

Vocabulary support for speaking tasks can be provided by using labels on pictures and diagrams.

Information transfer activities

Palmer (1982) describes a wide range of information transfer activities which involve the learner turning a diagram, chart, table or form into written or spoken text. For example, a learner may have a map of a country with a route marked on it in various ways to indicate travel by car, train, ship or plane. The learner describes the holiday route to another learner who marks it on his own map. The learner is helped in the spoken description by the vocabulary used to label the diagram. Further help can be provided by providing an opportunity for preparation and practice. This can be done using an expert group/family group procedure. Two different information transfer tasks are prepared. All the learners who have one task get together to practise it. All the learners who have the other task get together and practise theirs. These are the expert groups. After this practice, the learners form pairs (family groups) with one learner from each of the two expert groups. They then do the information transfer task.

Split information tasks

In a split information task each learner has unique, essential information. They must not show their pictures to another learner. Nation (1990) describes split information tasks where learners decide if pictures are the same or different. The learner who begins describing the picture has labels on her picture. The other learner does not.

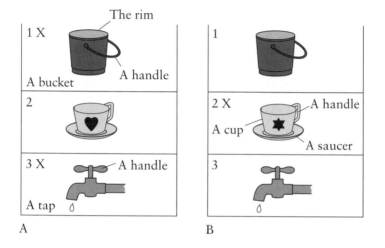

The set of pictures is made up so that the same labels occur on several different pictures and the same label will be on a picture where learner A starts speaking and on another picture where learner B starts speaking. This ensures that each learner makes both receptive and productive use of the words.

Hall (1992) used split information tasks that focused on particular mathematics vocabulary including *diagonal* and *perimeter*. The same words appeared in a variety of tasks. Here is a sample task and the discussion that resulted from it.

A: Which is quicker?   B: Which is quicker?
   Your way or B's?   Your way or A's?

Here is a sample of the discussion that occurred during the task.

A: Which is quicker? Your way or B's?
B: Which is quicker? Your way or A's? Go!
A: Which is quicker? Your way or B's?
B: Which way does your way go?
A: This way.
B: No. Just say it. Go. Tell me.
A: It's going here.
B: How? How? It's how? My way cause its going diagonally. Mine's . . .
A: Why? Is it around the edge?
B: B's quicker. No. Hah. Put B.
A: I draw a line up there its B. It's A. A's a perimeter and the other diagonally. A is around.
B: Put B. Well put that. Say put that. Across diagonal. Not a perimeter.
A: B. What you got?
B: Quicker.

Using cooperative tasks to focus on vocabulary

Cooperating activities are particularly effective in getting learners to explore a range of meanings that a word has and the range of elements of meaning it contains. Here are two examples of ranking activities. One focuses on the word *cancel* and the other on *instruction*.

- *Cancel.* Your team is supposed to play in a game on Saturday. List the reasons why the game might be cancelled. Rank them according to how likely they are to happen. (The vocabulary to be used can be included in the items to rank.)

The following example is based on the word *instruction* which occurred in a text in the phrase *reading instruction*.

- *Instruction.* You are about to begin studying at university for the first time. Before the university year begins you have a chance to receive instruction in a variety of skills. Rank them in order of value to you for university study.
  Instruction in writing assignments
  Instruction in taking lecture notes
  Instruction in using the library
  Instruction in organising and planning your time
  Instruction in making use of university clubs and facilities

The two examples are ranking activities, but problem solving activities, classification activities and brainstorming activities can also be used with a focus on a particular word. Activities which focus on a word are easy to make and can be very effective in helping learn the word. Learners should be told of the learning goal of the activity.

Notice that the activity can explore the meaning of the word or it can provide opportunities for the word to be repeated. Here are some more activities based on a reading text about an immigrant studying to become a nurse (*New Voices*, July 1997). The target word is italicised.

- Why do people become *refugees*? List as many causes as you can.
- Group these jobs according to the skills they *involve*: nurse, teacher, shop assistant, builder, computer programmer, factory worker, taxi driver.
- A group in your community has decided to *sponsor* a refugee family. List all the things that the sponsorship will involve.
- Using the text and your experience, list and group things you would need to do to become a *registered* nurse. Which one would you find the most difficult?

While the activities are being done, the teacher would look for the number of repetitions of the target word, the number of generative uses, and direct questions and statements about the meaning of the word.

How can a teacher design activities to help incidental vocabulary learning?

Speaking tasks such as mini-lectures, ranking activities, split information tasks, role play and problem solving discussion are not usually thought of as having vocabulary learning goals. One of the reasons for this is that it seems difficult to plan vocabulary learning as a part of a syllabus using activities that are largely productive, unpredictable, and dependent on the people who happen to be in the discussion group.

However, such activities are a very useful means of vocabulary learning and a vocabulary goal can be effectively incorporated into many speaking activities. It is also possible to plan what vocabulary is likely to be learned although this may be an incidental goal in speaking activities. Such activities can achieve a range of goals and several may be achieved in the same activity.

Here is part of the transcript of a problem solving discussion by three learners (S1, S2, S3) about redesigning a zoo (Newton, 1995). The task comes from Ur (1981).

S3: All enclosures should be filled

S2: Enclosures should be filled enclosure, do you know?

S1: What means enclosure? Do you know?

S3: Close ah— should be filled

S2: No I don't know enclos— enclosed

S1: Filled what means fill? Oh oh all enclosed, I think that all enclosed that means enclosed

S2: Fill

S3: Filled, filled

S2: Ohh

S1: Every every area yes should be filled

S2: Should be filled

S3: Should be put put something inside

S1: Yes because yes yes because you know two? the-

S2: I see. No empty rooms ahh

S3: No empty rooms yeah

S2: Two is the empty I see

S1: Yeah empty so we must fill it O.K.

The word *enclosures* comes from the handout that the learners are looking at. One of the points of information on this handout states, 'All the enclosures should be filled.' The learners S3 and S2 repeat the sentence from the handout and then S1 asks 'What means *enclosure?*' This then starts a discussion about the word. Notice that the form *enclosed* is also spoken although this does not appear on the handout at all.

What is clear from this example is that what is written on the handout has an effect on what is said during the discussion. It is also clear that the discussion involves the learners explaining the vocabulary to each other. The written input to the activity can play a major role in determining what is learned, if it includes vocabulary that is important for the speaking activity. Let us now look at vocabulary learning through a range of activities.

Retelling

As we shall see, retelling activities can take many forms. What is common to all of them is that learners read a text (usually about 100 to 200 words long), and retell it. From a vocabulary learning point of view, the text provides new vocabulary and a context to help understand it, and the retelling gives learners the chance to productively retrieve the vocabulary and ideally make generative use of it. Research by Joe (1998) indicates that absence of the text during retelling encourages generative use, but that having the text present during retelling ensures that more of the target vocabulary is used. As having the text present during retelling provides poor conditions for retrieval (the form which should be retrieved is already present in the text that the learner can look at), until further research is done on this technique, it is probably best not to have the text present during retelling.

Other forms of retelling include '4/3/2' (Maurice, 1983; Arevart and Nation, 1991), and 'Read and retell' (Simcock, 1993). 4/3/2 involves a learner giving the same talk to three different listeners one after the other, but with four minutes to give the first delivery of the talk, three minutes for the delivery of the same talk to the second listener, and two minutes for the third. The talk can be a retelling of a previously studied text. The repetition would not be expected to increase the range of generative use, but would provide opportunity for more fluent retrieval.

Eller, Pappas and Brown (1988) observed native-speaking kindergarten children's vocabulary development on three separate occasions one day apart as they listened to and then retold the same picture book story. Eller, Pappas and Brown were able to show that the children's control of particular words increased from one listening and retelling to another. Although the study had some weaknesses, particularly in that the vocabulary observed was not pretested, this type of longitudinal process study has much potential in vocabulary acquisition research. The results of the study support the idea that knowledge of particular words gradually increases as a consequence of repeated encounters.

The Read and retell activity involves retelling a written text, but the listener has a set of guiding questions to ask the reteller so that it seems like an interview. The design of the questions can encourage the use of the target vocabulary from the written text and ensure that all the important parts of the text are retold. Both the listener and the reteller study the text and the questions before the retelling, and they can rehearse the retelling to perform in front of others.

When observing retelling activities, the teacher would look for the use of the wanted vocabulary, particularly to see if it was in a salient enough position in the text to encourage its use in retelling, and to see if it was being used generatively in the retelling.

Role play

Role play activities can involve a written text on which the role play is based and may involve written instructions to the role players. The

'Say it!' activity combines these features and is a simple introduction to role play. In Say it! learners read a short text such as a newspaper report containing the wanted vocabulary. They can read it and discuss it together if they wish. Then they look at a grid containing short tasks for them to perform. The columns in the grid are labelled with the letters A, B, C and the rows are numbered. The first learner in the group says the reference of a square, for example, B2, and the second learner in the group has to perform the task contained in that square. After that the second learner says a square reference and the third learner has to perform that task. This continues around the group. The same task may be performed more than once by different learners in the group.

Here is the newspaper report on which the following Say it! is based. The learners need to read the report carefully and discuss it before doing the activity.

CASTAWAYS SURVIVED ON SHARK'S BLOOD
Three fishermen who drifted on the Pacific for four months told yesterday how they drank shark's blood to survive.

The fishermen from Kiribati told their story through an interpreter in the American Samoa capital of Pago Pago after being rescued by the ship Sakaria.

Kautea Teaitoa, Veaieta Toanuea, and Tebwai Aretana drifted 400 kilometres from home after their outboard motor failed on February 8.

They said four ships had refused to help them during their ordeal.

When they were picked up on June 4 they had eaten the last of a one-metre shark four days before and drunk all of its blood.

'I have not prayed so much in all my life,' Mr Aretana said.

	A	B	C
1	You are Kautea. Say what helped you survive.	You are Tebwai Aretana. How did you feel when the ships refused to help you?	You are a sailor on the Sakaria. What did you do to help the fishermen?
2	You are Tebwai. Explain why you were in the boat and what happened after it broke down.	You are Kautea. How did you feel when you caught the shark?	You are the captain. Explain why you stopped?
3	You are Veaieta. Explain what caused the problem.	You are the interpreter. Describe the feelings and appearance of the three men.	The journey was called an ordeal. Why was it an ordeal?

Notice that the tasks in each square are designed to encourage use of the wanted vocabulary and that they require the learners to reshape what was in the text to suit the viewpoint of the task. If the text is read, discussed, understood and then put away before doing the activity, then retrieval is encouraged. The role play nature of the tasks encourages generative use of the vocabulary.

Larger problem solving role play activities can involve substantial written input that needs to be processed in a similar way (Nation, 1991b). Learners need to read about the background to the problem, the problem, the constraints on the solution, and their own roles.

Ranking

Newton (1995) found that shared tasks where learners all had equal access to the same information resulted in more negotiation of word meaning than split tasks where each learner had different information. Split tasks had more negotiation overall but most of this was not negotiation of word meaning. Vocabulary which is placed in the list of items to rank is most likely to be used in the activity, particularly if the items are difficult ones for the learners to agree upon. Words occurring in the description of the background and the instructions are less likely to be used and learned. Clearly the places where words occur on the worksheet have a major effect on whether they will be learned. Although Newton found that negotiation was an important contributor to learning, most words learned were used in the task but were not negotiated for word meaning. If a word was negotiated, there was a 75% chance that it would be learned. If it was simply met in the input there was a 57% chance that it would be learned. However, 80% of the vocabulary learned in the task was not negotiated. Negotiation makes learning more certain, but it still accounts for only a small amount of the vocabulary learning in conversation activities. Very few words were learned by simply seeing them in the written input but not using them or hearing them used in the task.

Other activities

There are numerous other speaking activities which make use of written input. These include split information tasks (Nation, 1977), interview activities, and information transfer activities (Palmer, 1982). Thoughtful design of the worksheets and careful observation of their use can maximise the opportunities for incidental learning of useful vocabulary while learners are involved in a meaning focused speaking task.

Designing and adapting activities

Let us look at a task and consider how it could be redesigned to create more favourable opportunities for vocabulary learning.

Learners work in groups to solve the following problem.

You have just seen one of your friends stealing things from a local shop. What will you do?

1. Inform the shop owner immediately.
2. Tell your friend to put it back.
3. Discuss it with your friend later to discourage him from doing it in the future.
4. Just ignore it.
5. Discuss it with your parents.

The following words in the written input are unknown to many of the learners: *local, inform, discourage, ignore. Inform* and *ignore* are important ideas in the text and the likelihood of them being noticed, discussed and used in the activity is quite high. *Local* and *discourage* may not get the same attention.

There are several important ways in which the activity could be improved for vocabulary learning. First, the numbers in front of the choices should be removed. If they are left there, then the learners will say things like 'I think four is the best choice' instead of saying 'I would just ignore it' which makes use of the target word *ignore*.

Second, the written input is quite short and does not contain a lot of useful new vocabulary. The written input thus needs to be increased in quantity and additional useful words to learn should be included. This can be done in several ways: by increasing the amount of description about each choice, by giving more description of the background to the task (more information about the friend and what was stolen, for example), or by adding more choices. Probably the most effective way will be to turn the activity into a role play. This would involve providing each player with a role card describing their role and goals, and adding descriptions of constraints to the activity (your friend's parents punish him severely for bad behaviour) (Nation, 1991b).

Third, some changes could make more certain that the wanted vocabulary was used. The activity could be made into a ranking activity rather than a choosing activity. This might get more evenly spread discussion of the choices. Each learner in the group could be given responsibility for a different choice. They should make themselves very familiar with that choice and while they do not have to make it their first choice, they have to ensure that it gets sufficient discussion

Table 4.3. *Features to improve vocabulary learning from speaking tasks*

1. Make sure that the target vocabulary is in the written input to the task and occurs in the best place in the written input.

    Have plenty of written input.

    Make sure about 12 target words occur in the written input.

    Try to predict what parts of the written input are most likely to be used in the task and put wanted vocabulary there.

2. Design the task so that the written input needs to be used.

    Avoid the use of numbering in lists of items or choices.

    Use retelling, role play, problem solving discussion based on the written input.

    Have a clear outcome to the task, such as ranking, choosing, problem solving, completion.

3. Get each learner in the group actively involved.

    Split the information.

    Assign jobs or roles.

    Keep the group size reasonably small (about four or five learners).

    Have learners of roughly equal proficiency in a group who feel comfortable negotiating with each other.

4. Ensure that the vocabulary is used in ways that encourage learning.

    Use tasks such as role play that require changing the context of the vocabulary.

    Use a procedure such as the pyramid procedure or reporting back to get the vocabulary reused.

    Remove the input so that recall is required, or after looking at the detailed sheet, use a reduced one for the task.

    After the task is completed, get the learners to reflect on what vocabulary they learned.

and consideration during the activity. It may be more effective to get them to memorise their option and then remove the written input.

Fourth, some changes could be made to give the wanted vocabulary the chance of being used *often* in the activity. These could include getting learners to report back to other groups on their decision and reasons for the decision, and moving through a pyramid procedure from pairs to fours to the whole class.

Table 4.3 lists changes that could be made to improve the vocabulary learning potential of a communication activity.

The effectiveness of the changes may be seen by testing the vocabulary learning from the activity, or more informally by observing whether the learners are negotiating and using the wanted vocabulary during the activity.

Adapting the activity

Here is an example of adaptations made to the shoplifting problem.

The italicised words are the target words for learning. Note that the adapted version contains about twelve. Note also that there are now more choices and a lot of background information. You may wish to check the changes made against the list in Table 4.3.

You have a friend who comes from a poor family. One day when you were in a supermarket you saw your friend *conceal* a packet of sweets under his *jacket*. He thinks you did not see him steal them. You know that the *manager* of the supermarket is very *strict* about shop-lifters and always calls the police and *prosecutes offenders*. You also believe that the shop has some kind of system for catching shop-lifters. What will you do?

- *Inform* the manager immediately and ask him not to *prosecute* your friend.
- Tell your friend to return the sweets to the *shelves*.
- Discuss it with your friend later to *discourage* him from doing it in the future.
- Just *ignore* it.
- Discuss it with your parents.
- Ask your friend for half of the sweets.
- Leave the shop immediately so that you are not *connected* with your friend's actions.
- *Forcibly* take the sweets from your friend and put them back on the shelves.

Split the choices between the members of the group taking two each. Form groups of the people with the same pairs of choices. In these expert groups discuss: (1) what your choices mean, (2) the advantages, and (3) disadvantages of each choice. Then split into groups of four with a person from each expert group in the new group. Alternatively or additionally, the activity could be role played with each learner taking a role (friend's parents, worker in the supermarket, police, the friend, you) or a job. During the activity, each learner can take on one of the following jobs:

- Encourage others to speak by asking, 'What do you think?' 'Do you agree?' 'Which one do you *favour*?'

- Summarise what others have said beginning with phrases like, 'So you think that . . .' or 'So we have decided that . . .'
- *Deliberately* disagree with some of the group members by saying things like, 'No. That's not a good idea. I think . . .' or 'I'm opposed to that. I think we should . . .'
- Keep each group working towards the answer by saying things like, 'Let's decide what we *definitely* won't do,' or 'Let's decide on the best *solution*.'

After each group has decided on a course of action, get them to prepare a list of reasons why they chose this one and why they did not choose the others. Ask them to report these reasons to the other groups.

Teachers who are serious about planning vocabulary learning should give careful attention to the design of speaking activities; without compromising their communicative nature it is easy to increase the opportunity for planned vocabulary learning.

It is worthwhile noting that speaking activities do not always have to be carried out in the second language in order to help second language vocabulary learning. Knight (1996) found that although learners used the first language a lot, they were actually discussing unknown second language words. Lameta-Tufuga (1994) deliberately introduced a discussion activity in the first language about the task that the learners were going to do. The discussion was used to get learners to clarify what they needed to know in order to do the task. After the discussion in the first language, the learners did the writing task in the second language. Learners who were given the opportunity to discuss the task in their first language did better on the writing task than learners who discussed it in the second language. The transcripts of the first language discussion show that a lot of second language vocabulary and phrases are embedded in the first language discussion.

- *um e pei o mea ei lalo e malo i le* pressure *ao mea ei luga e* semi-fluid. (It's like the things below are rigid due to pressure and those above are semi-fluid.)
- Because *o le* membrane, *magakua le* membrane *le* cell membrane *lea e* allowiga *le vai e alu mai leisi iku lea e kele ai le vai i le mea lea e kau leai se vai*. (Because of the membrane, remember the membrane, the cell membrane that allows water to move from one side with higher water concentration to where there is less water.)

This discussion gets attention to both the form and meaning aspects of important words in the text and places the English words in a rich, meaningful context.

In spite of the transitory nature of listening and speaking, it is possible to encourage vocabulary learning through these skills by increasing the opportunity for deliberate generative attention. While doing this it is also important to make sure that the vocabulary demands of listening and speaking are not overwhelming, so that work in these skills can contribute to learning through meaning focused attention and fluency development.

5 Vocabulary and reading and writing

Just as the oral skills of listening and speaking can contribute to vocabulary growth, so can the written skills of reading and writing. Indeed, control of the reading skill can be a major factor in vocabulary development for both native and non-native speakers.

Research on L1 reading shows that vocabulary knowledge and reading comprehension are very closely related to each other (Stahl, 1990). This relationship is not one directional. Vocabulary knowledge can help reading, and reading can contribute to vocabulary growth (Chall, 1987).

Vocabulary size and successful reading

There has been continuing interest in whether there is a language knowledge threshold which marks the boundary between not having and having enough language knowledge for successful language use. There are at least two ways of defining what a threshold is. One way is to see a threshold as an all-or-nothing phenomenon. If a learner has not crossed the threshold, then adequate comprehension is not possible. If the learner has crossed the threshold, then, other things being equal, comprehension is possible for all learners. This is the strong view of a threshold and the one that corresponds to its traditional meaning.

Another way is to see a threshold as a probabilistic boundary. That is, if a learner has not crossed the threshold, the chances of comprehending adequately are low. If the learner has crossed the threshold, the chances are on the side of the learner gaining adequate comprehension. This second definition of a threshold is the way that Laufer uses the term.

Laufer and Sim (1985a) used comprehension questions and interviews with learners to determine a threshold score where learners could be said to be able to comprehend an English for academic purposes text in the Cambridge First Certificate in English exam. They concluded that a score of 65–70% was the minimum necessary. As a result of interviews which involved seeing how learners dealt with the text, and supplying needed items to see how comprehension was affected, Laufer and Sim determined that the most pressing need of the foreign language learner was vocabulary, then subject matter knowledge, and then syntactic structure.

Laufer (1989b) then went a step further to see what percentage of word tokens (running words) needed to be understood in order to ensure 'reasonable' reading comprehension of the text. Laufer set reasonable comprehension as a score of 55% or more. Percentage of word tokens known was found by getting learners to underline unfamiliar words in the text and adjusting this score by the number of words mistakenly said to be known as determined by a translation test. The rest was converted to a percentage of total word tokens in the text which were known. This calculation should be expressed in 2 stages:

1. The number of words known in the text is:
   Total words in text – [words reported as unknown + words reported as unknown × (number of discrepancies × 100/40)].
2. The coverage is the number of words known in the text × 100/
   Total number of words in text

In the first stage of the calculation, the number of discrepancies x 100/40 is 'the bluff index' i.e. what percentage of vocabulary is not reported as unknown. When multiplied by the reported number of words, we get the number of words that was not reported as unknown but should have been. Therefore to calculate how many words in the text are *really* unknown, we add the number of reported words to those that should have been reported. Then to see how many words were known, this number is subtracted from the number of words in the text. The second stage converts the number of known words into the percentage of the total number of words in the text and this is the coverage.

Let us take an example. Say a person reports 20 unknown words, then in the translation test we find 10 discrepancies (that is, ten words said to be known, but which were not translated correctly. So the bluff index is 10 × 100/40 = 25%. This means he should have reported as unknown 20+ 20 × 25/100 = 25. If the text has 200 words, then the number of words known is 200 − 25 = 175. The coverage is 175 × 100/200 = 87.5% (Laufer, personal communication).

Laufer found that the group that scored 95% and above on the vocabulary measure had a significantly higher number of successful readers (scores of 55% and above on a reading test) than those scoring below 95%. The 90% level did not result in significant differences between those above and below. A comparison of the 95% and above group with the 90–94% group revealed a significant difference in comprehension scores. In this study, Laufer does not justify the 55% threshold of comprehension (it does not agree with the 65–70% threshold determined in the Laufer and Sim (1985a) study) except to say it is the lowest passing grade in the Haifa University system. Laufer sees this as minimally acceptable comprehension.

The next step is to determine what vocabulary size (number of word types, lemmas, or families) will provide 95% coverage of academic text. Laufer (1989b) accepts Ostyn and Godin's (1985: 353) evidence that the 4,839 words (types? lemmas? families?) in the Dutch school books that they had written provide 95–98% coverage of three randomly chosen newspaper clippings. There are several problems with this. First, evidence from frequency studies of Dutch is being applied to English. Second, the unit of counting is not specified; is it types, lemmas, or families? Third, newspapers are not academic text; and fourth, three newspaper clippings make a very, very small corpus.

Corpus studies of English can provide better estimates. Such studies show that the number of word families needed to cover a set percentage, say 95%, of the tokens in a text depends on: (1) type of text – novel, newspaper, academic text, spoken informal conversation, etc., (2) length of text, and (3) homogeneity of text; is it on the same topic and by the same writer? See Table 1.7 page 17 for examples.

Laufer (1992b) in a further study looked at the relationship between reading comprehension score (as measured by an English test produced in the Netherlands or the English subtest of the Israeli entrance examination) and vocabulary size, as measured by the *Vocabulary Levels Test* (Nation, 1983) or the *Eurocentres Vocabulary Size Test* (Meara and Jones, 1990). The minimal vocabulary level where there were more readers' than non-readers (56% in the reading comprehension test) was 3,000 word families.

Laufer has approached the vocabulary threshold question from several directions: by looking at the relative contributions of vocabulary, grammar and background knowledge to reading comprehension, by looking at vocabulary coverage and reading comprehension, and by looking at vocabulary size and reading comprehension. Her main interest has been in determining the minimal language proficiency level where teachers can usefully switch from concentrating on language development to the development and transfer of reading skills. Her studies have consistently shown the 3,000 word family level to be a minimum for the reading of unsimplified text.

The safest measure to use in defining the threshold is the coverage (word token) measure which Laufer found to be around 95%. As we have seen (Table 1.7) the same number of word types or word families will give different coverage of different kinds of text with academic texts requiring the larger vocabulary size.

It is useful to understand why coverage of tokens is important. Eighty per cent coverage of a text means that one word in every five is unknown (about two words per line). Ninety per cent means one in every ten is unknown (about one word per line), and 95% coverage means one in every twenty is unknown (about one unknown word in every two lines). Hirsh and Nation (1992) suggest that for ease of reading where reading could be a pleasurable activity, 98–99% coverage is desirable (about one unknown word in every 50–100 running words). To reach 95% coverage of academic text, a vocabulary size of around 4,000 word families would be needed, consisting of 2,000 high-frequency general service words, about 570 general academic words (the *Academic Word List*) and 1,000 or more technical words, proper nouns and low-frequency words.

Hu and Nation (in press) compared the effect of four text coverages on reading comprehension of a fiction text. In the 100% text coverage, no words were unknown. In the 95% text coverage version, one word was unknown, on average, in every twenty. In the 90% version there was on average one unknown word in every ten running words, and in the 80% text coverage there was one unknown word in every five running words. Hu and Nation found a predictable relationship between text coverage and comprehension, with comprehension improving as the text coverage by the known words increased. At the 95% coverage level, some learners gained adequate comprehension but most did not. At the 90% coverage level a smaller number gained adequate comprehension, and at the 80% level none did. Hu and Nation concluded that for largely unassisted reading for pleasure, learners would need to know around 98% of the running words in the text.

Hu and Nation's study suggests that the all-or-nothing threshold is around 80% vocabulary coverage for fiction text. No learner reading the text with this coverage achieved adequate comprehension. The probabilistic threshold is around 98%. With this coverage almost all learners have a chance of gaining adequate comprehension. If, instead of adequate comprehension, a standard of minimally acceptable comprehension is applied (as Laufer did in her study), then 95% coverage is likely to be the probabilistic threshold.

Hu and Nation found a predictable relationship between percentage coverage of known words and comprehension. Most learners in this study needed 98% coverage to gain adequate comprehension of a fiction text. At 95% coverage some gained adequate comprehension but most did not.

Table 5.1. *The number of unfamiliar tokens per 100 tokens and the number of lines of text containing one unfamiliar word*

% text coverage	Number of unfamiliar tokens per 100 tokens	Number of text lines per 1 unfamiliar word
99	1	10
98	2	5
95	5	2
90	10	1
80	20	0.5

There is evidence from a study with native speakers to support 99% coverage for pleasure reading. Carver (1994: 432) concluded that in easy material, nearly 0% of the words will be unknown. In difficult material, around 2% or more of the words will be unknown. In appropriate material, around 1% of the words will be unknown.

Carver argues that for learners to use reading to increase their vocabulary size, they need to read material that is not too easy for them, otherwise they will meet few unknown words. Easy reading may increase depth of vocabulary knowledge, but it is unlikely to increase breadth of vocabulary knowledge. Learners need to know a substantial amount of vocabulary in order to read unsimplified material, especially academic text. If we relate text coverage to the strands of learning from meaning-focused input and fluency development, then learners would need to have 95% coverage for learning vocabulary from meaning-focused input, and 98–100% coverage for fluency development. This means that learners need to have simplified reading material of various levels in order to learn from meaning-focused input and to develop fluency in reading if they are to learn from these strands at all stages of their second language development.

It is important that teachers match learners and reading material to suit the various goals of learning vocabulary through reading, developing fluency in reading, reading with adequate comprehension and reading for pleasure. There are several ways of doing this matching. One way is to let learners select the material that they want to read on a trial and error basis. This could work well if the learners have an understanding of the different types of reading and the vocabulary requirements of each type. Another way is to test learners' vocabulary knowledge using receptive vocabulary measures like the *Vocabulary Levels Test* and then advise learners. It is also possible to get learners to look at a page or two of a text and indicate the unknown words. A rough percentage coverage can be worked out from this. This is not a very reliable method but may be sufficient.

Learning vocabulary through reading

The research on learning second language vocabulary through reading is reviewed in the chapter on guessing words from context (chapter 7). Generally, this research shows that small amounts of incidental vocabulary learning occur from reading. These small amounts can become big if learners read large quantities of comprehensible text.

Usually a distinction is made between intensive reading and extensive reading. Intensive reading involves the close deliberate study of short texts, sometimes less than a hundred words long, but usually around 300–500 words long. Although the aim of intensive reading is to understand the text, the procedures involved direct a lot of attention to the vocabulary, grammar and discourse of the text. This deliberate attention to language features means that intensive reading fits within the strand of language-focused learning.

Paribakht and Wesche (1993) report on an experiment comparing the effects on vocabulary learning of reading plus vocabulary exercises with repeated opportunities to meet the same vocabulary while reading. The learning was not incidental in that learners would be aware that they were going to be tested on comprehension and vocabulary knowledge after each activity. Both approaches resulted in vocabulary learning, but the reading plus exercises group learned more vocabulary than the reading only group. Paribakht and Wesche attempted to equalise the time taken for the two treatments and to match the additional exercises for the reading plus group with additional reading for the reading only group. This experiment agrees with other studies largely comparing incidental and intentional learning (Hulstijn, 1988) which show more learning for a deliberate intentional focus on vocabulary.

Paribakht and Wesche's study focuses largely on how much learning occurred. It is likely that different kinds of attention to vocabulary result in learning different aspects of word knowledge (see chapter 2). Later in this chapter we will look at typical vocabulary exercises that accompany a text for intensive reading. Extensive reading involves reading with the focus on the meaning of the text. In general, extensive reading does not involve much additional language use other than filling out a brief book report form. From a vocabulary perspective, it is useful to distinguish two types of extensive reading: one which aims at vocabulary growth and one which aims at fluency development. For

Table 5.2. *Types of reading and vocabulary coverage*

Type of reading	Learning goals	% vocabulary coverage
Intensive reading	Developing language Developing strategy use knowledge	Less than 95% coverage
Extensive reading for language growth	Incidental vocabulary learning Reading skills	95–98% coverage
Extensive reading for fluency development	Reading quickly	99–100% coverage

vocabulary growth, extensive reading texts should contain no more than 5% unknown tokens (excluding proper nouns) and preferably no more than 2% to ensure that comprehension and guessing can occur, and no less than 1–2% to make sure that there is new vocabulary to learn. Texts which provide repetition of unknown vocabulary, that is, continuous texts on the same topic, provide favourable conditions. If graded readers are used, learners should be reading at the level just beyond their present vocabulary knowledge.

For fluency development, learners need to read texts that contain little or no unknown vocabulary. Unknown vocabulary slows down learners' reading and makes it more difficult to gain the smoothness and flow needed for pleasurable reading. If graded readers are used, learners should be reading very easy texts, at least one level below their present vocabulary knowledge.

The distinctions made in Table 5.2 are mainly for planning a reading or vocabulary programme to ensure that there is an appropriate range and balance of types of reading.

Vocabulary and extensive reading

Experimental studies of extensive reading have used unsimplified texts written for young native speakers and simplified texts written for non-native speakers. Both of these kinds of texts provide favourable conditions for language learning. The studies show that extensive reading benefits quality of language use, language knowledge and general academic performance. To be effective an extensive reading programme needs to involve large quantities of reading at an appropriate level.

The idea that learners can develop their language knowledge

through extensive reading is attractive for several reasons. Firstly, reading is essentially an individual activity and therefore learners of different proficiency levels could be learning at their own level without being locked into an inflexible class programme. Secondly, it allows learners to follow their interests in choosing what to read and thus increase their motivation for learning. Thirdly, it provides the opportunity for learning to occur outside the classroom.

However, before investing time and money in an extensive reading programme, it is necessary to be sure that the learning that occurs from it is not restricted solely to the improvement of reading fluency, even though this in itself is a useful goal.

Extensive reading by non-native speakers of texts written for young native speakers

The 'book flood' studies reviewed by Elley (1991) show striking increases made on measures of language use, language knowledge and academic performance. The studies of extensive reading that Elley participated in have been the most substantial in terms of length (12–36 months) and number of students (from over a hundred to several thousand). The book flood studies involved learners spending the greater part of their foreign language class time reading books that interested them.

The measures of language use in Elley, and Elley and Mangubhai's (1981) studies included measures of oral language, reading comprehension, and writing. An interesting finding in some of the studies was the improvement made in writing, which appeared most dramatically in the tests given two years after the beginning of the book flood. Elley and Mangubhai (*ibid.*: 23) suggest that this may have happened because learners' language knowledge had passed a threshold which was enough to allow them to produce their own ideas. Improvements in reading, listening and oral language were equally striking but not so unexpected, because the 'shared book' approach used in one of the groups of classes involved learners in listening, reading, and orally joining in with the reading of a story.

The language knowledge measures included word recognition (where learners had to read aloud a list of words) vocabulary knowledge and grammar. The vocabulary knowledge measures did not measure total vocabulary size or vocabulary growth. The measures of academic success involved the examinations used across the school system. Learners in the book flood groups had a greater than normal success rate in these examinations. Although there were no formal measures of learners' attitudes to reading, informal observation and teacher reports indicated that book flood learners enjoyed reading.

These studies present compelling evidence of the improvements in second language acquisition that can be brought about by such programmes. Elley (1991: 378–379) attributes the success to five factors: extensive input of meaningful print; incidental learning; the integration of oral and written activity; focus on meaning rather than form; high intrinsic motivation. The control groups in the studies were classes following a syllabus of language items that were presented one by one with substantial amounts of form focused activity.

The books used in the experiments generally contained a lot of pictures and were not controlled according to a word list but were written appropriately for young native speakers (Elley and Mangubhai, 1981: 26); they were not graded readers. The children in the book flood studies were aged from 6 to 12 years old.

Let us look at two books written without formal vocabulary control for young native speakers: *The Three Little Pigs* in the Ladybird series which seems to have been used in the Fiji book flood study (Elley and Mangubhai, 1981: 26) and *Dry Days for Climbing George* by Margaret Mahy (1988); and compare them with a graded reader written to fit into a prescribed vocabulary level: *Indonesian Love Story* (Meister and Nation, 1981, Longman Singapore). Table 5.3 presents the vocabulary profile of the three texts showing the percentage of running words in the 1,000 most frequent words (according to West's (1953) *General Service List*) the percentage in the second 1,000 most frequent words and the percentages for names of characters and places, and remaining words.

In *The Three Little Pigs*, *pig*, *wolf*, and *(Mr) Smith* make up the total of names. *Pig* is actually in the second 1,000 words but for comparison purposes it was counted as a name. Note that the names of the characters and places make up a large proportion of the words not in the first 2,000 words.

We can see from Table 5.3 that the graded reader *Indonesian Love Story* provides greater control with 99% of the words coming from the most frequent 2,000 words of English plus names. But the figures of 96.7% and 93.6% are still good coverage figures. In *The Three Little Pigs* just one word in every 30 will be outside the lists and in *Dry Days for Climbing George* one word in every 22. In addition, several of the words outside the lists were repeated several times (*huff*, *puff*, *chinny*, *chin*). Elley and Mangubhai's motivation for choosing books written for young native speakers was probably that these were much more attractively illustrated, and interesting for young readers. It also seems that in terms of vocabulary control such texts compare favourably

Table 5.3. *The percentage coverage (and cumulative coverage) of three texts by the high-frequency words of English, names, and all the remaining words*

Books	1st 1,000	2nd 1,000	Names	Remaining words
Dry Days for Climbing George	76.8%	11.7% (88.5%)	5.1% (93.6%)	6.4% (100%)
The Three Little Pigs	78.1%	11.1% (89.2%)	7.5% (96.7%)	3.3% (100%)
Indonesian Love Story	82.7%	8.4% (91.1%)	7.9% (99%)	1.0% (100%)

with graded readers. A study of texts aimed at teenage native speakers of English showed that such texts are not as accessible for non-native speakers as graded readers (Hirsh and Nation, 1992).

Extensive reading with graded readers

In two experiments, one conducted with second language learners in England for a maximum of 60 hours (Tudor and Hafiz, 1989; Hafiz and Tudor, 1989) and one with learners in Pakistan for a maximum of 90 hours (Hafiz and Tudor, 1990), Hafiz and Tudor looked at the effect of extensive reading of graded readers on learners' language use. The study in England used standardised reading and writing measures and analyses of the students' writing, while the study in Pakistan used only analyses of students' writing. Even with these limited and indirect measures, improvement was seen, particularly in writing. There was no significant change in the vocabulary used in writing for the group in England, but this is not surprising as the vocabulary of the graded readers was probably far below the learners' vocabulary level (Hafiz and Tudor, 1990: 36). There were some indications that the simplified syntax of the graded readers seemed to encourage the learners to simplify the syntax in their own writing. All of Hafiz and Tudor's measures were of language use. It is likely, had they included more direct measures of vocabulary size, word recognition and English structures, as Elley and Mangubhai did, that there would have been even more signs of improvement. Tsang (1996) also found very positive effects of simplified reading on learners' writing performance.

Extensive reading of unsimplified texts

Several correlational studies looking at the effect of a variety of factors on L2 proficiency have shown the importance of extensive reading. Huang and van Naerssen (1987) found that reading outside class was the most significant predictor of oral communicative ability. Green and Oxford (1995), in a study of the effect of learning strategies on language proficiency, found that reading for pleasure was most strongly related to proficiency. Gradman and Hanania (1991) found that out of class reading was the most important direct contributor to TOEFL test performance. This study raised the important issue of causality through the use of the *LISREL* program for analysing the data. Gradman and Hanania found the strongest connection going from individual out of class reading to TOEFL results. They also found that oral exposure, speaking and listening outside class and communicative oral use affected out of class reading.

It is clear from these studies that extensive reading can be a major factor in success in learning another language. It is likely that the relationship between extensive reading and language proficiency is changing and complex. Success in formal study may make reading more feasible. Success in reading may increase motivation for further study and reading. These correlational studies are supported by Pickard's (1996) survey of the out of class strategies used by a group of German learners of English in Germany, where extensive reading of newspapers, magazines and novels ranked very high on the list of strategies used for learning English. Use of reading and other input sources may be the only practical options for out of class language development for some learners.

In a study using Science Research Associates reading boxes, Robb and Susser (1989) found extensive reading of SRA material and readers written for American teenagers produced several results superior to a skills focused reading course involving less reading. The extensive reading programme also gave the learners more enjoyment both of reading and writing. The effects of extensive reading were thus both cognitive and affective.

Extensive reading and vocabulary growth

Experimental studies of second language learners' vocabulary learning from reading have not come near to approaching the careful design of first language studies best exemplified by the work of Nagy, Herman and Anderson (1985). The second language studies (Saragi, Nation and Meister, 1978; Pitts, White and Krashen, 1989; Day, Omura and Hiramatsu, 1991) used tests that were not sensitive to small amounts of learning, did not adequately control text difficulty, and generally lacked careful control of the research design.

In spite of these shortcomings, there is no reason to doubt the finding that learners incidentally gain small amounts of vocabulary knowledge from each meaning focused reading of an appropriate text. The most important finding from first language studies is that this vocabulary learning is not an all-or-nothing piece of learning for any particular word, but that it is a gradual process of one meeting with a word adding to or strengthening the small amounts of knowledge gained from previous meetings. The implications of this finding are very important for managing extensive reading. Essentially, vocabulary learning from extensive reading is very fragile. If the small amount of learning of a word is not soon reinforced by another meeting, then that learning will be lost. It is thus critically important in an extensive reading programme that learners have the opportunity to keep meeting words that they have met before. This can be done in two ways: by doing large amounts of extensive reading at suitable vocabulary levels so that there are repeated opportunities to meet wanted vocabulary, and by complementing the extensive reading programme with the direct study of vocabulary. A well-balanced language programme has appropriate amounts of message directed activity and language focused activity.

The research on extensive reading shows that a wide range of learning benefits accrue from such activities. Experimental studies have shown that not only is there improvement in reading, but also in a range of language uses and areas of language knowledge. Although studies have focused on language improvement, it is clear that there are affective benefits as well. Success in reading and its associated skills, most notably writing, helps learners enjoy language learning and value their study of English.

However the figures on repetition indicate that teachers need to be serious about extensive reading programmes, particularly in ensuring that learners do large amounts of reading. The benefits of extensive reading do not come in the short term. Nevertheless, the substantial long-term benefits justify the high degree of commitment needed.

Intensive reading and direct teaching

Commercially published reading courses usually include reading texts accompanied by a variety of exercises focusing on vocabulary, grammar, comprehension and discourse. There is considerable debate in the research on L1 reading about the value of deliberately spending time on vocabulary teaching, which includes direct teaching and vocabulary exercises. Nagy (1997) and his colleagues take the position that it is a waste of time teaching vocabulary. The two main justifications given for this position are the large number of words in English and the large amounts of time needed to deliberately teach vocabulary: because it takes such a long time to effectively teach a word, and because there are so many thousands of words, direct teaching can at best only account for a very, very small proportion of native speakers' vocabulary growth.

This is a strong argument and is well supported by L1 research. However, it does not apply quite so strongly to second language learners. There are two reasons for this. Firstly, there is the high-frequency/low-frequency distinction. Native speaking children beginning school already know close to 5,000 word families including the high-frequency words. New vocabulary learning will largely be the low-frequency words of the language. Non-native speakers however need to learn the high-frequency words. As we have seen, these make up a relatively small group of words which deserve time and attention. The arguments against direct teaching apply to low-frequency words.

The second reason in favour of some direct teaching for second language learners is that direct teaching can add to incidental learning of the same words and can raise learners' awareness of particular words so that they notice them when they meet them while reading. This consciousness-raising does not require much teaching time to be spent on each word. The results are best seen from a long-term perspective – as one of the many meetings which will eventually lead to the word being well known.

Preteaching

If vocabulary is an important factor in reading and readability measures, then it is tempting to conclude that preteaching vocabulary in a reading text should increase the readability of the text. This has been very difficult to show experimentally in first language studies. Tuinman and Brady (1974), for example, found that substantial preteaching of vocabulary resulted in little change in comprehension. Other studies (McKeown, Beck, Omanson and Pople, 1985) have shown positive effects.

There have been several attempts to explain the inconsistent findings. One explanation is that vocabulary knowledge in itself is not the critical factor. Vocabulary knowledge is a symptom of wide reading, knowledge of the world and reading skill. Teaching vocabulary alone is ignoring the important world knowledge that lies behind it and which is critical for effective reading. Wixson (1986) points out methodological difficulties in measuring the effect of preteaching, particularly the importance of the pretaught vocabulary for the message of the text, and the relationship between the pretaught vocabulary and the comprehension measures. Graves (1986), in a substantial review of first language vocabulary learning and instruction, notes that several of the studies are poorly reported, so that it is difficult to evaluate the quality of the research. However, the well reported and well conducted studies show that preteaching vocabulary helps comprehension if the preteaching involves rich instruction. That is, the preteaching involves several meetings with the word, focuses on many aspects of what is involved in knowing a word including fluency of access to the word (Mezynski, 1983) and meeting the word in several sentence contexts (Stahl, 1990: 21), and gets the learners actively involved with processing the word.

Stahl and Fairbanks (1986), in a meta-analysis of first language studies of the effect of vocabulary teaching on comprehension, found a strong effect of vocabulary teaching on comprehension of passages containing taught words, and a slight effect of vocabulary teaching on comprehension of texts not designed to contain the target words. In one of the few second language studies, Johnson (1982) found no significant differences in comprehension between learners who studied relevant vocabulary before reading, learners who had glosses available while reading, and learners who had no planned vocabulary support. The study of vocabulary before reading did not meet the criteria of rich instruction.

Vocabulary difficulty and preteaching of content do not seem to interact with each other for first language learners. Preteaching of background knowledge related to the content of a text does not compensate for unknown vocabulary in the text (Stahl, Jacobson, Davis and Davis, 1989). Vocabulary difficulty and prior knowledge affect different aspects of the reading process. Laufer (1992c) similarly found that academic ability as measured by a university entrance test did not compensate for lack of vocabulary in reading for second language learners.

Stahl, Jacobson, Davis and Davis (1989) found that vocabulary difficulty affects literal comprehension of a text as measured by textually explicit questions, comprehension of central and supporting information, and exact cloze replacement of function words. That is, vocabulary knowledge affected the development of the microstructure of the text. Background knowledge was helpful in grasping the macrostructure of the text.

It seems then that difficulty with vocabulary must be dealt with by vocabulary focused means not by dealing with background knowledge. Because preteaching requires rich instruction and thus considerable time, it should focus on high-frequency words that will be useful for other texts as well. Stahl (1990: 17) suggests that preteaching an unimportant word may misdirect learners' reading of the text. In general, research on vocabulary instruction has shown that mixed methods which provide both contextual and definitional information are more effective both on reading comprehension and vocabulary learning than definitional methods (Stahl and Fairbanks, 1986). However, McDaniel and Pressley (1989) found that thirty seconds concentrated learning on each word had positive effects on the subsequent comprehension of a text.

Vocabulary exercises with reading texts

To classify vocabulary exercises that accompany reading texts Paribakht and Wesche (1996) used Gass's (1988) five levels in learning from input. This classification relates vocabulary exercises to the conditions under which learning might occur. Let us look at each of the five levels.

1. Gass's most basic level is called 'apperceived input' or noticing. There are several factors that can affect noticing including repetition, salience and prior knowledge. Vocabulary exercises that make use of the noticing condition (selective attention) include listing words to notice at the beginning of the text and using highlighting in the text: underlining, italics, bolding, asterisks. Glossing items may have a similar effect. The major effect is consciousness raising which will make the word more salient the next time it is met.
2. The next of Gass's levels is 'comprehended input'. This may be the first step towards receptive retrieval. Vocabulary activities at this level (recognition) involve matching words with first or second language synonyms, definitions or pictures.
3. Paribakht and Wesche's (1996) 'manipulation' level corresponds to Gass's 'intake'. Vocabulary activities at this level involve morphological analyses of words resulting in forming words of different word classes by the addition of affixes.
4. The fourth level is called 'interpretation' (Paribakht and Wesche) or 'integration' (Gass) and involves activities like guessing from context, matching with collocates and synonyms, and finding the odd word out in a set.
5. The production level, which Gass calls 'output', involves recall of the target word form as in: labelling activities, finding the form in the text to match with definitions given after the text, and answering questions requiring use of the target word.

It is also possible to classify such exercises according to the learning goal of the activity, that is, the aspect of vocabulary knowledge that the exercise contributes to. In chapter 2, knowing a word, these aspects have been described as form, which includes pronunciation, spelling and word parts; meaning, comprising concept, form–meaning connection and associations; and use: grammar, collocations and constraints.

Analysis of vocabulary exercises

In chapter 3 on teaching vocabulary, four questions were used to analyse teaching techniques to see if they were doing their job well.

1. What is the learning goal of the activity?
2. What are the psychological conditions that assist learning?

3. What are the observable signs that learning might occur?
4. What are the design features of the activity which set up the
   conditions for learning?

Using these questions, let us look closely at a few vocabulary activities that might accompany a reading text. The purpose of such an analysis is to see how each activity might work and how teachers could use it most effectively.

Matching definitions to words in the text

This activity involves finding words in the text which match definitions given after the text. Often the definitions are listed in the same order as the words occur in the text. The activity has a meaning goal: linking form and meaning. The conditions leading to learning are either noticing or retrieving, depending on whether the word was known before reading the text or not. There will probably be few observable signs that the conditions will be met beyond successful completion of the task. If the learner can complete the task without looking back at the text, then the activity involves retrieval of previously known vocabulary. The design features of the task include: the ordering of the definitions, the possible use of an initial letter cue to encourage retrieval, and the placement of the definitions on a different page from the text to encourage rehearsal. The activity is suited to individual work, and can easily be adapted to learners with a wide range of proficiency levels.

Collocational matching

Learners have two lists of words which they must match to result in a set of collocations. The goal of the activity is collocational use. The learning condition is receptive generative use drawing on L1 knowledge, real world knowledge or previous L2 use. If the activity is done in pairs or groups then the content of the discussion will provide useful clues to what is going on. If it is done as an individual activity, then the speed with which the learner finds the answers, and any signs of retrieval of the answers may be useful. The major design feature is the closeness in meaning of the items within each list. If the items are very similar in meaning – *sparkle, glitter, shine, twinkle* – then the task will be much more difficult. This activity, when done as group work, makes good use of learners with different first languages, because they can use a variety of first language parallels to predict English collocations.

Answering questions

After reading the text, learners answer comprehension questions which encourage use of the target vocabulary. The learning goal is strengthening the meaning–form connection. If the answer requires repetition of part of the text, then the learning condition is productive retrieval. If the answer requires the learners to use the information from the text in a creative way, then the learning condition is productive generative use. There are many important signs to look for: Is the learner using the word in the answer? How different is the context provided in the answer from the context provided in the text? (How generatively is the word used?) Was the word recalled or searched for in the text? Design features include the use of inferential questions to encourage generative use, taking the text away to encourage retrieval and getting learners to share their answers to get receptive generative use. If the answers are shared this makes good use of learners at different levels of proficiency in the same class.

Readability

In his classic study of readability, Klare (1963) notes that the word is the most important unit in measuring readability and the characteristic most often measured is frequency. However, the factors affecting the readability of a text obviously involve much more than the vocabulary. Chall (1958) points out that the vocabulary factor is an indicator of conceptual knowledge. Carrell (1987), in a very useful review of readability in ESL, considers a range of factors including motivation, prior knowledge, propositional density and rhetorical structure.

Readability formulas focus on what is easily measurable; word length and sentence length are attractive measures. The Flesch Reading Ease Formula (Carrell, 1987), for example, in its simplified version looks like this.

RE = .4(words/sentences) + 12(syllables/words) − 16

This means that with this formula the readability of a text is calculated by seeing how long the sentences are (words/sentences) and how long the words are (syllables/words). So a text 357 words long containing 16 sentences and with a total of 483 syllables would receive a score of 9.12.

Elley (1969) explored an easily applied measure of readability for reading material intended for native speaking children, with very promising results. Elley used a graded frequency list based on writing done by children. The list consisted of eight levels. Readability measures were gained in the following way.

1. From each story or selection, take three passages each long enough to contain at least 20 nouns.
2. Using the graded word list, record the frequency level of all the nouns in the passage. That is, each noun appearing in the highest frequency level will receive a score of one, those in the second highest level will receive a score of two. Those not in the eight levels receive a score of nine.

   Use these rules:

   (a) do not count people's names
   (b) count lemmas not types or tokens
   (c) count each lemma once only
3. Add up the frequency level numbers and divide by the number of nouns.

Elley's measure performed better than a range of other readability measures and it (or a variation) could be easily computerised, though the practicality of the measure is such that checking the nouns manually could take less time than typing the texts into a computer.

Such readability measures however only consider the symptoms of some of the more important underlying factors affecting readability. Moreover, they may mislead their users into thinking that simply by adapting texts using the factors involved in readability formulas, texts can be made easier to read. This is not necessarily so. However, readability measures underline the importance of vocabulary knowledge in reading.

Brown (1997), in a substantial study carried out with Japanese university students, compared students' cloze scores on fifty passages with first language readability measures and linguistic characteristics of the texts. Brown found that the first language readability indices were only weakly related to the EFL students' scores on the cloze test and that four of the linguistic characteristics (number of syllables per sentence, the average frequency of lexical items elsewhere in the passage, percentage of words with seven or more letters, and percentage of function words), when combined were more highly related to EFL difficulty.

What are graded readers?

Graded readers are complete books, usually but not exclusively novels, that have been prepared so that they stay within a strictly limited vocabulary. They are typically divided into several levels.

Table 5.4. *The vocabulary levels in the
Oxford Bookworms series*

Level	New words	Cumulative words
1	400	400
2	300	700
3	300	1,000
4	400	1,400
5	400	1,800
6	700	2,500

Here is the vocabulary grading scheme of the Oxford 'Bookworms' series.

There are six levels in the series. To read the books at level 1, a learner would need a vocabulary of around 400 words. Some of the titles available at this level are *White Death*, *Mutiny on the Bounty*, *The Phantom of the Opera*, and *One Way Ticket*. Level 2 adds another 300 words making a total of 700 words; all of the books at level 2 are within this vocabulary. Some topic words not in the vocabulary and proper nouns are also allowed. Some of the titles are simplifications and abridgements of well known works (*Sherlock Holmes Short Stories*, *Dracula*) while others are original pieces specially written for the series. This has prompted some to call graded readers 'language learner literature' (Day and Bamford, 1998). The Bookworms series includes fiction, a series for younger readers, and 'factfiles' non-fiction titles.

Graded readers can fit into a course in many ways. They can be a means of vocabulary expansion; by reading them learners increase their vocabulary size. Because vocabulary is controlled, it is possible for elementary learners to read books where 95% of the vocabulary is already familiar. They can thus learn remaining words through guessing from context or dictionary use under conditions which do not place a heavy learning burden on them. They can be a means of establishing previously met vocabulary; learners can enrich their knowledge of known vocabulary and increase the fluency with which the vocabulary is retrieved. Nation and Wang (1999) concluded that the graded reading scheme that they studied was designed to reinforce and establish previously met vocabulary. This is probably the way most publishers regard graded readers and fits with West's (1955: 69) view of them as 'supplementary' readers, which provide reading practice, enrich known vocabulary and provide motivation to continue study through success in use.

Nation and Wang found that when learners move to a new level in their graded reading, it is likely that they will meet quite a high proportion of unknown words. At this point it would be wise to supplement the learning through reading with direct study of the new vocabulary, using word cards. This is best done as an individual activity with learners making their own cards and choosing words from the books to put on the cards. Teachers can give useful advice and training in how to go about this learning. Cards may need to be made for only the first one or two books at a level. After that the density of unknown words will be light enough to allow more fluent reading.

Graded readers can also play a role in the development of reading skills, particularly the development of reading fluency.

Designing and using a simplified reading scheme for vocabulary development

There are now several excellent substantial reviews of graded readers (Bamford, 1984; Hill and Thomas, 1988a, 1988b, 1989; Thomas and Hill, 1993; Hill, 1997) mainly deriving from the Edinburgh Project on Extensive Reading. They consider a wide range of factors: the attractiveness of the covers, the length of the texts, illustrations, degree of vocabulary and grammatical control, number of levels, accompanying exercises, subject matter and interest. Unfortunately, there has been little hard research on important questions critical to the development of an effective series of graded readers. These questions include the following.

What is the optimum proportion of unknown to known words in a graded reader? Hill and Thomas (1988: 45) suggest that there should be no more than one unknown word in every ten running words. Hirsh and Nation (1992) suggest one or two in every 100 running words. In supplementary readers West considered that the ratio of unknown words to known should be one in fifty running words (West, 1955: 21).

Holley (1973) tried to find the best ratio experimentally. She investigated the relationship between new word density (the ratio of unknown words to the total length of a text) on the one hand and vocabulary learning, reading time, comprehension, and student ratings of difficulty and enjoyability on the other, using a 750-word text with a glossary. Instead of finding a favourable new word density beyond which learning suffered, Holley found that vocabulary learning continued to increase even up to a new vocabulary density of one new word per fifteen known words. Scores on reading time, comprehension, and student ratings of difficulty and enjoyment were not significantly related to new word density. One reason for Holley's finding may be that her text was short (750 words) compared with the length of most simplified reading books which are several thousand words long. In Holley's short text a high ratio of unknown words to known may be acceptable because the total number of unknown words in the text is not high. In a longer simplified reading book this high ratio would result in an unacceptably high total number of unknown words. Another reason was that each new word also appeared in a glossary and the learners had plenty of time to learn these by rote learning techniques.

Hu and Nation (in press) compared four densities of unknown words: 80% of words familiar (one in five words was unknown), 90% (one in ten was unknown), 95% (one in twenty) and 100% (no unknown words). Second language learners' comprehension of a fiction text was tested by a multiple-choice test and a cued written recall test where learners responded to brief written questions to recall as much of the text as they could. It was found that comprehension increased in a predictable way as the density of unknown words decreased. To gain adequate comprehension of the text, most readers would need to know 98% of the running words in the text. At the 95% density level, most learners did not gain adequate comprehension. In this study, learners were not provided with a glossary and did not have access to dictionaries; they had to read the text unassisted.

Densities of one unknown word in ten running words or one unknown word in fifteen running words are not suitable for the goals of extensive reading. One unknown word in ten means that there is an unknown word in every line of text and twenty to thirty unknown words per page. Even one unknown word in twenty means an unknown word in every two lines. A density of one unknown word in fifty is more suitable for pleasurable extensive reading.

What is the optimum spacing of vocabulary levels in a series? Ideally the steps between the levels would allow a learner who has learned all the vocabulary at one level to read the next level within the desired proportion of known words. That is, when moving from one level to another having learned all the words at the previous level, the learner should have 98% coverage, for example, of the running words at the new level. Research by Wodinsky and Nation (1988) suggests that the steps are likely to be quite small. In a study of two graded readers at the 1,100-word level (Longman Level 4) they found that the move from the previous 750-word Longman Level 3 (a gap of 350 words) gave 93.1% and 96.5% coverage of the new level. This was only a

Table 5.5. *The ideal text coverage by different types of words in a graded reader*

Words	Percentage coverage	Cumulative % coverage
Previous levels	90.5%	90.5%
Proper nouns	4.5%	95.0%
Current level vocabulary	4.0%	99.0%
Others	1.0%	100.0%

small study done before desktop computers were readily available, but it suggests that at the lower levels of a scheme a gap of 350 words may be too large. Given the nature of vocabulary coverage with the less frequent words providing less coverage of text, the steps between the levels would become bigger from one level to another.

Nation and Wang (1999) examined a corpus of forty-two graded readers (seven readers at each of six levels in the same scheme). Ideally, in terms of percentage coverage of text, the levels in a graded reading scheme should be roughly equal. That is, when a learner moves from level 2 readers to level 3 readers, the new words at level 3 should cover the same percentage of running words as the words at level 2 did when the learner moved up from level 1. If this was so, then the vocabulary burden of each level would be equal in terms of assisting comprehension. Ideally, the percentage coverage of text by the newly introduced words should be 4% or less, because then the words from the previous levels and the proper nouns could cover 95% or more of the text, making comprehension and guessing from context easier (Laufer, 1992b; Liu Na and Nation, 1985). Table 5.5 suggests what the proportions of different types of words in a graded reader should be.

Using the coverage data from their study, Nation and Wang suggested the following set of levels.

Level	Number of word families
1	500
2	700
3	1,000
4	1,500
5	2,000
6	3,000
7	5,000

Some level 6 and 7 graded readers in this scheme should be non-fiction and should focus on academic vocabulary as exemplified by the *Academic Word List* (see appendix 1). The levels differ considerably from those used in most graded reading schemes, although some schemes come very close. The stages are small at the earlier levels, and become very large later on. Another way of spacing the levels is to base them on a manageable set of words that could be learned within a set time. It is likely that the size of the levels is not as important as controlling the vocabulary in the readers so that no more than a small percentage is not covered by previous levels.

Using performance on cloze tests taken from various levels of a set of graded readers, Cripwell and Foley (1984) investigated the effectiveness of the grading scheme. They found that scores on the cloze tests decreased as the texts came from levels with increasing numbers of words indicating that the steps in the grading scheme resulted in an increase in the difficulty of the texts. What was alarming in the study was the low level of reading proficiency of EFL learners even after four and five years of study.

What is the highest vocabulary level that a series of readers should reach? Ideally, after the highest graded reader level, a learner should be able to move to friendly unsimplified texts and not face too large a proportion of unfamiliar words. Some series stop around the 2000 word level, others go to the 3000 and 5000 word levels. Research by Hirsh and Nation (1992) suggests that there should be readers at the 2600 word level and the 5000 word level. This recommendation is based on the idea that for extensive reading learners should know 98–99% of the running words in a text. That is, there should be one or two unknown words in every 100 words, roughly one in every 5–10 lines of text.

Nation and Wang (1999) looked at the coverage of various types of unsimplified texts by the list used by a graded reading scheme. When comparing the graded reader list with the *General Service List* (West, 1953), it was found that 84.7% of the words in the *GSL* appeared in the graded reader list. Graded readers are thus an effective way of meeting most of the high-frequency words of English.

Table 5.6 shows that the graded reader list used in the Nation and Wang study covers 85.6% of the fiction section of the *Wellington Corpus of Written New Zealand English* (WCWNZE) (a corpus paralleling the *LOB* and Brown corpora). The graded reader list provides fractionally better coverage than the *GSL*. This can be accounted for by the greater number of words in the graded reader list, some of these words in the *Academic Word List*. The graded readers deal well with

Table 5.6. *Coverage of various types of text in the WCWNZE by the GSL, AWL, and graded reader list*

Lists	Fiction	Popular	Newspapers	Academic
Readers	85.6%	81.9%	80.1%	76.3%
GSL	85.5%	81.5%	79.7%	76.4%
GSL + AWL	86.4%	86.4%	84.9%	85.1%

the high-frequency words and provide the beginnings of knowledge of other vocabulary including academic vocabulary.

Even if around 5% coverage is allowed for proper nouns, the coverage figures by the graded reader list and the *GSL* are still a long way from the minimum 95% coverage needed for reading with not too heavy a vocabulary load. This indicates that with a top limit of 2,400 words or even 3,000 words, most graded reader schemes do not come close enough to the vocabulary size needed for comfortable reading of unsimplified text.

Should there be graded readers around the 4,000 and 5,000 word levels? The answer to this question is clearly yes. If there are no graded readers around these levels, then learners will not be able to read with comfort and pick up vocabulary without interfering too much with the reading. They will also have difficulty in reaching a good degree of fluency with the vocabulary they already know.

However, after the 2,000 word level, learners need to start specialising in their vocabulary learning to suit their language use goals. If learners carry on learning generally useful vocabulary, this will help with reading fiction but will not be an effective way to help with reading academic texts. Table 5.6 shows that the 570 words of the *Academic Word List* are a useful goal for learners wanting to read newspapers (5.2% coverage) and academic text (8.7% coverage). In comparison, the third 1,000 most frequent words in the *Brown* corpus provide less than 4.3% coverage. Graded readers should specialise after the 2,000 word level.

How many readers should be read at each level? How many readers need to be read at each level in order to: (1) meet all of the words at that level and (2) have a good chance of learning most of the words at that level? Wodinsky and Nation's (1988) study showed that reading two texts at the 1,100 word level resulted in meeting only 57% of the unfamiliar words at that level. Similarly, reading only two readers provided little repetition of the unfamiliar words. Only 56 out of the 350 available words occurred ten times or more in the two readers studied.

Nation and Wang (1999) calculated that learners would need to read around five books at each level to meet most of the words introduced at that level and to meet many of them several times. They found that most repetitions occurred at later levels of the scheme, so it was best not to stay too long at the early levels. By working their way through the levels of a scheme, learners would gain a very large number of repetitions of the words in the scheme, particularly the words at the earlier levels. Nation and Wang found that about three quarters of the words in the graded reading scheme occurred at least ten times in their corpus of 42 readers (seven readers at each of six levels).

How many readers should learners be reading within a set time at each level? The idea behind this question is that learners need to get repetitions of vocabulary in order to help learning. There is a rough way of providing a guideline for deciding how much extensive reading learners at a particular level should be doing. The two factors determining the necessary amount of reading are (a) the frequency level of the learners' vocabulary, and (b) the length of time that the memory of a meeting with a word is retained. For example, if a learner has a vocabulary of around 1,000 words and is thus expanding her vocabulary at the 1,001–2,000 word level, on average each word at this word level will appear once in every 10,000–15,000 running words (see Table 5.7). If, for example, the memory of a meeting with a word lasts for one week, then the learner will need to read at least 10,000 words per week (40 pages of 250 words per page) to ensure that there is another meeting with the word before the memory of it is lost. At this level, this is the equivalent of one graded reader every one to two weeks. As learners' vocabulary gets bigger, the new vocabulary is of lower frequency, and therefore the amounts of extensive reading would need to be greater. The length of graded readers increases as the vocabulary level increases, so up to the 2,000 word level about a book every one or two weeks is about right.

Table 5.7 shows for example that each word at the 1,500 word level occurs 75 times per million running words. This means that a learner with a vocabulary of the most frequent 1,500 words would need to read 13,000 running words in order to meet a repetition of words at this level to reinforce a previous meeting.

The figures in column two are from Francis and Kučera (1982). Column three converts the figures in column two to a ratio. The lengths in column four are from the *Longman Structural Readers Handbook* (1976). The weakness of this analysis is that the figures of occurrences per 1,000,000 running words are based on unsimplified texts. Simplified texts, especially long ones, provide more repetitions of high-frequency words (Wodinsky and Nation, 1988). Nation and

Table 5.7. *Word frequency level and the average number of running words needed to meet each word again*

Vocabulary frequency level	Word frequency in 1,000,000 running words (Kučera and Francis, 1982)	Average number of running words between repetitions of each word	Graded reader length (Longman Structural Readers)
1,000 word level	113 per 1,000,000	1 per 10,000	20,000
1,500	75	1 per 13,000	35,000
2,000	56	1 per 20,000	up to 50,000
3,000	34	1 per 30,000	
4,000	23	1 per 43,000	
5,000	16	1 per 62,500	
6,000	8	1 per 125,000	

Wang (1999) in a study of graded readers largely confirmed these figures. They calculated that learners needed to read one book per week at the early levels and around two books per week at the later levels.

Is vocabulary learning helped by indicating the new words at a level in a text? New vocabulary can be indicated in the text by bold letters and by providing glossaries. There is evidence from learning from listening (Elley, 1989) and from studies comparing incidental and intentional learning (Hulstijn, 2001) that drawing attention to new words can increase the chances of them being learned. Bramki and Williams' (1984) study of lexical familiarisation in academic text shows that many of the important new words that are defined in the text are written in bold or italics or in quotation marks to draw the readers' attention to them. The effect of this on learning is not known.

Is careful grammatical control necessary to produce readable readers? A criticism often made of simplified texts is that the simplification of vocabulary results in more difficult grammar. Another criticism is that strict control of grammar results in unnatural, awkward text. Many of the simplified reader schemes control not only vocabulary but also grammar. The Longman Structural Reader Series, for example, has a detailed scheme of grammatical control. Readability studies place grammatical features well below vocabulary in determining the readability of a text. However, grammatical features can play a significant part in determining readability (Tweissi, 1998). Research is needed to determine how much grammatical control is needed to make readers accessible for second language learners. It may be that rough control of sentence length and complex sentences is sufficient.

How to simplify

Simensen (1987) describes the criteria used by publishers in preparing simplified and adapted readers. What is interesting is that a few graded reading schemes do not use word lists but rely on writers' intuitions. Some series use existing course books rather than frequency counts to determine the grading of grammatical structures. Simensen also notes how some publishers make sure that grammatical and discourse signals are as explicit as possible, particularly with regard to pronoun reference, direct and indirect speech, and conditional sentences. Some of these guidelines resemble suggestions for elaboration more than simplification.

Dolch (1951: 147) describes three ways of producing simplified texts.

- Take a piece of reading material, check the vocabulary with a list and substitute easy words for the hard words. This has the disadvantages of not adapting the presentation to the audience, not taking account of grammatical difficulties and upsetting the idiom and flow of the language. It may however be a feasible strategy when simplifying for learners of quite high proficiency to simplify only the words outside the 5,000 word level and to provide a glossary for words in the 3,000 to 5,000 level.
- Rewrite the material in easier language keeping an eye on the vocabulary list. This often results in lame wooden writing typical of a large proportion of graded reader texts.
- Get a feeling for the audience by looking at their normal level of language use, then write something directly for them. When it seems right, check it against a word list and if necessary make a few changes.

Dolch regards this third option as the most effective in producing interesting readable material. Goodman and Bird (1984: 144) argue against word list-based simplification of texts for native speakers. They consider that writing to a word list makes texts strange and unpredictable. Words should be used not because they are in a list but because they are needed to express a message. It is much better for a writer to have a reader in mind than a word list.

Their detailed comparison of the wording of six texts is used to support this position. Day and Bamford (1998) make a similar point for non-native speakers. They see simplified material as language learner literature. Just as there is literature for children, teenagers and adults, there is literature specially written for second and foreign language learners which takes account of the language proficiency, age level and background of the readers. Word lists have a role to play in guiding the production of this literature, but they are only one (and not the most important) of the factors which should affect its production.

Simplification is an important tool in second language learning. It may be that the use of the term with its implications of reducing text is unsuitable and something like 'roughly tuning input' will get simplification the respectability it deserves. Without simplification, the strands of meaning-focused input, meaning-focused output, and fluency development become impossible for all except advanced learners.

We need to see simplification as one of a range of options for making text accessible. Each of the options – simplification, elaboration, easification, negotiation – has its own particular strengths and values. Rather than focusing on which one is best, we need to look at what each has to offer and how each can be used to best effect. Teachers need an expanded range of options not a reduced one.

Many of the criticisms of simplification are criticisms of bad simplification. We need to have standards of good simplification and praise those texts that exemplify them. The late Colin Mortimer used to draw an analogy between Shakespeare and the second language materials writer. Shakespeare wrote for a stage where there were no flashbacks, no voice-overs to reveal thought, little scenery and so on and yet with all these restrictions created masterpieces. The second language materials writer is also working with severe limitations, but within these limitations it should also be possible to create small masterpieces. We need to see more of these masterpieces.

Alternatives to simplification

Some writers and teachers are uncomfortable with simplification, largely because they feel that the authenticity of the text is lost. This is a mistaken view as authenticity lies in the reader's response to the text and not in the text itself (Widdowson, 1976). There are alternatives to simplification, but they are best regarded as complementary alternatives rather than substitutes.

Elaboration

Elaborative modification of a text usually results in a text that is larger than the original. This is because an elaborative modification involves preserving as much of the original text as possible, and making its meaning more accessible to a second language learner by the addition of redundancy and a clearer signalling of the thematic structure (Parker and Chaudron, 1987). Redundancy is created by the addition of paraphrasing, synonyms, optional syntactic markers, and the repetition of items to make coherence more apparent.

Advocates of elaborative modification (Long and Ross, 1993; Yano, Long and Ross, 1994) have seen it as a replacement for simplification. They criticise simplification because it results in stilted text which is not cohesive, because native speakers do not normally simplify by controlling vocabulary and grammatical structure, and because it removes access to linguistic forms that learners need to develop their proficiency. These arguments are easily rebutted. While there are too many poor simplifications, there are many good ones too (see the appendix in Day and Bamford, 1998, for a list of the best graded readers). Simplification, especially of vocabulary, is a normal process, and the study of vocabulary frequency and coverage shows the enormous number of low-frequency items occurring only once in a text that make reading unsimplified text for pleasure impossible for many learners.

Attempts to show that elaboration results in better comprehension than simplification have been largely unsuccessful (Parker and Chaudron, 1987; Long and Ross, 1993; Yano, Long and Ross, 1994). It is best to view elaboration as another way of making texts accessible for learners. Where it is important to retain as much of the original as possible, elaborative modification will be preferable to simplification. Where however large quantities of pleasurable reading are needed, simplification should be the preferred strategy.

Easification

Easification (Bhatia, 1983) involves making a text easy to read, not by changing the wording of the text, but by adding different kinds of support such as diagrams, pictures, charts and tables, text summaries, glossaries, guiding questions and headings.

Negotiation

Another way of making a reading text accessible is to read it with the help of others, negotiating the meaning of the text through discussion. Palincsar and Brown's (1986) interactive teaching procedure is an example of this.

Ellis (1995) compared the effect of premodified input (simplification and elaboration) and interactionally modified input on vocabulary learning. Ellis's study involved spoken language not reading. He found that although more word meanings were learned from the interactionally modified input, this was slow. Words were learned faster in premodified input. Over-elaboration of input reduced learning. Clearly each form of adaptation brings its own strengths and disadvantages. The teacher needs to match the form of adaptation of text to the learning goal and environmental constraints.

Glossing

Unknown words are sometimes glossed in texts for second language learners. A gloss is a brief definition or synonym, either in L1 or L2, which is provided with the text. Sometimes the words in the text are marked to show that they are glossed. Here is an example based on *Animal Farm*.

small holes in the door of a hen-house

walked unsteadily

room joined to the kitchen for washing dishes

Mr Jones, of the Manor farm, had locked the hen-houses for the night, but was too drunk to remember to shut the *pop-holes. With the ring of light from his lantern dancing from side to side, he *lurched across the yard, kicked off his boots at the back door, drew himself a last glass of beer from the barrel in the *scullery, and made his way up to bed, where Mrs Jones was already snoring.

Glossing has certain attractions. Firstly, it allows texts to be used that may be too difficult for learners to read without glosses. This means that unsimplified and unadapted texts can be used. Secondly, glossing provides accurate meanings for words that might not be guessed correctly; this should help vocabulary learning and comprehension. Thirdly, glossing provides minimal interruption of the reading process, especially if the glosses appear near the words being glossed. Dictionary use is much more time-consuming. Fourthly, glossing draws attention to words and thus may encourage learning. Research has focused on the effects of different types of gloss, and the effects of glossing on vocabulary learning and reading comprehension.

Types of gloss

Are words best glossed in the learners' first language, that is using a translation, or in the second language? Jacobs, Dufon and Fong (1994) found no difference between L1 and L2 glosses in their effect on comprehension and vocabulary learning. Learners were happy with L2 glosses as long as they could be easily understood. Myong (1995) found that L1 glosses resulted in better vocabulary learning but did not differ from L2 glosses in their effect on comprehension. It seems that the first requirement of a gloss is that it should be understood. The choice between L1 and L2 does not seem to be critical as long as the glosses are clear.

Where should glosses occur? The choices include: (1) in the text directly after the glossed word, (2) in the margin on the same line as the glossed word, (3) at the bottom of the page containing the glossed word, and (4) at the end of the whole text. Watanabe (1997) found that glossing immediately after the glossed word did not work so well. In the case of the gloss immediately after the word, learners have to realise that the following definition is in fact a definition and not new information. In some technical texts this is explicitly signalled by bolding or italicising defined words or by grammatically signalling the definition. In all the gloss conditions, the presence of the gloss (which included both the word form and its definition) drew learners' attention to the word and thus encouraged seeing the word as an item to learn and not just as a part of the message. Because the gloss contained the word form, looking at the gloss gave another repetition of the word. Long in Watanabe (1997) suggests that this could involve three meetings with the word: see it in the text, see it in the gloss, look back at it in the text to see how the meaning in the gloss fits the context. In a study that looked at the effect of glossing on vocabulary learning and comprehension, Holley and King (1971) found no difference between glosses in the margin, at the foot of the page and at the end of the text. Jacobs, Dufon and Fong (1994) found that learners expressed a clear preference for marginal glosses. It would seem best to follow this preference, particularly where vocabulary learning is one of the goals of glossing.

Should glosses involve learners in decision making? Hulstijn (1992) suggested that providing multiple-choice glosses where the choices were reasonably close in meaning to each other could result in more thoughtful processing of the vocabulary and thus improve vocabulary learning. Hulstijn found that choices did make a significant difference, but Watanabe (1997) did not find any difference. Hulstijn (1992) however suggests that choices are dangerous in that some learners made incorrect choices and thus upset learning. The effort of creating the multiple-choice glosses is probably not repaid by dramatic increases in learning. This, combined with the possibility of learners making wrong choices, suggests that single glosses should be used.

Effects of glossing

Most studies have found that glossing has a positive effect on vocabulary learning (Hulstijn, Hollander and Greidanus, 1996; Jacobs, Dufon and Fong, 1994; Myong, 1995; Watanabe, 1997). Hulstijn (1992) found that although learners without glosses did not differ from learners with glosses on items correctly translated in the vocabulary post-test, learners without glosses made many more incorrect translations. The lack of glosses led to incorrect guesses from context. In a carefully controlled study, Hulstijn, Hollander, and Greidanus (1996) compared the effect of L1 marginal glosses, dictionary use, and no glosses or dictionary use on incidental learning of vocabulary from text. Learners in the dictionary group consulted the dictionary infrequently with the result that there was little difference in vocabulary learning between the dictionary group and the control group. However, the few words that were looked up had a good chance of being learned. The study also looked at the effect of frequency of occurrence in the text (one occurrence or three occurrences). Frequency was found to have a significant effect on learning especially for the group who had marginal glosses. Marginal glosses encouraged learning. Learners in the marginal gloss group made greater gains than the dictionary or no gloss or dictionary group.

The effects of glossing on comprehension are mixed. This may be because in all published experiments on glossing for second language learners, the glossed words made up less than 5% of the running words and in most experiments less than 3%, allowing learners 95–98% coverage of the unglossed parts of the text. Laufer (1992b) presents evidence that 95% coverage is needed for adequate comprehension. Comprehension may be more likely to be affected by glossing if there are larger numbers of unknown glossed words so that the glosses allow learners to gain the 95% coverage.

Davis (1989) found that glossing was more effective than preteaching vocabulary. Watanabe (1997) found a positive effect of glossing on open ended comprehension questions. Myong (1995) and Jacobs, Dufon and Fong (1994) found no effect for glossing on comprehension.

Overall, research on glossing shows that it contributes to vocabulary learning and occasionally to comprehension. Glosses are best in the margins of the text and can be in the L1 or L2 as long as they are easily understood. Because learning from glosses is largely incidental (the main focus is usually on comprehension of the text), learning from glossing is not great (Hulstijn, 1992). Glossing however is another useful tool in helping learners in the gradual process of strengthening and enriching their knowledge of particular words.

There is clearly a wide range of opportunities for learning vocabulary through reading, with both simplified and unsimplified texts. While writing does not offer the same range of opportunity, it can still be a means for vocabulary growth.

Vocabulary and the quality of writing

Holistic assessments of ESL learners' writing generally relate well to some form of vocabulary analysis of the writing. Astika (1993) found, when using Jacobs, Zingraf, Wormuth, Hartfiel and Hughey's (1981) ESL composition scale, that the vocabulary section accounted for the largest amount of variance by far. Santos (1988) found that lexical errors were rated as the most serious in EFL students' writing by university professors.

Vocabulary choice is a strong indicator of whether the writer has adopted the conventions of the relevant discourse community. Corson (1997) argues that, for writers with academic purposes, it is essential to gain productive written control of the Graeco-Latin vocabulary of English in order to be recognised as a member of the academic writing community. Laufer's (1994) studies show that university students generally show progress in this area by an increase in the amount of academic vocabulary in their academic writing. Leki and Carson (1994) found that second language learners see lack of vocabulary as the major factor affecting the quality of their writing.

Comparisons between native speakers' and second language learners' writing show not surprisingly that native speakers use a much wider range of vocabulary (Harley and King, 1989; Linnarud, 1986). Engber (1995) compared measures of lexical richness with teachers' ratings of composition quality, finding that counting the number of error-free content word lemmas gave the strongest correlation (.57) with teachers' ratings. Engber's findings support Laufer and Nation's (1995) decision to exclude lexical errors from analysis of writing. Clearly, vocabulary plays a significant role in the assessment of the quality of written work.

Measures of vocabulary size and growth in writing

There are several ways of measuring the productive written vocabulary of a language learner. One is to measure it directly and overtly using a discrete point vocabulary test. Laufer and Nation (1999) have developed and trialed such a test which is a productive parallel of the receptive *Vocabulary Levels Test* (Nation, 1983). The test is divided into word frequency levels (2,000, 3,000, *University Word List* (Xue and Nation, 1984), 5,000 and 10,000) and uses a completion item type where the first few letters of the word are provided to cue the tested word. Here are some examples.

- I'm glad we had this opp_____ to talk.
- There are a doz_____ eggs in the basket.
- Every working person must pay income t_____.
- The pirates buried the trea_____ on a desert island.

Laufer and Nation (1995) found substantial and significant correlations between total scores on the active levels test and the proportion of words in learners' written compositions at: (1) the 1,000 word level (negatively correlated with total scores), (2) the *University Word List* level and, (3) beyond those levels. That is, the higher a learner's vocabulary size as measured by the active levels test, the fewer words used at the 1,000 word level and the more used from the *University Word List* and low-frequency levels in their written work. This shows that appropriate vocabulary tests can reflect language use (Arnaud, 1984, 1992; Laufer and Nation, 1995).

A second way to measure vocabulary size and growth in written work is to analyse the vocabulary of learners' written compositions. Numerous measures have been suggested for doing this including: lexical variation (also known as the type/token ratio), lexical original-ity, lexical density, lexical sophistication and lexical quality. In all of these measures it is important to keep text length constant (Richards and Malvern, 1997) as a change in text length will affect the measures. Laufer and Nation (1995) provide a critique of these measures showing that each contains inherent weaknesses and propose a new measure, the 'Lexical Frequency Profile', which avoids the weaknesses of the other measures. Like the others mentioned above, this requires the use of a computer and provides an analysis of the percentage of word families at various frequency levels in a piece of written work. The frequency levels are determined by reference to frequency counts: the *General Service List of English Words* (West, 1953), and the *University Word List* (Xue and Nation, 1984) now replaced by the *Academic Word List* (Coxhead, 1998). The computer program which does the analysis is available free at http://www.vuw.ac.nz/lals/ and is called Range. The proper nouns and severe lexical errors are removed from the compositions, typed into the computer and saved. The program is run over the files to gather the data.

Laufer (1994) has arranged the data in two ways. One way is as a full profile with the percentages of word families at the 1,000, 2,000, UWL and other levels. The other way is to use a condensed profile. This can be of two types: the 'Beyond 2000' measure (Laufer, 1995) which simply looks at the total percentage of word families not in the 1,000 and 2,000 levels, and a condensed measure for more advanced learners which looks at the percentage of word families not in the 1,000, 2,000 and UWL levels. Because the studies that Laufer has been involved in have looked at learners who are in the early stages of university study, the Beyond 2000 measure has been the more effective because significant changes occur in the proportion of words used from the *University Word List*. Table 5.8 contains some typical figures from Laufer's studies.

Laufer (1994) has shown that:

- The Lexical Frequency Profile of learners' writing changes as a result of continuing contact with English. The proportion of words used from the first 2,000 becomes less and the words from the *University Word List* (and words not in the first 2,000) increase.

Table 5.8. *Lexical frequency profiles of the compositions of various native speaker and second language learner groups*

Learners	Percentage of word families in the first 2,000 words according to West (1953)	Percentage of word families beyond the first 2,000 words
18-year-old native speakers (Laufer, 1994)	75%	25%
Israeli university entrants (Laufer, 1994)	90%	10%
The same Israeli learners one semester later (Laufer, 1994)	87%	13%
ESL learners (Laufer and Paribakht, 1998)	88%	12%

- The Lexical Variation measure (number of types × 100 ÷ the number of tokens) does not change over one or two semesters' contact with English.
- There is a relationship between vocabulary size as measured by direct testing and learners' Lexical Frequency Profiles (Laufer and Nation, 1995).
- The Lexical Frequency Profile is similar between similar kinds of writing done by the same learners within a few days of each other. That is, it is a stable measure (Laufer and Nation, 1995).

A third way of measuring vocabulary use in writing is to use a rating scale that focuses on vocabulary. Jacobs, Zingraf, Wormuth, Hartfiel and Hughey (1981) include a vocabulary scale as one of five scales in their ESL composition profile. The vocabulary scale is worth a total of 20 points out of 100. The other scales are content (30 points), organisation (20), language use or grammar (25), mechanics or spelling, punctuation etc. (5). Table 5.9 lists the four levels in the vocabulary scale.

Bringing vocabulary into productive use

Learners' written vocabulary can be increased by a general focus on vocabulary size and by a focus on particular words for particular activities. Two studies (Laufer, 1998; Laufer and Paribakht, 1998) compared three measures of vocabulary size. The first, the *Vocabulary Levels Test* (Nation, 1983, 1990), is a measure of receptive knowledge

Table 5.9. *Jacobs* et al.'s *(1981) vocabulary scale from their ESL composition profile*

Points out of 20	Descriptors
20–18	Excellent to very good: • sophisticated range • effective word/idiom choice and usage • word form mastery • appropriate register
17–14	Good to average: • adequate range • occasional errors of word/idiom form, choice, usage *but meaning not obscured*
13–10	Fair to poor: • limited range • frequent errors of word/idiom form, choice, usage • *meaning confused or obscured*
9–7	Very poor: • essentially translation • little knowledge of English vocabulary, idioms, word form • *or* not enough to evaluate

and includes items like the following in which learners have to match the three definitions on the right with three of the words on the left. Learners write the number of the appropriate word next to its definition, so *4* should be written next to *look closely*.

1. file
2. involve   _____ look closely
3. oblige   _____ stop doing something
4. peer   _____ cry out loudly in fear
5. quit
6. scream

The second measure, the *Productive Levels Test* (Laufer and Nation, 1999), described earlier in this chapter, is a measure of productive (Laufer calls it 'active') vocabulary knowledge.

1. The child pee_____ at the stranger curiously.
2. He qu_____ his job when he found a better one.
3. She scr_____ all through the horror film.

These two measures are discrete point measures with a deliberate focus on vocabulary. They test the same words. The third measure, the Lexical Frequency Profile (Laufer and Nation, 1995), involves computer analysis of learners' free writing and is a measure of vocabulary in use.

Laufer (1998) found a high correlation between the two discrete point measures (.67/.78), a large increase in vocabulary size over the period of a year on each of the two measures, but no correlation between these measures and the learners' Lexical Frequency Profile (the size of their free productive vocabulary in use), and no change in the Lexical Frequency Profile over a year.

While it is possible to make significant changes in vocabulary knowledge, it is not easy to move this knowledge into productive use. Laufer suggests that one cause of this may be a lack of encouragement and suitable activities to push receptive and productive knowledge into active use. Laufer also suggests that perhaps the receptive and active knowledge increases were not large enough to influence active use. This last explanation is unlikely as the increases in her study were substantial.

Laufer and Paribakht (1998), in a study involving a wider range of learners including ESL and EFL learners, found significant and moderate correlations between the receptive and productive discrete point measures and the Lexical Frequency Profile. They found that the development of active vocabulary was slower and less predictable than the development of passive vocabulary. In both studies learners' vocabulary size as measured on the receptive test was larger than vocabulary size as measured by the productive test. Laufer and Paribakht's experiments indicate that it is not an easy job to bring receptive vocabulary into productive use, particularly for low-frequency words.

Research with native speakers indicates that even when the focus is on specific words to be used for a particular writing task, considerable preteaching of an intensive kind is needed to establish words and bring them into free productive use. Duin and Graves (1987) examined the effects on vocabulary knowledge, use of vocabulary in writing and writing performance of preteaching 13 words over a six-day period. The more the treatment was focused on writing, and was intensive and rich, the better the results.

There seem to be (at least) two important factors affecting productive vocabulary use: knowledge and motivation. Productive knowledge of vocabulary requires more learning than receptive knowledge. There is plenty of evidence for this both from experimental studies of receptive and productive learning (see chapter 2) and from measures of learners' receptive and productive vocabulary size. Table 2.1 (see p. 27) outlines the additional kinds of knowledge needed for production through the receptive/productive division in each of the nine sections of the table.

The second factor affecting productive vocabulary use is motivation. The term is used here in Corson's (1985) sense which includes the desire and opportunity to use a word. We may know vocabulary but, because the opportunity and wish to use a particular word does not arise, that word remains as part of our 'unmotivated' vocabulary. That is, it could be used but it is not.

Activities that try to move vocabulary into productive use need to take account of these two factors. Let us now look at a range of these activities, starting with those that involve a great deal of teacher control over the writing and moving to those that involve more learner choice.

Reading and sentence completion

There are several varieties of completion activities; they can follow a reading text and use words that occur there. Completions range from copying from the text to having to use words with a different inflection or derivational affix, or to express an idea not in the text.

Paraphrase

Learners read sentences that they then have to re-express using a target word which is provided for them. The teacher will need to model the use of the word first or provide some example sentences.

Everybody will be helped by the changes.
(benefit)_____

Translation

Learners translate sentences or short texts from their first language. The target vocabulary may be provided.

The second-hand cloze

Pre-reading and translation are usefully linked in the second-hand cloze (Laufer and Osimo, 1991). This technique involves learners placing previously taught words into gaps in a text which summarises the content of a previously studied text. The formal context for the words is new. Learners are guided by having a dictated list of first language meanings which will fill the gaps but which have to be translated into the appropriate second language word.

Dictionary use

Learners need to be trained in dictionary use so that they can readily find words that they need in their writing (see chapter 8). Harvey and Yuill (1997) investigated the monolingual dictionary use of learners engaged in a writing task. They found that the most common reasons, in order of frequency, for using a dictionary were: to find the correct spelling (24.4%), to check on a meaning (18.3%), to see if the word exists (12.8%), to find a synonym (10.6%) and to check on the grammar (10.5%). The length of an entry was seen as the major challenge in finding needed information about a word.

Reading like a writer

The teacher and the learners work together through a reading text noting features of the text that typify that style of writing. From a vocabulary perspective these features can include the degree of formality of the vocabulary, the use of lexical chains, lexical cohesion through the use of related words, and signals of changes in the stages of the text. Chapter 6 looks at these features in more detail. The learners are encouraged to use some of the features in a writing task.

The dicto-comp and related activities

In the dicto-comp (Ilson, 1962) the learners listen to a text and then write it from memory. They can be encouraged to use target words by: seeing the words on the board as the text is read and having them remain there; seeing the words on the board as the text is read, then having all except the first two letters of each word rubbed off; having translations of the target words put on the blackboard.

Activities related to the dicto-comp (Nation, 1991a) include: dictation, delayed copying, the reproduction activity (read a text, put it away, write it from memory) and the dicto-gloss where learners work together to reconstruct a previously heard text.

Guided semantic mapping

Learners work with the teacher to develop a semantic map around a topic. The teacher deliberately introduces several target vocabulary items and puts them on the map as well as elaborating on them with the learners who then use the semantic map to do a piece of writing. If the writing is done in small groups, a learner in the group can be given the responsibility of ensuring that the target words are used.

Using written input to affect vocabulary use in writing

In chapter 4, we looked at how written input can be designed and used to affect vocabulary use in speaking. The same guidelines can be applied to encourage the use of particular vocabulary in writing. These guidelines include: providing plenty of written input to the task, designing the task to make use of the written input, using recall and adaptation of the input to encourage generative use.

Using speaking activities to affect vocabulary use in writing

Speaking activities designed to encourage the use of certain vocabulary can be used as the first stage of a writing task. The learners do the specially designed speaking task which encourages spoken productive use of the target vocabulary. Then they report back orally on the results of their speaking task to the class. Finally, they prepare a written report on the conclusions of the speaking task. If these tasks have been well designed, the target vocabulary will occur in the speaking task, the oral reporting and the written report.

Issue logs

Each learner decides on an interesting topic and over a period of several weeks collects information on this topic from newspapers, radio and television news, books, magazines, interviews, etc. Each week the learner reports orally to a small group and every two weeks produces a written report summarising the information gathered so far. The learner is told to deliberately incorporate into the written summaries new vocabulary which has been met in the information gathering for the topic. The final outcome is a comprehensive written report.

Responding to vocabulary use in written work

When learners hand in written work to be marked, the teacher can use this as an opportunity to encourage vocabulary development.

Vocabulary use in written work can be viewed from several perspectives. The following piece of writing was done by a reasonably advanced second language learner. The vocabulary in the piece of writing has been marked up to show which words are in the 1,000 most common words of the English language (not marked), in the second 1,000 (underlined), in the *University Word List* (**bold**), and not in any of these lists (*italics*).

Should a government be allowed to limit the number of children a family can have? Discuss this idea considering basic human rights and the danger of population explosion.

This depend on different countries' situation. In some countries there is a few population and shortage of working forces so it is *OK* to have as many children as you want. But in some countries there are a large population and people still want to <u>birth</u> more so the <u>government</u> must do something to control this situation. For example in India now there are one billion people and the country cannot provide enough food, <u>medical</u> care, education to her people. I think for this situation it is allowed that <u>government</u> can limit the numbers of children a family can have. But should not only limit I think, control is <u>suitable</u>. After limiting the numbers of children the country can do better about <u>education</u>, *nutrition* and <u>medical</u> care. so this young **generation** will become more healthy and higher class. Then after maybe ten years the population <u>explosion</u> will disappear and the quality of people will increase. On the other hand, if we just think about rights and <u>birth</u> as many children as we want but cannot <u>responsible</u> of them so the *kids* cannot get enough caring when they grow up maybe they cannot find a **job** and live in a **stressful** life also the average living standard will drop down. That is mean we are <u>selfish</u> people. Human rights do not just mean we can do everything we want and it must *associate* with the society. If not why we still <u>obey</u> lots of <u>moral</u> standards? But I don't think the <u>government</u> are allowed just simply order people to do something. It should through a lot of **research** and give a average standard. In my *opinion* I think two children in a family is better than just one child. Because the children can got a *partner* and learn how to *cope* with relationship with others. Also children's supporting is not very expensive to the family. so they can get a good <u>education</u> and their <u>parents</u> can pay more <u>attention</u> to them.

It is interesting to look at the vocabulary use from the viewpoints of accuracy, clarity and liveliness. A careful study of the text shows that there are very few errors with low-frequency words; most occur with high-frequency words. There are a few points in the text where it is not clear what the writer means – 'higher class' (line 11) 'give a average standard' (line 21) – but once again these are with high-frequency words. There are also some points where the text comes alive through the use of a really appropriate word or phrase such as 'nutrition', 'generation', 'stressful', and 'cope', and in most cases these are low-frequency words. A teacher's response to the vocabulary use in this piece of writing would be 'Keep taking risks with the words you know, and try to use words that you have recently met.' This advice might be different for other learners depending on how they used the various types of words in their writing. This approach to commenting on vocabulary use in writing is frequency based. In the next chapter, we will look at vocabulary in text from a different viewpoint.

6   Specialised uses of vocabulary

When learners have mastered the 2,000–3,000 words of general use-fulness in English, it is wise to direct vocabulary learning to more specialised areas. Depending on the aims of the learners, it is possible to specialise by learning the shared vocabulary of several fields of study, for example academic vocabulary. Subsequently, the specialised vocabulary of one particular field or part of that field can be studied. Because many courses focus on learners who will do academic study in English, we will look first at academic vocabulary.

Academic vocabulary

Academic vocabulary is variously known as 'generally useful scientific vocabulary' (Barber, 1962), 'sub-technical vocabulary' (Cowan, 1974; Yang, 1986; Anderson, 1980), 'semi-technical vocabulary' (Farrell, 1990), 'specialised non-technical lexis' (Cohen, Glasman, Rosenbaum-Cohen, Ferrara and Fine, 1988), 'frame words' (Higgins, 1966), and 'academic vocabulary' (Martin, 1976; Coxhead, 2000). The division of the vocabulary of academic texts into three levels – general service or basic vocabulary, sub-technical vocabulary and technical vocabulary – is commonly made (although this distinction ignores low-frequency vocabulary with no technical or sub-technical features). Dresher (1934) made such a three-part division when looking at mathematics vocabulary for native speakers. Other writers have independently made a similar distinction. Typically, academic vocabulary lists include words like *accumulate*, *achieve*, *compound*, *complex* and *proportion* which are common in academic texts and not so common elsewhere.

Flood and West (1950) posed the question 'How many words are needed to explain everything in science to someone who has little or no training in science?' They answered this question by compiling a dictionary for readers of popular science and determining how large a defining vocabulary was needed. The resulting defining vocabulary numbered just under 2,000 words – 1,490 words which made up the defining vocabulary of the *New Method Dictionary* (West, 1935), and 479 additional words needed for scientific terms. A revised version of this vocabulary can be found in an appendix to West's (1953) *General Service List* (*GSL*). Sixty of the 479 words are scientific terms like *alkali, cell, nucleus* and *molecule*; 125 are semi-scientific terms like *absorb, bulb, image* and *revolve*; the remainder are non-scientific words. It seems that a well-selected vocabulary of 2,000–2,500 words could be used to write popular scientific English, defining needed terms as they occurred.

There have been several studies that have investigated the vocabulary needed for academic study. Two of them (Campion and Elley 1971; Praninskas 1972) assumed that learners already knew a general service vocabulary and looked at academic texts to see what words not in a general service vocabulary occur frequently across a range of academic disciplines. Two other studies (Lynn 1973; Ghadessy 1979) looked at the words that learners of English wrote translations above in their academic texts. There were considerable overlaps between these four lists and they were combined into one list, the *University Word List* (*UWL*), by Xue and Nation (1984; also in Nation, 1990). This combined list of academic vocabulary was designed to consist of words not in the *GSL* but which occur frequently over a range of academic texts. Some examples: *acquire, complex, devise, fallacy, goal, imply, intelligent, phase, status*. This academic vocabulary, which contains over 800 word families, gives an 8.5% coverage of academic texts. Its low coverage of non-academic texts shows its specialised nature: 3.9% coverage of newspapers and 1.7% coverage of fiction (Hwang 1989).

The *University Word List* has been replaced by the *Academic Word List* (Coxhead, 1998). This list of 570 word families is based on a 3,500,000 token corpus of academic English which is divided into four groupings – Arts, Science, Law and Commerce – with each grouping consisting of seven sub-groupings such as psychology, mathematics, history, etc. Both range and frequency were used in choosing words for the list, with all word families in the list occurring in all four groupings and occurring at least 100 times in the total corpus. The frequency of each of the words in the list was compared with their frequency in a 3,500,000 corpus of novels. This was done to see which words in the list were truly academic words and which were general service words not in West's (1953) *GSL*. The list appears to provide slightly better coverage of academic text than the *UWL* even though it contains fewer words. The list is divided into ten sub-lists of 60 words each based on range and frequency criteria (see appendix 1).

The importance of academic vocabulary

There are several reasons why academic vocabulary is considered to be important and a useful learning goal for learners of English for academic purposes.

First, academic vocabulary is common to a wide range of academic texts, and not so common in non-academic texts. One of the earliest studies to look at this (Barber, 1962) is typical of the many small-scale studies that followed it. Barber compared three academic texts ranging in length from 6,300 to 9,600 tokens. This was done before computers were available for such research and, although the corpus was small, the analysis was very time-consuming and very carefully done. The finding of academic words common to the texts influenced a lot of thinking about English for Specific Purposes. Several subsequent studies have confirmed that it is possible to create an academic vocabulary common to a range of academic writing (Campion and Elley, 1971; Praninskas, 1972; Hwang, 1989). There has been little research comparing the frequency of specific academic words in academic and non-academic texts (Cowan, 1974), but the studies that have done this (Coxhead, 1998) show a big contrast in frequency.

Second, academic vocabulary accounts for a substantial number of words in academic texts. There are two ways of measuring this: by looking at the number of tokens (coverage) academic vocabulary accounts for; and by looking at the number of types, lemmas, or word families. Sutarsyah, Nation and Kennedy (1994) found that academic vocabulary (the *University Word List*) accounted for 8.4% of the tokens in the Learned and Scientific sections (Section J) of the *LOB* and *Wellington corpora*, and 8.7% of the tokens in an economics text. Coxhead (1998) found that her academic word list (the *Academic Word List*) covered 10% of the tokens in her 3,500,000 running word academic corpus and around 8.5% in an independent corpus. These are substantial percentages given that a general service third 1,000 word list would only cover around 4.3% of the same corpus.

Farrell (1990: 31), using a different classification of general service, semi-technical and technical vocabulary, found that out of 508 lemmas occurring more than five times in his corpus of electronics texts, 44% of the lemmas were semi-technical, and 27.7% technical. Sutarsyah, Kennedy and Nation (1994) found that in a 295,294 token economics textbook, there were 1,577 general service word families, 636 *University Word List* families, and 3,225 other families which included proper nouns, technical words and low-frequency words.

The coverage of each of the sublists in Coxhead's *Academic Word List* shows how even this specially selected list contains words with a

Table 6.1. *Coverage of the* Academic Word List

Sublists and number of words	% coverage	Number of tokens per 350 word page
1 60 words	3.6%	12.3 words per page
2 60	1.8%	6.0
3 60	1.2%	4.2
4 60	0.9%	3.2
5 60	0.8%	2.7
6 60	0.6%	2.4
7 60	0.5%	1.7
8 60	0.3%	1.3
9 60	0.2%	1.0
10 30	0.1%	0.5
Total 570 words	10.0%	35.1

wide range of frequencies. Table 6.1 shows that the first sublist contains 60 word families and covers 3.6% of the running words of each page of an academic text which is equivalent to 12.3 tokens per page. That is, on average, just over 12 words per page of an academic text will be made up of words from sublist 1. Around 35 tokens per page of most academic texts will be from the *Academic Word List*.

Third, academic vocabulary is generally not as well known as technical vocabulary. In a small-scale investigation of difficulties found by second language learners reading academic texts, Cohen, Glasman, Rosenbaum-Cohen, Ferrara and Fine (1988) found that non-technical vocabulary like *essential, maintain, invariable* was more often unknown than technical vocabulary. Cohen *et al.* identified some problems with such vocabulary in addition to simply not knowing the words.

- It was sometimes used with a technical meaning and sometimes not, and learners were not always aware of this.
- Learners were often not aware of related terms being used to refer to the same thing. That is, they did not pick up instances of lexical cohesion through paraphrase.

Anderson (1980) also found that sub-technical terms were the words most often identified as unknown by her learners in academic texts. Many learners get low scores on the *University Word List* section of the *Vocabulary Levels Test* (see appendix 3). In a study with native speakers of English, Cunningham and Moore (1993) found that the presence of academic vocabulary in questions made those questions more difficult to answer.

Fourth, academic vocabulary is the kind of specialised vocabulary that an English teacher can usefully help learners with. This is in contrast to technical vocabulary where the teacher can often do little because of: lack of background knowledge in the subject; the need to learn technical vocabulary while learning the content matter of the technical field and; the mixture of specialist disciplines within the same group of English students. From this perspective, an academic vocabulary list represents an extension of the general service vocabulary for learners with academic purposes. It is a list of words that deserves a lot of attention in a variety of ways from both learners and teacher, no matter what their specialist area of academic study.

Trimble (1985: 129–130) suggests that a difficulty with some academic vocabulary is that it takes on extended meanings in technical contexts, and in different technical contexts there may be quite different meanings. For example, *fast* means 'resistant to' in medicine, 'a hard stratum under poorly consolidated ground' in mining, and 'said of colours not affected by light, heat or damp' in paint technology.

For the words making up an *Academic Word List*, it is important to discover if the list consists of words whose form is similar across disciplines but whose meanings are quite different, or if it contains words that draw on the same underlying meaning for their different uses. One way of comparing whether the same word form is used with a similar meaning in a different subject area would be to use a rating scale like that used by Nagy and Anderson (1984). Another way would be to look at elements of meaning. For example, Memory (1990) used a scoring key for scoring recall of definitions where one or two marks were allocated for each 'meaning element' (usually a content word) of a definition. So, for the term *wealth*, the presence of the word *product* or a close synonym in the recall of the definition was given two marks, *any* (1 mark), *economic* (2), *tangible* (2), *useful* (1), *scarce* (1), *transferable* (1). The original definition was 'any economic product which is tangible, in addition to being useful, scarce and transferable.' (*ibid.*: 44).

Making an academic vocabulary list

Academic vocabulary lists are usually made by analysing a corpus of academic English. This can be done in several ways. One way is to take an area of specialisation such as electronics (Farrell, 1990) or medicine

(Salager, 1983 and 1984) and classify the kinds of vocabulary found. Farrell (1990) drawing on Cowan (1974) defines semi-technical vocabulary as formal, context-independent words with a high-frequency and/or wide range of occurrence across scientific disciplines, not usually found in basic general English courses. This definition seems to hedge on range ('and/or wide range') but Farrell's later discussion makes it clear that range is a critical part of the definition, although he did not seem to use it when constructing his own list. Farrell created a semi-technical list consisting of 467 types from Section J of the *LOB Corpus*, using his intuition to remove the general words. Section J of *LOB* contains around 160,000 running words (eighty 2,000-word texts).

Salager (1983) used a comparison of the frequencies in the Kučera and Francis (1967) count with frequencies of words in a 100,000 running word corpus of medical English to divide the vocabulary of a medical corpus into three categories: Basic English, Fundamental Medical English, and Specialised Medical English. Fundamental Medical English largely corresponds to the *University Word List* and includes items such as *evaluate, differ, presence, factor, serve*. Salager classified the Fundamental Medical English terms into functional and notional categories such as description of process, cause and effect, measurement, description of illness or injury, in order to see what role these words played in medical discourse. Salager's (1983) study is noteworthy because of its comparison of a specialised corpus with a diverse corpus to highlight specialised vocabulary, and its attempt to explore the role that sub-technical vocabulary plays in academic discourse.

Ward (1999) suggests that it is not necessary and perhaps not desirable to set up the three levels of general purpose vocabulary, academic vocabulary and specialised vocabulary for learners who have clear specialised goals right from the early stages of their study. Ward created a list of frequent words from an engineering corpus (without distinguishing general purpose, academic and specialised vocabulary) and then applied this list to an independent set of engineering texts. He found that a 2,000 word family vocabulary was sufficient to provide over 95% coverage of the texts. This was much better coverage than that provided by the 2,000 words of the *GSL* and the 836 words of the *UWL*. Early specialisation helps strip away items that are useful in less specialised uses of the language but which may not occur in the specialised texts.

Another way of making an academic vocabulary list is to take a diverse academic corpus and see what words occurring with wide range and reasonable frequency are not part of general service high-frequency vocabulary (Campion and Elley, 1971; Praninskas, 1972; Coxhead, 1998).

Coxhead's count was based on a 3,500,000 running word collection of recent academic articles and books. It was divided into four main faculty divisions: humanities, science, commerce and law. Each faculty was further divided into seven disciplines – history, education, etc. Range and frequency criteria were used in describing what words would be in the *Academic Word List*. The list, which we have already met several times, is called the *Academic Word List*; it assumes knowledge of the *GSL*.

A third way to make an academic vocabulary list is to collect words that learners write first language translations above in their academic texts (Lynn, 1973; Ghadessy, 1979).

There tends to be substantial overlap between these types of lists (Xue and Nation, 1984), indicating that there exists a general academic vocabulary which causes problems for second language learners.

Sequencing the introduction of academic vocabulary

Worthington and Nation (1996) examined the occurrence of academic vocabulary (the *University Word List*) in several series each consisting of 12 texts to see if the natural occurrence of such vocabulary in texts was sufficient for: providing coverage of the whole list and; providing a suitably gradual introduction to the words by not having too many or too few new items from the list in each text. They found that there were two major difficulties involved in using the natural occurrence of vocabulary in texts to determine the quantity and sequencing of vocabulary.

- An impossibly large number of texts would be needed to cover all of the vocabulary of the *UWL*. If texts were used as a means of sequencing vocabulary, it would be possible to do this for only a part, say 50%, of the *UWL*. Other ways of meeting the remaining vocabulary would have to be devised. These might include adaptation of texts, learning from lists, using specially prepared exercises, or simply leaving it somewhat to chance by encouraging extensive reading. This may be less of a problem for the *Academic Word List*.

- A very large amount of unfamiliar *UWL* vocabulary is met in the first three or four texts. This is far too much to be usefully dealt with in a few lessons and so there would need to be vocabulary learning preparation before meeting these texts.

It is clear from the difficulties involved in using texts to sequence the introduction of vocabulary that there would need to be a three step approach to sequencing.

1. First, the learners would need a gradual introduction over about five texts to the high-frequency, wide range 100–200 items in the *UWL*. This could be done by judicious selection or partial simplification of academic texts. The glossing could be done outside the text by the addition of glossaries at the side of the page or at the end of the text (Jacobs, Dufon and Fong, 1994), or a form of elaboration could be used where the words are explained in the text itself (Long and Ross, 1993). The partial simplification would involve the replacement or glossing of *UWL* words not in the first 100–200 items in addition to the replacement of some of the words not in the first 2,000 and *UWL*. At this step the sequencing is based on frequency and range.
2. Then, about 12 or more unadapted texts could be used to cover a further 200 or 300 items resulting in coverage of about half of the *UWL*. At this step the occurrence of vocabulary in texts determines the sequencing of the vocabulary.
3. Then, because the unknown academic vocabulary load of the texts would not be so heavy, learners could be encouraged to do large amounts of extensive reading of academic texts, both within and outside their subject areas. This could be accompanied by decontextualised learning of *UWL* words and study through formal exercises such as those involving word parts. At this step both frequency and range information, and occurrence in texts are used independently of each other to determine the sequencing of items to be learned.

The assumption behind this sequencing is that the occurrence of vocabulary in texts is the initial opportunity to meet the words but these then need to be learned to some degree so that they are not unknown items when met in subsequent texts. It is not sufficient to assume that simply meeting the items in a text is enough to ensure learning. This meeting would have to be accompanied or followed up by intensive study and opportunity for use, so that the knowledge of each item of vocabulary would be cumulatively enriched.

The nature and role of academic vocabulary

There have been attempts to study the role that academic vocabulary plays in an academic text. At one level the Latinate nature of the vocabulary adds a tone of formality and learnedness. It is this aspect that Corson (1985 and 1997) describes in his work on the lexical bar. Some writers have also tried to examine the kinds of language functions and notions that academic vocabulary represents. Strevens (1973) suggests a classification of concepts which are general to science and technology and which reflect and convey the philosophy and methodology of science.

Discrimination and description imply concepts of *identity* and *difference, processes, states, changes of state, quantification*;
Classification implies concepts of *taxonomies* and the *co-occurrence of features*;
Inter-relation implies concepts of *causality, influence*, and *interaction*;
Explanation implies concepts of *evidence, intuition, hypothesis, experiment, models, theory*; etc

(Strevens, 1973: 226–227)

Martin (1976) classifies academic vocabulary into: (1) the research process, (2) the vocabulary of analysis, and (3) the vocabulary of evaluation. These categories correspond to parts of a typical report of experimental research.

In a fascinating and insightful paper, Meyer (1990) suggests that there is a process of delexicalisation or grammaticisation going on in English where words which used to carry a full lexical meaning are now becoming more like function words. These include words like *affecting, barring, concerning, fact, process, matter* whose jobs in some other languages are done by function words or inflections. These words are becoming more grammatical and less lexical. Meyer classifies these words into three major categories.

1. Vocabulary relating to the domain of the text and the linguistic acts performed in it. This includes words like *argue, examine, survey, recommendation* which tell us what the authors are doing in their texts and what they ascribe to other authors.
2. Vocabulary describing scientific activities. This includes words like *analyse, examine, survey, implementation*. They relate closely to the categories described by Strevens (1973) above.
3. Vocabulary referring to the subject matter of scientific activities. This includes technical vocabulary but is by no means restricted to that. Meyer describes three main groups as examples:

   - Lexical expression of tense, aspect, modality, etc.: *current, present, recent, ability, impossibility, likely*.
   - Classification of states of affairs: *change, development, process, structure, quality*. Meyer notes that many of these words seem to be taking on the role of classifiers, that is,

general words to characterise a group of related items or a
state of affairs. Classifiers can act as shorthand anaphoric
items, act as general terms to be elaborated on later, and
act as a kind of proper name for something already
defined.

• Relations between states of affairs: this is a very diverse
group. It can include quantitative changes *expansion,
increase, decline, reduction,* causal relations *arising,
affecting, contribute,* set inclusion *include, comprise,* and
many others.

The academic vocabulary of texts allows the writer to generalise
talk about scientific activities. Viewed from this perspective, academic
vocabulary performs important roles in helping academics do what
they need to do. 'Context-independent' vocabulary is an important
tool of the writer in doing learned and scientific things.

Testing academic vocabulary

The *Vocabulary Levels Test* (appendix 3) contains a section based on
the *Academic Word List*. If a learner intends doing academic study in
English in upper secondary school or at university, then a score of at
least 25 out of 30 is desirable. If a learner has a lower score than this
then study of the items in the *Academic Word List* will be very useful.
Academic vocabulary needs to be used productively as well as receptively so it is important to monitor learners' productive knowledge of
these words. The productive levels tests devised by Laufer and Nation
(1999) and the Lexical Frequency Profile (Laufer and Nation, 1995),
which measures the proportion of various types of words in learners'
free writing, are useful measures for this.

Learning academic vocabulary

For learners studying English for academic purposes, academic vocabulary is a kind of high-frequency vocabulary and thus any time spent
learning it is time well spent. It is therefore important to have lists of
academic vocabulary to help in planning and assessing learning. The
four major strands of a language course – meaning-focused input,
language-focused learning, meaning-focused output, and fluency
development – should all be seen as opportunities for the development
of academic vocabulary knowledge. Thus there should be listening and
reading activities that encourage the learning of academic vocabulary
and also language-focused activities such as direct teaching, learning
from word cards, and word part analysis. Academic vocabulary is

largely of Latin or Greek origin and so learners can use word part analysis to help learn the vocabulary. Chapter 8 on word parts contains a variety of suggestions and exercise types. Farid (1985) uses a word part approach to words in the Praninskas (1972) list.

Because academic vocabulary is useful in speaking and writing, learners need the opportunity to use it in meaning-focused output activities, that is in speaking and writing in academic contexts. Corson (1995: 149) argues that using academic (Graeco-Latin) vocabulary helps users by letting them put their knowledge on display. Productive use of academic vocabulary is an important component of academic success. This can be encouraged through the presentation of prepared formal talks, discussions based on texts, writing summaries and critical evaluations of articles, and reviewing the literature of a topic.

Being able to use words fluently is part of vocabulary knowledge. Being able to access words quickly means that more processing time is available for concentrating on what to say rather than how to say it. Fluency is encouraged by repeated opportunities to work with texts within the learner's proficiency. One way that fluency can be encouraged is through the use of issue logs, an idea developed by Nikhat Shameem and Alison Hamilton-Jenkins at the English Language Institute at Victoria University of Wellington. Each learner chooses a topic to follow and become an expert on over several weeks during a pre-university English course. These topics might be terrorism, the Bougainville–New Guinea conflict, global warming or Thai politics. Each learner regularly finds and reads newspaper reports on their topic, listens to TV and radio news and writes a weekly summary of recent events related to their topic. They present a weekly oral report to members of their small group who discuss their report. These activities involve the learners using the four skills of listening, speaking, reading and writing with repeated attention to the same topic area. They thus soon bring a lot of background knowledge to their reading and discussion – ideal conditions for fluency development.

Knowing academic vocabulary is a high priority goal for learners who wish to do academic study in English. After gaining control of the 2,000 high-frequency words, learners need to then focus on academic vocabulary. Knowing the 2,000 high-frequency words and the *Academic Word List* will give close to 90% coverage of the running words in most academic texts. When this is supplemented by proper nouns and technical vocabulary, learners will approach the critical 95% coverage threshold needed for reading.

For native speakers, knowledge of academic vocabulary is a sign that they have been involved in academic study of various kinds. The vocabulary is the result of the experience. For second language learners who do not know the academic vocabulary of English it is important to determine if they have gained academic skills and experience in their first language. If they have, then direct learning of the *Academic Word List* is one of a variety of useful ways to get control of this vocabulary. If however, second language learners of English have not done academic study in their first language, simply learning academic vocabulary will not make up for this lack of experience. They need to learn the academic vocabulary as they develop skill and experience in dealing with the appropriate range of academic discourse.

The research on academic vocabulary is encouraging, although much still remains to be done. It has been shown that it is possible to devise lists of academic words which are small enough to be feasible learning goals and which provide enough coverage of academic text to make them a very valuable part of a learner's vocabulary.

Technical vocabulary

The motivation for distinguishing technical vocabulary from other vocabulary is similar to that for distinguishing academic vocabulary from general service words, that is, to identify words that will be particularly useful for learners with specific goals in language use – reading academic texts in a particular discipline, writing technical reports, participating in subject specific conferences, and so on.

Having distinguished such a group of words it is possible to see how they affect language learning goals, particularly the number of words that need to be known to be able to cope effectively with language in use. The approach taken here is to use percentage of text coverage as an indicator of this. Having distinguished such a group of words it is also possible to examine how they would be learned and the role of teaching in the learning process.

Distinguishing technical vocabulary from other vocabulary

In essence, a technical word is one that is recognisably specific to a particular topic, field or discipline. There are degrees of 'technicalness' depending on how restricted a word is to a particular area. These degrees can be shown by classifying and exemplifying technical vocabulary in four categories, with Category 1 being the most technical and Category 4 the least. The four categories depend on the criteria of relative frequency of form and meaning.

Category 1. The word form appears rarely if at all outside this particular field.

> Law: *jactitation, per curiam, cloture*
> Applied Linguistics: *morpheme, hapax legomena, lemma*

Electronics: *anode, impedance, galvanometer, dielectric*
Computing: *wysiwyg, rom, pixel, modem*
Category 2. The word form is used both inside and outside this
particular field but not with the same meaning.

Law: *cite* (to appear), *caution* (vb)
Applied Linguistics: *sense, reference, type, token*
Electronics: *induced, flux, terminal, earth*
Computing: *execute, scroll, paste*

Category 3. The word form is used both inside and outside this
particular field, but the majority of its uses with a particular meaning
though not all, are in this field. The specialised meaning it has in this
field is readily accessible through its meaning outside the field.

Law: *accused* (n.), *offer, reconstruction* (of a crime)
Applied Linguistics: *range, frequency*
Electronics: *coil, energy, positive, gate, resistance*
Computing: *memory, drag, window*

Category 4. The word form is more common in this field than
elsewhere. There is little or no specialisation of meaning, though
someone knowledgeable in the field would have a more precise idea
of its meaning.

Law: *judge, mortgage, trespass*
Applied Linguistics: *word, meaning*
Electronics: *drain, filament, load, plate*
Computing: *print, program, icon*

Words in Category 1 are clearly technical words. They are unique to
a particular field in both form and meaning. Yang (1986) suggests that
these words could be found by computer analysis using figures based
on frequency and range. Someone who knows these words is likely to
have knowledge of that field well beyond knowing the words. Indeed,
it is likely that these words can only be learned and really understood
by studying the field. They could not sensibly be pre-taught. Words in
Category 2 are clearly technical words as the more general meaning of
the word when used outside the field does not provide ready access to
its technical use.

Words in Categories 3 and 4 are less obviously technical because
they are unique neither in form or meaning to a particular field. The
words, particularly in Category 4, are readily accessible through their
use outside the field. A glance at a list of Category 4 words is sufficient
to quickly identify what field is being examined. Murphey (1992), in a
study of pop songs, found that the word *love* was extremely frequent,
in fact among the top ten words along with *the, be, you. Love* is probably not a technical word, although it meets the criterion for Category

4, because pop songs are not considered an area of technical knowledge.

Categories 2 and 3 indicate that range based on form alone is not
sufficient to make sensible decisions between what are technical words
and what are not. In many cases, meaning must also be considered.
The cline which exists from Categories 2 to 4 raises the question of
whether a technical word needs to have a technical meaning, that is a
meaning which is different from its uses outside a particular field, and
if so how different the meaning needs to be. The cut-off point distinguishing technical words from non-technical words could come after
category 2, 3 or 4.

Several researchers have used relative frequency or range as a way of
distinguishing technical vocabulary. Bečka (1972) distinguished three
types of words in specialised discourse: grammatical words and two
kinds of lexical words – non-terminological words and terminological
words. Grammatical words (sometimes called function words) are a
small group of around 270 types (176 word families, see appendix 6),
if numbers are included. They are generally of very high-frequency and
very wide range. They consist of words that are not nouns, verbs,
adjectives and adverbs. They include words like *the, of, she, but,* and
might. Only a few function words (*hence, hither, thither, thrice,
whereas, whither*) fall outside the most frequent 2,000 words.
Terminological words (which could also be called terminology or technical terms) are words whose meaning requires scientific knowledge.
To use them well we must know the science involved (Bečka, 1972:
48). Terminological words, because of their specialised meaning, are
generally of moderate to low-frequency in texts and more importantly
have very narrow range. In groups of texts classified under a range of
different disciplines, terminological words will be among the lower-
frequency words and will occur in a limited range of texts and disciplines. The critical statistical signal that a word is a terminological
word is that it has narrow range (low textual and register frequency) –
it occurs in only a few texts and disciplines – in relation to its frequency
of occurrence. For example, *bargain* and *styrene* have the same frequency in Francis and Kučera (1982), but *bargain* occurs in eight different texts in seven different disciplines. *Styrene* occurs in only two
different texts in two different disciplines. *Styrene*'s narrow range
marks it as a technical word. Bečka's data is a compelling argument for
the need to take account of range in the construction of word lists.

A study of the 6,000 lemmas in the ranked list of higher frequency
lemmas in Francis and Kučera (1982) however indicates that most
words with low range compared to other items of the same frequency
are not technical terms. However a corpus of 2,000-word texts may
not be the best kind of corpus to reveal striking differences in range

between terminological words and non-terminological words. Longer texts would give technical terms a chance to attain a frequency comparable to moderate frequency non-terminological words.

Sutarsyah, Nation and Kennedy (1994), in a study of an economics text, found that a group of around 30 words that were obviously related to the field of economics accounted for over 10% (1 in every 10) of the running words in the text. These were words like *cost*, *demand*, *price* (see Table 6.2). Over half of the 34 words from Table 6.2 are in the first 1,000 of the *General Service List* (West, 1953) and four-fifths are in the complete *GSL* or the *University Word List*.

Making lists of technical vocabulary

There are two systematic ways of developing lists of technical vocabulary: through the use of technical dictionaries, and through the use of corpus based frequency counts. Technical dictionaries can be regarded as technical vocabulary lists, but they do not contain frequency information useful in assessing the relative usefulness of the words, and they give little indication of how the words listed were chosen.

Using a dictionary

Using a dictionary to create a technical vocabulary list involves the methodological problems of sampling, defining what is actually being counted (what is counted as a word) and classification described in Nation (1993c). There is also the problem of choice of dictionary, because working from a dictionary means that the base data has been compiled by someone other than the researcher and the principles underlying its compilation are not likely to be described or apparent. Does the dictionary adequately represent the field which is being examined? Is the dictionary up to date? Is it as complete as possible? Does it reflect a US or UK bias?

Using a corpus-based frequency count

It is possible to use an existing frequency count that distinguishes range figures from frequency figures – the best example is the *American Heritage Word Book* (Carroll, Davies and Richman, 1971) – or to carry out a range and frequency count comparing a general corpus with a specialised corpus (see Sutarsyah, Nation and Kennedy, 1994). Some studies dispense with the general count (Farrell, 1990), but then there is greater dependency on intuitive judgement. Farrell created a list of technical vocabulary for the field of electronics based on a 20,017 token corpus containing 1,258 lemmas. The division of

Table 6.2. *Words in the most frequent 1,000 of the economics text that occur much more frequently than in the general academic corpus (from Sutarsyah, Nation and Kennedy (1994))*

Word family	Frequency in the economics text	Frequency in the general academic corpus
Price	3,080	90
Cost	2,251	91
Demand	1,944	102
Curve	1,804	83
Firm	1,743	41
Supply	1,590	86
Quantity	1,467	53
Margin	1,427	24
Economy	1,353	172
Income	1,183	96
Produce	1,237	167
Market	1,104	110
Consume	955	70
Labour	1,004	131
Capital	907	50
Total	946	114
Output	861	50
Revenue	763	10
You	866	118
Profit	733	27
Production	772	84
Average	777	90
Goods	705	21
Product	749	106
Trade	621	85
Buy	521	35
Wage	522	75
Monopoly	454	13
Percent	450	41
Million	445	42
Household	360	41
Equilibrium	328	21
Choice	339	39
Elasticity	333	34
Total frequency	3,080.00	2,322

Notes:
Words not marked are in the first thousand words of the GSL (19 out of 34 words)
Words marked <u>word</u> are in the second thousand words of the GSL (3 words)
Words marked **word** are in the *University Word List* (6 words)
Words marked *word* are not in any list (6 words)

the lemmas into basic, semi-technical and technical terms seems to have been largely done on an intuitive basis although frequency and range information were also consulted. The data in the Farrell study agrees with other studies of specialised corpora (Sutarsyah, Nation and Kennedy, 1994).

- A small group of highly topic related words (*current, fig., voltage, circuit*) occurs very frequently, accounting for at least 10% of the running words in the corpus.
- Several of the words in this high-frequency group are in West's *General Service List of English Words* or the *University Word List* with related meanings (*circuit, field, energy, plate, connected, supply, positive, flow*). They are not completely technical but are also known in some form in non-specialised language.
- A few of the highly frequent words stand out as reflecting the nature of the discourse (*fig., if, we* – the most frequent pronoun).
- Several words are clearly technical in form and meaning but have a very low-frequency of occurrence in the corpus. This would make it difficult to distinguish technical words purely on the basis of frequency.
- Several technical words have very low range *within* a specialised corpus (Farrell, 1990: 30). This means that the occurrences of a particular technical word are not spread evenly through a text, but cluster in a particular chapter or section. This reflects the occurrence of some proper nouns in novels (Hirsh, 1992), with some characters appearing for a short time and then never being mentioned again.

Learning technical vocabulary

Several writers (Cowan, 1974; Higgins, 1966; Barber, 1962) consider that it is not the English teacher's job to teach technical words. The words are learned through study of the field. As we shall see later, the use of general service words and academic words as technical words (*resistance* in electronics; *wall* (cell wall) in biology; *demand* in economics) means that the English teacher may be able to make a useful contribution to helping the learners with technical vocabulary. Strevens (1973: 228) points out that learners who know the scientific field may have little difficulty with technical words; a teacher who does not may have a great deal.

Godman and Payne (1981: 37) argue that a technical term only makes sense when other related terms are also known. This is perhaps another way of saying that knowing a technical word involves knowing the body of knowledge that it is attached to. Flowerdew (1992: 208) notes that definitions in science lectures to non-native speakers occur systematically. The lecture may be organised around definitions of key terms in that topic area. This discourse role of definitions underlines the point that knowing the technical vocabulary is very closely related to knowing the subject area.

Considering the large numbers of technical words that occur in specialised texts, language teachers need to prepare learners to deal with them. Chapter 1, on the goals of vocabulary learning, presented some information on the statistical nature of technical words. From the learner's point of view, unknown technical words usually cannot be ignored when reading because they are closely connected to the topic being discussed. They are also difficult to guess from context if the reader does not already have a good background in that technical area. For the same reason, looking the word up in a dictionary does not bring much satisfaction. Clearly, learning technical words is closely connected with learning the subject.

Although English teachers are not usually well equipped to work with technical texts and the technical vocabulary they contain, they can help learners get accustomed to the idea that different uses of words may have a shared underlying meaning. The *wall* of a living cell shares important features with the *wall* of a house. Visser (1989) devised the following kind of exercise to deal with this. Learners can work individually or in pairs on the exercises.

interpret/intɜːrprɪt/verb	interpret/intɜːrprɪt/verb	What is the core meaning of this word?
If you **interpret** something in a particular way, you decide that this is its meaning or significance. *Even so, the move was interpreted as a defeat for Mr Gorbachev . . . The judge says that he has to interpret the law as it's been passed . . . Both of them agree on what is in the poem, but not on how it should be interpreted.* **How would you interpret the meaning of this sign?** ▶	If you **interpret** what someone is saying, you translate it immediately into another language. *The woman spoke little English, so her husband came with her to interpret . . . Three interpreters looked over the text for about three or four hours and found that they could not interpret half of it.* **Interpret this sentence into your language: 'I really like chocolate cake.'**	

These exercises are easy to make and as well as improving knowledge of particular words, they get learners used to the idea that words 'stretch' their meanings. The sample sentences come from the *COBUILD* dictionary.

Memory (1990), in a study of 15- and 18-year-old native speakers, looked at whether technical vocabulary was best taught before, during or after reading and found no significant difference. Learning was tested by recall of definitions. The argument for learning technical vocabulary during reading emphasises the importance of seeing how a technical term fits into a framework of knowledge. It may thus be more revealing to also test using semantic mapping or some other measure that looks at how knowledge of a technical term is integrated into a field of knowledge. Learners should approach specialised vocabulary strategically, considering whether particular words are worth learning, and considering how they can be most efficiently learned.

The main purpose in isolating an academic or technical vocabulary is to provide a sound basis for planning teaching and learning. By focusing attention on items that have been shown to be frequent, and in the case of academic vocabulary of wide range, learners and teachers can get the best return for their effort.

Technical vocabulary however is only one kind of specialised vocabulary, and its occurrence is affected by factors that influence the use of all vocabulary. We will now look at these factors.

Vocabulary in discourse

So far in this book we have looked mainly at vocabulary as isolated words or in phrase and sentence contexts. But the main role of vocabulary is to convey messages in extended spoken and written texts. We will now look at the part played by vocabulary in discourse.

Vocabulary use in a text arises from the communicative purposes of the text. There are two related aspects to consider. First, vocabulary use signals and contributes to the uniqueness of the text, that is, what makes this text different from all other texts. Second, vocabulary use carries general discourse messages which are shared with other texts of similar types. Thus, when we examine what vocabulary use does in a text, we can look at the special features of the text, and we can also look at how these special features are examples of general language constraints and discourse requirements. We will look at the general discourse messages that vocabulary can carry and see how these can affect particular texts. Table 6.3 lists the communicative messages of vocabulary in a text, classified according to Halliday's (1994) three major divisions of field, tenor, and mode.

Let us now look in more detail at each of the three sets of discourse functions.

Vocabulary and the information content of the text

Function words

It might be expected that because the function words of English are a small, largely closed group their frequency would be constant across a range of texts. However, this turns out not to be so. Although it is possible to predict that a small number of function words will account for a significant proportion of the running words of a text, the particular nature of the text will determine how frequent each function word is and its frequency relative to other function words.

The approximately 270 function word types (176 word families) account for 43–44% of the running words in most texts (Johansson and Hofland, 1989; Francis and Kučera, 1982). The unusually high-frequency of some function words in a text may indicate important features of the discourse. In the economics textbook used in the Sutarsyah, Nation and Kennedy (1994) study, *you* had a frequency much higher than its frequency in the general academic corpus, because the writer typically addresses his message directly to the reader to involve the reader in the topic: 'You have just been named chief economic strategist for OPEC.' Newton and Kennedy (1996) found different occurrences of prepositions and conjunctions in split information tasks compared with shared information tasks.

Topic related vocabulary

Goodman and Bird (1984) argue that there are two major kinds of word frequency studies, each giving quite different information. The most common kind of word frequency study examines a large range of texts to establish general service high-frequency words. A more neglected kind of frequency study looks at the frequency of words within a particular text. If we want to understand why and how particular kinds of words are used, we must study individual texts intensively. The frequency with which words occur in a text is a result of the characteristics of the particular text itself.

The most immediately striking finding when looking at a frequency ranked list of the vocabulary in a text is the way that topic related

Table 6.3. *The discourse functions of vocabulary*

The information content of the text
1. The vocabulary reflects the topic of the text through the frequent use of particular words.

2. The vocabulary shows the formality of the text through use of *Academic Word List* vocabulary and other Latinate vocabulary.

3. The vocabulary shows how technical the subject matter is through the use of technical vocabulary and deep taxonomies.

4. The vocabulary shows the writer or speaker's ideological position (Fairclough, 1989: 113–116), often through metaphor.

The relationship between the writer or speaker and the reader or listener
5. The vocabulary shows the power relationships and frequency of contact relationships between the writer and reader or speaker and listener through the use of vocabulary over the range of colloquial, spoken vocabulary to very low-frequency, learned vocabulary.

6. The vocabulary shows the writer or speaker's attitude to the subject matter or to others through the use of vocabulary over the range of emotionally involved to uninvolved.

7. The vocabulary shows the writer's wish to make the text accessible or inaccessible to certain readers or the writer's wish to communicate with the already initiated (Corson, 1985) through the selection of vocabulary and through defining in the text.

8. The pronoun use shows the writer's stance with regard to the audience.

The organisation of the text
9. The vocabulary signals the rhetorical stages or semantic structure of the text (e.g. problem-solution) (McCarthy, 1991).

10. The vocabulary shows the most important sentences in terms of drawing the main topics together (Hoey, 1991).

11. The vocabulary shows the connections between parts of the text through lexical cohesion (Halliday and Hasan, 1976), and use of 'grammaticised' words (Winter, 1978; Meyer, 1990).

words occur among the very high-frequency words. A brief glance at the most frequent content words in the list is usually sufficient to determine what the text is about. The following list contains the most frequent content words from part of a well known story.

little	25
pig	22
house	17
said	14

wolf	9
build	8
straw	7
man	6
catch	5
bricks	4
built	4
now	4
sticks	4

Typically, the most frequent content words in a text occur with a frequency per 1,000 words that is very much higher than their frequency per 1,000 words in other texts or in a collection of different texts. Sutarsyah, Nation and Kennedy (1994) found that a group of 34 words in an economics textbook were so frequent that they accounted for 10% (one word in every line) of the running words in the text. These words occurred with a frequency of up to sixty times the frequency with which they occurred in a more general corpus of similar size. Here are some of those words: *price, cost, demand, curve, firm, supply, quantity, margin, economy, income, produce, market, consume, labour, capital, total.*

Each text has its own topic vocabulary which occurs because of the message the text is trying to convey. The vocabulary gives the text part of its unique flavour. This has several important messages for language teaching. First, in the production of simplified material, it is important that any vocabulary grading scheme used is flexible enough to allow the use of topic related vocabulary that may not be in the lists used to guide the grading of the material. There can be rules regarding the repetition of these additional words to make sure that they have a chance of being learned and that they do not act as a burden to the reader. If a particular word occurs only once then it may be a burden but if it is repeated several times in the book then the initial learning effort is repaid by the opportunity to use that learning again when the word reoccurs. Most well designed graded reader schemes have rules of this kind.

Second, when learners are being asked to speak or write on a topic, their language production is likely to be more apt if they are given the chance to meet relevant topic related vocabulary before they produce. This can be done in a variety of ways – through topic related reading, discussion, direct teaching, or accompanying support materials.

Third, from a course design perspective, learners may need exposure to a range of topics if they are to develop a rich vocabulary. In the

Sutarsyah, Nation and Kennedy (1994) study of an economics text, only 548 of the second 1,000 words of the *GSL* occurred, compared to 796 in the more general corpus.

Fourth, as we have seen in Table 1.7 (see p. 17), different texts contain quite different amounts of academic vocabulary. This shows that the general topic of the text influences the type of vocabulary that occurs. In an unpublished study, Jenkins (1993) developed a vocabulary of children's books, and in a similar study Hwang (1989) found evidence of a newspaper vocabulary. Courses focusing on a limited range of text types could benefit from the development of a specialised vocabulary.

Fifth, teachers need to be careful when focusing on vocabulary in intensive reading. The content words that occur most frequently in a particular text may not be useful words when learners face a different text. Teachers may need to give most attention to less frequent words in a particular text that are high-frequency words across a range of texts. Today's teaching needs to help tomorrow's tasks.

Vocabulary and the relationship between the writer or speaker and reader or listener

Corson (1997) presents arguments to support the view that use of academic vocabulary is taken as evidence of being in control of the academic meaning systems, and is thus essential to academic success.

Academic vocabulary is overwhelmingly Graeco-Latin and is not easy to learn because words refer to abstract ideas, they are infrequent, and their forms do not reveal their meaning. Thus learners need to have 'a rich acquaintance with the specialist areas of discourse in which they appear, as well as frequent and motivated contact with the words themselves' (*ibid.*: 701). Corson argues that meeting words receptively is insufficient for using them well. They need to be used in motivated talk about text. Not all learners have access to this experience.

Studies involving the *University Word List* and the *Academic Word List*, have shown the very uneven spread of this vocabulary across different types of writing. It is uncommon in fiction (1.7% text coverage), moderately frequent in newspapers (3.9% text coverage), and very frequent in academic texts (8.5% text coverage). The frequent occurrence of this vocabulary is a sign of the formal academic nature of a text, or in Corson's (1997) terms, that the text is drawing on different meaning systems from those texts with little academic vocabulary.

Some work has been done on examining the way vocabulary reflects academic meaning systems. One area of attention has been in the use of reporting verbs as in 'Barrington (1967) *states* that . . .' Thompson and Ye (1991) look at the way the wide range of reporting verbs in English can be used to reflect evaluation of the citations reported. There have also been attempts to relate the kind of academic vocabulary used to what academic discourse does: citing, evaluating, hypothesising, contrasting, relating and explaining (Strevens, 1973; Martin, 1976; Meyer, 1990).

The amount of technical vocabulary in a text and presence or absence of explanation of this vocabulary is a sign of the intended audience for the text. It is not always easy to decide what is a technical term, and there are degrees of 'technicalness'.

Vocabulary and the organisation of the text

The frequency of topic-related words is only one aspect of their occurrence in a text. In an insightful book, Hoey (1991) shows that by examining the number of lexical links between sentences in a non-fiction text, it is possible to: identify the sentences which are central to the topic of the text (these also tend to provide a reasonable summary of the text); identify the sentences which are marginal to the topic of the text; and identify where a topic is introduced and ends.

These lexical links include repetitions of words (in either the same form or in inflected or derived forms), paraphrase of various kinds (which includes synonyms and hyponyms), substitution (including pronouns) and ellipsis (Hoey, *ibid.*: 83). Essentially, sentences which are central to the topic of the text have more lexical links to other sentences, that is, they share more vocabulary that refers to the same ideas. In terms of discourse analysis, a major strength of Hoey's lexically based analysis of relationships is that it shows relationships between sentences that may be separated by several intervening sentences. These links often occur with the topic-related words and they can form 'lexical chains'. They can occur within a text and also between speakers in a conversation (McCarthy, 1991: 69).

Learners need to be able to see the links between the various forms of topic-related vocabulary; for example, they need to see that *biologist* and *scientist* are in fact referring to the same person in a particular text. For this reason, Hoey (1991: 241) suggests that topic-related words which form links should be given priority when glosses are provided to accompany a text. This would have the effect of helping the learner quickly make sense of the text, because the sentences central to the topic would be understood.The learning of unknown words would also be helped if their relationship with synonymous known items was clarified. In addition, links through synonymy and paraphrase not only show shared aspects of meaning, but also highlight differences. Each new link can be part of a developing enrichment (McCarthy, 1991: 66). The results of Hoey's study can be used to justify:

- non-linear note-taking from the text
- looking for lexical links in order to understand the structure of the text
- not needing to understand every sentence to get the important ideas in a text
- the importance of stressing lexis as a prerequisite for reading
- teachers focusing on word families and lexical sets
- writers making clear connections between related parts of their text using lexical repetition

Discourse-organising vocabulary

McCarthy (1991: 78–84) and McCarthy and Carter (1994: 105) drawing on the work of Winter (1977, 1978) and Hoey (1983) show how certain words are strongly associated with certain patterns of information. These patterns involve stages in a piece of discourse such as: (1) stating the problem, (2) suggesting solutions, (3) evaluation of the solutions. Vocabulary like *problem, crisis, dilemma, issue* is associated with the problem stage, while words like *address* (vb), *justifiable, effective, manage*, and idioms are associated with the evaluation stage. McCarthy (1991) gives most attention to the problem/solution/evaluation and hypothetical/real (claim/counter-claim) patterns, but as McCarthy suggests, there are numerous other patterns whose parts may be signalled by the occurrence of certain vocabulary. These include:

1. the various topic types (Johns and Davies, 1983; Nation, 1993b) such as description of physical structure and characteristics (what something is like), instruction (how to do something), state/situation (what happened) and process (what happens)
2. the various genres (Derewianka, 1990) such as narratives, arguments, instructions, information reports, recounts and explanations
3. the classical rhetoric classifications such as argument, narrative, exposition and description
4. the various clause or conjunction relations (Winter, 1977 and 1978; Hoey, 1983; Halliday and Hasan, 1976; Nation 1984) such as cause and effect, contrast, exemplification, and inclusion,

especially when they relate several sentences rather than just clauses within a sentence

Some of this discourse-organising vocabulary consists of words that act a little like pronouns in that they refer back or forward in the text to another part of the text. These have been called 'anaphoric nouns' (Francis, 1994) and more generally 'discourse-organising words' (McCarthy, 1991: 75). They include words like *question*, *issue*, *assumption*, *hypothesis*, *position*, *case*, *situation* when they refer to another piece of text. Here are some examples from one text (Parkin, 1990: 101):

- 'If the supply of a good falls, its price rises. But by how much? To answer this *question*'
- 'You are trying to decide whether to advise a cut in output to shift the supply curve and raise the price of oil. To make this *decision*'
- 'Let us compare two possible (hypothetical) *scenarios* in the oil industry'

Meyer (1990) sees this discourse-organising vocabulary as becoming to some degree 'delexicalised', that is, depending more for its meaning on what it does or refers to in the text than what it carries with it. When learners meet these words in texts they need to be sensitive to their many functions which include referring to other parts of the text and signalling a stage in the discourse.

Ivanič (1991) calls these words 'carrier nouns' and typifies them as countable abstract nouns which are like pronouns in that they have a constant meaning and a variable context-dependent meaning. Ivanič (*ibid*.: 108) notes that these nouns often play an important role in exam questions ('Describe three factors that . . .') because they can be accompanied by a number but they do not give anything away about the content of the answer. Because these nouns are not topic specific, they are important candidates for a general academic vocabulary like the *Academic Word List*. Their strengths as discourse organising vocabulary are that they have a referential function and variable meaning like pronouns but, unlike pronouns, they can be modified by demonstrative pronouns, numbers, and adjectives, they can occur in various parts of a sentence and they have a significant constant meaning. Francis (1994) describes the function of these nouns as **'labelling'**: they tell the reader what to expect when they occur before their realisation and they encapsulate and classify what has been said when they occur after their realisation. They thus play an important role in the organisation of discourse.

Table 6.4. *Examples of different markers of the same clause relationship*

Vocabulary 1	Vocabulary 2	Vocabulary 3
though	nevertheless	concede
if, unless	otherwise	condition
so that	for this purpose	purpose
whereas	however	contrast

Winter (1977) notes that the relationships between clauses and sentences are largely unsignalled, but when they are signalled there are three kinds of vocabulary that do the signalling, which he refers to as Vocabulary 1, Vocabulary 2 and Vocabulary 3.

Vocabulary 1.   Subordinators like *after, although, as, at the same time as.*
Vocabulary 2.   Sentence connectors like *accordingly, in addition, all the same, also.*
Vocabulary 3.   Lexical items like *achieve, affirm, alike, cause, compare, conclude, consequence, problem.*

Winter argues that this third group, although it consists of nouns, verbs and adjectives, has many of the characteristics of closed class or function words. The words in this group make up a small and fairly closed set, are to varying degrees delexicalised, and their meaning is realised by words occurring before or after them. Winter (*ibid.*: 20) lists 108 headwords for Vocabulary 3. Of these, 92 can be seen as paraphrases of words in Vocabulary 1 and Vocabulary 2 (see Table 6.4).

These 108 headwords are not the complete list as many of them can be expressed by synonyms, but the relationships they signal make up a closed set. Because these delexicalised words can play an important signalling role in clause relationships, they play an important signalling role in discourse structure.

Marco (1998) sees 'procedural' vocabulary (lexical words which structure discourse and establish meaning relationships) as consisting of two main groups: procedural organising vocabulary and procedural defining vocabulary. Procedural organising vocabulary is involved in clause relations and the structure of schemata. Procedural defining vocabulary includes formal signals of the act of defining (*is defined as, means*) and signals within the act of defining, namely category words and descriptions of attributes which relate to the parts of the classical definition pattern. Teachers need to be sensitive to the discourse functions of these discourse organising words and draw attention to them in intensive reading.

Words in discourse

Let us now look at a short piece of academic text to see how vocabulary occurs in the text and to pull together the points made about vocabulary so far in this chapter. The text is taken from *Macroeconomics* (Parkin, 1990). Here is the text with the words marked in bold which occur with a very high-frequency in this book but with a much lower frequency in other texts. This is the book used in the Sutarsyah, Nation and Kennedy (1994) study whose results are shown in Table 6.2 (p. 202).

Chapter 5 Elasticity
OPEC's Dilemma
If the **supply** of a **good** falls, its **price** rises. But by how much? To answer this question, **you** will have to don a flowing caftan: **You** have just been named chief economic strategist for OPEC – the Organization of Petroleum Exporting Countries. **You** want to bring more money into OPEC. Would **you** restrict the **supply** of oil to raise **prices**? Or would **you produce** more oil? **You** know that a higher **price** will bring in more dollars per barrel, but lower **production** means that fewer barrels will be sold. Will the **price** rise high enough to offset the smaller **quantity** that OPEC will sell? As OPEC's economic strategist, **you** need to know about the **demand** for oil in great detail. For example, as the world **economy** grows, how will that growth translate into an increasing **demand** for oil? What about substitutes for oil? Will we discover inexpensive methods to convert coal and tar sands into usable fuel? Will nuclear energy become safe and cheap enough to compete with oil?

In this chapter, **you** will learn how to tackle questions such as the ones just posed. **You** will learn how we can measure in a precise way the responsiveness of the **quantities bought** and sold to changes in **prices** and other influences on **buyers** or sellers.

Price Elasticity of Demand
Let us begin by looking a bit more closely at **your** task as OPEC's economic strategist. **You** are trying to decide whether to advise a cut in **output** to shift the **supply** curve and raise the **price** of oil. To make this decision, **you** need to know how the **quantity** of oil **demanded** responds to a change in **price**. **You** also need some way to measure that response.
Two Possible Scenarios
To understand the importance of the responsiveness of the **quantity** of oil **demanded** to a change in its **price**, let us compare two possible (hypothetical)

scenarios in the oil industry, shown in Fig.5.1. In the two parts of the figure, the **supply curves** are identical, but the **demand curves** differ.

Focus first on the **supply curve** labelled *So* in each part of the figure. This **curve** represents the initial **supply**. Notice that *So* cuts the **demand curve** in both cases, at a **price** of $10 a barrel and a **quantity traded** of 40 **million** barrels a day.

Now suppose that **you** contemplate a cut in **supply** that shifts the **supply curve** from *So* to *S1*. In part (a), the new **supply curve** *S1* cuts the **demand curve** *Da* at a **price** of $30 a barrel and a **quantity traded** of 23 **million** barrels a day. In part (b), the same shift in the **supply curve** results in the new **supply curve** cutting the **demand curve** *Db* at a **price** of $15 a barrel and a **quantity traded** of 15 million barrels a day. (Parkin, *ibid.*: 102–103)

Firstly, note the very frequent occurrence of the marked words. There are 34 words in the book in this group (see Table 6.2) and these 34 word families account for 10% of the running words in the text. There is on average one in every line of Parkin's book.

Secondly, notice the part of the text where these words do not occur. This is where a range of examples is being presented. Examples help bring a message alive but they also impose a vocabulary load because they move outside the normal vocabulary of the text.

Thirdly, notice that one of these highly frequent words is a function word – *you*. This is the only function word in the list of 34 words. Notice that it is frequent because of the way the writer treats the relationship between himself and the reader. He directly addresses the reader, involving the reader in the text and directing the reader in a polite version of the imperative ('you will have to learn . . .').

Let us now look at the lexical chains in the text. Notice the relationship between the lexical chains and the very high-frequency vocabulary. Here are two related chains.

1. price rises
   raise prices
   a higher price
   will the price rise high enough
   raise the price
   change in price

2. supply of a good falls
   restrict the supply
   lower production
   smaller quantity that OPEC
   will sell
   a cut in output
   shift in the supply curve

Notice that by the end of the text the discussion has moved from actions (restrict the supply) to abstract representation (shift in the supply curve); this is the point of the whole book: learning the principles behind economic activity.

Notice the variety of forms and uses to convey the same idea.

Because this text is introductory, the writer is very aware of and friendly to the reader (*you*). As a result the vocabulary used is largely accessible and not highly technical. There are few words that have forms unique to the field of economics (*elasticity* perhaps). Most are slightly narrowed uses of common words: *price, supply, demand, margin*. The whole book has a vocabulary of only 5,438 word families indicating once more its role as an accessible, introductory text.

The example text contains some discourse-organising words – *question, decision, scenarios* – that could be related to the problem/ solution/evaluation pattern. There are also several anaphoric nouns that are very clearly formally related to what they refer to: *production, growth, response*. This clear relationship reflects once more the writer's intention to keep the text accessible.

This chapter has tried to show that vocabulary does more than convey particular meanings; it plays an important part in making a text cohesive and coherent so that the text conveys a range of different messages to the reader or listener.

7 Vocabulary learning strategies and guessing from context

Vocabulary learning strategies are a part of language learning strategies which in turn are a part of general learning strategies. Schmitt (1997) provides a very useful overview of the rise in importance of strategy use in second language learning, noting that it grew out of an interest in the learner's active role in the learning process.

It is not easy to arrive at a definition of what a strategy is, but to deserve attention from a teacher a strategy would need to:

1. involve choice, that is, there are several strategies to choose from
2. be complex, that is, there are several steps to learn
3. require knowledge and benefit from training
4. increase the efficiency of vocabulary learning and vocabulary use

There are numerous strategies which have these features. Learners not only need to know about these strategies, but need to have skill in using them.

A taxonomy of vocabulary learning strategies

There have been a number of attempts to develop a taxonomy of vocabulary learning strategies, usually as part of a piece of research into learners' strategy use. Schmitt (1997) developed an extensive taxonomy organised around Oxford's (1990) social, memory, cognitive and metacognitive categories. Gu and Johnson (1996) also developed a substantial list divided into: beliefs about vocabulary learning, metacognitive regulation, guessing strategies, dictionary strategies, note-taking strategies, memory strategies (rehearsal), memory strategies (encoding) and activation strategies.

Williams (1985) identifies five potentially trainable strategies for working out the meaning of unfamiliar words in written text. These include: inferring from context, identifying lexical familiarisation, unchaining nominal compounds, synonym search and word analysis. Williams suggests that these become the focus of deliberate, intensive

Table 7.1. *A taxonomy of kinds of vocabulary learning strategies*

General class of strategies	Types of strategies
Planning: choosing what to focus on and when to focus on it	Choosing words Choosing the aspects of word knowledge Choosing strategies Planning repetition
Sources: finding information about words	Analysing the word Using context Consulting a reference source in L1 or L2 Using parallels in L1 and L2
Processes: establishing knowledge	Noticing Retrieving Generating

teaching. What is interesting about several of these strategies, particularly lexical familiarisation and unchaining nominal compounds, is how they involve reinterpreting *known* words. That is, a known word like *snap* (to break) may be used in the phrase *snap election*. Thus, they offer a different kind of challenge to a second language learner who might not know any meaning for the words than for a native speaker who has to extend the reference of known words.

The following taxonomy tries to separate aspects of vocabulary knowledge (what is involved in knowing a word) from sources of vocabulary knowledge, and learning processes.

Let us now look at each of these types of strategies in turn.

Planning vocabulary learning

The strategies in this category involve deciding on where to focus attention, how to focus the attention, and how often to give attention to the item.

Choosing words

In chapter 1 we looked at the various levels of vocabulary (high-frequency, academic, technical, low-frequency) and the different returns for learning effort. Learners should know what their vocabulary goals are and should choose what vocabulary to focus on in terms of these goals. Gu and Johnson's (1996) study noted that this evaluative selective attention was a noted characteristic of successful learners.

It is important that learners have access to lists of high-frequency and academic words and are able to obtain frequency information from dictionaries. Learners should have a clear strategy for deciding what vocabulary to focus on and where to find this vocabulary.

Choosing aspects of word knowledge to focus on

In chapter 2 we looked at what is involved in knowing a word. Learners need to be aware of these aspects of word knowledge. Most often the main concern will be knowing the meaning of the word, but the need to use a word in speaking or writing will require attention to other aspects.

Choosing strategies

Gu and Johnson's (1996) most successful learners were those who actively drew on a wide range of vocabulary learning strategies. Their least successful used a much more limited range. Successful strategy users need a strategy for controlling their strategy use. This involves choosing the most appropriate strategy from a range of known options and deciding how to pursue the strategy and when to switch to another strategy. For example, consulting a dictionary could be followed by the use of word cards to establish knowledge of the word.

Planning repetition

Most vocabulary learning requires repeated attention to the item. One of the most important strategies to encourage remembering is the use of increasingly spaced retrieval (Baddeley, 1990; Pimsleur, 1967). This can involve an informal schedule for returning to previously studied items on word cards and the recycling of old material, or it can involve more organised review using a computer or filing system (Mondria and Mondria-de Vries, 1994). The role of repetition was looked at in more detail in chapter 3.

Sources: finding information about words

In order to cope with new vocabulary when it occurs and to learn unfamiliar vocabulary, learners have to be able to get information about the words. This information may include all of the aspects involved in knowing a word. It can come from the word form itself, from the context in which the word occurs, from a reference source or from drawing on analogies and connections with other languages.

Analysing word parts

Because a large proportion of English words are derived from French, Latin or Greek, they are made up of word parts: affixes and stems. Being familiar with common word parts can provide a useful basis for seeing connections between related words, checking guesses from context, strengthening form and meaning connections, and in some cases working out the meaning of a word. Word parts are looked at more closely in chapter 8.

Using context

Gu and Johnson (1996) subdivide the strategy of using context into the various kinds of cue that a learner could draw on, including background knowledge and linguistic cues. Guessing from context is examined in detail later in this chapter.

Consulting a reference source

There is a variety of reference sources available for gaining information about vocabulary. They can be subdivided into: formal sources, usually written, (dictionaries of various kinds, glossaries, lists, concordances) and more spontaneous sources, usually oral, including asking teachers, native speakers or other learners for information. Chapter 8 looks at various strategies for dictionary use and discusses the effects of glossing. Negotiating unknown vocabulary is examined in chapter 4 on listening and speaking.

Using parallels with other languages

The learning burden of a word depends on how much its various aspects are similar to patterns and items that the learner already knows from previous study of the second language, from the first language, or from other languages. These parallels can occur with all aspects of knowing a word and are most striking with cognate words. Swan (1997) provides a wide range of examples of helpful and unhelpful relationships between the first and second language. Kellerman's (1985) research shows that learners become more cautious about using first language patterns in the second language as they learn more about the second language.

Swan (1997: 166) presents several versions of the 'equivalence hypothesis' that second language learners might use when drawing on L1 patterns to use in L2, for example:

- Foreign words look different from mother tongue words but work in the same way (semantically and grammatically).
- Regard everything as the same unless you have a good reason not to.

More sophisticated versions of learners' equivalence hypotheses take account of linguistic and cultural distance.

Processes: establishing vocabulary knowledge

The third major set of strategies involves ways of remembering vocabulary and making it available for use. The major categories used here relate to the conditions for vocabulary learning described in chapter 3: noticing, retrieving and generating. These conditions can apply to all aspects of vocabulary knowledge, and are ordered here from the least to the most effective with generation being the most effective for learning.

Noticing

Noticing involves seeing the word as an item to be learned. Strategies at this level include: putting the word in a vocabulary notebook or list, putting the word on to a word card, orally repeating the word and visually repeating the word. These strategies tend to be largely recording strategies, but they are a very useful first step towards deeper processing of words.

Retrieving

Retrieval involves recall of previously met items. Each retrieval strengthens the connection between the cue and the retrieved knowledge. Receptively, the cue may be the written or spoken form of the word and the retrieved information may be its meaning or use. Productively, the cue is the meaning or use and the retrieved information is the word form. There are thus many kinds of retrieval: receptive/productive, oral/visual, overt/covert, in context/decontextualised. Retrieval can occur across the four skills of listening, speaking, reading and writing; it involves recalling knowledge in the same form in which it was originally stored.

It is important for learners to realise that there is a substantial qualitative difference between (1) studying words in lists and notebooks where the form, meaning and use of the word are all on display and need not be retrieved, and (2) retrieving previously met information where only a cue is present (such as the word form) and the other information has to be recalled by the learner. Retrieval strategies (2) are superior to noticing strategies (1). If learners keep vocabulary notebooks, they should become familiar with ways of covering up part of the entry so that they are encouraged to retrieve that information.

Generating

Like retrieving, this group of strategies to establish vocabulary knowledge includes many kinds of generation: receptive/productive, oral/visual, overt/covert, in context/decontextualised. From an instructional viewpoint, generating involves 'rich instruction'. Generation strategies include: attaching new aspects of knowledge to what is known through instantiation (visualising examples of the word), word analysis, semantic mapping, and using scales and grids. It also includes rule-based generation by creating contexts, collocations and sentences containing the word, mnemonic strategies like the keyword technique, and meeting and using the word in new contexts across the four skills of listening, speaking, reading and writing.

The three major categories of vocabulary strategies – planning, finding information, establishing knowledge – include a wide range of strategies of different complexity. In this chapter and the following chapter, we will look at them in more detail.

Training in strategy choice and use

Most vocabulary learning strategies can be applied to a wide range of vocabulary and are useful at all stages of vocabulary learning. They also allow learners to take control of learning away from the teacher and allow the teacher to concentrate on other things. Research shows that learners differ greatly in the skill with which they use strategies.

For these reasons, it is important to make training in strategy use a planned part of a vocabulary development programme. This planning involves:

1. deciding which strategies to give attention to
2. deciding how much time to spend on training the learners in strategy use
3. working out a syllabus for each strategy that covers the required knowledge and provides plenty of opportunity for increasingly independent practice
4. monitoring and providing feedback on learners' control of the strategies

For each of the strategies like guessing from context, using word parts, dictionary use and direct learning, learners need to spend a total of at least four or five hours per strategy spread over several weeks. There is little research to guide teachers in deciding how much time to spend on strategy training, but it is certainly not sufficient to demonstrate and explain a strategy to learners and then leave the rest to them. Learners need to understand the goal of each strategy and the conditions under which it works well; they need to gain the knowledge which is needed to use the strategy, and they need enough practice to feel comfortable and proficient in it. This all takes time, but it is repaid by the continuing gains that the learners get from being able to use the strategy well.

It has been argued at several points in this book (see p. 20) that strategies are particularly useful for dealing with the low-frequency words of the language. There are so many low-frequency words that teachers cannot possibly teach them all. Learners need to keep learning them however, and strategies provide the essential means of doing this. No matter how much a learner knows, there will still be words that are unknown and strategy use provides a way of coping with these unknown words.

Teachers need to understand and rehearse the arguments for giving time to strategy training. This is because they need to convince learners of the value of working on strategies and they may need to convince other teachers.

There are many options to choose from when designing a mini-syllabus for strategy development. The following list includes most of the options. Teachers need to choose from these and sequence them in a suitable way.

- The teacher models the strategy for the learners.
- The steps in the strategy are practised separately.
- Learners apply the strategy in pairs supporting each other.
- Learners report back on the application of the steps in the strategy.
- Learners report on their difficulties and successes in using the strategy outside class time.
- Teachers systematically test learners on strategy use and give them feedback.
- Learners consult the teacher on their use of the strategy, seeking advice where necessary.

Porte (1988) suggests that learners should be encouraged to examine the effectiveness of their vocabulary coping strategies. This can be done by working through activities like guessing from context to see what learners do and what options are available.

Learners' use of strategies

Studies of strategy use can observe learners in several ways.

Studies can gather information about what learners say they usually do. Such information is usually gathered through written question-naires or oral interviews. Written questionnaires are easy to adminis-ter to large groups of people but the data gathered is retrospective and may be not a true reflection of what actually happens when a learner tackles a word.

Studies can gather information about what learners are able to do. This information is usually gathered by getting learners to perform learning tasks, perhaps getting them to speak aloud while doing them, and observing them closely while they do the task. The learners are aware that they are being observed and may be aware of what the observer is investigating. Such data gathering is time consuming and observation can influence the learners' performance, encouraging them to do things they do not normally do.

Studies can gather information about what learners say they did. Such information is gathered by getting learners to perform a task under normal conditions, and then when they have finished they are asked to think back and describe what they did and what they were thinking about. This recall could be cued by a videotape of the task performance. It is time consuming to gather such data although written recall could be used. Again, the retrospection might not be a true reflection of what actually happened.

Studies can gather information about what learners actually do. This information has to be gathered while the learners are unaware of being observed or unaware of the goal of the observation. The diffi-culty with such data gathering is that it can only look for external signs of what is happening and thus may require high degrees of interpreta-tion by the observer.

These four ways of data gathering differ in reliability, validity and practicality, with the more practical and reliable ways tending to be less valid in gaining information about normal behaviour.

Ahmed (1989) used observation of learners doing think aloud tasks and a structured interview to gather data on Sudanese learners' vocab-ulary learning strategies. The learners were divided into good learners and underachieving learners as determined by school officials on the basis of school records and subjective assessment. Cluster analysis was then done on the data to see how these two groups of learners per-formed. The clusterings clearly distinguished good and underachiev-ing learners and also showed different patterns of strategy use at different levels of the school system. The good learners saw other learners as a resource for vocabulary knowledge. One cluster, predominantly of good learners, made full use of monolingual dictionaries, using them as a source of many kinds of information. Another high achieving cluster made good use of bilingual dictionaries. Generally, the underachieving learners used a smaller range of strategies than the good learners and tended to avoid active practice.

Gu and Johnson (1996) used a questionnaire to investigate advanced learners' use of English vocabulary learning strategies. They then correlated this information with the learners' scores on tests of vocabulary size and general English proficiency to see the statistical relationships between reported strategy use and these measures. Gu and Johnson used their data in two ways: (1) to see what strategies correlated well with previous learning, and (2) to see what clusters of strategies different learners used and what types of learners they were.

There were small but significant positive correlations between vocabulary size and self-initiation strategies (.35) (seeking out personally relevant and interesting vocabulary), activation strategies (.31) (deliberately using the vocabulary that had been studied), selective attention (.24) (knowing which words to give attention to), dictionary look-up strategies (.24), semantic encoding (.24) (creating semantic associations and networks), extended dictionary strategies (.23) (looking at examples of use in the dictionary), and meaning oriented notetaking strategies (.23) (writing down meanings and synonyms). Visual repetition (memorising spelling and writing the word repeatedly) correlated negatively ($-.2$) with vocabulary size.

Generally, memorisation and attention to form strategies did not correlate positively or well with vocabulary size and proficiency. Vocabulary size and general English proficiency correlated reasonably highly with each other (.53) and many of the same factors that correlated significantly with vocabulary size also correlated with proficiency at roughly the same order of magnitude. Overall students' beliefs about vocabulary and their strategies explained only about 20% of the variance in either vocabulary size or English proficiency (Gu and Johnson, 1996: 660).

Gu and Johnson distinguished five different types of learners by looking at the clustering of the various beliefs and strategies they examined. The types are listed in order of their scores on the proficiency and vocabulary size measures.

1. Readers. These were the best students and a very small group. They believed in learning through natural exposure, as in reading, and careful study, but not memorisation. They sought words that *they* considered to be useful and dealt with words in context.

2. Active strategy users. These were the next best students in terms of vocabulary size and proficiency. They were hard working and highly motivated. They used a variety of strategies to learn the words they considered important. These included natural exposure, memorisation, dictionary use, guessing, etc. They generally used strategies more than other learners.

These first two groups (readers and active strategy users) accounted for less than 11% of the learners in the study.

3. Non-encoders.
4. Encoders.

These two groups were very similar to each other in that they made average use of the various strategies. The only difference between them was that the encoders used more deliberate memorisation strategies like association, imagery, visualising the form of a word and breaking the word into parts. These two groups accounted for 87% of the learners.

5. Passive strategy users. This group accounted for less than 2% of the learners and was the least successful. They strongly believed in memorisation but were well below other learners in their use of strategies. They were the reverse image of the active strategy users.

Some caution needs to be shown in interpreting the Gu and Johnson study. Firstly, it is based on self-report questionnaire data. What learners say they do does not always represent what they actually do. Secondly, there is no way in the study of determining how well learners used the strategies they said they used. There is plenty of evidence from other research that learners use strategies like guessing from context, memorisation and the keyword technique badly; learners usually need considerable training in the keyword technique before they can use it comfortably and well. Thirdly, the data gained depends on the selection, classification, grouping and labelling of the various sub-strategies. Gu and Johnson (*ibid.*: 673–679) list all the questions they used and these should be looked at when examining the results. Some of Gu and Johnson's questions grouped under the same heading may draw on opposing rather than complementary features and have not been given a reversed value. For example in the section on 'Guessing strategies: using background knowledge/wider context', use of topic knowledge is listed with lexical familiarisation and wider context. Haastrup (1989) suggests that using topic knowledge may result in good guessing but little vocabulary learning, while using language cues (like lexical familiarisation and wider context) will help vocabulary learning. Similarly, using lists and cards are grouped together, although they may draw on different kinds of memory process. Fourthly, the questionnaire was very long – 108 items plus personal data – and a fatigue factor may have accounted for 87% of the learners clustering around the average scores. However, this is a substantial and comprehensive study with important messages for teachers and learners.

- Some of the strongest correlations in the study involved learners making decisions about what vocabulary was important for them. Relating learning to personal needs and goals is at the centre of taking responsibility for learning.
- Memorisation is only useful if it is one of a wide range of actively used strategies. It should not be the major means of learning. This fits well with the viewpoint taken in this book that vocabulary learning should be balanced across the four strands of learning from meaning-focused input, direct learning, learning from output and fluency development. Memorisation is one part of the direct learning strand.
- There is a very wide range of strategy options to draw on, and learners draw on these with varied success and skill. Learners could benefit from being made aware of these strategies, how to use them well, and how to choose between them.

Lawson and Hogben (1996) got learners to think aloud while they learned twelve new words in another language. Thus, this investigation looked at what learners can do, rather than at what they say they do. Lawson and Hogben also measured how well each word was learned, and correlated strategy use with recall of the word's meaning. Their findings are largely supported by other strategy studies.

1. Learners who recalled more words used a greater range of strategies and used strategies more often than learners who recalled fewer words. This seems to be a robust finding of strategy studies.
2. In general, elaboration strategies are more effective than repetition and word feature analysis strategies.
3. Repetition strategies were the most frequently used strategies. Simple rehearsal was effective but other repetition strategies were not.

Lawson and Hogben's (1996) study not only gathered data about what learners could do, but also to a degree gathered data on how well the strategies were applied. Only three of the fifteen students used a special mnemonic strategy.

Schmitt compared Japanese learners' strategy use at four different age levels. He found that there was a trend away from form-based memorisation towards more meaning-based processing from the lower age groups to the higher.

Schmitt used a questionnaire to survey learners' reported strategy use and how useful they rated each strategy. The ratings for helpfulness almost always were higher than the amount of use, perhaps indicating that learners are aware of the value of an organised approach to vocabulary but do not organise themselves well. The study revealed a strong preference for bilingual dictionaries and a focus on word form to consolidate learning. Some of the consolidation strategies that learners rated highly (written repetition, oral repetition) did not correlate well with proficiency or vocabulary size in Gu and Johnson's (1996) study. This indicates learners could benefit from advice on strategy choice and use.

Sanaoui (1995) conducted a series of intensive longitudinal case studies investigating the approaches to vocabulary learning taken by learners of French as a second language.

Sanaoui saw her subjects fitting into two major categories: those who used a structured approach to their learning and those who used an unstructured approach. Some learners planned and organised the way they approached vocabulary learning; they took control of the learning rather than relying on what the language course provided. They used their own initiative in regularly creating opportunities for vocabulary learning by listening to the radio, watching videotapes, speaking with friends, making tapes for use while jogging or driving, reading and doing self-study. They kept systematic records of their vocabulary learning by using notebooks and lists. They reviewed what they had done several times a week and took their notebooks with them for review during spare moments. They deliberately sought out opportunities to use the items they had learned.

The learners who followed an unstructured approach relied mainly on the course material. If they made lists, they did not review them and occasionally lost them. Their attention to vocabulary outside class tended to be opportunistic rather than planned. It seems that learners who organised their vocabulary learning made better progress than those who did not.

Similarly, Moir (1996) examined the vocabulary learning behaviours of ten adult learners of English who were all committed, conscientious, hard-working learners of English who spent several hours a week outside class working on vocabulary. Moir found that only one showed a high level of responsibility for his learning and an awareness of what was involved in learning vocabulary. The less effective learners:

- spent more time on vocabulary learning outside class than the effective learner
- selected the words to learn from class texts rather than from a range of sources of interest and value to them
- selected words simply because they were unknown rather than considering frequency, area of specialisation (academic or non-academic vocabulary), personal goals or previous meetings with the words
- were aware that the words they selected were of limited use to them
- focused on the meaning of the words in copied sentences rather than also exploring the range of collocations and uses, and creating their own sentences
- used rote learning rather than strategies they were taught (the keyword strategy, word cards and trying to use the words in conversation)
- limited their learning to the short-term goals of the weekly test rather than focusing on their long-term goals
- did not revise the words any more after the weekly test
- knew that they were not learning efficiently but did not alter their selection of words or learning procedures
- did not feel very satisfied with their vocabulary learning
- did not retain many of the words they studied

Moir saw the causes of the poor approaches to vocabulary learning as: a poor awareness of what is involved in learning a language; limited control of language learning strategies; trying to meet the perceived expectations of the teacher; the influence of the weekly tests; the carry-over of perceptions, expectations and strategies from previous learning experience. Moir concluded that learners need a strong meta-cognitive understanding of the nature and purpose of the learning task, an awareness of a range of appropriate strategies and a clear understanding of their own needs. It is also clear that teachers and tests play a critical role in directly and indirectly shaping approaches to learning.

In general, the strategy studies show that there is value in being able to use a wide range of strategies and that many learners are restricted to too narrow a range. Strategy training seems to have a very useful role to play in second language vocabulary development.

Procedures that integrate strategies

Several writers (Kramsch, 1979; Mhone, 1988; McComish, 1990) describe procedures for getting learners to select their own vocabulary for learning, record it, learn it, share it with others, and be monitored and assessed on their learning. These procedures also relate to the use of vocabulary notebooks (Schmitt and Schmitt, 1995) in that they aim at learners taking responsibility for their own learning and developing the necessary skills to do this.

Let us look closely at Kramsch's (1979) procedure and consider and expand on the options available at each point.

1. *Selecting the words.* The learners are told that they need to learn five words a day – three chosen by them and two chosen by the teacher. Kramsch suggests that the learners look for vocabulary that they can readily use in talking or writing, and words that are easily adaptable to any context. The learners need to develop a feeling for which words are low-frequency and which are more useful. Now learners can more readily gain information about which words are particularly useful by consulting the frequency markings in the later editions of the *COBUILD Dictionary* or the Longman *Dictionary of Contemporary English*, or by consulting word lists such as West (1953) or Hindmarsh (1980). Kramsch points out that sometimes a word is chosen for aesthetic reasons: because it sounds nice, because it represents an unusual concept or because it has personal associations. McKenzie (1990) and Carroll and Mordaunt (1991) suggest that learners should choose words that are 'semi-familiar' to them, that is, words that are partly known and that they can imagine themselves using in the future. This is largely to help receptive vocabulary become productive.

   Robinson (1989) argues that more attention should be given to getting learners to use the high-frequency, non-context dependent vocabulary that can be used to paraphrase and define. This allows learners to cope with breakdowns in communication and to more effectively engage in the negotiation of meaning.

2. *Recording the words and monitoring the recording.* Kramsch (1979) suggests writing the words on index cards along with a synonym, antonym or translation and an example sentence. The way the word is recorded will have a strong effect on how it is learned. The teacher can check the cards to ensure that the words are useful and that the information recorded (such as the context sentence) is correct. Carroll and Mordaunt (1991) also suggest noting definitions, etymology, the sentence the word occurred in, a sentence created by the student, and synonyms and antonyms. Schmitt and Schmitt (1995) suggest elaborating the information

over a period of time by listing derivatives, collocates, mnemonic cues and stylistic information. McComish's (1990) word spider is a way of helping learners remember the various types of information to look for, and largely corresponds to the various aspects of what is involved in knowing a word.

3. *Learning the words.* If words are recorded on small cards with the word on one side and its translation on the back, then learners can be instructed in the best ways to apply rote learning procedures. Similarly, generative procedures like the keyword technique and mental elaboration through self-created contexts, cause–effect chains (Sokmen, 1992) and situational links can be used. Learners need to be aware of the ways they can enhance learning and the principles which lie behind the techniques.

4. *Sharing with others.* Learners should regularly present a word or a few words to others by writing it on the board, defining it and saying where they met it, why it's worth learning and how they remembered it, and giving some example sentences containing it. Learners get a boost when they find that others add the word to their own store of items to learn. The class can question the presenter about the word and make suggestions for learning. This is also a useful opportunity for the teacher to provide comments. These presentations could only deal with a very small number of words but they can be very useful in reinforcing what can be known about a word and how it can be learned, and in developing an enthusiasm for vocabulary.

5. *Assessing and monitoring learning.* Kramsch (1979) suggests the following procedure for testing learning: the learners work in pairs or small groups and exchange sets of cards; each learner is tested on five words by his or her partner; the learner has to define the tested word and give a sample sentence containing it; points are awarded. This testing provides another opportunity for sharing words. An alternative approach is for learners to supply the teacher with a list of say, 20 words each week. The teacher makes a brief note next to ten of the words. If the teacher writes *der.* after a word, the learner has to write three derived forms of the word. If the teacher writes *coll.*, the learner has to provide three collocates. If the teacher writes *sent.*, the learner has to write a sentence using the word.

6. *Recycling the vocabulary.* Learners are encouraged to indicate in their writing, by using an asterisk, the words that they have used which were on their cards. They are also encouraged to make conscious and deliberate efforts to use the vocabulary they have

learned. To a very small degree this can be done through classroom games and activities, but primarily it depends on each learner's initiative.

Schmitt and Schmitt's (1995) description of the principles lying behind vocabulary notebooks and the ways in which they can be used is an excellent guide for teachers wishing to develop a strategy programme. Let us now look at the most important of all of the vocabulary learning strategies in detail.

Learning words from context

Incidental learning via guessing from context is the most important of all sources of vocabulary learning. This is particularly true for native speakers learning their first language. It should also be true for second language learners, but many do not experience the conditions that are needed for this kind of learning to occur. A major goal of the rest of this chapter is to look at these conditions and see how they can be established. We will look at how successful learners can be at guessing from context, how much and what kind of learning can occur from this guessing, and the kinds of clues available for guessing. We then look at how learners can be helped to become skilful at guessing from context.

Intentional and incidental learning

Learning vocabulary from context is often seen as something opposed to the direct intentional learning and teaching of vocabulary (Kelly, 1990). This is an unfortunate view and the position taken in this book is that they are complementary activities, each one enhancing the learning that comes from the other. A well-designed language learning programme has an appropriate balance of opportunities to learn from message-focused activities and from direct study of language items, with direct study of language items occupying no more than 25% of the total learning programme.

In this chapter, learning from context is taken to mean the incidental learning of vocabulary from reading or listening to normal language use while the main focus of the learners' attention is on the message of the text. The texts may be short or long. Learning from context thus includes learning from extensive reading, learning from taking part in conversations, and learning from listening to stories, films, television or the radio. Learning from context does not include deliberately learning words and their definitions or translations even if these words are presented in isolated sentence contexts (see, for example, Gipe and Arnold, 1979). This kind of learning is looked at in chapter 8. Context sentences and phrases are valuable aids in intentional, language-focused vocabulary learning, and part of the confusion behind the learning from context/learning from lists argument is to see the difference as relying on the presence or absence of context, rather than the distinction made in this chapter of being between message-focused, incidental learning and language-focused intentional learning. As we shall see, however, this distinction of incidental and intentional is not easy to maintain, particularly if we accept that all learning involves conscious attention.

Hulstijn (2001) argues that the terms 'intentional' (the learners are aware that they will be tested on particular items) and 'incidental' (the learners are not aware of a later test) are not particularly relevant to studies of vocabulary learning. What is more important is the quality of the mental processing that takes place during learning.

Although learning vocabulary from context should be largely incidental learning, a deliberate, intentional focus on developing the skills and strategies needed to carry out such learning is required. Because of the importance of guessing from context, it is worthwhile for both teachers and learners to spend time working on guessing strategies.

What proportion of unknown words can be guessed from context?

To answer this question properly, we need to look at guessing from context which occurs under realistic and favourable conditions. Firstly, we need to look at guessing where learners already know a large proportion of the words in the text. This is necessary for learners to be able to use the clues for guessing the unknown words. It is likely that at least 95% of the running words need to be already familiar to the learners for this to happen (Liu and Nation, 1985). 95% coverage means that there is one unknown word in every 20 running words, or one in every two lines. This is still a heavy load of unknown vocabulary and probably densities like 1 in 50 (98% coverage) are optimal. Studies which use higher densities of unknown words, for example one in every ten running words, have shown little successful guessing, and set up conditions that make successful guessing unlikely (Laufer and Sim, 1985b; Bensoussan and Laufer, 1984). A critical factor in successful guessing is the learners' vocabulary size, because this will affect the density of unknown words in a text. In most studies of second language learners, getting the optimal ratio of unknown to known running words may involve using simplified or adapted texts.

Secondly, the estimates of guessing need to be based on the actual words not known by each learner. This means that the choice of words to be examined needs to take account of actual learner knowledge, and cannot rely on teacher intuition or the unsystematic choice of words from a text. If the choice of words was carried out properly, then more readily generalisable statements about the percentage of text coverage and chances of guessing, or vocabulary size and the chances of guessing could be made. Schatz and Baldwin (1986) argue that most experiments on success in guessing from context are flawed because they use a mixture of high-frequency and low-frequency words most of which are already known to the learners. To truly test the availability of context clues, experimenters would need to focus on unknown words at the appropriate frequency level for the learners being tested. Schatz and Baldwin worked with native speakers aged between 16 and 17. They found no significant difference between learners who had context to help them guess and learners who were tested on words in isolation. Schatz and Baldwin's tests were multiple-choice and asked learners to provide a definition. The forms of the tests and the ways in which they were marked did not give credit for partial knowledge.

Thirdly, learner skill is a critical factor in guessing. Gibbons (1940), Cook, Heim and Watts (1963) and many other studies have found a wide variation in the ability of learners to guess from context. From an optimistic viewpoint, if some learners can guess large numbers of words successfully, then potentially most learners can if they develop the skill. Studies of guessing should thus report performances of the best guessers as well as averages.

Fourthly, learners must be given credit for guesses that are not 100% correct but which make a small but positive contribution to knowledge of the meaning of the word. Learning by guessing from context is a cumulative procedure by which learners gradually develop their knowledge of words. It is likely, at least for some words, that the initial meetings with a word in context simply give rise to a vague knowledge of the form of the word and the awareness that it is unfamiliar and thus should get some attention next time it occurs. Beck, McKeown and McCaslin (1983) in an article subtitled 'All contexts are not created equal' argue that there is a range of helpfulness in natural text contexts for unknown words. They range from misdirective contexts where learners are likely to infer the opposite meaning, through non-directive contexts where no help is given, to general contexts where general aspects of word meaning are inferable, and end with directive contexts which could lead learners to a specific, correct meaning for a word. Beck, McKeown and McCaslin are probably correct in saying not all contexts are equally informative, but by seeing the goal of one meeting as a specific correct meaning, they underestimate what can be learned from context. For instance, here is their example of a misdirective context (the least helpful in the scale) for the word *grudgingly*:

Sandra had won the dance contest and the audience's cheers brought her to the stage for an encore. 'Every step she takes is so perfect and graceful,' Ginny said *grudgingly*, as she watched Sandra dance.

There is useful partial information available from this context. First, there is the form of the word. Second, it has clear affixes and a stem form. Third, it functions as an adverb. Fourth, it can relate to the way people say things. Knowing these bits of information is still a long way from knowing the word, but they are initial, useful steps in the right direction.

Fifth, in discussions of learning from context, it is important to distinguish between guessing from natural contexts and deliberate learning with specially constructed or chosen contexts.

Most studies of guessing from context do not take account of all of these five factors and thus tend to give misleading results.

With these five cautions in mind, let us now look at the results of studies of second language learners' guessing from context. Seibert (1945) found high rates of success (around 70%) in intensive guessing with learners who knew French guessing Spanish words in context. The similarities between these two closely related languages clearly helped the guessing. Bensoussan and Laufer's (1984) learners worked on a difficult text – around 12% of the running words were unknown to the learners. They were able to guess only a small percentage (13%) of the unknown words. Bensoussan and Laufer estimated that clues were not available for around 40% of the words that they considered to be problem words for the learners in the text.

Parry's (1991) longitudinal study of four adult learners guessing from context supports earlier non-native speaker studies in showing reasonable success in guessing from context: a range of 12% to 33% of guesses classified as correct and a range of 51% to 69% of guesses either partly correct or correct. Most words found to be unknown were not particularly subject-matter related but were in the register of formal expository prose. Horst, Cobb and Meara (1998) found gains of around 22% in vocabulary knowledge. Knight (1994) found that second language learners learned words from context while reading, on average 6% of the unknown words on an immediate translation test and 27% on an immediate multiple-choice test (corrected for guessing) were learned while reading. Comparable scores were found on a delayed test two weeks later. The twelve unknown words in each of the tests occurred at a density of approximately one unknown word in twenty running words, meaning that the known words gave approximately 95% coverage of the text.

The findings from the few reasonably well conducted studies of guessing by non-native speakers have not shown large amounts of successful guessing and learning from guessing. This may be partly due to poor design, but it is also the effect of the cumulative nature of such learning involving only small gains per meeting for most words.

'What proportion of unknown words can be guessed from context?' is probably not the right question. It should be 'Is it possible to use context to keep adding small amounts of information about words that are not yet fully known?' The answer to this question is clearly 'Yes'. It is likely that almost every context can do this for almost every word, but this has not yet been investigated experimentally.

How much vocabulary is learned from context?

There are several important factors to keep in mind when trying to answer this question. First, it is important to distinguish working out the meaning of a word from context and remembering the meaning of a word worked out from context. Second, it is important to see learning as involving even small increases in knowledge of a word. Learning from context is a cumulative process where meaning and knowledge of form are gradually enriched and strengthened. Tests of learning from context need to be sensitive to small amounts of learning (Nagy, Herman and Anderson, 1985). Third, it is important to see if the contexts and conditions for learning are typical of normal reading. Nagy, Anderson and Herman (1987) note that several studies use specially created contexts, combine contexts and definitions, or replace known words with nonsense words. These kinds of studies may provide useful information about the nature of learning from context but they cannot be used to estimate how much learning occurs from normal reading.

Studies with young native speakers of English using text which has not been specially modified (Nagy, Herman and Anderson, 1985; Nagy, Anderson and Herman, 1987; Shu, Anderson and Zhang, 1995) have found that there is between a 1 in 10 and 1 in 20 chance of an unfamiliar item being learned to some degree. The range of chance of learning in the experiments depended partly on how soon learning was measured after the reading occurred. Nagy, Herman and Anderson (1985) tested vocabulary learning 15 minutes after the reading and got a 1 in 10 rate. Nagy, Anderson and Herman (1987) tested vocabulary learning six days after the reading and got a 1 in 20 rate. A meta-analysis of 20 studies involving native speakers (Swanborn and de Glopper, 1999) confirmed these findings with students incidentally learning an average of 15% of the unknown words they met while reading. In all of these studies, the unknown words made up 3% or less of the running words. Smaller proportions of unknown words typically resulted in more learning. As we shall see later, quantity of reading (with the opportunity for previously met items to recur within a certain time) may be an important factor in learning from context. Even with rich specially constructed contexts, up to ten repetitions and some preteaching, learning is still low (Jenkins, Stein and Wysocki, 1984).

There are several things that can happen to an item met in context.

- It is guessed correctly to some degree and at least partially learned. This may happen for 5% to 10% of the words.
- It is guessed correctly to some degree but nothing about it is learned. This probably happens to many words.
- It is guessed incorrectly.
- It is ignored, possibly because it is not important for the wanted message in the text.

Studies with second language learners have generally not been as carefully conducted as the studies with native speakers (Saragi, Nation and Meister, 1978; Pitts, White and Krashen, 1989; Day, Omura and Hiramatsu, 1991; Dupuy and Krashen, 1993). However, Horst, Cobb and Meara (1998), in a study using a long text (a graded reader) and two kinds of vocabulary test, found that about one in five of the unknown words were learned to some degree. In terms of actual words, this averaged about five words.

The higher gains in the Horst, Cobb and Meara study are due partly to the effect of the length of the text, but also to the use of a simplified reader where the unknown words do not occur too densely and the conceptual knowledge that learners bring from their first language. Nagy, Anderson and Herman (1987) found that a major factor affecting learning from context was whether the word represented an unfamiliar concept. Shefelbine (1990) similarly found greater difficulty with new concepts. In his study, however, the chances of learning vocabulary from natural contexts were higher than other studies because there was a deliberate focus on guessing vocabulary.

Incidental vocabulary learning from context in all these experiments is small, not only in the likelihood of words being learned but also in the actual number of items learned. This low rate has to be balanced against other considerations:

1. Incidental vocabulary learning is only one of the various kinds of learning that can occur when learners read. Not only can they begin to learn new words and enrich known ones, they can also improve grammatical knowledge, become more familiar with text structure, improve reading skills, learn new information and learn that reading can be an enjoyable activity.
2. Small gains become large gains if learners do large quantities of reading. If learners read thousands or millions of running words per year, then considerable vocabulary learning is possible. Nagy (1997: 75) estimates that if a learner reads a million running words of text a year, and if two per cent of these words were unknown, this would amount to 20,000 unknown words per year. If one in twenty of these were learned, the annual gain would be 1,000 words a year. One million running words is roughly equivalent to three or four undergraduate textbooks (Sutarsyah, Nation and Kennedy, 1994), or ten to twelve novels, or 25 complete *Newsweek* magazines (Kennedy, 1987), or 65 graded readers of various levels (Nation and Wang, 1999).
3. Learning rates can be increased considerably by some deliberate attention to vocabulary (Elley, 1989; Hulstijn, 1992).

There are several conclusions to be drawn from the findings on the rate of vocabulary learning from context. First, it is important that learners do large quantities of interesting reading. Large quantities for second language learners means something like a graded reader of a suitable level every week. Second, second language learners should not rely solely on incidental vocabulary learning from context; there needs to be judicious attention to decontextualised learning to supplement and be supplemented by learning from context. Direct vocabulary learning and incidental learning are complementary activities.

The low amount of learning from normal incidental guessing from context could be a benefit rather than a cause for concern as a single context generally provides an inadequate source of information about a word. It is particularly difficult to distinguish between core aspects of the meaning and those peculiar to the particular context. It may thus be good that learners do not quickly decide on a meaning and remember it well. Van Daalen-Kapteijns and Elshout-Mohr (1981) found that high-ability students remained flexible in the meanings they attached to unfamiliar words so that they were ready to make later revisions if they proved necessary. The small, gradual increments of learning a word from context under normal conditions of incidental learning encourage a flexible approach to finally determining the meaning and make it unlikely that an initial, strong but wrong interpretation will be made and maintained.

It has been argued (Haastrup, 1989: 319–320) that words are likely to be remembered better if there was some difficulty in interpreting them. This hypothesis is based on studies by Cairns, Cowart and Jablon (1981) and Jacoby, Craik and Begg (1979) which suggest that decision-difficulty results in a more distinctive memory trace. Cairns, Cowart and Jablon suggest that items met in highly predictable contexts may be easily processed but have low saliency in memory. This means that if learners read texts that they bring a lot of world knowledge to, they may be able to easily cope with unknown words but retain little memory for these words. That is, guessing will be easy but learning of vocabulary will be poor. If on the other hand learners have to rely heavily on linguistic bottom-up interpretation of the context and have to puzzle over the interpretation, guessing may be more laborious but learning of vocabulary may be greater.

Texts on unfamiliar topics could thus be better sources of learning from context. This is an intriguing hypothesis which has very important implications for teachers and learners, particularly with regard to choice of text and preteaching about the information in the text. So far, no L1 or L2 study has directly investigated this, although Parry's (1991) study provides some support for Haastrup's idea.

Fraser (1999) found more vocabulary was retained from inferring from context when:

- The inferring was followed up by consulting a dictionary (this almost doubled retention). Dictionary use makes an important contribution to vocabulary growth, and learners can benefit from training in dictionary use.
- First language based word identification was used. That is, the learners retrieved an L1 synonym for the unknown word. Finding an L2 synonym was also effective but not as effective for retention as an L1 synonym, and creating a paraphrase for the meaning was the least effective for retention. This supports previous studies showing that a simple expression of word meaning is most effective for learning.
- Learners remembered that they had seen the word before meeting it again but before the second meeting they could not recall its

meaning. This shows that vocabulary learning is best regarded as a cumulative process with subsequent meetings building on previous meetings, even though previous meetings only resulted in very small amounts of learning.

Fraser found a very wide range of individual differences in retention.

What can be learned from context?

A critical factor in guessing from context is what is being learned. At the simplest level, the unknown word may represent a familiar concept and so the new label for that familiar concept is being learned. If the concept is an unfamiliar one, then both the concept and the label need to be learned. There is plenty of experimental evidence to show learners' difficulty with new concepts (Nagy, Anderson and Herman, 1987). Although the word form and its meaning are among the most important things to know about a word, there are many other kinds of information that can be learned from context that are important in the receptive and productive use of the word. These are outlined in chapter 2 and include: the part of speech of the word, its collocates, the things it can refer to and the various forms the word can take. These different kinds of information are all closely related to each other and come together to enrich a learner's knowledge of a word: the range of collocates that a word has helps specify its meaning; the grammatical patterns a word takes are closely related to its collocates; the affixes a word can take may affect its grammatical functions, its meaning and its range of collocates.

Anderson and his colleagues (Anderson and Ortony, 1975; Halff, Ortony and Anderson, 1976; Anderson, Stevens, Shifrin and Osborn, 1978; Anderson and Shifrin, 1980) make the point that in language comprehension readers and listeners use their knowledge of the world and analysis of the linguistic context to create particular instantiations of the words and phrases they comprehend. That is, they think of detailed particular instances guided by the words they read or hear and their knowledge of the world. So, when they see the sentence *The golfer kicked the ball* they think of a particular kind of ball, most likely a golf ball. When they see the sentence *The baby kicked the ball* their instantiation of *ball* will be different. The same applies to their instantiations of *kicked*. Word meanings are context sensitive.

The point of Anderson and his colleagues' investigations into instantiation is that knowing a fixed core of meanings for a word is not sufficient for language use. People have a range of meaning representations for each word which they draw on with the help of context when they comprehend. Instantiation is usually necessary for full comprehension.

One very important value of context in learning vocabulary is that a variety of contexts will evoke a variety of enriching instantiations. Paired-associated learning is not likely to do this. Each paired-associate repetition is likely to strengthen but not enrich.

There is experimental evidence to show that providing a sentence context, or several contexts, as well as a definition, helps word learning. Gipe and Arnold (1979) found contexts and definition to be superior to synonym or short definition, a classification task or using the dictionary. Nist and Olejnik (1995) found that when learners saw the word in context and then looked at a definition, the context helped their performance on a multiple-choice test which required them to choose an appropriate situation to which the word would apply.

An example of *aberration* would be:
a. having a glass of cold milk with freshly baked cookies
b. going to bed every night at exactly the same time
c. a 16-year-old who didn't want her own brand new car
d. an infant who woke up every four hours to eat

Prince (1996) looked at weak and advanced learners learning from context. The learning from context condition involved specially constructed sentences but did not provide an accompanying translation or definition; learners had to use the context to discover the meaning of the word. In the translation condition, learners saw an L1 word and its L2 translation. Learning was tested in two ways: by translation of isolated words and by having to fill a blank in a sentence. The sentences were not those which acted as the context during learning from context. Learning from translations resulted in higher scores than learning from context for both weak and advanced learners and, overall, learners found the translation test easier than the sentence completion test. Those in the advanced group who learned through context however did slightly better in the sentence completion test than in the translation test. Prince interprets this as indicating that this group were better able to transfer their knowledge to new applications. The weak group outperformed the advanced group where no transfer of learning was required, that is, where learning by translation was tested by translation.

When deliberately learning vocabulary where the meaning is already provided by a translation or definition, well chosen contexts can provide information about grammatical features of the word, typical collocates, situations of use and finer aspects of meaning.

What clues does a context provide and how effective are they?

The major motivation for analysing and classifying the various kinds of context clues is to provide a checklist for training learners in the skill of guessing from context. If teachers have a well established list to work from, then they can be systematic and consistent in the way they draw learners' attention to clues and in training them to recognise and use the clues. Furthermore, if the relative frequency and effectiveness of the various clues have been established, then it is possible to design a well graded programme of work covering the range of clues.

Haastrup (1985, 1987 and 1989) used think-aloud introspection and retrospection to study L2 learners' inferencing procedures to see what knowledge sources they used and how they combined knowledge from various sources. Haastrup classified the knowledge sources using Carton's (1971) three categories (which are not mutually exclusive):

- interlingual: cues based on L1, loan words in L1 or knowledge of other languages
- intralingual: cues based on knowledge of English
- contextual: cues based on the text or informants' knowledge of the world

The most careful and systematic attempt to come up with a system of clues for native speakers was carried out by Ames (1966). Ames used texts with every 50th word (provided the word was a content word) replaced by a nonsense word. Native speaking Ph.D. students introspected while they guessed each word. Ames's study has the strengths of systematically sampling content words and using several readers' performance. Its major weakness is that the majority of the words being guessed were already very well known to the students. That is, even though the words were replaced by nonsense words, they represented known concepts in familiar collocations. In spite of this weakness, Ames's study provides a very useful survey of available clues.

Rankin and Overholser (1969) used Ames's (1966) classification system of contextual clues and devised test items to test the effectiveness of each type of clue. They found a wide range of effectiveness of the various clues but a highly consistent rank order of difficulty among grade levels and reading levels. Learners' reading ability was a good predictor of the ability to use each of the types of clue.

Care needs to be taken in using Ames's system as the names for some of the categories, for example 'language experience', and 'tone, setting, mood', do not clearly reflect the types of clues included. Ames provides plenty of examples in his article of the types of context clues.

Table 7.2 lists Ames's categories with the rankings of effectiveness obtained by Rankin and Overholser. There are other ways of classifying context clues. Sternberg and Powell (1983) use eight functional categories which describe the type of information conveyed rather than the devices used to convey the information. Their categories are: temporal, spatial, stative (physical properties), functional, value (worth or desirability), causal/enablement, class membership, and equivalence.

The italicised word in Table 7.2 is the word to be guessed. In Ames's study it was replaced with a nonsense word.

Ames (1966) and Sternberg and Powell (1983) describe clues in the linguistic context of the unknown word. There is a variety of other factors that can affect guessing from context. Artley (1943) includes typographical aids such as the use of italics, quotation marks or bolding; word elements such as the stems and affixes of words; and pictures and diagrams. Artley calls most of the kinds of clues described by Ames 'structural clues'.

In addition to these clues, there are what Jenkins and Dixon (1983) and others call 'mediating variables'. These mediate between the learners and the information in the text, strengthening or weakening the chances of guessing and learning from context. They include the following:

1. Number of occurrences. The more often an unknown word occurs the greater the chance of guessing and learning it (Horst, Cobb and Meara, 1998; Stahl and Fairbanks, 1986).
2. Proximity of recurrence. The closer the repetitions the more likely the clues from each occurrence will be able to be integrated.
3. Variability of contexts. The more different the contexts in which a word recurs the greater the range of clues available.
4. Presence of relevant clues. Some contexts have useful clues, some do not.
5. Proximity of relevant clues. The nearer the clues are to the unknown word, the more likely they are to be used (Carnine, Kameenui and Coyle, 1984).
6. Number of relevant clues. The more clues there are, the easier the guessing.

Table 7.2. *Ames's (1966) categories of context clues with Rankin and Overholser's (1969) rankings of effectiveness in providing correct responses*

Ames's category	Example	Number of items in Ames's study (n = 334)	% correct in Rankin and Overholser
Words in series	sonnets and *plays* of William Shakespeare	31	69
Modifying phrases	*slashed* her repeatedly with a knife	31	62
Familiar expressions	expectation was written all over their *faces*	26	61
Cause and effect	He reads not for fun but to make his conversation less *boring*.	10	59
Association	All the little boys wore short *pants*.	19	59
Referral clues	Sweden 15.3 etc. These *statistics* carry an unpleasant message.	13	55
Synonym clues	it provokes, and she *provokes* controversy	36	52
Definition or description	some looked alive, though no *blood* flowed beneath the skin	22	51
Preposition	He sped along a *freeway*.	20	50
Question and answer	Now, what about *writing* . . . ?	9	43
Comparison or contrast	Will it be a blessing or a *bane*?	37	39
Main idea and detail	I soon found a *practical* use for it. I put orange juice inside it.	17	30
Non-restrictive clauses	24 hours – *hardly* a significant period of time	9	26

7. Explicitness of relevant clues (Carnine, Kameenui and Coyle, 1984). A clearly signalled synonym within context helps learning.
8. Density of unknown words. If many unknown words are close to each other, they will be harder to guess. Horst, Cobb and Meara (1998) found that successful guessing related to second language learners' vocabulary size. This is at least partly because the greater the learners' vocabulary size, the greater the number of known words in the surrounding context.
9. Importance of the unknown word to understanding the text. The more needed a word is, the more likely a learner will put effort into the guessing.
10. Prior knowledge of the topic. Real world knowledge can play a vital part in guessing. Learners who already have a topic-related script or schema can use this to help guessing.
11. Familiarity of the concept. If the concept is already known, guessing is easier (Nagy, Anderson and Herman, 1987). If the concept is strange and unusual, guessing is difficult (Daneman and Green, 1986).
12. Familiarity of the referents. If the ideas in the clues are familiar to the learners, guessing is easier (Jenkins and Dixon, 1983: 251–252).
13. Concrete vs. abstract referents. If the ideas in the clues are not abstract, then guessing is easier.
14. Amount of polysemy (having several related meanings). If the word is not polysemous, then guessing is easier (Saemen, 1970).

Studies of guessing from context have shown that there are high correlations between guessing skills and vocabulary knowledge, reading skill (Herman, Anderson, Pearson and Nagy, 1987), reading comprehension and verbal IQ (Hafner, 1967). This suggests that an alternative to a direct focus on guessing skills would be a more general focus on improving reading skills. This more general focus is also suggested by the diversity of context clues that learners need to be able to draw on. There are so many clues that could be specifically taught and these appear in such a variety of forms that attention to individual clues may be bewildering and demotivating. However, if there are specific aspects to guessing that are not included in general reading proficiency, then a focus on guessing could be an effective way of getting competent readers to gain more vocabulary knowledge from context.

On evidence from the study of cloze tests (Leys, Fielding, Herman and Pearson, 1983; Rye, 1985; Chihara, Oller, Weaver and Chavez-Oller, 1977), it seems that most of the clues for guessing word meanings from context will come in the immediate context, that is within the same sentence as the unknown word. Attempts to show that cloze items are affected by constraints across sentence boundaries have had mixed results (Rye, 1985). At most, it seems that context clues from other sentences are likely to account for much less than 10% of those available. Cziko (1978) suggests that sensitivity to discourse clues develops after sensitivity to syntactic clues in second language learners.

What are the causes of poor guessing?

A major difficulty faced when guessing words from context is the form of the word to be guessed. Laufer and Sim (1985b) and Bensoussan and Laufer (1984) found that second language learners produced many responses based on known words that had some formal resemblance to the unknown word. Sometimes, these incorrect form-based guesses resulted in learners reshaping the grammatical context to fit their incorrect guess.

Laufer and Sim (1985b) looked at errors learners made in trying to interpret a difficult unsimplified text, and described a faulty approach that learners adopted to interpreting the text. In this approach, step one was to interpret the meanings of the words, often relying on formal similarity to known words. Step two involved adding textual and extratextual knowledge. Step three involved imposing a sentence structure on the parts of the text to fit with the lexical clues and knowledge of the word gained from Steps one and two. This approach resulted in considerable misinterpretation of the text. Laufer and Sim argue that guessing from context should not be focused on until learners have a sufficiently large vocabulary to support such guessing.

Saemen (1970), in a study of young native speakers, found that uncommonly known meanings of polysemous words were harder to guess from context when the real word form was used compared with the use of a nonsense word. That is, the known form led learners towards a known but inappropriate meaning. Fraser (1999: 239) suggests that although word form clues can be misleading, it may be impossible to train learners to hold off using such clues because they are accessed in a such a fast, automatic manner.

Wittrock, Marks and Doctorow (1975) found that if young native speakers read a story containing familiar words and then read the same story again but this time with some unfamiliar words replacing some of the familiar words, they learned some of these unfamiliar words. The establishment of the familiar context on the first reading seemed to make it easier to learn the unfamiliar words on the later reading.

An important factor affecting guessing from context is the similarity between the learners' first language and the second language. Palmberg (1988b) found that young Swedish speakers were able to comprehend much of a specially prepared English text even though they knew almost no English. This can be a dangerous strategy however and in general it seems best to let context guide the guess rather than form.

Neuman and Koskinen (1992) looked at the effect of captioned television, television alone, simultaneous listening and reading, and reading alone on the learning of unknown vocabulary from context for ESL learners. They found the captioned television condition to be superior to the other conditions and also evidence of a 'Matthew effect', learners of higher English proficiency learning more words and the lower proficiency learners learning less. Li (1988) compared second language learners' guessing from context in repeated contrived contexts through listening and reading and found greater successful guessing from reading.

Do different learners approach guessing in the same way?

We have looked at variables affecting guessing which are a result of the word itself and the context in which it appears. We have also looked at 'mediating' variables related to the context such as the number of times the word is repeated and distance between the clues and the word to be guessed. There are also variables that relate to the person doing the guessing. There is evidence that there are different ways of approaching the guessing task (van Daalen-Kapteijns and Elshout-Mohr, 1981) and different ability, knowledge and skills that learners bring to the guessing task.

There are several studies that examine second language learners' approaches to guessing from context (Homburg and Spaan, 1982; Walker, 1983; Parry, 1991; McKeown, 1985; Laufer and Sim, 1985b; Bensoussan and Laufer, 1984; Haastrup, 1989; van Parreren and Schouten-van Parreren, 1981; Haynes, 1993; Morrison, 1996; Huckin and Bloch, 1993; Arden-Close, 1993). In general, a good guesser uses a variety of clues, checks various types of clue against each other, does not let the form of the word play too large a part and does not arrive at a guess prematurely. Proficiency in L2 is a major factor in successful guessing.

We need to be careful in interpreting the result of such studies because it is clear that procedures used to investigate the guessing process influence what happens. At the very least, the investigative procedures of introspection and writing down the cues used, substantially increase the amount of time that a reader would normally spend on guessing a word from context. In addition, the investigative procedures transform incidental learning into an intentional, problem-solving activity and often encourage definite guesses instead of allowing incremental learning.

These studies show that there are substantial clues in the context that are available to the sensitive reader but also that not all readers can make good use of these clues.

Van Daalen-Kapteijns and Elshout-Mohr (1981) compared high and low verbal native speakers' performance on a deliberately focused guessing from context task. High and low verbal learners were distinguished by measures that looked at quantity of word knowledge. High verbal learners tended to use an analytic strategy, choosing an initial model of the word meaning and transforming additional information to fill out and refine the initial model. The transforming (reshaping) part of the process was seen as being a critical feature of the analytic process. Low verbal learners also set up an initial model but tended to remember the various additional cues discovered from other contexts with little or no reworking or transformation of the initial model. Any final summing up of a definition then tended to rely on memory for the model and additional clues and required a weighing up of the various bits of information at that point.

Van Daalen-Kapteijns and Elshout-Mohr also found differences between high and low verbal learners in the quality of the form of the definition that they arrived at as a result of guessing. Low verbal learners tended to use a less standard form of definition compared to the succinct classic form of superordinate plus essential defining features. This same difference was also found when the high and low verbal learners were asked to define common words that were well known to them. The study showed that learners may approach guessing in different ways and this may result in qualitatively different outcomes. Although the study does not discuss this, it may be that there is a causative connection between the approach taken to guessing and vocabulary size.

Shefelbine (1990) found that native speakers with higher levels of general vocabulary were able to guess more words than learners with lower levels. This vocabulary size difference was both quantitative (lower vocabulary students knew fewer words) and qualitative (they knew some words less well than the higher vocabulary students). Lower vocabulary size means that: there are more words to guess; there is less comprehensible context to support the guesses and; learners bring less background knowledge to the texts they read.

Daneman and Green (1986) argue that learners' success in guessing from context will vary according to the size of their working memory. Working memory can be measured by getting learners to perform a reading span test. In this test learners are given increasingly longer sets of sentences to read aloud and at the end of each set they try to recall the last word of each sentence in the set. Their reading span is the maximum number of sentences they can read aloud while still being able to recall all of the last words in the sentences.

The size of working memory and success in guessing from context are related because guessing from context involves integrating information from successively met context clues (*ibid.*: 8). If these clues are no longer available in memory then guessing will be poor. As well as finding a significant correlation (.69) between reading span and success at guessing from context, Daneman and Green found a significant correlation (.58) between skill at guessing and vocabulary knowledge. Sternberg and Powell (1983) found a similar correlation and argued that a vocabulary test measures past acquisition from context, while a learning-from-context task measures present acquisition.

Daneman and Green (1986) suggest that the capacity of working memory will vary according to how efficient a learner is in using the specific processes which are needed in the task they are working on. An optimistic view would be that training in these processes would increase the amount of information that could be held in working memory; training in the processes needed for guessing from context could increase the space available in working memory for effective application of this skill.

Arden-Close (1993) examined the guessing from context strategies of second language learners of different proficiency levels by getting learners to write their thoughts while they guessed. He found that even proficient learners were distracted by the form of the unknown words (contamination = contain, spas = space). Arden-Close used three kinds of texts: texts with words underlined, texts with words left out and texts containing nonsense words. In both the underlined and non-sense word texts, the forms of the words tended to distract the learners. In the blank-filling texts, there was a higher success rate, presumably because only context and not word form clues could be used. Learners' guessing was limited by their knowledge of English, but where they could bring background features to bear they could make good use of it and made more successful guesses. The lowest proficiency students often gave the meaning of neighbouring words as the guess for the unknown word. Arden-Close's analysis shows the complexity of the guessing skill and the close relationship it has to general language proficiency and reading proficiency. While training is likely to improve skill at guessing, it is unlikely to adequately compensate for low language proficiency.

How can teachers help learners improve learning from context?

The most important ways in which teachers can help learners improve learning from context are:

1. helping them to find and choose reading and listening material of appropriate difficulty
2. encouraging them to read a lot and helping them gain a lot of comprehensible spoken input
3. improving their reading skills so that they read fluently and with good comprehension
4. providing training in guessing from context

These ways are ranked in order of importance with the most important first. The reason for this ranking is that guessing from context seems to be a sub-skill of reading and seems to draw heavily on other reading skills. Good guessers are good readers (McKeown, 1985). The four ways described above can be more generally described as: matching learner and text, quantity, general skills approach, and a particular skill.

It may be that training in guessing helps vocabulary learning simply because it encourages learners to give deliberate thoughtful attention to vocabulary items.

How can learners be trained to guess from context?

Carnine, Kameenui and Coyle (1984) gave young native speakers training in guessing from context by teaching them a rule, 'When there's a hard word in a sentence, look for other words in the story that tell you more about that word,' and giving practice in applying the rule with corrective feedback. The training involved three sessions, dealing with a total of 33 unknown words. The trained learners outperformed the control group which received no training. The rule was not as important as the practice in bringing about improvement.

Like Haastrup (1989), Morrison (1996) used pairs of learners introspecting with each other, cooperating to work out the meaning of a word from context. Morrison suggests that as well as being a productive research procedure it is also a useful training procedure, as a wide range of clues are covered and the learners in a pair tend to lift each other's performance.

Jenkins, Matlock and Slocum (1989) looked at three different intensities of: (1) training on guessing words from context and (2) learning words from direct teaching with native speakers. With direct teaching, more teaching resulted in substantially stronger knowledge. This finding agreed with earlier studies by Pany and Jenkins (1978) and Pany, Jenkins and Schreck (1982). Training in guessing from context improved up to a point with increased training. The low training group received nine sessions of 10 minutes each with five words in each session. The medium training group had eleven sessions with fifteen words practised each session for around 20 minutes per session. The high training group had twenty sessions with 15 words practised each session. The medium training group performed better on the guessing from context post-tests than the low or high training groups. In general, the scores on deriving meanings were low. Jenkins, Matlock and Slocum explain the low achievement of the high training group by suggesting that they may have become weary of the training. They also calculate that the training almost doubled the medium training group's skill at guessing.

Hafner (1965), in a study of young native speakers, spent a total of six hours and 20 minutes over a month teaching the use of contextual aids. Some small progress was found in vocabulary size but there was no measure of the change in accuracy of guessing.

Buikema and Graves (1993) found positive effects for training teen-aged native speakers in guessing from context. The training involved introducing the learners to the idea of using clues to guess and the value of looking for many clues. Buikema and Graves saw the strengths of the instruction as being: planned, focused, concentrated, explicit, motivating and involving transfer of responsibility.

Fukkink and de Glopper (1998) in a meta-analysis of 21 studies involving native speakers found that training resulted in better guessing, particularly if learners' attention was directed to clues in the context. Kuhn and Stahl (1998), in a review of 14 studies, also found improvement as a result of training.

Learning from context and attention-drawing activities

There is some evidence that a combination of attention-drawing activities such as presenting words to learners before reading (Jenkins, Stein and Wysocki, 1984) and defining words as they occur in context (Elley, 1989) increases the amount of vocabulary learning. Swanborn and de Glopper (1999) in a meta-analysis of 20 studies of learning from context found that the nature of the vocabulary pretest affected the amount of words learned. Laufer and Hill (2000) suggest that having words highlighted in their computerised text probably increased dictionary look-up and therefore learning. Drawing attention to words increases the chance of them being learned but it is important to distinguish between the effects of these kinds of activity on vocabulary learning and on comprehension of the text. Jenkins, Stein and Wysocki (1984), studying young native speakers of English, found no direct effect of preteaching on comprehension, but there was a marked effect on the learning of the words from context.

Attention-drawing can be done in the following ways:

1. Drawing attention to the word
   pretesting
   preteaching
   seeing a list before reading
   highlighting (colour, bold, italics) in the text
   having a list while reading

2. Providing access to the meaning
   glossing
   teacher defining through preteaching
   teacher defining while listening to the text
   hyper-text look-up
   dictionary look-up

3. Motivating attention to the word
   warning of a test
   providing follow-up exercises
   noting contexts while reading (e.g. filling in a notebook)

Several of these methods have been tested in experimental studies, but many have not.

Do glossing and dictionary use help vocabulary learning?

There is now considerable evidence that when learners' attention is drawn towards unfamiliar words and there are clear indications of meaning, vocabulary learning is much greater than when learners read without deliberately focusing on new vocabulary.

Nist and Olejnik (1995) examined the procedure of meeting a word in context and then looking up its meaning in the dictionary. Four different kinds of tests were used to measure the learning of each word. They found that there was no interaction between the meeting in context and the looking up of the word, and that the quality of the dictionary definition determined the quality of learning. Nist and Olejnik argue that dictionaries can be substantial contributors to the process of vocabulary learning. Hulstijn's (1993) study of inferencing and dictionary look-up behaviour found that learners who were good at inferring preferred to confirm their guesses by consulting a dictionary. Learners differed greatly in their skill at inferring. There was a modest correlation (.50) between inferring ability and overall vocabulary size.

Watanabe (1997) compared three forms of vocabulary glossing in texts on second language learners' vocabulary learning. The three forms of glossing were: (1) inserting a brief explanation of the word in the text immediately after the word (Bramki and Williams, 1984, call this 'lexical familiarisation'), (2) glossing the word in the margin '(crib = baby's bed)' and (3) providing two-choice multiple-choice glosses in the margin. Hulstijn (1992) has suggested that multiple-choice glosses supplement contextual information, encourage mental effort by having to choose and avoid incorrect inferences by providing a meaning. Glossing appeared to improve comprehension. The two conditions involving glosses in the margin of the text resulted in higher scores in the immediate and delayed post-tests compared to (a) providing the meaning in the text and (b) having no glosses or meaning provided in the text. Learning from the single gloss treatment was higher than the multiple-choice gloss treatment in all post-tests but not significantly so. The slightly lower scores for multiple-choice may have come from learners making the wrong choice. Glossing almost doubled the learning (17 words) compared to learning from the text with no glosses or lexical familiarisation (10 words).

Mondria and Wit-de Boer (1991) used specially constructed, isolated sentences to investigate second language learners' learning from context. The experiment involved three stages: (1) a guessing stage where the context sentences were shown and learners guessed the translation of the target words, (2) a learning stage where the learner saw the correct translations of the target words and had to learn them, and (3) a testing stage where the learners saw the words in new non-informative contexts and had to translate them. Mondria and Wit-de Boer found no relationship between success at guessing and retention. It is likely that the learning stage overwhelmed the effects of guessing.

Formats for testing or practising guessing

Researchers have used a variety of formats for testing or practising guessing. These range from fixed deletion cloze procedures where the missing item is a blank, to unaltered texts where learners guess words with the real word form present.

There are several factors that need to be considered when deciding on a format for guessing:

The effect of the word form. Several studies (Bensoussan and Laufer, 1984; Laufer and Sim, 1985b) have shown that learners are often influenced by the actual form of the word. If the word resembles a known word, the form may lead them to a wrong guess. If the form contains familiar parts, then these may be used to guide the guess. One of the most difficult things to learn when becoming proficient at guessing is to let the context rather than the form guide the guess. Formats which use a blank remove this distraction. This may be useful at the early stages of developing a guessing strategy but it is important at some stage that learners get practice in suspending form-based guesses while they use the context to guess. When learners' guessing skills are tested, it is useful to see if they have control of this aspect of the strategy. It may also be useful to see if learners can deal with homographs when only one member of a pair of homographs is known and learners meet the unknown member.

Previous knowledge of the word to be guessed. When testing the guessing skill, it is necessary to be sure that learners do not already know the word that is to be guessed. One way of solving this problem is to replace the words to be guessed with nonsense words. This means that any answer is truly a guess. Leaving blanks also achieves this purpose. However, there are several context clues that are available for known words that are not available for unknown words. These clues make guessing easier and not representative of guessing truly unknown words. For example, there are Ames's (1966) clues of familiar expressions (collocations), for example, 'Who spends one evening a week *thacing* the fat with the boys?' Because the collocation is known, the word is easily guessed, but if 'chewing the fat' was not known before, then it would not be guessable.

There are thus two kinds of previous knowledge to consider: the knowledge of the form itself, and the collocational, grammatical knowledge. Using nonsense words deals with the problem of knowledge of the form but it does not deal with the other kinds of knowledge. The validity of Ames's (1966) study is severely compromised by not taking account of this kind of knowledge.

The density of unknown words and the size of the context. An important factor affecting success at guessing is the ratio of known words to unknown words. Liu and Nation (1985) suggest that a ratio of one unknown to 24 known is needed for successful guessing. That is, at least 95% of the words in the text must be familiar to the reader. If the density of unknown words is too great then learners do not have a chance to show their guessing skill.

Guessing can be tested or practised with isolated sentences or with continuous text. As we have seen, it seems that only a small proportion of the clues needed for guessing occur outside the sentence containing the unknown word. It thus may be acceptable for practical reasons to practise or test some guessing in isolated sentences. However, at some stage in a learner's development of the guessing strategy it is important that the few clues from the wider context are given attention.

The types of words to be guessed. Words that represent unfamiliar concepts are more difficult to guess than words that represent known concepts (Nagy, Anderson and Herman, 1987). It is likely, especially for second language learners, that the majority of words to be guessed represent known concepts. However, some, especially technical words, will also require learners to develop new concepts. Second language learners in their later meetings with words in context will also need to see distinctions between the second language word and the nearest first language equivalent. When testing the guessing skill it is thus important to see if learners are able to deal with unfamiliar concepts.

Different parts of speech are not equally represented at the various frequency levels. There tend to be more nouns among lower-frequency words, for example. If a true measure of the learners' guessing skill is needed, it is important that the kinds of words to be guessed represent the kinds of words that a learner with a given vocabulary size would need to guess. A strength of Ames's (1966) study was that he tried to get a representative sample of words to guess by using a cloze procedure. Unfortunately he did not take the vocabulary size of his learners into account and so did not restrict his sample to words outside their level of vocabulary knowledge.

It should be clear from the discussion of these four factors that the validity of a practice or testing format for guessing from context would be enhanced if: the actual word form appeared in the context, the learners did not already know the word, there was a low density of unknown words, the unknown words were in a continuous text and the unknown words were typical of those a learner of that vocabulary size would meet. This is the ideal and for a variety of reasons, many of them related to pedagogical, reliability and practicality issues, other formats have been used. Table 7.3 lists the possibilities.

When practising and testing guessing from context it may be effective to draw on a variety of formats to focus attention on particular aspects of the guessing skill.

Dunmore (1989) reviewed exercise types for practising guessing from context in five course books and found four major exercise types:

Table 7.3. *Features of formats for testing or practising guessing*

---

1. Word form
    a blank space instead of the word
    a nonsense word
    a real word

2. Selection of words and contexts
    real randomly sampled contexts
    real selected contexts
    contrived contexts

3. Size and relationship of contexts
    isolated sentence contexts
    isolated paragraph contexts
    continuous text contexts

- matching a given synonym with a word in the text
- filling a blank with a suitable word
- providing words before reading and then seeing if the learner can use context to find the meanings of the words
- developing awareness of text features that could help guessing

Dunmore is critical of the various exercise types because they tend to test rather than train guessing, and encourage a belief that synonyms are sufficient to express the meanings of unknown words. This last criticism may be a little harsh as finding a first language translation or a second language synonym may be a reasonable first approximation of the meaning of a word.

Steps in the guessing-from-context strategy

There is no one procedure for guessing from context but most procedures draw on the same kinds of clues. Some procedures work towards the guess in an inductive approach. Others work deductively from the guess. A deductive approach is more suited to younger learners who will be less analytical in their approach and to advanced learners who are familiar with the various clues and wish to concentrate on developing fluency in guessing. An inductive approach, such as that described by Clarke and Nation (1980) is useful for making learners aware of the range of clues available and for developing the sub-skills that may be needed to make use of the clues. The aim of all guessing procedures is to help learners become fluent and skilful at guessing from context so that the guessing does not interrupt too much the normal flow of reading.

Let us look first at Clarke and Nation's five-step inductive procedure. Further discussion of it can be found in Nation (1990) and Nation and Coady (1988).

Step 1. Decide on the part of speech of the unknown word.
Step 2. Look at the immediate context of the word, simplifying it grammatically if necessary.
Step 3. Look at the wider context of the word, that is the relationship with adjoining sentences or clauses.
Step 4. Guess.
Step 5. Check the guess.
   Is the guess the same part of speech as the unknown word?
   Substitute the guess for the unknown word. Does it fit comfortably into the context?
   Break the unknown word into parts. Does the meaning of the parts support the guess?
   Look up the word in the dictionary.

This procedure is strongly based on language clues and does not draw on background content knowledge. There are two reasons for this. First, linguistic clues will be present in every context, background clues will not; this procedure aims at being as generalisable as possible. Second, using background knowledge as the main source of information is likely to result in less vocabulary learning than more system-focused sources of information.

The procedure moves from a narrow focus on the word in Step 1 to a broader view in Step 3. Van Parreren and Schouten-van Parreren (1981) suggest that there are various levels of information with the grammar level being lower than the meaning level. This higher, meaning level can only be used if the lower, grammar level does not cause problems. Making a guess involves choosing the appropriate level at which to seek information and moving to another level if this proves to be the wrong one (*ibid.*: 240).

Step 1 in Clarke and Nation's procedure encourages the learner to focus on the unknown word and ensures that the right word is focused on. Note that word-part analysis does *not* occur at this step. Arriving at a correct guess from word-part analysis is less sure than using context clues, and getting learners to delay using word-part clues is the most difficult thing to achieve when developing skills in guessing from context.

Step 2 looks at the immediate context, that is, the clause containing the unknown word. This source of information will contain most of the clues needed to guess most words correctly. Sometimes the immediate context is difficult to interpret because it is in the form of a passive with a missing agent, because the subject and verb are separated by a relative clause or through nominalisation, or pronouns are present which need to be interpreted. Learners can practise clarifying the immediate context by unpacking nominalisations, turning the passive construction into an active one, and by interpreting reference words. There is an exercise called 'What does what?' which gives this practice. Here is an example of the exercise applied to a text. The exercise is very easy to prepare.

The teacher chooses an appropriate text, preferably with line numbers. The teacher then writes the line number and word and the learners have to ask 'What does what?' about the word. In the example below, the 'What does what?' questions have been added to clarify the procedure. Usually the learners will have to make the questions themselves. More information on 'What does what?' can be found in Nation (1979).

We live in a style that most of our grandparents could not even have *imagined*. Medicine has cured diseases that *terrified* them. Most of us live in better and more spacious homes. We eat more, we grow taller, we are even born larger than they were. Our parents are amazed at the matter-of-fact way we handle computers. We casually use *products* – microwave ovens, graphite tennis rackets, digital watches – that did not *exist* in their youth. Economic growth has made us richer than our parents and grandparents. But economic *growth* and technical change, and the wealth they *bestow*, have not *liberated* us from scarcity. Why not? Why, despite our immense wealth, do we still have to face costs? (Parkin, 1990: Chapter 3)

> Who imagines what?
> What terrifies who?
> Who produces what?
> What did not exist?
> What grows?
> What bestows what?
> What liberates who?

Step 3 involves looking at the wider context. A conjunction relationship activity can be used to practise this part of the procedure. In this activity, the learners have to see what joining word can be put between the clause containing the unknown word and the adjoining clauses. Sometimes the relationship will already be marked by a conjunction, adverbial or some other sign of the relationship, but these will still have to be interpreted. Learners can be helped with this by having a list of prototypical conjunction relationship markers as in the left-hand column of Table 7.4. The learners may need to become familiar with the kinds of information that each of these markers provides which is outlined in the right-hand column of the table, and they need to know the range of words that signal these relationships.

See Nation (1979, 1984, 1990: Appendix 6) and Halliday and Hasan (1976) for further information on conjunction relationships.

Learners can practise Step 3 by interpreting the relationship between pairs of sentences in a text. This is usefully done by learners working in pairs or small groups initially. Step 4 is the guess: the moment of truth. When this is done as a class activity, the teacher can award percentage points for the guesses with 100% (or 110%) for a fully correct guess, 90% for a very good guess, 80% for a guess that comes close to the meaning and so on. This is not the last step.

Step 5 involves checking the guess to see if it is on the right track. Comparing the part of speech of the guess with the part of speech decided on at Step 1 makes sure that the learner is focusing on the unknown word. Sometimes incorrect guesses are simply the meaning of an adjoining word. The second way of checking – substitution – makes sure that the context has been considered, because the word will not fit if it has not. The third way of checking involves word part analysis (looked at in detail in chapter 8). This comes at this stage to make sure that the learner does not twist the interpretation of the context on the basis of what the word looks like. Laufer's (1988, 1991) study of synforms shows that this is a very common problem. The learner analyses the word parts and sees if the meaning of the parts relates to the guess. If they do, the learner can feel happy. Looking up the word in a dictionary is the last way of checking. It should be easy to choose the appropriate meaning from the dictionary if several meanings are listed there, because the guess will have given a good indication of which one to choose.

The deductive procedure (see, for example, Bruton and Samuda, 1981) involves the following steps:

Step 1. Guess the meaning of the word.
Step 2. Justify the guess using a variety of clues.
Step 3. Readjust the guess if necessary.

The advantage of this procedure is that it places the guess at the forefront of the activity and allows intuition to play a part. It also works well as a group and class activity.

Whichever approach learners tend to favour, they need not follow a rigid procedure when guessing but they should be aware of the range of possible clues and should have the skills to draw on them.

Table 7.4. *Conjunction relationships and their meaning*

Prototypical marker	Other markers	The meaning of the relationship between the clauses
and	furthermore, also, in addition, similarly . . .	The clauses joined together are in a list and share similar information.
but	however, although, nevertheless, yet . . .	The clauses are in contrast to each other. One may be negative and the other positive. They may contain opposing information.
then	next, after, before, when, first . . .	The clauses are steps in a sequence of events. They might not be in the order in which they happened.
because	thus, so, since, as a result, so that, in order to, if . . .	One clause is the cause and the other is the effect.
for example	e.g., such as, for instance . . .	The following clause is an example of the preceding more general statement, or the following clauses describe the general statement in more detail.
or	nor, alternatively . . .	The clauses are choices and they will share similar information.
in other words	that is (to say), namely . . .	The following clause has the same meaning as the preceding clause.
in short	to sum up, in a word . . .	The following clause summarises what has gone before.
instead	rather than, on the contrary	The following clause excludes what has just been said. That is, it has the opposite meaning.

Training learners in the strategy of guessing from context

Guessing from context is a complex activity drawing on a range of skills and types of knowledge. It is worth bearing in mind that it is a subskill of reading and listening and depends heavily on learners' ability to read and listen with a good level of proficiency. Learning a complex guessing strategy will not adequately compensate for poor reading or listening skills and low proficiency. Developing these reading and listening skills is the first priority.

When learners are given training in guessing from context, they should work with texts where at least 95% of the running words are familiar to them. This will allow them to have access to the clues that are there. In addition, the words chosen should be guessable. Not all words have enough clues: adjectives are usually difficult because they enter into few relationships with other words; nouns and verbs are usually easier.

Training in guessing should be given plenty of time. In a pre-university course, it could be practised three or four times a week for about ten minutes each, for at least six weeks, preferably longer. The aim of the practice is to get learners guessing quickly without having to go deliberately through all the steps. Fraser (1999) found that making learners familiar with the strategies of ignore, consult (a dictionary), and infer, using about eight hours of instruction, resulted in a decrease in the amount of ignoring and an increase in the amount of inferring. The success rates were over 70% for consulting a dictionary and inferring from context, if partially correct inferences were included. A further eight hours of instruction on linguistic context clues may have helped maintain the success rate of inferring especially for inferring where learners created a paraphrase for the meaning of the unknown word.

Involving the class working together with the teacher, in groups, pairs and then individually, training can focus on the subskills: determining part of speech, doing 'What does what?', interpreting conjunction relationships and doing word-part analysis. Training should also involve going through all the steps, gradually getting faster and faster. The teacher can model the procedure first, gradually handing over control to the learners. Learners can report on guessing in their outside reading and listening and others can comment on their attempts. There can be regular guessing-from-context tests using isolated sentences and connected texts. Learner improvement on these tests can be recorded as a means of increasing motivation.

Teachers should be able to justify the time and effort spent on guessing strategy to themselves, their learners and other teachers. These justifications could include:

- the value of the strategy for both high-frequency and low-frequency words
- the strategy accounts for most vocabulary learning by native speakers
- the enormous number of words that can be dealt with and perhaps learned through this strategy
- the effectiveness of the strategy
- the benefits of the strategy in contributing to reading and listening comprehension
- the fact that learners differ widely in their control of this skill, and training can narrow these differences
- the need for this skill in dictionary use

Teachers should also be able to look critically at the various activities suggested for improving guessing (Honeyfield, 1977; Dunmore, 1989).

In any list of vocabulary learning strategies, guessing from context would have to come at the top of the list. Although it has the disadvantages of being a form of incidental learning (and therefore being less certain) and of not always being successful (because of lack of clues), it is still the most important way that language users can increase their vocabulary. It deserves teaching time and learning time. A well planned vocabulary development programme gives spaced, repeated attention to this most important strategy.

8 Word study strategies

This chapter looks at the word study strategies of using word parts, dictionaries and word cards. These are all intentional approaches to vocabulary learning and fit within the strand of language focused learning.

Word parts

Most of the content words of English can change their form by adding prefixes or suffixes. These affixes are typically divided into two types: inflectional and derivational. The inflectional affixes in English are all suffixes. They include -s (plural), -ed, -ing, -s (3rd person singular), -s (possessive), -er (comparative), -est (superlative). Unlike most derivational suffixes, inflections do not change the part of speech of the word or word group they are attached to and are added after a derivational suffix, if the word has one.

Derivational affixes in English include prefixes and suffixes. Most of the derivational suffixes and a few prefixes change the part of speech of the word they are added to (happy (adjective) / happ*iness* (noun); able (adjective) / *en*able (verb)). Some of the affixes, especially prefixes, also alter the meaning of the word in a substantial way (judge/*pre*-judge; happy/*un*happy; care/care*less*). Words which contain affixes are sometimes called complex words.

Researchers on the vocabulary growth of native speakers of English usually distinguish three main ways in which a learner's vocabulary increases: through being taught or deliberately learning new words, through learning new words by meeting them in context, and through recognising and building new words by gaining control of prefixes, suffixes and other word building devices. In this chapter we look at the extent to which word building affects vocabulary size, the psychological reality of the relationship between inflected and derived words and their stem form, and the teaching and learning options for gaining control of English word building processes.

A knowledge of affixes and roots has two values for a learner of English: it can be used to help the learning of unfamiliar words by relating these words to known words or to known prefixes and suffixes, and it can be used as a way of checking whether an unfamiliar word has been successfully guessed from context.

Is it worthwhile learning word parts?

One way to answer this question is to approach it in the same way we approached the learning of vocabulary, that is, from the point of view of cost/benefit analysis. Is the effort of learning word parts repaid by the opportunity to meet and make use of these parts?

There are numerous studies of English affixes. Some have attempted to calculate the proportion of English words originating from Latin, Greek, Anglo-Saxon, Celtic and other sources (Grinstead, 1924; Roberts, 1965; Bird, 1987 and 1990). Their studies relate to affixation because a large proportion of the words coming from Latin or Greek make use of affixes. Other studies (Nagy and Anderson, 1984; White, Power and White, 1989) look at the proportion of words with affixes in a particular corpus. Other studies (Thorndike, 1941; Stauffer, 1942; Bock, 1948; Harwood and Wright, 1956; Becker, Dixon and Anderson-Inman, 1980; Bauer and Nation, 1993) give the frequency of particular affixes within a corpus. They all confirm the frequent, widespread occurrence of derivational affixes. White, Power and White's (1989) study of the four prefixes *un-*, *re-*, *in-*, *dis-* found that approximately 60% of words with those prefixes could be understood from knowing the commonest meaning of the base word. Allowing for help from context and knowledge of the less common meanings of the prefixes, approximately 80% of prefixed words could be understood.

Studies of the sources of English vocabulary

Bird (1987 and 1990) after a careful and detailed analysis of the 7,476 word type entries in the ranked vocabulary list of items with a frequency of ten per million and above in the *LOB* corpus, (Johansson and Hofland, 1989) concluded that 97% of these words were derived from approximately 2,000 roots. He found, as Roberts (1965) did, that the most frequent one thousand words of English contain around 570 words of Germanic origin, but thereafter the Germanic words drop to around 360 per thousand. The words derived from French and Latin make up 36% of the first 1,000 and thereafter about 51% (see Table 8.1).

Some of the word parts that Bird (1987) analysed have a form that

Table 8.1. *Sources of the most frequent 7,476 words of English (from Bird, 1987)*

	1st 100	1st 1,000	2nd 1,000	from then on
Germanic	97%	57%	39%	36%
Italic	3%	36%	51%	51%
Hellenic	0	4%	4%	7%
Others	0	3%	6%	6%

does not change in different words, such as *-ness*. Many of the others require considerable imagination and effort to see a connection, for example, *cap(ut)* = 'head', which occurs in *capital, cap, cape, escape, cattle, chapel, chief, achieve*. Bird's figures roughly parallel the findings of Roberts (1965) and Grinstead (1924), with words of Germanic origin predominating in the first 1,000 and Italic and Hellenic words predominating from the second 1,000 onwards, averaging around 60% of English vocabulary.

Studies of the proportion of affixed words

Nagy and Anderson's (1984) study of the word families in a section of the list based on the *American Heritage* corpus (Carroll, Davies and Richman, 1971) is a classic of its kind. Their goal was to see how many word families the sample, and by extrapolation all printed school English, contained. To find this they classified the formally related words in their sample into word families using a scale of meaning relatedness. In doing the classification, they carefully distinguished the different types of word family members. Table 8.2 presents some of their data for types involving affixes.

Table 8.2 shows that 21.9% (roughly one fifth) of the different types in a written text are inflected and 12.8% (roughly one eighth) have a derivational affix.

Table 8.3 shows how affixation affects the membership of a typical word family.

'Other minor variations' includes alternative spellings and pronunciations, capitalisation, truncations and abbreviations.

Table 8.3 gives figures for the average number of affixed members in a word family. The first column of figures uses an inclusive flexible definition of what can be in a word family, including less transparent derivatives such as *visual/visualize, percent/percentile, fend/fender*. The second column uses a more exclusive definition, allowing only

Table 8.2. *Percentage of inflected and derived types in a corpus of texts*

Suffixation	7.6%
Prefixation	4.0%
Derived proper names	1.2%
Total derived forms	12.8%
Regular inflections	16.9%
Irregular inflections	0.3%
Inflections with proper names	4.7%
Total inflections	21.9%

Table 8.3. *The base and affixed members of a typical word family*

Word type	Inclusive definition	Only closely related items	Examples 1.	2.
Base word	1.00	1.00	think	sure
Regular inflections	1.90	1.16	thinks, thinking	surer, surest
Irregular inflections	0.70	0.20	thought	
Transparent derivatives	2.57	1.57	thinker, unthinking	surely, ensure
Less transparent derivatives	1.65		unthinkable	surety, assure
Other minor variations	1.46	0.89	t'ink	Sure
Total types in a family	7.64	4.66		

very transparently related family members. The figures for each category of word type differ because in the second column the less transparent derivatives are excluded, being considered base words with their own set of family members. Thus the total number of word families is much greater in the second column for the same number of types, and so the average is smaller. For each base form there are on average between 1.5 and 4 derived forms (i.e. excluding inflections) depending on whether the inclusive or more strict definition of a family is used.

The evidence of the origins of English words and analysis of word forms in a corpus show that word parts are a very common and important aspect of English vocabulary.

Studies of the frequency of affixes

Thorndike's (1941) study of 90 English suffixes, like many subsequent studies, made use of his studies of word frequency. For each suffix,

Thorndike indicates how many words it occurs in – in total, and at various word frequency levels. He provides an average analysis score which represents the likelihood that a 16-year-old American child would recognise the affix in a word. Thorndike also provides an average inference score which is the ease of inferring what the word means from knowing that it equals the stem plus the suffix. Thorndike also lists the various meanings of the suffix showing how many suffixed words have that meaning and a word times frequency figure. Thorndike's monograph is a rich source of information about the value of the various suffixes and their particular uses in written English. Thorndike also makes recommendations for the teaching of the individual suffixes.

Bauer and Nation (1993) set up seven levels of affixes based on the criteria: frequency (the number of words in which the affix occurs), regularity (how much the written or spoken form of the stem or affix changes as a result of affixation), productivity (the likelihood of the affix being used to form new words) and predictability (the number and relative frequency of the different meanings of the affix).

Thorndike's study considered not only the number of words with a particular affix but also the frequency of each affixed word. Thorndike did not consider productivity. A comparison of Thorndike's figures with Bauer and Nation's levels shows a high degree of agreement. Bauer and Nation's levels 2 to 6 only include affixed forms where the stem can exist as an independent word (a free form). For example, *pretty* as in *prettyish* is a free form but *-ceipt* as in *receipt* is a bound form, not a free form, because *ceipt* cannot exist as an independent word.

The frequency studies of Stauffer (1942), Bock (1948), Harwood and Wright (1954) and Becker, Dixon and Anderson-Inman (1980) simply consider the frequency of affixes with no consideration of different meanings, predictability, regularity or productivity. They show that a small number of affixes occur very frequently and account for a very high percentage of affix use. Stauffer (1942), for example, found that the 15 most common of the 61 prefixes he studied accounted for 82% of the total number of prefixed words in Thorndike's (1932) *Teacher's Word Book of 20,000 words*.

These studies all show that there is a relatively small group of very useful accessible affixes that learners could be introduced to at appropriate levels of their language development. Table 8.4 contains a recommended list divided into five stages. Stage 1 can be used with low intermediate learners.

The first four stages are based on levels 3 to 6 of Bauer and Nation (1993). Stage 5 is based on Stauffer (1942), Bock (1948) and

Table 8.4. *A sequenced list of derivational affixes for learners of*
English

Stage 1

-able, -er, -ish, -less, -ly, -ness, -th, -y, non-, un- (all with restricted uses)

Stage 2

-al, -ation, -ess, -ful, -ism, -ist, -ity, -ize, -ment, -ous, in- (all with restricted uses)

Stage 3

-age (leakage), -al (arrival), -ally (idiotically), -an (American), -ance
(clearance), -ant (consultant), -ary (revolutionary), -atory (confirmatory),
-dom (kingdom, officialdom), -eer (black marketeer), -en (wooden), -en
(widen), -ence (emergence), -ent (absorbent), -ery (bakery, trickery), -ese
(Japanese, officialese), -esque (picturesque), -ette (usherette, roomette), -hood
(childhood), -i (Israeli), -ian (phonetician, Johnsonian), -ite (Paisleyite; also
chemical meaning), -let (coverlet), -ling (duckling), -ly (leisurely), -most
(topmost), -ory (contradictory), -ship (studentship), -ward (homeward), -ways
(crossways), -wise (endwise, discussion-wise), anti- (anti-inflation), ante-
(anteroom), arch- (archbishop), bi- (biplane), circum- (circumnavigate),
counter- (counter-attack), en- (encage, enslave), ex- (ex-president), fore-
(forename), hyper- (hyperactive), inter- (inter-African, interweave), mid- (mid-
week), mis- (misfit), neo- (neo-colonialism), post- (post-date), pro- (pro-
British), semi- (semi-automatic), sub- (subclassify, subterranean), un- (untie,
unburden)

Stage 4

-able, -ee, -ic, -ify, -ion, -ist, -ition, -ive, -th, -y, pre-, re-

Stage 5

-ar (circular), -ate (compassionate, captivate, electorate), -et (packet, casket),
-some (troublesome), -ure (departure, exposure), ab-, ad-, com-, de-, dis-, ex-
('out'), in- ('in'), ob-, per-, pro- ('in front of'), trans-

Harwood and Wright (1956) who all analysed the Thorndike lists.
Teachers may wish to be selective at the later stages of the table as the
items are a mixture of high-frequency irregular items and low-
frequency items. Thorndike (1941: 59), for example, recommends
that the best way to learn what -some means is to learn the meanings
of twenty or more words made with it. Similarly with -ure, Thorndike
recommends that learners simply spend five minutes looking at a list of
words ending in -ure.

There is no evidence to show that the stages in this list represent the
order in which learners acquire a knowledge of affixes. There is also
no reason to expect that there is an invariant order in which they are
acquired. The list however indicates an order for teaching and learning that will give the best return for learning effort.

Do language users see words as being made of parts?

There has been continuing experimentation on whether native speakers of English and other languages treat words which contain prefixes and suffixes as set units or whether they reconstruct these complex words each time they use them by adding affixes to the stem. That is, do we store and retrieve *government* as a single form, or do we make it out of *govern* plus *-ment* each time we use it? This question is not a simple one because there are many variables that can influence the way language users store and retrieve words, and many ways words can be stored. Marslen-Wilson, Tyler, Waksler and Older (1994) list the important variables which include: the particular language involved, whether spoken or written use is investigated, whether prefixes or suffixes are being considered, whether inflectional or derivational affixes are considered, whether the affix and stem combinations are seman tically transparent (the meaning of the whole equals the sum of the parts) and whether the forms of the parts are easily recognisable in their spoken or written forms.

There are several kinds of evidence that indicate that at least for lower-frequency, regularly formed, semantically transparent suffixed words, and possibly for some other kinds of complex words, they are recomposed each time they are used. Nagy, Anderson, Schommer, Scott and Stallman (1989) investigated whether the speed with which a word is recognised depends on the frequency of the word form alone or whether it depends on the combined frequency of the members of the word family. For example, does the speed at which a learner recognises the word *argue* depend only on the frequency of *argue* or does it depend on the combined frequency of *argue, argues, arguing, argument*, etc.? If the speed of recognition depends on the combined frequency of members of the word family, then this is evidence that morphological relations between words are represented in the lexicon. To make sure that it really was morphological relationships and not simply similar spelling, Nagy *et al.* also checked to see if the recognition of a word like *fee* was influenced by the frequency of words like *feet, feel, feed* which share the same letters but which are not morphologically related. Nagy *et al.* found that both inflected and derivational relationships significantly affected speed of recognition, suggesting that inflected and derived forms are stored under the same entry or are linked to each other in the mental lexicon. This underlines the importance of making learners aware of morphological relationships and of considering words to be members of word families when teaching or testing.

Several researchers point out that there are differences between what etymological, linguistic and synchronic analysis reveal as being word parts, and what language users actually operate with as they construct complex words. A young native speaker of English, who is half-Thai and half-Caucasian, at the age of five told me he was 'half-Buddhess, half-Goddess'. Most native speakers do not realise that the words *rank* and *arrange* are etymologically related. Although *business* is regularly related to *busy*, *organisation* to *organ*, few native speakers would realise the connection.

Interpretation of interview data on vocabulary knowledge in Anglin (1993) suggests that derivational affixes may be implicitly learned. In their descriptions of derived words, six-, eight- and ten-year-old children rarely explicitly described derived words in terms of their root and affix. 'Children more often figure out an inflected or derived word by isolating its corresponding root word, identifying its meaning, and then casting the whole inflected or derived word appropriately into an illustrative sentence' (Anglin, *ibid.*: 145).

In this typical example from Anglin (*ibid.*: 96), I is the interviewer and C is the child.

I. The next word is *unbribable*. What does the word *unbribable* mean?
C. Um . . . people try to bribe you and sometimes like they try to . . . say somebody had like $2,500.00 maybe and someone . . . say their friend who never cared for them or something . . . they would give you flowers and chocolates and they would say, 'I want to be your friend,' and all that, but they're just trying to bribe you. But *unbribable*, they won't do it, they just, you won't fall for it anymore. Like you won't get bribed; you'll be unbribable. You'll say no.
I. OK. Can you tell me anything more about the word *unbribable*?
C. Like I'm probably unbribable because I don't let anybody bribe me or anything to take my toys and money or something away. So I wouldn't let them do it to me. I'd just say like, 'I can't. I'm unbribable.'

There is also plenty of evidence (Nagy, Diakidoy and Anderson, 1993) that native speakers' use and awareness of morphological relationships develops from the very early stages of language use to at least their teenage years. Table 8.5 lists the language factors that affect the likelihood of learners noticing and using word parts.

Let us look at two examples to make Table 8.5 clearer.

1. *-ness* as in *slowness* is an affix that meets many of the criteria in Table 8.5.
   - It appears in many words (*happiness, sadness, tenseness*); there are 307 different word types with this affix in the *LOB Corpus*.
   - It has a high frequency; some of the word types containing *-ness* are very frequent.

Table 8.5. *Factors affecting the ease of perceiving and using word parts (technical terms given in brackets)*

USE	The affix appears in many words.	(frequency)
	The affix appears in frequent words.	
	The affix continues to be used to form new words.	(productivity)
	The affixed word is the same form class as the base.	
	The affix attaches to a base of known form class and produces a word of known form class.	(regularity of function)
MEANING	The meanings of the stem and affix are closely related to the meaning of the complex word.	(semantic transparency)
	The affix has only one meaning or one very common meaning.	(predictability)
	The affix has both a semantic and grammatical meaning.	
FORM	The base is a complete word in its own right.	(a free form)
	This combination of letters only occurs as an affix.	
	The spoken form of the base does not change when the affix is added.	(regularity of the spoken base)
	The spoken form of the affix does not change when the affix is added.	(regularity of the spoken affix)
	The written form of the base does not change when the affix is added.	(regularity of the written base)
	The written form of the affix does not change when the affix is added.	(regularity of the written affix)

Note: Neutral affixes have a high degree of regularity. Non-neutral affixes are less regular.

- *-ness* is still used to make new words, such as *deadness*. It is very productive.
- It is generally but not always added to adjectives to make nouns. It has a high but not perfect regularity of function.
- Words made with *-ness* are semantically transparent. Thorndike (1941) says that 'the quality, state, or condition of being x' accounts for about 95% of its uses and 'x behaviour', as in *brusqueness* and *kindness*, accounts for the rest. It has high predictability. Exceptions are *witness*, *business* and *(Your) Highness*.
- *-ness* does not add more than its syntactic meaning. *-ful* as in *cupful* or *un-* as in *unhappy*, on the other hand, add a clear semantic meaning.
- *-ness* is only added to free forms. If we take *-ness* away, the remaining base is always a word in its own right.
- The word *lioness* has a final *ness* which is not the affix *-ness*. This instance is unlikely to cause confusion.

- *-ness* is very regular in both spoken and written forms and with reference to both affix and base. The spelling rule 'y becomes i' as in *happy – happiness* applies. It is a neutral suffix.

2. In contrast to *-ness*, the suffix *-ee* as in *appointee* and *payee* has less systematic patterning. The *LOB Corpus* has 25 examples. None are of high frequency.

  - It is occasionally used to form new words, so is still productive.
  - *-ee* makes nouns usually from a verb base.
  - *-ee* has several meanings and the most regular pattern 'one who is x-ed' as in *payee* only accounts for a small number of its uses. Unpredictable examples include *bargee, absentee, goatee, bootee, committee*, etc.

Word stems

The stems of complex words may be bound or free forms. Free forms can occur as words with no affixes. Bound forms can only occur with a prefix or a suffix. Advanced learners of English can usefully study small numbers of bound stems. One way of checking whether these stems are worth learning is to try to make substitution tables around them. If the stem can combine with many affixes to make a large number of words, it deserves attention. Here are some examples. In the table for *port* (see Table 8.6), we can make the following words, *export, exportable, exporter, exportation*, and so on. Other useful stems include: *fer (refer, prefer), form (deform, reform), ject (reject, injection), pos (oppose, propose), plic (complicated, applicable), scrib (scribble, subscribe), spect (inspect, spectacles), sta (circumstance, constant)* and *tract (tractor, subtract)*.

If learners have special purposes for learning English, it is worth investigating to see if there are affixes and stems which are important in their areas of specialisation. Students of medicine, botany and zoology, for example, will find that there are affixes and stems like *-itis, haemo-* and *photo-* that can give them access to many technical words in their fields.

The knowledge required to use word parts

To make use of word parts learners need to know several things. For receptive use, they have to be able to recognise that a complex word, such as *unhappiness*, is made up of parts, and that these parts can

Table 8.6. *Word stems and affixes*

═══════════════════════════════════════

1. *-port* – (to carry)

ex-		[0]
im-		-able
trans-		-er
		-ation

[0]		[0]
re-	*port*	-able
sup-		-er

| de- | | [0] |
| | | -ation |

| sup- | | -ive |

[Other useful words with *port*:
important, insupportable]

2. *-struct* – (to build)

con-		[0]
de-		-ion
in-		-ive
ob-		
	struct	
[0]		
re-		-ure

3. *-vers* – (to turn)

a-		
ad-		
con-		
ob-		-e
per-		
re-		

a-		
con-	*vers*	-ive
sub-		-ion

di-		
extra-		
in-		-ion
intro-		
per-		
retro-		

═══════════════════════════════════════

occur in other words, such as ***unpleasant, happily*** and *sadness.* Tyler and Nagy (1989) call this 'relational knowledge'. Learners also need to know what the parts mean. In addition, they have to be able to see how the meanings of the stem and affix combine to make a new but related meaning. In the case of most suffixes this is largely syntactic, but particularly with prefixes, the affix can contribute significantly to the meaning of the complex word. An important extension of this to help learning is for the learners to be able to see how the meaning of the parts relates to the dictionary meaning of a new word. This then allows the parts to act as mnemonic devices for the meaning.

For productive use, the learner needs a more detailed awareness of the formal changes to the stem and the affix that can occur when they are combined to form a complex word. These formal changes can affect the pronunciation: *flirt/flirtation* (stress change), *quantity/quantify, describe/description.* They may also affect the written form: *sacrilege/sacrilegious, legal/illegal.* Some changes in the written form are covered by regular spelling rules. Also for productive use the learner needs to be aware which form class of stem can take certain affixes. For example, *-ly* can be added to adjectives but not to nouns. Tyler and Nagy call this 'distributional knowledge'.

Before looking at activities to develop each of these kinds of knowledge, it is worth considering some general principles. Firstly, it is probably most efficient to begin to deal with word parts after learners have already learned a substantial number of complex words as unanalysed wholes. These can act as familiar items to attach their new knowledge of word parts to. Secondly, it is important to see the development of knowledge of word parts as being a long-term process. Basing it on a 'mini-syllabus' such as the levels described by Bauer and Nation (1993) is a useful way of systematically sequencing the teaching. Thirdly, like all vocabulary learning, there is the danger of interference between items if formally or functionally similar items are focused on at the same time. It is probably wise to deal with one affix at a time as the opportunity arises, rather than having intensive word building sessions where a range of new affixes is introduced. Fourthly, the use of word parts in understanding and producing words is essentially a creative activity. Anglin (1993) and others call it 'morphological problem solving'. Learners should therefore be encouraged to see the regular form and meaning patterns that lie behind the use of many word parts, and to take risks. Fifthly, there are large numbers of stems and affixes but some are much more useful than others. When giving attention to stems and affixes some thought should be given to their frequency, so that the learning and teaching effort is well repaid by many opportunities for use. Finally, it needs to be realised that many complex words are not based on regular, frequent patterns and are best learned as unanalysed wholes. Part of the learners' and teacher's skill is being able to recognise when this is the case.

Monitoring and testing word building skills

There are four aspects of word building knowledge that are worth monitoring by a teacher. Monitoring can be done in a rather informal way through classroom tests, sometimes with the learners contributing items, or it can be done more formally through carefully designed tests that will be used with different classes and by different teachers. The four aspects are listed in order of importance with each accompanied by some testing procedures.

Learners need to be able to recognise word parts in words

1. Learners are given words that they break up:

    unhappiness   *un*/happi/*ness*

    Learners' knowledge of the meaning of the parts can also be tested by asking them to label the affixes.

    not ← *un*/happi/*ness* → noun

    This test is simple to make, a little time-consuming to mark, and requires the learners to have explicit knowledge of the tested items. It is a good classroom test.

2. Learners group words according to their parts. Carroll (1940) developed the following item type for formal testing of learners' skill in recognising parts and identifying their meaning. Carroll's test contained 36 items like the following:

    ☐ 1. ready   ☐ 1. writing
    ☐ 2. read
    ☐ 3. regression   ☐ 2. back, again
    ☐ 4. region
    ☐ 5. repeat   ☐ 3. true
    ☐ 6. return
    ☐ 7. rectangle   ☐ 4. very

    The instructions are as follows:
    In the LEFT-HAND column of each problem there are several words which have some common element of meaning. This common element of meaning is represented by groups of letters in the words. But the group of letters which is found in each word *does not have the same meaning in all*

of them. You are to find all the words in which the group of letters has the *same* meaning. Place a cross (✘) in the box to the left of all the words which have that common element of meaning. In the RIGHT-HAND column of the problems are four words or phrases, *only one* of which is the English equivalent or meaning of the language unit common to the words you have just marked. Place a cross in the box to the left of the correct word or phrase. *(ibid.: 104–105)*

Carroll found correlations higher than .9 between the learners' scores on choosing the correct examples in the left hand column and choosing the right meaning in the right hand columns of the items.

Learners need to be able to recognise what the affixes mean and do

There are two approaches to testing this: one which requires explicit knowledge and one which does not.

1. The learners are given a list of word parts and have to write their meaning or function. For example:

    -*ness*   _____
    -*less*   _____
    re-   _____

    These parts could be presented in words:

    happi*ness*   _____
    care*less*   _____
    *re*consider   _____

    To make the test a little easier and to make marking easier, choices could be provided:
    Copy the appropriate meaning from the answers next to each word.

    Answers: again, makes a noun, down, without, makes a verb

    happi*ness*   _____
    care*less*   _____
    *re*consider   _____

2. Tyler and Nagy (1989) devised the following item type to avoid the need for explicit knowledge:

    You can _____ the effect by turning off the lights.
    (intensify, intensification, intensity, intensive)

    To avoid the effect of previous knowledge of the whole word forms, in one version they used nonsense stems.

    I wish Dr Who would just _____ and get it over with.
    (transumpation, transumpative, transumpate, transumpatic)

In a later study Nagy, Diakidoy and Anderson (1993) developed another item type to avoid the weaknesses they saw in the previous items (that is, the possibility of knowing the whole unanalysed form *intensify*, and the distracting effect of nonsense words ('How can I choose if I don't know what the word means?').

Which sentence uses the word powderise correctly?
    a. First they had to find a powderise rock.
    b. First they had to powderise find the rock.
    c. First they had to find a powderise for the rock.
    d. First they had to find a way to powderise the rock.

Teachers may feel that this item type is undesirable for normal classroom use because of the effort required to prepare such items and the predominance of incorrect examples over correct ones. For Nagy *et al.*'s (1993) controlled experimental study however, it worked well.

Learners need to be aware of the changes of written and spoken form that occur when an affix is added to a word

1. The simplest way to test the written form is to give spelling dictation. That is, the teacher says words like *unhappiness* and the learners write them.

2. The teacher gives the learners a list of stems + affixes which the learners must combine:

happy   +   ness   =   _____

3. For some learners, the explicit testing of a spelling rule may be useful, for example: 'What happens when you add a suffix beginning with a vowel to a word ending in *y*?' 'Change the *y* to *i* and add the suffix.'

Learners need to know which classes of stems can take certain affixes

Tyler and Nagy (1989) tested this aspect of productive word building knowledge by giving learners a list of items consisting of well formed and ill formed items that the learners had to respond to by indicating 'Yes' or 'No'. All the stems were known items.

tameness   _____
repeatise   _____
harshful   _____
flattish   _____
centreless   _____

In the above examples *repeatise* and *harshful* should be responded to with 'No' because *-ise* is not added to verbs, and *-ful* is not added to adjectives.

If Corson's (1985) idea of the lexical bar is correct, learners may be reluctant to use derived forms wherever a simpler form is available. This avoidance could be picked up by researchers by counting the number of derived forms in learners' speech or writing and comparing that with equivalent native speaker use. This is an unresearched area.

The word part strategy

The word part strategy for learning new complex words involves two steps:

1. Break the unknown word into parts. This step requires learners to be able to recognise prefixes and suffixes when they occur in words.
2. Relate the meaning of the word parts to the meaning of the word. This step requires learners to know the meanings of the common word parts. It also requires learners to be able to re-express the dictionary definition of a word to include the meaning of its prefix and, if possible, its stem and suffix.

Here are some examples. The italicised words represent the meaning of the affix. Note how the dictionary definition does not usually give the meaning of the affixes.

Word	Dictionary definition	Reworded definition
unaccountable	does not seem to have any sensible explanation	*not able* to be explained
reshuffle	reorganisation of people or things, esp. jobs	change people or jobs *again*
community	people who live in a particular place or area	people who live *together* in a place
disperse	scatter	go *away* in many different directions
exhaust	drain the energy	make the energy go *out*
incessant	continual	*not* stopping

There are several ways of learning the meanings of prefixes and suffixes and becoming familiar with their forms. Basically, however, learners should deliberately learn the meanings of the most common affixes. The learning procedure can be the same as the deliberate learning of

Table 8.7. *A list of prefixes for a pair learning activity*

Prefix	Meaning	Example word
fore-	before	forename
bi-	two	biplane
en-	forms a verb	engage, enslave
ex-	former	ex-president
mis-	wrongly	misfit
pro-	in favour of	pro-British
semi-	half	semi-automatic
counter-	against	counter-attack
hyper-	above, over	hyperactive
inter-	between, among	inter-African, interweave
arch-	chief	archbishop
mid-	middle	mid-week
neo-	new	neo-colonialism
post-	later, after	post-date
anti-	against	anti-inflation
un-	reversal of action	untie, unburden
sub-	under	subclassify, subterranean

words using word cards as described later in this chapter. The list given in Table 8.5 provides a useful set of learning goals. Time should be provided in class to make sure they are learned and simple tests should be given to monitor and encourage learning.

After some affixes have been learned, there are various game-like activities that can be used to help establish the knowledge. These include 'word-making and word-taking' (Fountain, 1979), Bingo-type games (Bernbrock, 1980) and analysis activities (Nation, 1994: 182–190). Word-making and word-taking involves learners using cards with affixes and stems on them and trying to put them together to make words. Analysis activities involve learners in breaking words into parts, grouping words with similar parts and matching parts and meanings.

Learners can also teach each other prefixes and suffixes in pair work. One learner is the teacher and has a list of words with their prefixes and meanings of the prefixes listed. Table 8.7 is based on level 5 of Bauer and Nation (1993).

The learner folds his paper so he can only see the list of meanings. The 'teacher' says a word, says its prefix and then waits for the learner to find the meaning. The 'teacher' gives the learner three chances at finding the meaning in his list and then gives the answer. The 'teacher' then moves on to the next word. However, just before a new word on the list is presented all the previous ones are tested again. This revision is more important than the initial testing.

Teachers should model the analysis of words and re-expressing word meanings as much as possible. This strategy of re-expressing word meanings is essentially an application of the keyword technique. The affixes or stem act as the keywords and the re-expressing of the meaning represents the combined imaging of the meaning of the keyword and the meaning of the target word.

The justification for spending time helping learners gain control of the word part strategy is that it can help the learning of thousands of English words. The strategy is useful for both high-frequency and low-frequency words, and is especially useful for academic vocabulary.

It takes time to learn the important prefixes and suffixes and to learn to re-express meanings. A well developed vocabulary development programme makes sure that this time is planned and provided.

Some writers (Ilson, 1983; Pierson, 1989) suggest that learners should get information about the derivations of words; what languages they came from to English, and the form and meaning changes that occurred to them when they were adopted as English words. Pierson notes that this information is especially meaningful to Chinese learners as they are aware of the etymology of Chinese written characters and appreciate seeing a similar process of change in English words. An interest in etymology requires learners to have access to a dictionary that provides this information. Unfortunately, learners' dictionaries do not provide simple versions of etymological information. Ilson (1983) suggests that there are four kinds of etymological information: listing origins and cognates, breaking words into their parts, describing the processes by which particular words are formed (*brunch = breakfast + lunch*) and explaining the procedures in the development of particular words. The value of etymology for learners of English is that it is an interesting subject in its own right but, more importantly, it can help make some words more memorable. That is, it can help learning.

The study of cognates and loan words may be useful for some learners, especially where there are significant changes to the form of words after they have been borrowed. Daulton (1998) notes that although Japanese contains a large number of English loan words, the move to a syllabic spelling system has brought about striking formal changes. This means that there is a need for the deliberate pointing out of relationships.

The word building systems of English are very important ways of enabling learners to make the most effective use of the stem forms that they know. It is thus important to check that learners have the knowledge to use these systems and that (where appropriate) they are making use of that knowledge.

We have looked at the importance of prefixes, bases and suffixes for the learning of vocabulary. Using the information we have looked at so far, teachers should be able to: (1) decide which affixes their learners should know, (2) test to see if their learners know them and (3) design a range of activities to help them learn the affixes. Teachers should also be aware of the range of factors which cause difficulty in recognising and using word parts.

Using word parts to help remember new words is a major vocabulary learning strategy. It deserves time and repeated attention because it can involve such a large proportion of English vocabulary. Another important strategy, especially for accessing the meaning of words, is dictionary use, which we will look at now.

Using dictionaries

Dictionaries can be used for a wide range of purposes. Scholfield (1982a, 1997) has consistently distinguished between the different requirements and strategies for dictionaries which are to be used for comprehension (listening and reading) and dictionaries which are to be used for production (speaking and writing). As well as being sources of information, dictionaries can also be aids to learning (Nation, 1989). The following list covers most purposes for dictionary use.

Comprehension (decoding)

- Look up unknown words met while listening, reading or translating.
- Confirm the meanings of partly known words.
- Confirm guesses from context.

Production (encoding)

- Look up unknown words needed to speak, write or translate.
- Look up the spelling, pronunciation, meaning, grammar, constraints on use, collocations, inflections and derived forms of partly known words needed to speak, write or translate.
- Confirm the spelling, pronunciation, meaning, etc. of known words.

- Check that a word exists.
- Find a different word to use instead of a known one.
- Correct an error.

Learning

- Choose unknown words to learn.
- Enrich knowledge of partly known words, including etymology.

In the following sections we will look at these various purposes in more detail.

Is it necessary or worth training learners to use dictionaries?

This section looks at whether learners use dictionaries well, and looks at the value of being able to use a dictionary.

Do learners use dictionaries well?

Studies of second language learners' dictionary use have involved questionnaires (Béjoint, 1981; Tomaszczyk, 1979), analysis of filmed recordings (Ard, 1982), observing dictionary use (Atkins and Varantola, 1997), and filling out flow charts immediately after dictionary use (Harvey and Yuill, 1997).

Harvey and Yuill looked at learners' use of a monolingual dictionary (*Collins COBUILD English Language Dictionary*) while writing. Because a monolingual dictionary alone was used, this study was largely restricted to learners looking up words that they already partly knew, or that they thought might exist in a similar form to their first language. 10.6% of the look-ups however were to find a synonym to replace a known second language word.

Table 8.8 lists the reasons for looking up words and gives the percentage of successful searches.

A notable finding of the study was the number of times that the example sentences were used to get information on meaning, grammar and register. The study also indicated that learners made little use of the grammatical coding scheme in the dictionary. Béjoint (1981) found that learners said that they did not give much attention to the various coding schemes. Generally, for these learners the degree of success in their dictionary use was quite high.

The Atkins and Varantola (1997) study examined users (who were largely very advanced and lexicographically sophisticated users of English) performing a translation task. They had access to both

Table 8.8. *Reasons for and degree of success in looking up words in COBUILD during a writing activity (based on Harvey and Yuill, 1997)*

Reason for searching for the word	% of total look-ups	% success of the search
to check on spelling	24.4%	92.8%
to confirm the meaning	18.3%	87.1%
to see if the word exists	12.8%	77.0%
to find a synonym to use instead of the known word	10.6%	63.9%
to find out about the grammar of the word	10.5%	90.2%
to check on the constraints or register of the word	9.3%	92.1%
to find collocations	8.2%	78.6%
to find a correctly inflected form	5.9%	100.0%

bilingual and monolingual dictionaries. The vast majority of look-ups were to find or check on an L2 translation. Success rates were higher with bilingual dictionaries, and in L2–L1 translation.

Most studies of learners' dictionary use have involved advanced and sophisticated learners; this is partly because a reasonable level of proficiency is needed to use a monolingual dictionary. There is a noted lack of studies on less proficient learners and on the effects of training on dictionary use.

Do dictionaries help learners?

Dictionaries can help learners with understanding and producing text, and with vocabulary learning. Luppescu and Day (1993) looked at the effect of bilingual dictionary use on vocabulary learning while reading. Students using a dictionary gained higher scores on a vocabulary test given immediately after the reading than students who did not use a dictionary. However, some items in the vocabulary test were answered incorrectly by more learners who used a dictionary than those who did not. This seemed to occur for words where there were many alternative meanings given in the dictionaries. This suggests that learners' dictionary searches were not very skilful. It was also noted that learners who used a dictionary took almost twice as long to read the passage as learners who did not use a dictionary.

Some studies of dictionary use have used texts and dictionaries on the computer. This means that each look-up can be electronically recorded (Knight, 1994; Hulstijn, 1993). In a carefully designed experiment with learners of Spanish as a second language, Knight (1994) found that learners who had access to a dictionary learned more words in both immediate and delayed (two weeks later) tests than learners who had no access to a dictionary. Learners with access to the dictionary also gained higher comprehension scores. Access to the dictionary helped the lower verbal ability group most. Their scores with dictionary access were close to the high verbal ability group who also had dictionary access. Without dictionary access, relying only on guessing from context, the difference between the high and low verbal ability groups was greater. The dictionary use groups took longer to do the reading. A study of the amount of dictionary use suggested that high ability learners may have been using the dictionary when they did not need to. Hulstijn (1993) made a similar finding.

Knight (1994) suggests that Bensoussan, Sim and Weiss's (1984) finding that dictionary use had no effect on comprehension may have occurred because the learners in the Bensoussan *et al.* study were all high proficiency learners. Knight found no difference in comprehension scores with or without dictionaries for her high verbal ability group.

Hulstijn (1993) found a very wide range of amount of dictionary consultation between individuals. Learners were generally strategic with the words they looked up, giving most attention to those words that were most relevant to the reading comprehension task that they were set, and ignoring words which were not relevant to the task. Words that could be easily inferred were looked up almost as much as words that were difficult to infer. Learners do not seem to have great faith in their inferring skills.

Generally dictionary use takes time and some learners may spend more time on dictionary use than they need to. This may be a result of the tasks that were used in the experiments and learners' awareness that they were involved in an experiment. Dictionary use helps learning and comprehension, and is particularly useful for learners who do not cope well with guessing from context.

What skills are needed to use a dictionary?

Several researchers (Neubach and Cohen, 1988; Scholfield, 1982b) have noted the complex nature of dictionary use. The skills required differ according to whether the dictionary is used in conjunction with listening and reading (receptive use), or with speaking and writing (productive use). In the following sections these skills are described as steps in strategies for receptive and productive use. See Scholfield (1982b) for a detailed description of a similar strategy.

Receptive use

Receptive use of a dictionary largely involves looking up the meaning of a word that has been met while reading or listening. The following steps make up a strategy that can be the basis for learner training. As each step is described, the skills needed at each step are spelled out, tests of these skills are suggested, and suggestions for training learners in the skills are provided.

1. Get information from the context where the word occurred. The skills needed for this step include: (1) deciding on the part of speech of the word to be looked up, (2) deciding if the word is an inflected or derived form that can be reduced to a base form, (3) guessing the general meaning of the word and (4) deciding if the word is worth looking up by considering its relevance to the task and general usefulness.

Each of these skills can each be tested directly. Training in finding the part of speech can be done by intuitively classifying words in context into part of speech, or by following some rules that guide the classification. To gain skill in breaking words into parts learners can just practise doing so with feedback and guidance, or they can learn the commonest affixes. Clarke and Nation (1980) suggest a way of training learners in guessing from context (see also chapter 7).

2. Find the dictionary entry. Skills needed for this include: (1) knowing the order of the letters of the alphabet (some dictionaries do not follow a strictly alphabetic order), (2) knowing the dictionary symbols for the different parts of speech and (3) knowing alternative places to search, such as separate entries, sub entries, word groups, derived forms, variant spellings and appendixes.

Each of these skills can be tested separately by getting learners to say the alphabet, interpret dictionary symbols and describe different places to search. The combined skills can be tested by doing timed searches. Learners can be prepared for this step by practising saying the alphabet, studying and being taught about the various symbols used in the dictionary with some practice in using them, observing skilled dictionary users searching for a word, and analysing dictionary entries and classifying their parts. The following is a useful split information activity which can be used for gaining familiarity with the types of information that may be found in a dictionary entry.

Each learner has one of the following sentences to memorise. After memorising, each learner returns the piece of paper containing the sentence to the teacher. Then, without any writing, the learners put the sentences in order so that the description of a typical dictionary entry is correct. Here are the sentences.

a. The phonetic variations can then be shown. For example /klever/.
b. Next, the entry gives the part of speech of the word. For example, noun, verb, adjective.
c. The meaning of the word is the next part of the dictionary entry.
d. Frequently the entry shows how the word is used in a sentence. This is to help you use the word more easily.
e. The entry for each word has its parts arranged in a certain order.
f. Then the entry can show variant spellings of the word, e.g. colour/color.
g. Then the entry can have the information as to whether or not the word, if it is a noun is countable or uncountable.
h. This may be accompanied by the year or century in which the word was first used in English.
i. The dictionary entry can have the derivation (what language the word comes from). For example *sahib* IndE and EPak.
j. The phonetic guide to the pronunciation of the word follows. For example /klevə/.
k. The actual spelling of the word is first in the entry.

3. Choose the right sub-entry. Once the correct entry has been found there may be a need to choose between different meanings and uses listed within that entry. In order to make this choice, the information gained in step 1 from the context in which the word occurred will need to be used. This may involve quick scanning of all or most of the sub-entries to make sure that the most appropriate sub-entry is chosen. There are useful tests of this skill which can also be used for practice. In a text, the teacher chooses words that have several different meanings or related meanings. For example, the context may say 'He was scrubbing the *flags* in front of his house.' The learner then has to find the most suitable entry, which in this case is where *flags* stands for *flag-stones*. Learners can get guided practice in choosing between sub-entries through group discussion and systematic elimination of the inappropriate sub-entries. When they guess such words in context, learners can predict whether it is likely to be a common meaning or an uncommon meaning, because this will give some indication of how far in an entry they may need to search.

4. Relate the meaning to the context and decide if it fits. This step involves adapting the meaning found in the dictionary to the context of the word in the text. In many cases this will not be a big change. In a few cases some narrowing or stretching of the meaning may be necessary. Another skill at this step is evaluating the success of the search, that is, does the meaning found fit nicely with the message of the text? There are two ways of testing whether learners have completed this step well. One is to measure comprehension of the text with a focus on the parts containing the unknown words. Another is to get learners to do self-evaluation of their search. Training in this step can involve making use of definitions and the example sentences in the dictionary to interpret words in context. Training can also involve paraphrasing the original contexts with the meaning of the unknown words added.

These steps may seem complicated, but in practice learners should be able to follow them quite successfully. But before getting too far into a strategy training programme, it is important to check that learners do need practice and training, and to check what aspects of the strategy need attention. A technique used by some learners is to mark each entry they look up in the dictionary each time they do so. They will realise they have looked up the same item more than once and this can provide an incentive for deliberate learning of the item.

Productive use

Using a dictionary for productive use is sometimes called using a dictionary for encoding, that is, turning ideas into language. It involves finding word forms to express messages. Bilingual dictionaries which go from the first language to the second language are an efficient way of doing this. Some writers suggest using a combination of bilingual and monolingual dictionaries for this purpose in order to get the best value from both types (Scholfield, 1982a; Stein, 1988).

It is possible to devise a strategy for using a dictionary for productive use. Scholfield (1981) describes a similar strategy for the correction of errors in written work.

1. *Find the wanted word form.* The skills needed to do this include: bilingual dictionary use; using a dictionary like the *Longman Language Activator*; or using synonyms, opposites or related words in a monolingual dictionary. Using a monolingual dictionary requires considerable search skills and requires a reasonable proficiency level in the second language. The following steps assume that if the word is looked up in a bilingual dictionary, there may also be a need to look it up in a monolingual dictionary to gain more detailed information so as to allow productive use of the word.

2. *Check that there are no unwanted constraints on the use of the word.* This step involves the skills of interpreting the dictionary's style labels and codes. These labels include: indications of whether the word is in current use or archaic, whether it is formal or colloquial, whether it is only used in the US or UK, whether it is impolite, etc. Several writers have indicated the inconsistency with which dictionaries signal this information (Hartmann, 1981). Teachers can train

learners in the interpretation of these labels through explanation and practice.

3. *Work out the grammar and collocations of the word.* Some of this information can come from the example sentences in the dictionary. Research indicates that learners are more likely to make use of the example sentences than they are to try to interpret grammatical coding schemes. This indicates that practice and training would be of great value in this particular skill of dictionary use. Generally, the more detailed information given by a coding scheme, the more difficult it is to interpret. However, this grammatical information can be of great use in written and spoken production. Not only is it necessary to be able to interpret the codes (e.g. N COUNT), it is necessary to be able to apply this information. (N COUNT means that a noun can be plural, and a singular form must have *a, the*, or a similar word in front of it.)

4. *Check the spelling or pronunciation of the word before using it.* In most learners' dictionaries the working out of the pronunciation requires reading phonetic script. This is a skill requiring considerable practice.

The two dictionary use strategies just described comprise one of the four major options for learners to deal with unknown vocabulary. They are an essential complement to the other options: inferring from context, using word cards and using word parts. Because dictionary use provides access to so many words and to so much information about them, it deserves a considerable amount of classroom time. Teachers should be willing to spend up to an hour a week over several weeks checking that learners have control of these strategies and training learners in their use.

To put the dictionary use strategies into practice, it is necessary to have access to a good dictionary. The next section looks at what dictionary types are available and how teachers and learners can judge which ones they should own.

What dictionaries are the best?

There are three major kinds of learners' dictionaries in terms of the languages they use: monolingual, bilingual, and bilingualised. Monolingual dictionaries are written all in one language; an English monolingual dictionary has an English headword, an English definition, and all the examples and other information in English. Second language learners using a monolingual dictionary need to be able to interpret definitions and other information in the second language. Here is an example entry from the *Longman Dictionary of*

Contemporary English. W2 indicates that the word is in the second thousand most frequent words in written English.

in.creas.ing.ly /in_kriːsiŋli/ *adv* more and more all the time   W2
[+adj/adv]: *The classes at the college have become increasingly full over the past five years.* [sentence adverb]: *Increasingly, it is the industrial power of Japan and South East Asia that dominates world markets.*

In some monolingual dictionaries for learners of English the definitions are written within a controlled vocabulary of around two thousand words. Other learner dictionaries have a policy of making the definitions simple but not being limited by a fixed defining vocabulary. Learners seem to prefer dictionaries written in a controlled vocabulary (MacFarquhar and Richards, 1983).

Cumming, Cropp and Sussex (1994) compared the effect of phrasal definitions, sentence definitions, phrasal definitions with an example sentence, and sentence definitions with an example sentence. No difference was found on a production measure (write a sentence using the word) and a 'comprehension' measure (which of six sentences using the word are correct). Students indicated a clear preference for having examples with definitions and they favoured the sentence definition format.

In general, monolingual learners' dictionaries contain much more information about each word than bilingual dictionaries do, and some teachers recommend that bilingual dictionaries be used in conjunction with monolingual dictionaries for writing and speaking.

Bilingual dictionaries use two languages. The head word and the examples are in one language and the meaning is in another. Sometimes the example sentences are also provided in two languages. So, a bilingual dictionary for a French learner of English would have the head word in English, a French translation of the word to provide the meaning and example sentences in English with perhaps a French translation of those sentences. Another section of the dictionary might go the other way (for speaking or writing), with the head word in French and then English words that could be used to convey that meaning. Here is an example entry from *Collins German Dictionary* (Terrell, Schnorr, Morris and Breitsprecher, 1991).

Nachprägen *vt sep* (*nachträglich prägen*) to mint *or* strike some more; (*fälschen*) to forge. **es wurden 200 Stück nachgeprägt** a further 200 copies were struck.

Bilingual dictionaries are often criticised. It is said that they encourage the use of translation (thought to be counter-productive in the language classroom), that they encourage the idea that words in the second language are equivalent in meaning to words in the first language (a one-to-one relationship) and that they provide little information on how words are used. These criticisms are misguided and unfair, and they also ignore the advantages of bilingual dictionaries (Thompson, 1987); a more balanced view needs to be taken of the role of translation in the language classroom. As a way of communicating meaning, the first language has several advantages. However, there needs to be care that there are a lot of chances for second language use, and second language use at a fluent level. As Nation (1978b) points out, translation as a way of communicating meaning is in general no better or worse than other ways. It would be just as misleading for a second language learner to believe that words in a second language are equivalent in meaning to their dictionary definitions as to believe that they are equivalent to their first language translation. While many bilingual dictionaries contain little information about each word, they can be seen as a complement, rather than a competitor, to monolingual dictionaries. Moreover, some bilingual dictionaries provide substantial information about each word.

The major advantages of bilingual dictionaries are: (1) they provide meanings in a very accessible way, and (2) they can be bi-directional – English–first language and first language–English. Although most monolingual dictionaries use a controlled vocabulary in their definitions, a learner has to know this vocabulary and has to be able to cope with the grammatical difficulties of the explanation. Numerous research studies (Lado, Baldwin and Lobo, 1967; Laufer and Shmueli, 1997) have shown that vocabulary learning is much more effective using L2–L1 pairs than through L2–L2 definition pairs. There is also plenty of evidence that shows the difficulties native speakers (McKeown, 1993) and non-native speakers (Nesi and Meara, 1994) have in understanding definitions.

Dictionaries can be used for both receptive and productive use. Bilingual dictionaries which go from the first language to the second language provide easy access to vocabulary for productive use. This access is not easily provided in monolingual dictionaries. If bilingual and monolingual dictionaries are used to complement each other for productive purposes, then the best qualities of both can be used.

Bilingualised dictionaries contain the information that is in a monolingual dictionary plus a translation of the head word.

Evaluating dictionaries

Which of these three types – monolingual, bilingual, bilingualised – is the best? Which particular dictionary is the best one to buy? There are several ways of answering these questions. One is to examine and compare the kinds of information that dictionaries provide. A second is to see what learners prefer and actually use. A third is to look at the effects of use of the different types of dictionary on text comprehension, language production and understanding dictionary entries.

The kinds of information in dictionaries

One way of surveying the kinds of information that dictionaries provide is to relate it to what is involved in knowing a word (see chapter 2). Discussion of these various types of information can be found in the numerous reviews of particular dictionaries (for example, Bauer, 1980 and 1981; Hartmann, 1982; Benson, 1995), comparative reviews of dictionaries (Herbst, 1996; Bogaards, 1996; *International Journal of Lexicography* (1989) 2:1) and general discussions of learners' dictionaries (Béjoint, 1981; Tickoo, 1987; Hartmann, 1992).

Table 8.9 relates the various kinds of information in dictionaries to what is involved in knowing a word. The table does not include some types of information which occur in some dictionaries and which can help learners, particularly information about 'false friends' and common errors. Nor does the table deal with the way in which the various bits of information are structured and signalled in dictionaries.

The learner can benefit not only from the type of information in the dictionary but also from the way it is presented. Baxter (1980) argues that using a monolingual dictionary makes learners realise that meaning can be conveyed by a definition as well as by a single word. This provides learners with the basis for a strategy in their spoken English – using a paraphrase based definition to make up for gaps in their productive vocabulary. Bilingual dictionaries on the other hand encourage the idea that a meaning should be expressed through a single appropriate word; they discourage the use of paraphrase.

Laufer (1992a) compared example sentences made by lexicographers with those chosen from a corpus. She found that lexicographers' examples were better for comprehension, and similar to corpus based examples for production. Her study also suggested that understanding corpus based examples required a larger vocabulary size. Laufer (1993) found that examples alone did not provide as much help for comprehension as a definition. A definition plus examples gave greater help than either of these sources alone.

When evaluating dictionaries, considering the kinds of information presented in dictionaries and the ways in which the information is organised and presented, it is important to distinguish the goals of

Table 8.9. *Dictionary information and what is involved in knowing a word*

Form	spoken	R	
		P	pronunciation, alternative pronunciations
	written	R	
		P	spelling, hyphenation (syllabification)
	word parts	R	etymology
		P	inflections, derived forms
Meaning	form and meaning	R	derived forms, etymology, examples
		P	
	concept and	R	meanings, illustrations
	referents	P	examples
	associations	R	examples
		P	synonyms, opposites, superordinates
Use	grammatical	R	
	functions	P	grammatical patterns, examples
	collocations	R	
		P	collocations, examples
	constraints on use	R	
	(register,	P	frequency, register, style, etc. (see
	frequency . . .)		Hartmann, 1981)

Note: In column 3, R = receptive knowledge, P = productive knowledge.

dictionary use: comprehension, production and learning. It is also appropriate at this point to consider a few preliminary practical issues like the following.

- How much can learners afford to pay for a dictionary?
- Is the physical size of the dictionary an important consideration? Do learners have to carry it around? Does it have to be a pocket sized dictionary?
- Are learners of a high enough level of proficiency to be able to understand definitions in a second language? Usually this requires a vocabulary of 2,000 words or more.

Choosing a dictionary for comprehension. Using a dictionary for comprehension or decoding involves using the dictionary to look up the meanings of words which have been met in reading or listening. Such a dictionary should have the features described in Table 8.10. The features are ranked in order of their importance with the most

Table 8.10. *Features and ways of checking the features of a learners' dictionary to be used to look up word meanings*

Features	Tests
1. The dictionary should contain lots of words and word groups.	• See how many words the introduction says it contains. • Count ten pages at random calculating how many words per page there are and multiply by the total number of pages in the dictionary. • Look up words in one of Diack's (1975) tests. • Look up some useful word groups.
2. The meanings should be easy to understand.	• Look in the introduction to see if the dictionary uses a limited defining vocabulary. • Look at entries for ten words to see if the meanings are easy to understand, and to see if first language translations are provided.
3. Derived words and word groups should be easy to find.	• Look to see if derived forms, especially irregularly spelled ones, are listed separately. • Look to see if important idioms are entered under each of their parts.
4. The meanings should be easy to find.	• Look at some entries to see if the most common meanings are listed first. • Look at some entries to see if different parts of speech get separate entries or clear sub-entries.
5. There should be examples and collocations to guide the search and confirm that the appropriate meaning has been found.	• Look at some entries to see how many examples are given. Are the examples easy to understand? • Look at some entries to see if collocations are provided.

important first. This list of features is very short (see, for example, reviews by Bogaards (1996) and Herbst (1996) for very detailed consideration of an extensive range). The list is intended to cover the most important features, to be able to be applied reasonably quickly, and to not require great skill or background knowledge in application. Judgements based on the application of this list could be very usefully supplemented by reading more detailed reviews, especially comparative reviews of any dictionaries under consideration.

Choosing a dictionary for production. Table 8.9 (see p. 292) listed the features that could occur in a dictionary that aims to provide full information on the receptive and productive aspects of knowing a word. Table 8.11 indicates what a teacher or learner should look for when choosing a dictionary aimed at providing information for speaking and writing.

The first criterion, finding a word, may not be satisfied very well by most monolingual dictionaries. The *Longman Language Activator* attempts to provide access to unknown forms solely through the second language although it has been criticised as being a little complex to use (Benson, 1995). However, as most learners would benefit from training in dictionary use, it is reasonable to provide training in the use of more complex dictionaries if they provide the types of advantages that the *Activator* provides.

Learners' preferences

Surveys of learners' preferences and use indicate that bilingual dictionaries are the preferred option for most learners (see Laufer and Kimmel (1997) for a review; Atkins and Varantola, (1997)). Baxter's (1980) survey of his Japanese university students showed that the students overwhelmingly used bilingual rather than monolingual dictionaries.

Dictionaries and language use

In a study of bilingualised dictionaries, Laufer and Kimmel (1997) found that some learners used only the translation in the dictionary entry while others used only the monolingual definition, others varied for different words between using the translation and monolingual definition, and others used both. Laufer and Kimmel argue that, because people use dictionary information in such a range of different ways, a bilingualised dictionary is preferable because it allows for such use.

Laufer and Hadar (1997) found that bilingualised dictionaries

Table 8.11. *Features and ways of checking the features of a learners' dictionary to be used for writing or speaking*

Features	Tests
1. There should be ways of finding the appropriate word.	• See if the dictionary is bilingual. • See if the dictionary provides ways of accessing the word through thesaurus-like keywords (as in the *Longman Language Activator*). • See if the dictionary provides opposites, synonyms, superordinates and other related words as a part of an entry.
2. The dictionary should provide information about constraints on use of the word.	• See if the dictionary contains frequency information. • See if the dictionary contains codes telling if the word is formal, colloquial, rude or old fashioned. • Look in the introduction to see the range of codes used.
3. The dictionary should provide plenty of understandable example sentences as models for use.	• Count how many examples are provided for each word and different uses of a word. • Check if each of the examples for an entry is different enough to provide different kinds of information for use.
4. The dictionary should contain easily understood information about the grammar and collocations of the word.	• Look in the introduction to see the range of information provided. The minimum should be part of speech, count/non-count for nouns, and verbs should have their patterns indicated. • See how easy it is to understand the information provided.
5. The dictionary should show the spelling of inflected and derived forms.	• See if the entry for the base form provides access to the inflected and derived forms. • See if alternative spellings are provided.
6. The dictionary should show how the word is pronounced.	• See if the pronunciation of the word is indicated. • Decide if the pronunciation guide is easy to use.

generally gave better results than bilingual and monolingual dictionaries on comprehension and production tests. The more skilled users were, the better they performed with the monolingual dictionary. However, the bilingualised dictionary users still achieved better results.

Dictionary use and learning

Two major themes of this book are:

- Learning any word is a cumulative process. We cannot expect a word to be learned in one meeting and so we need to see each meeting as a small contribution to learning.
- Learning a word occurs across a range of different learning conditions. The position taken in this book is that those conditions should involve roughly equal proportions of the four strands of meaning-focused input, language-focused learning, meaning-focused output and fluency development. These strands provide partly overlapping, partly differing kinds of knowledge.

We can apply these two ideas to the role of dictionaries in language learning. Dictionary use is a kind of language-focused learning: the deliberate, explicit study of words. It is thus only one of a range of sources of information about words. Dictionary makers and their critics set a very high standard for dictionary production. This is admirable and worth keeping to, because it will improve the information available in dictionaries. Learners, however, will only gain a small amount of information from any one dictionary look-up. This information may usefully add to what is already known and may be added to in later meetings with the word in a variety of ways, including further dictionary use. Expectations of what will be learned about words from dictionary use should not be too high, and teachers and learners should make efforts to see that this knowledge is added to through other encounters with the word. One of the most effective ways of encountering words is through deliberate study, which we will now look at in the final part of this chapter.

Learning from word cards

The term 'learning from word cards' will be used to describe the formation of associations between a foreign language word form (written or spoken) and its meaning (often in the form of a first language translation, although it could be a second language definition or a picture or a real object, for example). This term has been deliberately chosen to connect this kind of learning with a particular strategy and to avoid confusion with other terms such as 'list learning' (Griffin and Harley, 1996), 'paired associate learning' (Carroll, 1963; Higa, 1965), and 'learning word pairs' (Nation, 1982). As we shall see, list learning is not a desirable strategy if the order of the items in the list cannot be easily changed. Paired associates – referring to the association between form and meaning – is not a very transparent term, and word pairs implies that the meaning has to be expressed as a single word.

In the simplest form of learning from word cards, a learner writes a foreign word on one side of a small, easily carried card and its first language translation on the other. The learner goes through a set of cards looking at each foreign word and trying to retrieve its meaning. If it cannot be retrieved the learner turns the card over and looks at the translation.

Criticisms of direct vocabulary learning

Many teachers and writers about vocabulary learning see the direct study of vocabulary not immediately connected to a particular text as being opposed to learning from context (Larson and Smelley, 1972: 263; Judd, 1978; Turner, 1983; Oxford and Crookall, 1990) and thus consider it not a useful learning activity. Oxford and Crookall's (1990: 9–10) definition of decontextualising techniques provides the basic reasons for this dismissal of learning from word cards. 'Decontextualizing techniques are those that remove the word as completely as possible from any communicative context that might help the learner remember and that might provide some notion as to how the word is actually used as a part of the language.'

This comment contains two criticisms: that learning from word cards is not good for remembering; that learning from word cards does not help with use of the word. Before looking at each of these criticisms, it is necessary to make the point that the use of word cards does not exclude the possibility of putting a sample sentence or collocations on the card. Oxford and Crookall (1990) and others however would still regard this as decontextualised learning and thus undesirable because the word is not in a 'communicative' context, that is, it is not being used for a communicative purpose.

Decontextualised learning and memory

The first criticism is that lack of context makes vocabulary learning difficult. Judd (1978: 73) comments that words taught in isolation are generally not remembered. There is evidence that the presence of a sentence context can help with making the word form–word meaning association (Laufer and Shmueli, 1997), but there is also an enormous amount of evidence that shows that even without a sentence context large numbers of words can be learned in a short time and retained for a very long time.

Teachers and course designers greatly underestimate learners' capacity for the initial learning of foreign vocabulary. Thorndike (1908) found that learners could average about 34 German–English word pairs per hour (1,030 words in 30 hours). The least efficient of his learners averaged nine per hour (380 words in 42 hours) and the most efficient 58 per hour (1,046 words in 18 hours). After 42 days more than 60% of the words were still retained. Webb (1962) gained even more spectacular results in a continuous six-hour learning session. Like Thorndike, Webb found wide variation in achievement among learners. Some learners mastered only 33 lists of six English–Russian pairs (198 words) in six hours, an average of 33 word pairs per hour. Other learners mastered 111 lists (666 words) in under four hours, an average of about 166 words per hour. Both Thorndike and Webb found no decrease in learning capacity as learning progressed. Webb found that after five hours of continuous learning, learning and recall were not less than in the first hour of learning. In fact, there was an increase in learning capacity as the experiment progressed. Thorndike (1908), and also Anderson and Jordan (1928), comparing tests covering several weeks, noticed that initially fast learners still retained a greater percentage of words than slower learners. That is, fast learners are not fast forgetters.

The data on the number of repetitions required for learning is just as surprising. Lado, Baldwin and Lobo (1967) found that college students who had completed at least six credits of college Spanish achieved recognition scores averaging 95% and recall scores averaging 65% after meeting each word pair once in a 100-word list. The word pairs were infrequent Spanish words with English translations accompanied by pictures. Crothers and Suppes (1967) found that after seven repetitions of 108 Russian–English word pairs almost all of the learners had mastered all of the words. After six repetitions of 216 word pairs most learners had learned at least 80% of the words. Learning rates also tended to increase as the experiments progressed, thus showing the existence of a 'learning to learn' effect. In their study of indirect vocabulary learning in context, Saragi, Nation and Meister (1978) found that on average the number of encounters required for most learners to recognise the meaning of a word was around sixteen. In this experiment the learners did not know that they would be tested on the new vocabulary and did not consciously study it while reading.

Studies of very long-term memory show that the results of deliberate learning persist over several years (Bahrick, 1984; Bahrick and Phelps, 1987). Beaton, Gruneberg and Ellis (1995) studied a learner who had learned a 350 word Italian vocabulary using the keyword technique ten years previously but who had not had any opportunity to use the knowledge (the trip to Italy did not happen!). Ten years later it was found he remembered 35% of the test words with spelling fully correct and over 50% with minor spelling errors. After looking at the vocabulary list for ten minutes, recall increased to 65% (fully accurate) and 76% (some minor spelling errors). After one and a half hours' revision, recall was near 100%.

There is thus plenty of evidence that, for the simple word form–word meaning aspect of vocabulary learning, direct learning from word cards is an efficient and highly effective practice. However, critics say that such learning has little to do with language use, the second major criticism of learning from word cards.

Decontextualised learning and use

In chapter 2 we looked at what is involved in knowing a word. In its simplest form, learning from word cards helps with learning the written form of the word, learning the concept of the word and making the connection between form and meaning. These are three of the nine aspects involved in knowing a word. Learning from word cards can also provide some knowledge of the grammar of the word, particularly its part of speech, its spoken form and perhaps one or two collocations.

There are many aspects of knowing a word that are not effectively covered by learning from word cards, especially constraints on use of the word, the full range of collocations and grammatical patterns in which it occurs, the variety of referents and related meanings the word can have and its various morphological forms. Table 8.12 lists the aspects of knowing a word indicating which ones are most helped by learning from word cards, which ones are partly helped, and which are poorly dealt with by this strategy.

Note that word cards can be used for both receptive and productive learning.

A similar table could be designed for incidental vocabulary learning from context where a different range of aspects would be marked. The

Table 8.12. *Aspects of word knowledge dealt with by learning from word cards*

Form	spoken	R	
		P	
	written	R	✓✓
		P	✓✓
	word parts	R	
		P	
Meaning	form and meaning	R	✓✓
		P	✓✓
	concept and referents	R	✓
		P	✓
	associations	R	
		P	
Use	grammatical functions	R	✓
		P	✓
	collocations	R	✓
		P	✓
	constraints on use (register, frequency . . .)	R	
		P	

Notes:
In column 3, R = receptive knowledge, P = productive knowledge.
In column 4, ✓✓ = well dealt with, ✓ = partly dealt with.

point of this kind of analysis is to show that any one way of dealing with vocabulary is not efficient in helping learners gain control of all aspects of word knowledge. It is necessary to see learning from context and learning from word cards as complementary ways of learning which overlap and reinforce each other and which also give rise to some different kinds of knowledge. The strength of learning from word cards is that it is focused, efficient and certain. The strength of learning from context is that it places words in contexts of use, so that the conditions of learning closely resemble the conditions under which the words will need to be used.

Part of the criticism that learning from word cards does not help with the use of the word relates to the nature of word meaning. Some writers take the position that the meaning of words comes from the context in which it occurs. Contexts, not dictionaries, determine meaning (Burroughs, 1982: 54). Firth (1957) however, saw collocation as only one kind of meaning. A similar position is taken in this book.

That is, learners need to know a generalised underlying concept for a word and also need to know the particular uses and range of referents of this underlying concept. Learning from word cards is a very effective way of learning the underlying concept. Meeting words in context makes learners aware of how this concept changes to suit particular contexts and the range of contexts in which the word can be used.

So far, we have looked at two important criticisms of learning from word cards. The first, that word cards are not good for remembering is simply wrong; the research shows otherwise. The second criticism, that word cards do not help with the use of words, is largely correct, but it takes the incorrect view that there are no other things to learn about words. Learning formal features of a word, its meaning, and connecting the form to the meaning are prerequisites for using a word. As well as learning through the use-based strands of meaning-focused input, meaning-focused output and fluency development, there is considerable benefit in learning through language-focused learning of which learning from word cards is one strategy.

The contribution of decontextualised learning

There is a third criticism of the direct study of vocabulary, one mainly put forward by first language researchers (Anderson and Nagy, 1992). Although this criticism focuses mainly on the teaching of vocabulary, it has had the effect of discouraging the teaching of *strategies* for direct vocabulary learning. The argument is that there are so many words in the language and it takes so much time to effectively learn a word that direct study is an inefficient procedure for vocabulary growth. Learners are better off concentrating on reading because their long-term vocabulary growth will be greater as a result of incidental learning from context.

This criticism is largely correct for native speakers of English, who begin school already knowing several thousand words. For the following reasons, it is certainly not true for non-native speakers of English who do not know the high-frequency words of the language, or who need to quickly increase their knowledge of low-frequency words.

Firstly, all words in English are not equally valuable. Higher frequency words are much more useful than low-frequency words; there is a very good return for the time and learning effort spent on high-frequency words. Secondly, learning from word cards can be a way of quickly raising learners' awareness of particular words so that when they meet these words in reading and listening they will be noticed and more easily learned. That is, direct learning is a very useful complement to learning from context, and just one step in the cumulative learning of a word. In general, critics of direct vocabulary learning need to take a broader view of what is involved in knowing a word and how vocabulary can be learned.

The values of learning from word cards

The values of direct learning of vocabulary are: (1) it is efficient in terms of return for time and effort, (2) it allows learners to consciously focus on an aspect of word knowledge that is not easily gained from context or dictionary use and (3) it allows learners to control the repetition and processing of the vocabulary to make learning secure.

In the section on repetition and learning in chapter 3 (see pp. 74–81), we looked at the amount of learning within a set time and the retention of this knowledge over long periods of time. There are also studies comparing incidental learning with intentional learning which invariably show that a deliberate, intentional approach results in much more learning in a set time than incidental learning. The spacing of repetition and the use of mnemonic devices is best done at learners' leisure when they can choose the most suitable time and the most suitable way to help learning stick. There is no doubt that for certain kinds of knowledge direct learning is highly efficient and enduring.

N. Ellis (1995) argues that learning word meaning and linking the word form to the meaning is especially suited to explicit conscious learning. One reason why this might be so is that learners can make use of deliberate mnemonic strategies like the keyword technique.

The use of word cards provides an opportunity for learners to focus on the underlying concept of a word that runs through its various related uses. This has several values. Firstly, it reduces the number of words to be learned. If a learner can see *kiss* as in *kiss someone's lips* and *kiss* as in *The wind kissed his face* as being essentially the same word even though they might be translated by different words in the first language, then there are fewer words to learn. Dictionaries do not encourage this view, rightly preferring to separate as many different uses as possible in order to make it easier for the reader to find the meaning for a particular context. For example, the entry for *knee* in *Collins COBUILD English Language Dictionary* has the following divisions:

1.1. the place where your leg bends
1.2. the place around or above your knee when you sit
2.   the knee in a piece of clothing

3.   to be on your knees
4.   to bring a person or country to their knees

All of these uses share a clear common meaning and learners should be aware of this. Learners can do this analysis of underlying meaning as a way of preparing their word cards.

Secondly, looking at the underlying meaning of a word has an educational value. It demonstrates to learners that there is not a one-to-one correspondence between a word in the second language and the first language word. It shows learners that different languages categorise the world in different ways. Deliberate attention to concepts can also reveal the metaphors that users of the second language accept as a normal part of their view of the world (Lakoff and Johnson, 1980).

The word card strategy

Learning from word cards is a way of quickly increasing vocabulary size through focused intentional learning. The strategy is one that many learners already utilise but often their use is not as effective as it could be. The design of the strategy draws heavily on research on paired associate learning, mnemonic techniques and vocabulary learning. In the final section of this chapter, we will look at how learners can be trained in its use but let us now examine the steps in the strategy.

Choosing words to learn

The first step is to choose suitable words to learn.

Learn useful words. Priority should be given to high frequency words and to words that clearly fulfil language use needs.

Avoid interference. Words that are formally similar to each other, or that belong to the same lexical set, or which are near synonyms, opposites, or free associates should not be learned together (Higa, 1963; Tinkham, 1993 and 1997; Waring, 1997b; Nation, 2000a).

Making word cards

The second step is to prepare the word cards. Small cards (around 5 × 4 cm) should be used so that they can be easily carried around.

Put the word on one side and the meaning on the other to encourage recall. The word or phrase to be learned is written on one side of the card and its meaning on the other. The word can be written in a sentence context instead of as a single item if this makes learning easier.

Use first language translations. Research shows (Lado, Baldwin and Lobo, 1967; Mishima, 1967; Laufer and Shmueli, 1997) that learning is generally better if the meaning is written in the learners' first language. This is probably because the meaning can be easily understood and the first language meaning already has many rich associations for the learner. Laufer and Shmueli found that L1 glosses were superior to L2 glosses in both short-term and long-term (5 weeks) retention, irrespective of whether the words were learned in lists, sentences or texts.

One of the criticisms made of bilingual dictionaries, learning from lists and learning from word cards is that the use of the first language encourages learners to think that there is a one-to-one correspondence between words in the second language and words in the first. Learners need to be shown that this is not so, and looking for underlying meanings is a good way of showing this. Learners also need to be shown that there is not a one-to-one correspondence between a second language word and a second language definition, and between a second language word and a picture. The representation of meaning is a very inexact process and learners should be aware of this.

Use pictures where possible. In some cases, the meaning of a word will be best expressed by a diagram or picture. Experiments involving pictures as a means of learning productive vocabulary indicate that questions like 'Which are more efficient, pictures or translations?' are not appropriate. Pictures and translations have different effects and so should be regarded as complementary sources of meaning rather than alternatives. Thus, for receptive learning, Lado, Baldwin and Lobo (1967) found that simultaneous presentation of both a written and spoken translation *accompanied* by a corresponding picture was superior to other arrangements and alternatives. Experiments by Kopstein and Roshal (1954) and Deno (1968), while favouring pictures over translations, noted the differing effects of pictures and translations under various learning and teaching conditions. Deno concluded that in his experiment pictures were not encoded in the same way as words (*ibid.*: 206). Webber (1978) similarly found a superior effect for pictures.

A further argument for regarding pictures and translations as complementary is that different learners prefer different sources of meaning. Kellogg and Howe (1971) compared pictures and translations for learning Spanish words. They concluded that learning was significantly faster with pictures than with written words (*ibid.*: 92). This however did not apply to all learners. Twenty-five out of 82 learners learned faster with words than with pictures. So, although on average picture stimuli gave better results than words, a significantly large group within the class learned better from words. A teacher would achieve better results for all the learners by providing both words and pictures rather than by providing the form favoured by the majority.

Not all words are picturable, but for those that are, the actual drawing of the picture on the card could improve memory. A suitable picture is an instantiation of the word and this may result in a deeper type of processing than a first language translation which does not encourage the learner to imagine a real instance of the meaning of the word.

Keep the cards simple. Other kinds of information – collocates, etymology, constraints, grammatical pattern – could be put on the word card, but it is best to see word cards as only one step in the cumulative process of learning a word and not expect too much from this strategy alone.

Suit the number of words in a pack to the difficulty of the words. In a series of experiments, Crothers and Suppes (1967) investigated the effect on learning of different numbers of Russian–English word pairs in a list. If, for example, learners are required to learn 300 foreign word pairs, is it better for the learners to study 100 of them several times first, then study the second 100 several times, and then the third 100, or is it better for the learners to try to learn all the 300 word pairs as one list? When 300 words are learned as one list, the learners go through the whole 300 words once, then start at the beginning of the list again and continue going through the list until all the words are known. Crothers and Suppes studied the following list sizes: 18, 36, 72, 100, 108, 216 and 300 word pairs.

When difficulty was low, it was more efficient to use the largest group of words. When difficulty was high, then the smallest group of words was the best. Difficulty here has several meanings: difficulty is high when there is limited time for learning and learners have no control over the time they can spend on each item; difficulty is high when learners must recall and not just recognise the new words; difficulty is also high when the words themselves are difficult because, for example, they are difficult to pronounce and their English translations are adjectives, adverbs or verbs, rather than nouns (see Rodgers, 1969; Higa, 1965).

Using the cards

The quality of learning from word cards will depend on the way that they are used.

Use recall. Writing the word on one side and its meaning on the other allows the learner to be able to retrieve the meaning of the word from memory. Having to retrieve the meaning results in far superior learning to seeing the word and its meaning at the same time (Baddeley, 1990; Landauer and Bjork, 1978). This is one reason why cards are better than vocabulary lists and vocabulary notebooks as a means of learning. In lists and notebooks, the word form and its meaning are usually both visible together. If lists and notebooks are to be used to help learning, then the meaning needs to be covered up so that learners have the chance to retrieve the item from memory.

Learn receptively, then productively. It is best to learn words receptively (see the word, recall the meaning) first, and then learn them productively (see the meaning, recall the word form). There are two factors to consider here: the difficulty of the learning, and the way the learning will be used. Receptive learning is usually easier than productive learning (but see Stoddard, 1929; Griffin and Harley, 1996; Waring, 1997b). That is, it is usually easier to learn to recall a meaning for a given word than it is to recall a word form for a given meaning. In the early stages of learning a language it is quite difficult to remember vocabulary because there is not much other knowledge of the second language for the vocabulary to fit into. It is thus better to learn vocabulary receptively first and then productively later. Learning productively means turning over the pack of word cards, looking at the meaning and trying to recall the second language word.

Numerous experiments have also shown that recall is better if the direction of learning (receptive or productive) matches the direction of testing. That is, receptive learning favours receptive testing, productive learning favours productive testing. This testing or use effect is much stronger than the learning effect (Stoddard, 1929; Griffin and Harley, 1996; Waring, 1997b). This means that if words are to be learned for listening or reading (receptive use) then receptive learning is best. If words are to be learned for speaking or writing (productive use), then productive learning is best. If both receptive and productive use is needed, then vocabulary should be learned in both ways. Griffin and Harley (1996) suggest that if, for motivational or time reasons, only one direction of learning is possible then learning productively (see the meaning, recall the second language word) is probably best. All the relevant experiments show that learning is bi-directional. That is, by learning productively, some receptive knowledge is also developed, and vice versa.

Keep changing the order of the cards in the pack and put difficult words near the beginning. Learning words from cards involves making connections, particularly between the word form and its meaning. However, when several words are learned at the same time then other associations may be made between the different words and some of these associations do not help learning. Learning related words together can make learning more difficult because the words interfere with each other. Learning words in a set order can result in serial learning where one word helps recall of the next word in the list. If lists are being learned to be recalled and used as lists, then serial learning is a useful thing. For vocabulary learning, however, serial learning is not useful because each word needs to be recalled independently of others without having to go through a series of words. The way to avoid serial learning is to keep changing the order of the words in the pack.

The order of the words in a list has other effects on learning. In general, items at the beginning and end of a list are learned better than items in the middle. These effects are called the primacy and recency effects (Baddeley, 1990: 52). Putting difficult words near the beginning is also a way of ensuring that they get more attention.

Atkinson (1972) studied the effects of four word sequencing strategies (two of which made use of a computer and so will not concern us here) in learning written English responses to written foreign nouns. In the random order strategy the learners studied the items with no control over the order of the items. In the other strategy the learners decided for themselves which item was to be studied: 'The learner rather than an external controller determines the sequence of instruction' (*ibid.*: 124). The learners could choose items to study that had given them difficulty in earlier trials, but all the words from the earlier trials, both easy and difficult, were tested in the retention test. The learner-controlled strategy resulted in a retention gain of 53% over the random strategy, as measured by a retention test given one week after the learning. Atkinson's experiment shows an advantage of writing each word pair on its own small card rather than learning from one large list: if words are on cards then learners can change their order as a result of previous learning, and can thus give more attention to the more difficult words.

Say the words aloud or to yourself. N. Ellis (1995 and 1997) presents evidence to show that putting items into the 'phonological loop' is a major way in which items pass into long-term memory. According to Seibert (1927), silent rote repetition of vocabulary lists is not the most efficient way of learning. If foreign vocabulary is to be learned for productive purposes, then saying the words aloud brings faster learning with better retention. Seibert found that the result obtained by studying aloud was, in every case, far better than the results obtained by studying aloud with written recall, and by studying silently. Seibert also measured the time required for relearning after two, ten and 42 days and found that after 42 days learning aloud produced a better result than the other two ways. Gershman (1970) also found that writing had no significant effect on learning. Thomas and Dieter (1987) found that practising the written form of words improved knowledge of the written form but did not contribute significantly to strengthening the word form–word meaning connection.

Put the word in a phrase or sentence or with some collocates. While there are numerous studies that examine the effect of context on vocabulary learning (Grinstead, 1915; Seibert, 1930; Morgan and Bailey, 1943; Morgan and Foltz, 1944; Gipe and Arnold, 1979; Pickering, 1982; Dempster, 1987; Griffin, 1992; Laufer and Shmueli, 1997), they differ so greatly from each other in method, quality of design and quality of reporting that it is impossible to regard them as either supporting or contradicting each other in addressing the question 'Does context help vocabulary learning?'

If we put aside the poorly reported and poorly conducted studies and take only those that: (1) defined **context** as the target word being in a sentence context, (2) did not involve guessing but provided a gloss of the target word (either in the first language, second language or both), and (3) compared learning in a sentence context with paired associate learning, we are left with only four studies: (Seibert, 1930; Dempster, 1987; Griffin, 1992; Laufer and Shmueli, 1997).

Laufer and Shmueli compared words in isolation, words in a sentence, words in a text and words in an elaborated text. All four treatments involved the learners having access to the word form plus a gloss of the word. The sentence and list presentations were superior in both short-term and long-term retention. Laufer and Shmueli explain this superiority as being one of focus, with list and sentence presentations providing a more direct focus on the words themselves. Laufer and Shmueli tested learning by using a multiple-choice test with only English (L2) synonyms and definitions. There were no other tests looking for other aspects of knowledge that may have particularly favoured learning in a sentence context. Such a measure, for example getting learners to suggest collocates, may have shown the sentence context condition to be even more favourable for learning.

Seibert (1930) compared productive learning of paired associates (English–French), words in a sentence context with a gloss in brackets after the word 'On met *le mors* ("bit") dans la bouche du cheval,' and a mixture of paired associates and context. The learning was tested by first asking the learners to translate the isolated first language word into the foreign language, and then getting them to translate the first language word given in the original foreign language sentence context into the foreign language. Tests were carried out at intervals of fifty minutes, two days, ten days and forty days. Paired associate learning gave higher scores than the mixed approach and the sentence context approach. No statistical procedures were used beyond finding the mean, standard deviation, and the standard deviation divided by the square root of the mean, and it is likely that the differences between the results of the treatments may not have been significant.

Griffin (1992) examined the effect of a context sentence on learning and testing. He saw the major issue in the use of context sentences as one of transfer. 'What is in question here is the ability of a word learned in a list of word-pairs to cue an appropriate response in a dissimilar test condition' (*ibid.*: 50). Griffin found that for some learners list learning may make transfer to productive use less effective but for others list learning was highly effective. The provision of a sentence context can enhance learning because more information is provided about the word; learners however have to have the ability and motivation to use this information. Griffin found that where the test involved recalling a first language translation for a second language word, there was no advantage for learning in context. The provision of a context sentence can have positive advantages for learners who can make use of it.

Dempster (1987) found no helpful effects for the use of definition plus sentence contexts compared with definition alone when measured by: (1) a definition recall test, (2) sentence completion involving recall of the form of the word and (3) writing a sentence using the word. What Dempster's results show is that presentation of words in multiple contexts does not improve definition recall. Context, however, may contribute to other aspects of word knowledge such as knowledge of the range of possible referents and collocational knowledge. Meeting the word used in different ways in a variety of contexts (Joe, 1998) may strengthen knowledge of the meaning of a word but this would require several measures of word knowledge for each word to determine the strength of the effect.

The few well-conducted relevant studies do not show a striking superiority for sentence context over isolated word but, because of the extra information that a sentence context can provide and the small amount of effort needed to add a sentence context to word cards, it is probably advisable to use such contexts on cards wherever possible.

Wang and Thomas (1995) compared the effect of the keyword technique with the 'semantic-context' strategy which involves seeing the word in a context sentence. Although the keyword technique gave superior learning, as measured by immediate testing, the memory for the words learned by the technique deteriorated more quickly so that, after a two day delay, the sentence context strategy learning was equal to or better than the keyword learning. The results of the keyword technique seem to be fragile over time.

Process the word deeply and thoughtfully. N. Ellis (1995) distinguishes between learning the form of a word (what he calls the input/output specifications) and linking that knowledge of the form to a meaning. Drawing on evidence from memory research and second language learning, he proposes that learning to recognise and produce the spoken and written forms of words in a fluent way is primarily an implicit learning process. That is, it depends on practice and use. Explicit knowledge can guide this learning 'but essentially we learn to drive by driving itself, just as we learn to spell on the job of spelling or speak by speaking' (*ibid.*: 16). Linking knowledge of word forms to meaning, however, is a strongly explicit process which benefits from the use of memory tricks, thoughtful processing, deliberate analysis and elaboration, and conscious connections to previous knowledge. Although these ideas have been around for hundreds of years, it was the levels-of-processing theory by Craik and Lockhart (1972) which brought them into recent prominence.

Experiments investigating the recall of familiar non-foreign words (Craik and Lockhart, 1972; Craik and Tulving, 1975) indicate that words which do not receive full attention and are analysed only at a superficial level do not stay long in the memory. On the other hand, words that are fully analysed and enriched by associations or images stay longer. Craik and Tulving consider (1975: 290) that what learners do while studying words is more important than how motivated they are, how hard they work, how much time they spend and the number of repetitions of each word. These findings cannot be totally applied to foreign vocabulary learning. Foreign vocabulary learning requires repetition even if only because one occurrence of a word will not contain enough information for a learner to master the word. Also, recalling an already known form is a simpler task than learning an unfamiliar word form and connecting it to a given meaning. However, Craik and Lockhart's (1972) theory of the importance of the kind of operations or processing carried out on an item does receive support from experiments on the keyword technique.

The keyword technique

The keyword technique is primarily a way of making a strong link between the form of an unknown word and its meaning. It involves two steps after the learner has met the unknown word and has found or been provided with its meaning. The first step is to think of a first language word (the keyword) which sounds like the beginning or all of the unknown word. The second step is for the learner to think of a visual image where the meaning of the unknown word and the meaning of the keyword is combined. Here is an example.

If an Indonesian learner wants to learn the English word *pin*, the learner could use the keyword *pintu* which is the Indonesian word for 'door'. The learner then thinks of an image involving a door and a pin.

The technique is more clearly seen as a four part process.

1.		2.		3.		4.
unknown word	➜	first language keyword	➜	a mental image combining the meaning of the unknown word and the meaning of the keyword	➜	meaning of the unknown word

Here are some further examples. The keywords have been chosen from a variety of languages including English. Bird and Jacobs (1999) suggest that for languages like Chinese with very limited syllable structure, it may also be useful to choose keywords not only from the first language but from known words in the second language.

1.	2.	3.	4.
fund	*fun* (Thai) meaning 'teeth' →	a fund of money being eaten by a set of teeth →	a supply of money for a special purpose
candid	*can* (English) meaning 'container' →	a can with a label which honestly shows its contents →	honest and truthful
core	*hor* (Serbo-Croat) meaning 'choir' →	a choir standing on the core of an apple →	the most important or central part

Step 2 provides a word form link between the unknown word and the keyword. Step 3 provides a meaning link between the keyword and the meaning of the unknown word. The whole sequence provides a link from the form of the unknown word to its meaning.

The unknown word, because of its formal similarity to the keyword, prompts recall of the keyword. The keyword prompts recall of the image combining the keyword meaning and the meaning of the unknown word. This image prompts recall of the meaning of the unknown word and completes the set of links between the form of the unknown word and its meaning. Instead of an image at step 3, some experimenters (Pressley, Levin and McCormick, 1980) have used a sentence which describes what the image might be, for example, 'There is a *pin* in the *pintu*.'

The keyword technique can be used with ready made keywords and images as in the examples above; this is generally recommended for younger learners and seems to work as well as self created keywords and images (Hall, 1988; Gruneberg and Pascoe, 1996). Some researchers (Fuentes, 1976; Ott, Butler, Blake and Ball, 1973) found that learners in the control group were spontaneously using keyword-like techniques.

There has been considerable research on the keyword technique. It has been found that the technique works with:

1. learners of differing achievement (Levin, Levin, Glasman and Nordwall, 1992; McDaniel and Pressley, 1984) although learners with low aptitude may find it more difficult to use the technique (McGivern and Levin, 1983)

2. learners at a variety of grade levels including very young children (Pressley, Samuel, Hershey, Bishop and Dickinson, 1981)
3. elderly learners (Gruneberg and Pascoe, 1996)
4. educationally disadvantaged learners

The technique has been used with a wide range of languages: English speakers learning English, Spanish, Russian, German, Tagalog, Chinese, Hebrew, French, Italian, Greek, and Latin words, Dutch speakers learning Spanish and Arabic speakers learning English.

The keyword technique can be used in L1 or L2 learning, for learning the gender of words (Desrochers, Gelinas and Wieland, 1989; Desrochers, Wieland and Coté, 1991) and with learners working in pairs or individually (Levin, Levin, Glasman and Nordwall, 1992). When it is used for L1 learning, the unknown word is an L1 word and the keyword is usually a higher-frequency L1 word, for example, *cat* could be the keyword for *catkin*.

The experiments evaluating the keyword technique have compared it with:

- rote learning
- use of pictures (Levin, McCormick, Miller, Berry and Pressley, 1982)
- thinking of images or examples of the meaning – instantiation – (Pressley, Levin, Kuiper, Bryant and Michener, 1982)
- context – the unknown word is placed in sentence contexts and the meaning of the word is provided – (Moore and Surber, 1992; Brown and Perry, 1991)
- added synonyms – the meaning is accompanied by other known synonyms – (Pressley, Levin, Kuiper, Bryant and Michener, 1982)
- guessing from context (McDaniel and Pressley, 1984)

The studies cited above generally show the keyword technique results in faster and more secure learning than other approaches.

The keyword technique has positive effects on both immediate retention and long-term retention (one week to ten years). This finding is not consistent as there are a few studies which suggest that long-term retention is not good with the keyword technique (Wang, Thomas, Inzana and Primicerio, 1993; Wang and Thomas, 1992 and 1995) and so such learning may need to be closely followed by some additional meetings with the words.

The effect of the keyword technique is not limited to receptive recall of a synonym. Studies have shown it to be effective for recall of definitions (Levin, Levin, Glasman and Nordwall, 1992; Avila and Sadoski, 1996), in sentence completion tasks (Avila and Sadoski, 1996), in story comprehension (Avila and Sadoski, 1996; Pressley, Levin and Miller, 1981; McDaniel and Pressley, 1984), in writing sentences using the words studied (McDaniel and Pressley, 1984) and in productive recall (Gruneberg and Pascoe, 1996; Pressley, Levin, Hall, Miller and Berry, 1980). The keyword needs to overlap a lot in form with the unknown word for productive recall to be successful and repetition may be more effective (Ellis and Beaton, 1993). Learners find using the keyword technique an enjoyable activity (Gruneberg and Sykes, 1991) and can achieve large amounts of learning with it (Gruneberg, 1992: 180; Gruneberg and Jacobs, 1991) with some learners learning 400 words in twelve contact hours and 600 words in four days. It is unlikely that these rates could be sustained but they represent very useful initial achievements.

To be effective, learners need extended training with the keyword technique. Hall (1988) spent a total of three hours over a period of four weeks training learners in the use of the keyword technique and even this was probably not enough. As with all major vocabulary learning strategies, learners need to be brought to a level of skill and confidence where they find it just as easy to use the strategy as not. If their grasp of the strategy is unsure, then it will be rarely used. A fault with many of the experimental studies of the keyword technique is that training seems to have been very short or is not described clearly in the reports.

Several studies show that the keyword technique works well on some words (usually where keywords are easy to find) and not so well on others (Hall, 1988). It would be interesting to see if extended training in the keyword technique results in ease of use with most unknown words or if there are still problems finding keywords for many words and with some languages whose syllable structure differs greatly from the first language. Gruneberg's *Linkword* books provide keywords for a wide range of vocabulary, indicating that the only limit on finding a keyword could be the learner's imagination. In the books learners are encouraged to spend about ten seconds thinking of the image so that there really is visualisation.

The results of the experiments on the keyword technique are not unanimous, but there is a very large amount of evidence supporting its use, and if it is fitted into a balanced programme any possible weaknesses, such as long-term retention and availability for productive use, will be lessened. Research on the technique has continued at a rate far greater than its importance in learning would seem to justify, particularly when one considers other areas of vocabulary learning where we lack the support of experimental findings. Keyword studies now number well over one hundred.

Training learners in the use of word cards

The research reviewed in this chapter shows that there is value in learning vocabulary using word cards. This learning, however, must be seen as part of a broader programme involving other kinds of direct learning as well as the strands of meaning-focused input, meaning-focused output and fluency development. The research also shows that there are ways of maximising learning and learners need to know about these and how to make use of them. Some of Griffin's (1992) studies suggest the importance of informing learners about how to go about learning so that factors like transfer of learning, serial position in a list and item difficulty are taken into account to suit the language learning goal.

- Learners should know about the importance of retrieval in learning and how word cards encourage this by not allowing the word form and meaning to be seen simultaneously. They should know about receptive retrieval and productive retrieval.
- Learners should know the value of repeating and spacing learning and to include long-term review in their learning.
- Learners should know what information to include on their word cards, particularly a sentence context or some useful collocations.
- Learners should know what words to choose to put on their cards, giving particular attention to high-frequency words.
- Learners should know what to do with each word, rehearsing its spoken form and using mnemonic techniques like the keyword technique whenever a word is difficult to remember.
- Learners should keep changing the order of the cards, avoiding serial learning and putting more difficult items at the beginning of the pack so that they get more attention. They should re-form packs, taking out words now known and inserting new items.
- Learners should use small packs of cards in the early stages of learning and bigger packs when learning is easier.
- Learners should be aware of interference effects between semantically and formally related words and avoid including such related items in the same pack.
- Learners should make deliberate efforts to transfer the learning from word cards to meaning-focused language use.
- Learners should know how to monitor and reflect on their own learning, and adapt their learning procedures on the basis of this reflection.

Some of these techniques are easy to learn and require only a little explanation and discussion. Others, like the use of mnemonic devices,

choosing words to go on the cards, avoiding interference and transfer-
ring knowledge, require much more time and attention. Training in
the techniques can involve:

1. Understanding what should be done. This can be tested by
    quizzes.
2. Observing and hearing about others' learning experiences and
    discussing strengths and weaknesses in what was observed.
3. Performing learning tasks using word cards and reporting and
    reflecting on the experience.
4. Monitoring and training others in the use of word cards.

This training requires planning and a suitable allocation of time.
The principle of spaced retrieval should be applied to the training procedure and teachers should plan a mini-syllabus spread over several
weeks to train learners in the effective use of word cards.

Teachers should be able to justify to themselves and to others the
value of spending time training learners in the use of word cards.
These justifications could include the following:

- The word card strategy can be applied to both high-frequency and
  low-frequency words. It is widely applicable.
- Direct deliberate learning is faster and stronger than incidental
  learning.
- Direct learning can help incidental learning by raising
  consciousness of particular words and providing knowledge that
  can be enriched and strengthened through incidental meaning-
  focused learning.
- Learners differ greatly in their skill at direct learning. Training is
  likely to reduce these differences.
- Learners spontaneously do direct learning but they do not always
  do it efficiently. Training can increase their efficiency.

Learning to use word cards should not be seen as an alternative to
other kinds of learning. It should be seen as a useful and effective complement and simply one part of a balanced vocabulary-learning programme.

The three word study strategies examined in this chapter: using word
parts, dictionary use and using word cards, are important in helping
learners quickly increase their vocabulary size. The deliberate nature
of the strategies results in substantial gains. When these are supplemented by opportunities to meet and use these words in listening,
speaking, reading and writing, the vocabulary programme has a very
strong base.

9 Chunking and collocation

The term 'collocation' is used to refer to a group of words that belong together, either because they commonly occur together like *take a chance*, or because the meaning of the group is not obvious from the meaning of the parts, as with *by the way* or *to take someone in* (trick them). A major problem in the study of collocation is determining in a consistent way what should be classified as a collocation. This is a problem because they occur in a variety of general forms and with a variety of relationships between the words that make up the collocation. In this book, the term collocation will be used to loosely describe any generally accepted grouping of words into phrases or clauses. From a learning point of view, it makes sense to regard collocations as items which frequently occur together and have some degree of semantic unpredictability. These two criteria justify spending time on collocations because of the return in fluency and nativelike selection.

Collocation is often described as a 'Firthian' term (Kjellmer, 1982: 25; Fernando, 1996: 29), but Palmer used it many years before Firth and produced a substantial report which used a restricted definition of collocation, focusing mainly on items whose meaning is not obvious from their parts. 'Each [collocation] . . . must or should be learnt, or is best or most conveniently learnt as an integral whole or independent entity, rather than by the process of piecing together their component parts.' (Palmer, 1933: 4)

Palmer discussed several terms including idiom, heteroseme, phrase and formula but decided on collocation because it was not a completely new word (Palmer refers to a use in 1750 noted in the *Oxford English Dictionary*), it had not become definitely associated with other meanings, it was an international word in that it was made of Latin parts and it could be used in a variety of disciplines. When language users segment language for reception or production or to hold it in memory, they typically work with meaningful groupings of items. The size of these groupings, called chunks, depends on the level of proficiency they have attained. At one level they are realised as collocations.

A range of arguments has been put forward to justify giving attention to word groups and some of them go to the heart of what it means to know a language. Here is a brief list of these arguments. We will look at each of them more fully in the rest of this chapter.

1. *Language knowledge is collocational knowledge.* N. Ellis (2001) argues that although it is possible for linguists to discover grammar rules in instances of language, language knowledge and language use can be accounted for by the storage of chunks of language in long-term memory and by experience of how likely particular chunks are to occur with other particular chunks, without the need to refer to underlying rules. Language knowledge and use is based on associations between sequentially observed language items. This viewpoint sees collocational knowledge as the essence of language knowledge.

2. *All fluent and appropriate language use requires collocational knowledge.* Pawley and Syder (1983) argue that the best way to explain how language users produce nativelike sentences and use the language fluently is that in addition to knowing the rules of the language, they store hundreds of thousands of preconstructed clauses in their memory and draw on them in language use. Thus each word in the language is likely to be stored many times, once as a single item and many times in memorised chunks.

3. *Many words are used in a limited set of collocations and knowing these is part of what is involved in knowing the words.* In some cases the collocations are so idiomatic that they could only be stored as memorised chunks. In others there are general collocational rules (prosodies).

Considering the role of collocational knowledge in language learning raises an important recurring issue in language study, namely, how much of language learning and language use is based on underlying abstract patterns and how much is based on memorised sequences? When we hear or produce a sentence like *It's really great to see you!*, do we subconsciously perceive its underlying grammatical structure, do we see it as two or more previously stored chunks (*It's really great* and *to see you*) or do we see it as one stored unanalysed chunk that we recognise or produce when needed? The answer to this question should affect what collocations we give attention to and the way we deal with them in language classrooms. In this chapter we are concerned with collocation but the argument about the units of language knowledge and the way they fit together applies at all levels of language. Let us look first at the units.

Table 9.1. *Examples of chunking at different levels of written language*

Level	Type of chunking	Examples
Letters	Each letter is processed as a unit not as a set of separate strokes.	*p* is processed as a unit, not as a small circle and a descending stroke on the left hand side
Morphemes	Each morpheme is processed as a unit rather than a set of letters.	*play* is processed as a unit not as a combination of *p, l, a, y*
Words	Complex words are processed as a unit rather than several morphemes.	*player* is processed as a unit not as a combination of two units *play* and *-er*
Collocations	Collocations are processed as a unit not as a group of two or more words.	*a player with promise* is processed as a unit

Chunking

In an influential paper, Miller (1956) distinguished 'bits' of information from 'chunks' of information. Our ability to make reliable one dimensional judgements, such as classifying tones, brightness and size, seems to be limited to around seven bits of information. Coincidentally, the span of immediate memory seems to be limited to the same number of items. We can overcome this limitation by 'chunking' the information. Bits of information are formed into chunks by the process of 'recoding', that is, creating larger meaningful chunks. These recoded items need to be capable of being accessed fluently as units in order for them to act as chunks.

N. Ellis (2001) sees the learning of collocation as one level of chunking, that is, the long-term storing of associative connections (*ibid.*: 5). This chunking occurs at all levels of language, and in both spoken and written forms. Table 9.1 has examples from written language.

Chunking can develop in two directions: memorised unanalysed chunks can be later analysed, or smaller chunks can be grouped into larger chunks. For the moment however let us look at chunking as a process that starts with knowledge of the smallest parts. These small parts are later chunked to become bigger parts and so on. When learning to read another language which uses a different script, for example an Arabic speaker learning to read English, the smallest units will be the parts or strokes making up the letters. Distinguishing *d*, *b*, *p*, and *g* will require a lot of practice. When the learner can see each letter as a unit rather than having to look carefully at the parts to distinguish the letters, then one level of chunking has occurred. Similarly, at a higher level involving more or bigger chunks, a reader may be able to recognise particular words without having to look carefully at each letter. Common combinations have been chunked as morphemes or words.

Chunking typically occurs where the same parts are often observed occurring together. In some cases this occurs solely because of frequency. For example, words like *the* and *soon* occur very frequently and may be thus more efficiently treated as one chunk rather than a sequence of letters. In some cases, parts are often observed as occurring together because they represent a regular pattern in the language. For example, the sequence *spl* represents a regular initial consonant cluster in English following the pattern /s/ + voiceless plosive + /l/ or /r/.

The advantages and disadvantages of chunking

The main advantage of chunking is reduced processing time. That is, speed. Instead of having to give close attention to each part, the chunk is seen as a unit; this represents a saving in the time needed to recognise or produce the item. Instead of having to refer to a rule or pattern to comprehend or produce the chunk, it is treated as a basic existing unit. The main disadvantage of chunking is storage. There are many more chunks than there are components of chunks, and if the chunks are also stored in long-term memory then there will be a lot of items to store. There may also be difficulty in finding an item in the store. If chunks are learned as unanalysed units, then another disadvantage of chunking is that the parts of the unit are not available for creative combination with other parts. For example, if *Please make yourself at home* is learned as an unanalysed unit, then the parts *make yourself* and *at home* are not available from this chunk to use in other patterns – *Make yourself comfortable, I really feel at home here* – and so on.

The alternative to chunking is rule based processing. In productive language use, this means recreating an item each time it is used. The best researched language area concerned with this issue is word building, that is, the use of complex words. When we produce a word like *unable* or *unambiguousness* do we create these words from their parts each time we use them (*un + able, un + ambigu + ous + ness*) or do we simply retrieve them as already created previously stored complete units? There is a very large amount of research that attempts to answer this important question (see Marslen-Wilson, Tyler, Waksler and Older (1994) for a review). At present, the research evidence shows that high-frequency complex units like *unable* are stored as whole chunks and low-frequency complex items like *unambiguousness* are re-created by rules each time we need them. If this conclusion is correct then it represents a nice compromise between the advantages and disadvantages of chunking. High-frequency items are chunked and stored separately thus reducing processing time, and, as we have seen, a small number of high-frequency items account for a large proportion of use. Low-frequency items are not stored as chunked units, thus reducing the need for lots of storage, and, as we have also seen, the very large number of low-frequency items which account for a very small proportion of use. So re-creation takes processing time but does not happen frequently (see Table 9.2). It is likely that this efficient frequency based balance of storage of chunks and rule based creation or analysis runs through all levels of language.

As chunks become bigger, their frequency of use becomes lower. There will be a point where the frequency of collocations of a certain length is so low that it is not efficient to store them as a chunk. This is a general principle and there will be exceptions where a long collocation is stored as a chunk because an individual uses it frequently. Poems, songs and some speeches are probably also stored in this way.

This explanation however still does not tell us what the rules are and if there is an interaction between rules and chunks. That is, are rule based chunks easier to learn? To examine these issues, let us now look in more detail at each of the three positions on collocation that were briefly described at the beginning of this chapter.

Language knowledge is collocational knowledge

The strongest position taken on the importance of collocational knowledge is that it is essential because the stored sequences of words are the bases of learning, knowledge and use. In several papers Ellis (2001; Ellis and Schmidt, 1997) argues that a lot of language learning can be accounted for by associations between sequentially observed language items. That is, without the need to refer to underlying rules. The major factor affecting this learning by association is frequency of meeting with instances of language use (the power law of practice). By having chunks of language in long-term memory, language reception and language production are made more effective.

If we accept this view of collocational knowledge as the basis of language learning and use, then all collocational sequences, both regular and idiomatic, are important for learning with the most frequent ones

Table 9.2. *Frequency, storage and processing of complex items*

Type of vocabulary	Number of different words	Coverage of text	Treatment
high-frequency words	a few items (not many to store)	a large proportion of text (too much to process)	store as complete items
low-frequency words	many items (too many to store)	a small proportion of text (not much to process)	apply rules to create them each time they are used

being the most important. Although the direct formal study of collocations has a role to play in this learning (Ellis, 2001), most learning
will take place through meaning-focused receptive and productive language use.

Fluent and appropriate language use requires collocational knowledge

Pawley and Syder (1983) consider that the best explanation of how
language users can choose the most appropriate ways to say things
from a large range of possible options (nativelike selection), and can
produce language fluently (nativelike fluency) is that units of language
of clause length or longer are stored as chunks in the memory. They
suggest that this explanation means that most words are stored many
times, once as an individual word and numerous times in larger stored
chunks.

The puzzle of nativelike selection is that by applying grammar rules
it is possible to create many grammatically correct ways of saying the
same thing. However only a small number of these would sound
nativelike. For example, all the following are grammatically correct.

- Please close the window.
- I desire that the window be closed.
- The closing of the window would greatly satisfy me.
- The window should be closed please.

Not all are nativelike.

The puzzle of nativelike fluency is that we can only encode one
clause at a time when speaking and we usually need to do so without
hesitations in the middle of the clause. Most of the language we use
consists of familiar combinations. Only a minority is entirely new.

Support for this position comes from a longitudinal study comparing learners of French as a second language before and after residence
in a French speaking country. Towell, Hawkins and Bazergui (1996)
concluded that the observed increase in fluency of the learners was the
result of proceduralisation of knowledge which, in turn, was the result
of learners storing memorised sequences. Towell, Hawkins and
Bazergui reached this conclusion by observing that mean length of run
(number of successive syllables unbroken by a pause) was the most
important temporal variable contributing to the difference between
pre- and post-test performance, and by analysing the qualitative
changes in some transcripts.

Pawley and Syder argue that memorised clauses and clause
sequences make up a large percentage of the fluent stretches of speech

heard in everyday conversation (1983: 208). They distinguish 'memorised sequences' from 'lexicalised sentence stems'. Lexicalised sentence stems are not totally predictable from their parts. They behave as a minimal unit for syntactic purposes and they are a social institution (a conventional label for a conventional concept). There are degrees of lexicalisation. Memorised sequences are transparent, regularly formed clauses. Lexicalised sentence stems and memorised sequences are the building blocks of fluent speech. Pawley and Syder (*ibid.*: 215) consider that by far the largest part of an English speaker's lexicon consists of complex lexical items including several hundred thousand lexicalised sentence stems. It is worth stressing that Pawley and Syder are talking about clause-length units, not two- or three-word phrasal collocations.

To develop fluency, all collocational sequences are important and need to be encountered many times, certainly in normal meaning-focused use with some pressure or encouragement to perform at a faster speed than a struggling learner usually performs at. Research on receptive and productive language processing indicates that learners may need to experience the language chunks in the medium in which they need to use them. That is, learners are unlikely to become fluent speakers by becoming fluent listeners. To develop speaking fluency they need to practise speaking.

Some words occur in a limited set of collocations

Sinclair (1987) describes two models of the way words occur in a text:

1. The 'open-choice principle' sees language text as a series of choices where the only limitation on choice is grammaticalness.
2. The 'idiom principle' sees the constraints and limitations being much greater. As well as limitations based on the nature of the word and choice of register, language users have a large number of memorised or partly pre-constructed sequences. (Sinclair, 1991: 110)

The widespread and pervasive nature of the idiom principle is used as a justification for the study of groups of words.

It is not sufficient to define a collocation as a group of words that frequently occur together. In frequency counts of corpora, the groups *although he*, *but if*, and *of the* frequently occur but do not intuitively fit our idea of what a collocation is. Collocations are closely structured groups whose parts frequently or uniquely occur together. We would also expect collocations to contain some element of grammatical or lexical unpredictability or inflexibility. It is this unpredictability or learning burden that provides some of the justification for giving collocations special attention in a vocabulary course.

This two part definition of collocation means that groups like *eat fish*, *cold day*, and *if they* would not be considered as collocations, but groups like *take medicine, How do you do?* and *thin soup* would. It is possible to specify further these two general criteria of (1) being closely structured and (2) containing some element of unpredictability, and later we will look at ten scales which can be used to classify and describe collocations.

However, just because a collocation exists does not mean that it deserves attention from a teacher. In order to decide if classroom time and effort should be spent on an item the criteria of frequency and range need to be considered. If the frequency of a collocation is high and it occurs in many different uses of the language, it deserves attention. But it must compete for this attention with other collocations and with other words. Frequent collocations deserve attention in the classroom if their frequency is equal to or higher than other high-frequency words. That is, if the frequency of the collocation would be sufficient to place it in the most frequent 2,000 words, then it clearly deserves classroom time. Table 9.3 lists the most frequent two word, three word, four word and five word collocations occurring in the *Brown Corpus* (http://homepages.infoseek.com/~corpuslinguistics/). Note that these are only collocations of immediately adjacent words. The cut-off point of fifty occurrences in the million word corpus was chosen because this is roughly the cut-off point of the 2,000 most frequent words.

Frequent collocations of frequent words also deserve attention The collocation itself may not be frequent enough to get into the most frequent 2,000 words, but because it is a frequent unpredictable use of a high-frequency word, it deserves classroom time. Most collocations deserving classroom time will be of this type, for example, *give up, get off, heavy rain*.

Let us now look again at the unpredictability aspect of collocations. The degree of learning burden of a collocation depends on the predictability of its form and meaning. Receptively, in listening and reading, the learning burden depends on whether the meaning of the collocation is understandable from the meaning of its parts. There are two aspects to this: semantic opaqueness and uniqueness of meaning. The scale of semantic opaqueness involves the degree to which the parts reveal the meaning of the whole. The collocation *take medicine* can probably be understood from the meaning of its parts with the help of context. *Take medicine* is not unique in its meaning however as it could mean 'consume medicine' or 'carry medicine somewhere'.

Table 9.3. *Immediate two- to five-word collocations in the* Brown Corpus

	Two adjacent items	Three adjacent items	Four adjacent items	Five adjacent items
Number of collocations occurring fifty times or more	1,287	121	10	0
The ten most frequent collocations	of the in the to the on the and the for the to be at the with the of a	one of the the United States as well as some of the out of the the fact that the end of part of the it was a there was a	of the United States at the same time the end of the in the United States at the end of from # to # on the other hand one of the most the rest of the on the basis of	(All the following would not be in the 2,000 most frequent words or phrases) at the end of the the United States of America government of the United States the government of the United of the United States of to the editor of the as a matter of fact on the part of the
The most frequent opaque collocations	of course so that	in order to in terms of with respect to		

Table 9.4. *Three positions on the role of collocation*

Role of collocational knowledge	Extent	Range of focus	Prototypical activities
Language knowledge = collocational knowledge	Collocational knowledge is the main knowledge	All language items	Unanalysed chunks Dividing up text
Fluent and appropriate use requires chunks	Collocational knowledge is additional knowledge	Many long stretches of items	Fluency activities
Some words have a limited set of collocates	Some words require collocational knowledge	Many words	Study of concordances

Productively, in speaking and writing, the learning burden of a collocation depends on the predictability of the co-occurrence of its members. Would collocations in the first language or previous learning of the second language allow a user to predict this collocation? *Take medicine* is not predictable from some learners' first language (they *drink* or *eat* medicine), but the collocations *take a pill, take a tablet* may be predictable from knowing *take medicine*.

From a vocabulary learning point of view, we need research into collocation:

- to tell us what the high-frequency collocations are
- to tell us what the unpredictable collocations of high-frequency words are
- to tell us what the common patterns of collocations are – where some examples of a pattern would need special attention but where others could be predicted on the basis of previous attention
- to provide dictionaries (or information for dictionaries) that help learners deal with low-frequency collocations

Knowing the typical collocations of a word is one important aspect of vocabulary knowledge. Firth (1957: 195) noted that part of a word's meaning is its collocations. Stubbs (1995: 51) notes that most of the collocates of *cause* are undesirable situations or events like *trouble, concern, problems,* or *embarrassment*. Stubbs argues that words like *cause* gain part of their meaning from the company they keep.

If collocations are studied because of their unpredictability and frequency of occurrence, we need to know what collocations need and deserve attention. It is this motivation that lies behind dictionaries of collocations and frequency studies of collocations.

Classifying collocations

There is considerable variety in the terms used to describe groups of words which seem to function as units and there are many criteria which are used to classify the groups. The criteria used depend on the types of groups that are focused on and the reasons for focusing on them. For example, in examining idioms, Fernando (1996) uses the criteria: compositeness (the words fit together as a group), institutionalisation (the words frequently occur together) and semantic opacity (the meaning of the idiom is not the sum of its constituents). Kjellmer (1984) uses six criteria to measure *distinctiveness*, or degree of lexicalisation. These are: absolute frequency, relative frequency, length of sequence (number of collocates in the collocation), distribution over texts (range), distribution over text categories (range), and structural complexity. This list is limited because of Kjellmer's aim of using computer-based procedures to find the collocations. Kennedy (1998: 108–121) notes the wide range of types of collocation and the difficulty in deciding what to classify as collocations. He considers Firth's (1957: 14) definition of collocation as being habitual actual associates central to the definition of collocation but cautions that very large corpora would need to be used to begin to gain reliable and valid data on 'habitual' company.

The most effective way of setting up criteria for classifying items as collocations (or not) and for setting up categories of collocation is to use a set of scales. The large number of scales needed is evidence of the range of items covered by the term. We will look at ten scales that have been identified by a variety of researchers. These scales indicate what is involved in learning collocations.

1. Frequency of co-occurrence

The most obvious scale ranges from 'frequently occurring together' to 'infrequently occurring together'. Many studies of collocation exploit this feature by doing computer-based frequency studies of corpora. This criterion is not as straightforward as it seems. For example, do the co-occurring items have to be immediately next to each other, can they change their forms by the use of inflections, do they have to have a strong grammatical relationship or are common co-occurrences like *and the* classed as collocations? Frequency of co-occurrence however is a very important criterion, especially in lists intended for the design of teaching materials. As in studies of vocabulary, in the study of collocation range needs to be considered along with frequency. Kjellmer (1982) provides some instances from the *Brown* corpus where there are some substantial collocations that occur only in a very limited set of texts. For example, 'Be it enacted by the Senate and House of Representatives of the United States of America in Congress assembled, that . . .'

Frequency and range are measured by counting and can be expressed in absolute or relative terms (Kjellmer, 1984: 166–168). Absolute frequency is the actual number of times a collocation occurs in a corpus. Relative frequency compares actual frequency of occurrence with an expected number of occurrences. The expected frequency can be calculated by multiplying the frequency of occurrence of item 1 of the collocation by the frequency of occurrence of item 2 of the collocation and dividing this by the size of the corpus. There are also other, more elaborate ways of taking account of range and relative frequency.

2. Adjacency

Collocates can occur next to each other as in *left handed*, or separated by variable words or phrases as in *little did* x *realise*. The scale ranges from 'next to each other' to 'separated by several items'. Renouf and Sinclair (1991) examine what they call 'collocational frameworks' like *be* + ? + *to* and *too* + ? + *to*.

3. Grammatically connected

Collocates are usually within the same sentence as a part of a grammatical construction. However it is possible to see items within the same text, not grammatically connected to each other but in a lexical cohesion relationship as collocates. The scale ranges from 'grammatically connected' to 'grammatically unconnected'. Kennedy (1998: 113) notes that *silk* often occurs with a colour and has found the example 'Her uniform was of rich raw silk in a shade which matched her hair.' Here *silk* and *shade* should be considered as collocates without a strong grammatical connection.

4. Grammatically structured

Kjellmer (1982: 25) points out that 'habitually co-occurring' is inadequate as a criterion because it includes cases like *although he*, *of the* and *but too*, and so it is necessary to have another criterion of grammatical structure. *Of the* and *although he* meet the previous criterion of being grammatically connected but they do not make up a collocation that takes account of the major divisions that would be made in analysing a clause. Kjellmer applied the grammatical structure criterion by using a list of permitted structures. The scale ranges from 'well structured' to 'loosely related'.

5. Grammatical uniqueness

Some collocations are grammatically unique: *hell for leather*. Others seem to be exceptions to rules (in *go to bed*, *bed* occurs without an article) and others follow regular patterns (*weak tea*). The scale ranges

from 'grammatically unique' to 'grammatically regular' with patterned exceptions like *go to bed/town/hospital* as the mid-point.

6. *Grammatical fossilisation*

Grammatically fossilised collocations do not allow any change to the
form of the collocation through a change in word order (for example,
by and large, law and order) or through grammatical change with
inflections or part of speech. Some allow small changes: *kick the
bucket* cannot be *The bucket was kicked* or *kicking the bucket*, but *He
kicked the bucket* and *When do you expect him to kick the bucket?* are
possible. Some allow substantial changes in word order: *to piece
things together* can be expressed as *things were pieced together, they
were piecing things together* etc. The scale ranges from 'no grammatical variation' to 'changes in part of speech', with 'inflectional change'
as a mid-point.

7. *Collocational specialisation*

Some collocates only occur together. That is, they never or rarely occur
without each other, for example, *Anno Domini, be-all and end-all,
hocus pocus*. Some collocations consist of one item that only occurs in
the presence of the other item, but the other item is not under the same
restriction, for example, in *kith and kin, kith* seems to be limited to
this phrase, while *kin* can occur in many other places. Other examples
include: *to and fro, leap year, bubonic plague*. Some collocations
consist of items that can also occur with a range of other collocates:
good answer, commit suicide. Aisenstadt (1981) calls collocational
specialisation 'restricted connectability'.

   The scale ranges from 'always mutually co-occurring' to 'all occurring in a range of collocations' with 'one bound item' as the mid-point.
Renouf and Sinclair (1991) measure the degree of specialisation of a
collocate by expressing the proportion of times a word occurs in a particular framework as a percentage of the total occurrences of the item.
There are now several formulae for calculating collocational specialisation.

8. *Lexical fossilisation*

Some collocations are made up of collocates that cannot be replaced
by other words, for example, *a bird's eye view, No fear!, by and large*.
Some collocations allow substitution by words of related meaning, for
example, *entertain a belief, entertain an idea, entertain a desire; last*

week, last month, last year; last Friday, last Saturday etc. Sinclair (1987) calls this 'internal lexical variation'.

The scale ranges from 'unchangeable' to 'allowing substitution in all parts' with 'allowing substitution in one part' as the mid-point. It is assumed that all substitutions are by semantically-related items, and there is some common meaning in items made on the same collocational frame. The criterion implies that when counting the frequency of collocations the total frequency of the range of permitted substitutions must be counted. See Kennedy (1990) for such an approach to the treatment of preposition-based collocations.

9. Semantic opaqueness

This criterion and grammatical fossilisation are the two most commonly used to define an idiom. The most idiomatic collocations are those where the meaning of the whole is not deducible from the meaning of the parts. Examples include *for good, under someone's feet, have a soft spot for someone, of course*. The scale ranges from 'semantically opaque' to 'semantically transparent'.

10. Uniqueness of meaning

Just as some words have only one meaning, some collocations have only one meaning, for example, *on behalf of, keep a secret, answer the door, full moon. Kick the bucket,* however, has two meanings: to die, and to kick the bucket with your foot. This criterion considers the difficulty learners may have in assigning the appropriate interpretation to a collocation. The scale ranges from 'only one meaning' to 'several meanings' with 'related meanings' as the mid-point.

The ranges in each of the ten scales described above have all been graded from most lexicalised to least lexicalised. A highly lexicalised collocation would be one like *hocus pocus* which: is frequent; consists of adjacently occurring items with a strong unique grammatical connection and structure which allows no grammatical and lexical changes; is made up of items that rarely occur individually or in other relationships; whose meaning is not deducible from its parts; and has only one meaning. Most collocations will be high on the scale for only some of these criteria. The choice, prioritisation and weighting of the criteria will depend on the purpose of the classification.

The evidence for collocation

There is considerable speculation that collocations may be important building blocks in language use and language learning. There are three major types of evidence to support this view.

First there is the intuitive feeling that certain phrases seem to act as units; lists of collocations are presented as evidence for this. The work by Pawley and Syder (1983) and Nattinger and DeCarrico (1992) is of this type.

Second, there is the evidence from corpus studies that certain groups of words recur. Lists with frequency data are presented as evidence for this. The work by Kennedy (1992) and Kjellmer (1984) is of this type. This evidence is not easily obtained as collocations are necessarily less frequent than their constituent collocates, and items which intuitively seem to be collocations often have a very low-frequency of occurrence in available corpora. Also, evidence using collocations where considerable substitution in the collocation is possible does not present a convincing case, because the example collocations are those involving very frequent fixed patterns with minimal variation allowed. The more variation and substitution there is in a pattern the more it is towards the grammatical or open-choice end rather than the idiom or lexical end of a collocation scale. Sinclair (1991: 53) argues that there is a close correlation between the different senses of a word and the structures in which it occurs. 'Structures' includes lexical structure (collocations and similar patterns). Pervasive evidence of this nature provides support for the importance of collocation in language use and language teaching.

Kilgarriff (1997: 145–147), when studying word frequencies including the frequencies of some multiword items in the *British National Corpus* (http://info.ox.ac.uk/bnc/) for the *Longman Dictionary of Contemporary English (LDOCE)* (Summers, 1995), noted that for a multiword item to be included in the most frequent 3,000 word list, all of its constituent words would each have to have a frequency high enough to be in the most frequent 3,000 words. The only multiword groups to get into the *LDOCE*'s top 3,000 were *ice cream, of course, all right*, and *according to*. It should be noted that phrasal verbs and most multiword items consisting largely of function words were not included in the *LDOCE* count. It is likely that several of these would be candidates for a high-frequency word list. The *British National Corpus* has about 750 items marked as multiwords. Table 9.5 gives the most frequent of these, all in the most frequent 2000 items in the *British National Corpus*. It is not clear what the

Table 9.5. *The most frequent items marked as collocations in the* British National Corpus

Item	Part of Speech	Rank	Frequency	No. of texts
out_of	prp	177	49038	3551
per_cent	nn0	222	38205	1677
such_as	prp	272	32060	2772
of_course	av0	285	30942	3116
at_least	av0	335	25713	3190
up_to	prp	356	24704	3280
for_example	av0	378	23829	2310
so_that	cjs	429	21513	3123
because_of	prp	532	17812	3020
rather_than	prp	536	17759	2761
as_well_as	cjc	584	16257	2668
according_to	prp	606	15722	2549
as_if	cjs	610	15633	2027
at_all	av0	619	15348	2806
in_order	av0	735	12878	2376
as_well	av0	789	11985	2557
away_from	prp	802	11756	2544
each_other	pnx	886	10759	2322
more_than	av0	906	10524	1973
in_terms_of	prp	962	9993	1767
no_longer	av0	1119	8828	2346
due_to	prp	1120	8814	2089
even_if	cjs	1126	8757	2365
on_to	prp	1173	8448	2197
as_to	prp	1229	8086	2058
no_one	pni	1351	7390	1743
for_instance	av0	1360	7343	1641
in_particular	av0	1474	6767	1918
apart_from	prp	1535	6534	2263
in_front_of	prp	1538	6523	1721
sort_of	av0	1648	6110	927
even_though	cjs	1706	5894	1938
together_with	prp	1722	5844	1895
all_right	av0	1725	5841	906
no_doubt	av0	1872	5421	1801
as_far_as	cjs	1875	5414	2000
as_though	cjs	1888	5368	1124
subject_to	prp	1981	5128	1389

various criteria used to define a collocation are, but they include adjacency (occurring immediately next to each other). Note that they are marked in the corpus as collocations by the use of the underscore.

Third, there is evidence from studies of learning and knowledge. The work by Towell, Hawkins and Bazergui (1996) is of this type. It shows that language users make use of unanalysed collocations, that analysed collocations are used with greater speed than would be possible if they were recreated each time they were used, and that there are errors which demonstrate that collocations are being used as lexicalised units. The evidence required is of the same kind that is called on in the debate about affixation. That is, are complex word forms like *development* and *developer* created from *develop* plus an affix each time they are used or are they stored for convenience sake as ready-made units? The answer to the question for collocation is likely to be the same as that for the better researched area of word formation. This would have to be checked by learners' reaction times to various groupings. Some frequent items are treated as lexicalised units, other less frequent items are re-created each time they are used. Items which are frequent and irregular are more likely to be treated as ready-made units. One problem with the study of collocation is discovering where the dividing line is.

Collocation and teaching

To simplify the discussion of teaching, let us consider three points along a scale of collocation. At one end we have idioms like *a red herring, you're telling me* and *be that as it may* which are largely fossilised and opaque. In the middle we have groups like *take medicine, for example* and *little did x know* which allow some substitution, are sometimes grammatically unique, are not necessarily adjacent and are at least partially transparent. At the other end we have items like *as a result, it is assumed that, Where was I?* which are grammatically well formed, allow a lot of substitution and grammatical change, and are transparent.

Idioms need to be dealt with as if they were words; they should be given attention on the basis of their frequency and range of occurrence. Learning their meaning should be enriched by analysis and explanation of their parts and history, and some attention should be given to the way they function in discourse.

Items like *take medicine*, which are to some degree unpredictable, need to be examined for any patterning that occurs (*take medicine, take a rest, take a break, take a holiday*). Very frequent collocations can be the starting point for dealing with the range of related collocates.

The very predictable collocations should be dealt with as part of the enrichment of the individual collocates that make them up. For example, when the learners meet a word like *clear*, they should be introduced to its more common collocates: *a clear day, a clear sky, a clear thinker, a clear road*. Some very frequent or immediately useful collocations like *Can you tell me where the toilet is, please?* can simply be memorised and used, and later be analysed when the learners' level of proficiency is more advanced.

The principle of learning burden applies just as much to collocation as it does to individual words. The learning burden of an item is high if its form, meaning and use are not readily predictable from previous first language or second language knowledge. Its learning burden is light if it follows regular predictable patterns. There are numerous patterns of regularity lying behind groups of collocations.

Encouraging chunking

Chunking can develop from known parts; it can also occur from the memorisation of unanalysed chunks. There are two major approaches to helping learners chunk known components. The first way is to encourage learners to make more fluent use of the language because this will result in them having to work with bigger units than a single word. This fluency development would have to go across the four skills of listening, speaking, reading and writing. Ellis and Laporte (in press) note that certainly for beginners there are strong benefits for vocabulary acquisition (including phrases and collocations) in having to produce language.

The second major approach to helping learners chunk known components is through language-focused practice in chunking text containing familiar items, and the deliberate teaching and learning of collocates of known items. This can include the use of concordances, matching activities, and the development of collocation tables.

The memorisation of unanalysed chunks is an important learning strategy, especially for a learner who wants to quickly gain a degree of fluency in limited areas. It has other learning benefits as well, particularly in that it quickly provides a fund of familiar items that can be later analysed to help support the development of rules.

Chunking through fluency development

Schmidt (1992) presents a comprehensive survey of theories which can be used to explain fluency development. The most accessible theory that describes the development of chunking through fluency development is McLaughlin's (1990) restructuring theory. McLaughlin (*ibid.*: 113) argues that the restructuring of language knowledge, which for our purposes we will see as chunking, occurs when learners reach a high degree of automatisation through practice. Learners can become fluent through practice at one level of knowledge. The only way they can improve further is to restructure that knowledge, perhaps into larger chunks. This will slow them down initially, but they will then be able to reach higher levels of fluency because of restructuring. McLaughlin thus sees fluency development playing a central role in chunking.

When examining activities to see if they are likely to help the development of fluency, a teacher should look for the following features:

- The activity should involve only known vocabulary and grammatical features, and preferably familiar content knowledge. This can be achieved by working with material that has already been studied in previous classes, by choosing very simple material, by allowing learners to control the task and by helping learners to plan.
- The activity should be meaning-focused. That is, the learners should be interested in, and focused on, the messages they are sending or receiving.
- There should be some encouragement to do the activity at a speed faster than learners' normal speed. This should be possible because the learners are working with familiar, simple material. The encouragement can be in the form of time pressure, competition (with own previous performance or with others), or the opportunity to repeat a task.
- The activity should involve a large quantity of language processing. That is, learners should be reading or writing texts several hundred words long, or speaking and listening for several minutes.

Here are some activities that meet these requirements and can therefore be considered fluency-development activities.

4/3/2 technique

The 4/3/2 technique was devised by Maurice (1983). Learners work in pairs with one acting as the speaker and the other as listener. The speaker talks for four minutes on a topic while her partner listens.

Then the pairs change with each speaker giving the same information to a new partner in three minutes, followed by a further change and a two-minute talk.

Listening corner

A Listening corner is a place where learners can listen to tapes as a self-access activity. The teacher makes a tape of a spoken version of some writing that the learners have already done. The writing could have been done individually or as group compositions. Alternatively, learners can listen in English to recordings of what they have read before (in English or the first language), such as the reading texts from earlier sections of the coursebook.

Listening to stories

This is particularly suitable for learners who read well but whose listening skills are poor. The teacher chooses an interesting story, possibly a graded reader, and reads aloud a chapter each day to the learners who just listen to the story and enjoy it. While reading the story the teacher sits next to the blackboard and writes any words that the learners might not recognise in their spoken form. Any words the learners have not met before may also be written, but the story should be chosen so that there are very few of these. During the reading of the first chapters the teacher may go fairly slowly and repeat some sentences. As the learners become more familiar with the story, speed increases and the repetitions decrease. Learner interest in this activity is very high and the daily story is usually looked forward to with the same excitement people feel about television serials. If the pauses are a little bit longer than usual during the telling of the story, learners can consider what has just been heard and anticipate what may come next. It allows learners to listen to language at normal speed without becoming lost. The graded readers *In the Beginning* (Longman Structural Readers, Stage 2), *Of Mice and Men* (Heinemann Guided Readers, Upper level) and *Animal Farm* (Longman Bridge Series) are particularly good.

Best recording

The Best recording is a useful fluency activity involving a tape recorder or the language laboratory. The learner records a tape, talking about some previous experience or describing a picture or set of pictures. The learner listens to his recording noting any points where improvements could be made. Then the learner re-records the talk. This continues until the learner is happy with the recording. This technique can involve planning and encourages repetition through the setting of a quality-based goal.

Rehearsed talks

These talks involve learners using the pyramid procedure of preparing a talk individually, rehearsing it with a partner, practising it in a small group and then presenting it to the whole class.

Speed reading and Extensive reading

Speed reading and Extensive reading of graded readers provide fluency improvement by getting learners to work on easy material and giving them large amounts of practice. To be effective, speed reading courses need to be written within a limited vocabulary so that learners can focus on the reading skill without having to tackle language difficulties. Speed reading courses also have the benefit of involving learners in keeping a running record of their speed and comprehension scores. Research on graded readers (Wodinsky and Nation, 1988) shows that reading only a few books at one level provides learners with contact with almost all the words at that level. This shows that graded reading can provide a reliable basis for systematic coverage of vocabulary for fluency development.

Repeated reading

This is one approach to developing fluency in reading (Dowhower, 1989; Rasinski, 1989). Learners read the same text several times and proceed in one of a number of different ways. In one way the learners have a new task to do every time so that each reading is for a different purpose; the tasks become more demanding with each repetition. Another way is to set a time goal for reading the text, say, three minutes for a 500 word text; the learners read the text until they can do it in the set time. An even simpler goal is to get the learners to just read the text a set number of times. Research suggests that four or five times is most effective (Dowhower, 1989).

Continuous writing

Continuous writing is an activity where learners are given a set period (usually 5–10 minutes) to write, with the aim of producing a large quantity of writing within the time. The learners can record the number of words they wrote on a graph. The teacher responds to the writing *not* by correcting errors but by finding something positive in the content of the writing to comment on.

These fluency development activities cover a range of skills and apply the four criteria of familiarity, meaning focus, pressure, and quantity described earlier in this section.

Chunking through language-focused attention

There are three groups of activities which deliberately draw attention to chunks. One group involves dividing up texts into chunks, another group looks at the patterns that lie behind chunks, and a third involves the deliberate learning of new collocates.

Dividing up texts

Dividing up texts into chunks can occur across all four skills. There is a set of activities related to dictation (Nation, 1991a) where learners have to hold spoken or written chunks in their working memory before they reproduce them in spoken or written form. Dictation involves listening to a chunked text and having to write the text, chunk by chunk; it is related to several other techniques described below which differ from each other mainly in respect of the mediums of input and output. Dictation itself has listening input and written output. Delayed repetition has listening input and spoken output. Read-and-look-up has reading input and spoken output, and delayed copying has reading input and written output. They all involve holding language material briefly in memory before producing it. Leaving dictation aside, we will now look at the three other techniques.

Read-and-look-up

Michael West (1960b) devised the read-and-look-up technique as a way of helping learners to learn from written dialogues and to help them put expression into their speaking. It uses reading input and spoken output. West regarded the physical aspects of read-and-look-up as being very important for using the technique properly. The learners each take a role in the dialogue and work in pairs facing each other, reading and listening. The reader holds the piece of paper or the book containing the dialogue at about chest level and slightly to the left. This enables the reader to look at the piece of paper and then to look at the listener, moving only her eyes and not having to move her head at all. The reader looks at the dialogue and tries to remember as long a phrase as possible. The reader can look at the paper for as long as is necessary. When ready, she looks at the listener and says the phrase. While she looks at the paper she does not speak; while she speaks she does not look at the paper. These rules force the reader to rely on memory. At first progress is a little difficult because the reader has to discover what length of phrase is most comfortable and has to master the rules of the technique. It can also be practised at home in front of a mirror. West sees value in the technique because the learner has to hold the phrase in memory and so the brain is actively involved. Because of this, West considered read-and-look-up to be the most useful of all learning activities (*ibid.*: 12).

Delayed copying

Delayed copying involves copying from a reading text (Hill, 1969), that is, reading input and writing output. An essential feature of the technique is that learners try to hold as large a phrase as possible in their memory before writing it. So, instead of copying word for word, the learners read a phrase, look away from the text, and then write it. Unlike dictation, this technique is ideal for individual practice.

Delayed repetition

In delayed repetition, the learner listens to a long phrase, waits for several seconds and then repeats it. The technique has sometimes been used as a language proficiency test. This is because the length of the phrase that a learner can hold in memory has been regarded as an indicator of language proficiency (Lado, 1965; Harris, 1970). It can also be used as an exercise, either with the whole class or in pairs. When it is used as a whole class activity, the teacher says a phrase, counts to three and then gets the class to repeat it. The length of the phrase and/or the pause between listening and speaking can gradually be increased.

As preparation for these activities, learners can practise dividing up written text into chunks and discussing the best places to make the divisions. For learners who see attention to grammar as an essential part of a course, this discussion can be a useful way of satisfying that expectation.

Seeing the patterns in chunks

It is likely that chunks are easier to remember as chunks if they are seen to fit a pattern or if there is some kind of logic underlying the chunk. A typical activity which draws attention to patterning is the study of a concordance. That is, many examples of the target word in context are classified and generalisations are drawn from the classification. These generalisations can involve information about the frequency and relative frequency of collocates and groups of collocates, the meaning relationships among the collocates, and the grammatical patterns involved. Summaries of concordances can also be studied. Here is an example from Kennedy (1990) based on *different*.

very different from	(3)
so different from	(3)
fundamentally different from	(2)
little different from	(1)
too different from	(1)
completely different from	(1)

A further step away from the original raw data is to look at entries in dictionaries like *COBUILD* (Sinclair, 1995) which provide example sentences. To get the most from looking at this range of data, learners need to have a system for recording the generalisations. This could take the form of a substitution table with frequencies in brackets if appropriate.

very (3)
so (3)
fundamentally (2)   different from
little (1)
too (1)
completely (1)

It will usually be necessary for learners to be familiar with the terms for the most common parts of speech such as *noun, verb, adjective, preposition*, and so on. These analytical activities are suited to cooperative work in small groups.

Deliberately learning new collocates

Learners can practise matching collocates using grids or other formats:

1. commercial 2. agricultural 3. redundant 4. public 5. inaccessible 6. structural 7. legal 8. isolated

area opinion economy company travellers vehicle patient linguist building term implement machinery miners alterations country information community meeting mineral words facts region claim library surplus television investment features (Brown, 1974).

Collocations can also be brainstormed in groups. Learners tend to be far too cautious in their use of collocates (Channell, 1981), although this may be proficiency related (Kellerman, 1985).

Memorising unanalysed chunks

A very useful strategy, particularly in the early stages of language learning, is to memorise useful unanalysed chunks. This strategy can be applied to both regularly formed and irregularly formed chunks. The regularly formed chunks may eventually be analysed and form the basis for learning grammatical patterns. Chunks can be most effectively memorised by following the same learning guidelines as for isolated words. These are:

1. Write each chunk on a small card with its translation on the other side so that there has to be active retrieval of its form or meaning.
2. Repeat the chunk aloud while memorising it.
3. Space the repetitions so that there is an increasingly greater interval between learning sessions.
4. Use mnemonic tricks like the keyword technique, putting the chunk into a sentence, visualising examples of the meaning of the chunk, and analysing its parts. This increases the quality of the mental processing and helps learning.
5. Don't learn chunks with similar words or meanings together. They will interfere with each other.
6. Keep changing the order of the word cards to avoid serial learning.

Teachers need to develop awareness of the difficulties that lie behind some collocations and the kinds of patterns that exist. This will enrich their teaching and allow them to focus their effort on productive patterns where possible. Teachers also need to know why attention to collocation is useful and have a balanced range of ways of giving this attention.

10 Testing vocabulary knowledge and use

Testing vocabulary is similar to testing in other areas of language knowledge and use. The same criteria of reliability, validity, practicality and washback need to be considered when designing and evaluating vocabulary tests. In some ways testing vocabulary is easier than testing grammatical knowledge or control of discourse because the units to test are more obviously separate; it is not too difficult to identify what a word type is. However, there are problems and issues and we will look at these in this chapter. Like much of this book, this chapter is organised around questions that teachers typically ask. This means that it is structured rather differently from some other discussions of language testing. Moreover, there is now an excellent book devoted solely to vocabulary testing (Read, 2000).

What kind of vocabulary test is the best?

There are many different kinds of vocabulary test item. The following set of examples covers many that are typically used in vocabulary tests.

A 1,000 word level true/false test (Nation, 1993a)

Write T if a sentence is true. Write N if it is not true. Write X if you do not understand the sentence.

> 1. We cut time into minutes, hours and days.   ——
> 2. Some children call their mother Mama.   ——
> 3. All the world is under water.   ——
> 4. When you keep asking, you ask once.   ——

A vocabulary depth test (Read, 1995)

Choose four words that go with the test word. Choose at least one from each of the two boxes.

Sudden

beautiful quick	change doctor
surprising thirsty	noise school

A definition completion test (Read, 1995)

**Choose one word from the list on the right to complete the sentence.
Do not use the same word twice.**

1. A journey straight to a place is _____
2. An illness that is very serious is _____
3. A river that is very wide is _____
4. Part of your body that is not covered by any clothes is ____
5. Something that happens often is ____

faint
acute
common
bare
alien
broad
direct

A sensitive multiple-choice test (Joe, 1994)

Circle the choice that best gives the meaning of the underlined word.

chronic means   a. lasting for a long time
             b. dissatisfied
             c. to greatly decrease
             d. effective and harmless
             e. don't know

A translation test (Nurweni and Read, 1999)

Translate the underlined words into your first language.

1. You can see how the town has <u>developed</u>.   _____
2. I cannot say much about his <u>character</u>.   _____
3. Her <u>idea</u> is a very good one.   _____
4. I want to hear only the <u>facts</u>.   _____

With so many possibilities available, it can be difficult to choose which type to use in a particular test. In general, a good vocabulary test has plenty of items (around 30 is probably a minimum for a reliable test). It uses a test item type which requires learners to use the kind of vocabulary knowledge that you want to test. It is easy enough to make, mark and interpret, and it has a good effect on the learning and teaching that leads up to the test and follows it.

The vocabulary test item types above differ in many ways. Some have choices; some use the first language; some put the word in a sentence context; some require the learner to use the word; some focus on meaning while others focus on the form of the word, its grammar, collocations or associations. Table 10.1 is an adapted version of the Table 2.1 (p. 27) which lists what is involved in knowing a word.

Table 10.1 is useful for deciding what aspects of vocabulary knowledge are to be tested and should help with the first and most important question to ask when testing which is 'What do I want to test?' This answered, the next questions are 'How difficult do I want the test to be?' and 'Do I want the test to give credit for partial knowledge or do I want to test if the vocabulary is really well known?' A teacher may want vocabulary test items to be easy so that learners feel encouraged, so that she can see if learners are progressing in the gradual cumulative learning of particular words, and so that she can see if there are even small amounts of knowledge that can be built on. There are several ways of making a test more sensitive to partial knowledge, and we will look at these later in this chapter.

The next decision is what item type to use. When the testing goal and degree of difficulty have been decided, then the choice of item types has been narrowed. In order to decide finally between different item types, let us look at research evidence about some of the important features of vocabulary test items.

Is it enough to ask learners if they know the word?

Yes/No or checklist tests have been gaining in popularity since Anderson and Freebody looked at them closely in 1983. Before then, such tests were lists of words that learners responded to by saying whether they knew each word or not (Bear and Odbert, 1941; Campion and Elley, 1971). Anderson and Freebody included some nonsense words in their test so that the accuracy of learners' responses could be measured: if a learner says they know a non-word then they are overstating their vocabulary knowledge. Here is an example of part of such a test from Meara (1989).

Tick the words you know.

adviser	____	moisten	____
ghastly	____	patiful	____
contord	____	profess	____
implore	____	stourge	____
morlorn	____	discard	____

Table 10.1. *Aspects of word knowledge for testing*

Form	spoken	R	Can the learner recognise the spoken form of the word?
		P	Can the learner pronounce the word correctly?
	written	R	Can the learner recognise the written form of the word?
		P	Can the learner spell and write the word?
	word parts	R	Can the learner recognise known parts in the word?
		P	Can the learner produce appropriate inflected and derived forms of the word?
Meaning	form and meaning	R	Can the learner recall the appropriate meaning for this word form?
		P	Can the learner produce the appropriate word form to express this meaning?
	concept and referents	R	Can the learner understand a range of uses of the word and its central concept?
		P	Can the learner use the word to refer to a range of items?
	associations	R	Can the learner produce common associations for this word?
		P	Can the learner recall this word when presented with related ideas?
Use	grammatical functions	R	Can the learner recognise correct uses of the word in context?
		P	Can the learner use this word in the correct grammatical patterns?
	collocations	R	Can the learner recognise appropriate collocations?
		P	Can the learner produce the word with appropriate collocations?
	constraints on use (register, frequency . . .)	R	Can the learner tell if the word is common, formal, infrequent, etc.?
		P	Can the learner use the word at appropriate times?

Note: In column 3, R = receptive knowledge, P = productive knowledge.

The learner's score is calculated by subtracting the proportion of non-words marked as known from the number of real words marked as known. Meara and Jones (1990), Meara (1990b and 1991) and Meara and Buxton (1987) have used this test format extensively with second language learners, finding it a reliable, valid and practical measure of second language vocabulary knowledge.

Meara, Lightbown and Halter (1997) examined the effect of large numbers of cognates in Yes/No tests. As in previous studies they found correlations of .65–.75 between the Yes/No tests and language proficiency tests. Large numbers of cognates (50%) had the effect of making the learners' scores higher than, and significantly different from, scores on a non-cognate version. The report on the experiment does not tell us if 50% of the non-words in the test were also items that looked like cognates. This would be essential if the test was to work properly as the non-words must appear to be like the real words in the test so that the only way of distinguishing real words from non-words is through familiarity with the real words. In a study of vocabulary distractor types, Goodrich (1977) found that words of roughly similar spelling (*bread, beard*) were not distracting. This suggests that the use of non-words that are based on real words in Yes/No tests is not unnecessarily distracting.

Yes/No tests of vocabulary size have been used as placement tests, that is, to decide what course level a learner should be placed in. The *Eurocentres Vocabulary Size Test* developed by Paul Meara and his colleagues (Meara and Buxton, 1987; Meara and Jones, 1987) is a computerised Yes/No test. Strictly speaking it does not measure total vocabulary size but measures knowledge of the 10,000 most frequent lemmas of English. However, for most learners of English as a second or foreign language in the intermediate stages of their learning, there is probably little difference between what the test measures and total vocabulary size. The test is extremely efficient, taking just a few minutes to sit, and is scored by computer. In the test, a word appears on the screen and the learner has to indicate whether that is a word he knows or not. Some of the words are nonsense words and the learner's performance on the nonsense words is used to adjust the score on the real words. The *Eurocentres Vocabulary Size Test* has been found to work well as a placement test. It certainly fills all the requirements of a placement test, taking very little time to sit, giving instant results and being easy to interpret. The biggest reservation most teachers and researchers have with Yes/No tests in general is that learners do not overtly demonstrate knowledge of the meaning of the tested words.

Should choices be given?

Multiple-choice items are popular because they are easy to mark and, if the choices are not closely related to each other, learners can draw on partial knowledge. They also have a degree of respectability because they have been used in standardised tests like TOEFL. Comparison with other item types like translation, asking the learners to use the word in a sentence, blank filling with choices and interview show that it is generally the easiest of the item types for first language learners to answer (Nist and Olejnik, 1995; Paul, Stallman and O'Rourke, 1990). Nist and Olejnik measured learning from context and dictionary definitions using four different tests for each word: (1) a multiple-choice test of meanings, (2) a multiple-choice test of examples, (3) asking learners to write a sentence to illustrate the word and (4) sentence completion. The multiple-choice tests were the easiest with the average item difficulties for the four tests with college freshmen being (1) .86, (2) .83, (3) .53, (4) .63 (the lower the score, the greater the difficulty).

Nagy, Herman and Anderson (1985) have shown how it is possible to design multiple-choice items of different degrees of difficulty by varying the closeness in meaning between the distractors and the correct answer. The use of multiple-choice can encourage guessing. Paul, Stallman and O'Rourke (1990) interviewed first language learners about the strategies they used to answer particular multiple-choice items classifying them into the following categories.

- Knowing the answer: the answer was chosen because learners said they knew it was correct.
- Association: the answer was chosen because it could be related in some way to something they knew about the word.
- Elimination: the answer was chosen by ruling out the other choices.
- Position of the options: the answer was chosen because it was first, last or in the middle.
- Readability of the options: the answer was chosen because it was the only one they could read and understand.
- Guessing: the learners did not know why they chose an answer or they said they just guessed.

Paul *et al.* found that for both high-ability and low-ability readers, over 50% of the answers were chosen because of association. Knowing the answer accounted for 16% of the items for the high-ability group and 8% for the low-ability group. The high-ability group guessed only 8% of the answers (with about a 50% success rate) while the low-ability group guessed 21% (with a 35% success rate). This indicated that guessing is not a major problem with multiple-choice items and that learners' responses are generally not random but largely driven by some knowledge of the words.

Goodrich (1977) studied eight different distractor types in multiple-choice vocabulary items and found the false synonym (a word with a similar meaning to one of the meanings of the correct word but not correct in the given context) the most distracting. This reinforces Nagy, Herman and Anderson's (1985) decision to make items more sensitive by having distractors with minimal meaning relationship to the correct answer.

An advantage of multiple-choice items is that they can focus on particular meanings where words have more than one meaning. There seems to be no major disadvantage in using multiple-choice except perhaps in the amount of work required to make the items. When they are being made, it is important to be consistent about the closeness of the relationship between the distractors and the correct answers in form and meaning, as this has a major effect on the difficulty of the item.

One way of reducing the amount of work involved in making multiple-choice items is to use a matching format (see appendix 3):

Write the number of the right word next to its meaning.

1. bench
2. charity   _____ long seat
3. mate   _____ help to the poor
4. jar   _____ part of a country
5. mirror
6. province

This not only reduces the number of distractors that have to be made, but also allows many more items to be tested within the same time. A disadvantage, though not a severe one, of the matching format is that the items tested within the same block can affect each other. Campion and Elley (1971) found that changing the block a word was placed in often resulted in a big change in the number of correct answers for the word. This effect can be reduced by checking items carefully when they are made, pilot testing the items to see if learners cluster around the same wrong answer, using small blocks (about six choices per block), and following well thought out criteria to guide what meaning and form relationships are not permitted between the correct choices and distractors in a block. Using first language translations for the meanings makes the test much more sensitive to partial knowledge.

Should translations be used?

There is a general feeling that first language translations should not be used in the teaching and testing of vocabulary. This attitude is quite wrong. Translation is one of a number of means of conveying meaning and in general is no better or worse than the use of pictures, real objects, definitions, L2 synonyms and so on (see chapter 3). Translation or the use of the first language may be discouraged for political reasons, because teachers do not know the learners' first language, or because first language use is seen as reducing opportunities for second language practice. However, the use of the first language to convey and test word meaning is very efficient.

The greatest value of the first language in vocabulary testing is that it allows learners to respond to vocabulary items in a way that does not draw on second language knowledge which is not directly relevant to what is being tested. For example, in vocabulary interviews learners may find it difficult to explain the meanings of words using the second language. Creating definitions in a second language is quite a sophisticated skill. When scoring an interview, it may thus be difficult to tell if a learner's shaky performance is because the word was not well known or because the word was known but was difficult to define in the second language.

Research with native speakers of English (Feifel and Lorge, 1950) found significant differences at different age levels for the types of definitions provided for known words. For second language learners, translation provides a much easier means of explaining the meanings of second language words. Although there is no research yet demonstrating this, it is highly likely that a multiple choice or matching test would be much easier for learners to do, and more valid, if the definitions were in the first rather than second language. The use of the first language meaning is like choosing a simple synonym, whereas a second language definition often involves a definition form including a relative clause or a reduced relative clause, and reading these requires greater grammatical skill.

First language translations provide a very useful means of testing vocabulary, both receptively and productively, and in recall and recognition items. The difficulties caused by no exact correspondence between meanings in L1 and L2 are probably less than the difficulties caused by the lack of correspondence between L2 definitions and the meaning they are trying to convey.

Should words be tested in context?

Words can be tested in isolation –

casualty   a. someone killed or injured
                b. noisy and happy celebration
                c. being away from other people
                d. middle class people

– in sentence contexts –

Each room has its own priv____ bath and WC.

– or in texts.

    In a study designed to evaluate vocabulary test item formats for the Test of English as a Foreign Language (TOEFL), Henning (1991) compared eight different multiple-choice item types. Note that because of the enormous number of tests that have to be marked, the issue of multiple-choice (recognition) or no choices provided (recall) was not even considered. The variables investigated included the amount of contextualisation and the choice of supply item or matching item test types.

1. Amount of contextualisation. The various types of context included isolated words, minimal sentence context, long sentence context, and passage embedded items.

ISOLATED WORDS,   MINIMAL CONTEXT,
MATCHING   MATCHING
   deliberately   He spied on them *deliberately*.
   a. both   a. both
   b. noticeably   b. noticeably
   c. intentionally   c. intentionally
   d. absolutely   d. absolutely

PASSAGE EMBEDDED, MATCHING

In a <u>democratic</u>[1] society suspected persons are presumed innocent until proven guilty. The <u>establishment</u>[2] of guilt is often a difficult task. One consideration is whether or not there remains a <u>reasonable</u>[3] doubt that the suspected persons committed the acts in question. Another consideration is whether or not the acts were committed <u>deliberately</u>[4]. Still another concern is whether or not the acts were <u>premeditated</u>[5].

    4. (A) both
          (B) noticeably
          (C) intentionally
          (D) absolutely

MINIMAL CONTEXT, MATCHING, INFERENCING
He was guilty because he did those things *deliberately*.

   a. both
   b. noticeably
   c. intentionally
   d. absolutely

2. Supply versus matching item types.

MINIMAL CONTEXT, SUPPLY
He planned the crimes _____.
   a. both
   b. noticeably
   c. intentionally
   d. absolutely

Matching item types were found to be easier than supply item types, were more reliable and had higher criterion-related validity. Supply item types may require the learner to draw on additional syntactic and collocational knowledge and this could affect learners' performance. Isolated word or phrase matching item types were consistently inferior to matching item types that used complete sentence contexts. The item type with a minimal non-inferencing sentence context was the easiest of all the types examined. The value of context may be to orient the learner to the correct part of speech and, by more closely resembling conditions of normal use, encourage normal access to the meaning. Therefore, to provide learners with the greatest chance of showing the vocabulary knowledge they have, it seems appropriate to use matching items with a sentence context. Although items with opportunities for inferencing also performed well, they measure other things besides previous vocabulary knowledge and, for estimates of vocabulary size, could be misleading.

The passage embedded items also performed well but present practical difficulties in constructing paragraphs for randomly selected items. If however an achievement test of vocabulary knowledge were based on themes or units of work, designing such items could be less problematic.

Watanabe (1997) found that testing words in the context in which they had occurred in a previously read text resulted in higher scores than when the words were tested in isolation. This suggests that the context had a cuing effect on recall. As Baddeley (1990: 268–270) points out, testing under the same conditions as those in which the learning occurred results in much better recall than testing under new conditions. In Watanabe's study, the increase by testing in the same context was over 50%.

The disadvantages of using sentence contexts include the extra time required to make an item, and the fewer items that can be tested within the same time. Where multiple-choice or matching items are used and where there is deliberately a big difference in meaning between the distractors, then contexts are difficult to devise. This is because each of the distractors would have to be able to fit sensibly within the context sentence. If they did not, the learner could choose the correct answer not by knowing the meaning of the tested word, but by using substitution within the context sentence to eliminate the distractors. For example, let us try to rewrite one of the *Vocabulary Levels Test* (see appendix 3) blocks using sentence contexts.

1. He saw a *bull*
2. She was a *champion*   _____ formal and serious manner
3 He lost his *dignity*   _____ winner of a sporting event
4. This is like *hell*   _____ building where valuable objects are
5. She liked the *museum*   shown
6. This is a good *solution*

Several of the six choices can be eliminated by substitution, for example, 'She was a *formal and serious manner*,' 'He lost his *winner of a sporting event*,' and so on.

However, where possible, particularly in receptive recall translation tests, sentence contexts should be used. They are also useful in multiple-choice recognition tests, but care has to be taken that all the choices are feasible within the sentence contexts. They thus may not be suitable for sensitive multiple-choice or sensitive matching items.

How can depth of knowledge about a word be tested?

Looking at how well a particular word is known is called measuring *depth* of knowledge which is contrasted with measuring how many words are known (*breadth* of knowledge). Table 10.1 (see p. 347) lists various aspects of what is involved in knowing a word. Most people consider that the most important aspect of knowing a word is knowing what it means but as Table 10.1 indicates there are many other things to know. As we have seen in chapter 2, some aspects of word knowledge may not need to be directly learned for a particular word because they are predictable from the first language or from known patterns within the second language.

When we test different aspects of word knowledge, we may be interested in two things: whether a particular word is well known, and whether learners show awareness of the systematic patterns that lie behind many words. For example, when testing spelling, we may be interested in whether learners can spell words like *agree, balloon* and *practice*. But we may also be interested in whether a learner knows when double consonants are needed in words like *swimming, occurrence*, or *spinner*. Finding out how much learners are aware of underlying regularities involves careful selection of test items to include items that involve a particular rule and items that are exceptions to the rule. It also requires interpreting the results of the test by classifying the correct answers and analysing incorrect answers. There is a notable lack of tests that measure patterns underlying vocabulary use.

The following test item types are arranged according to the parts of Table 10.1 which is itself based on aspects of word knowledge. R = receptive knowledge; P = productive knowledge.

- Spoken form
  (R) Word or sentence dictation / hear the word and choose the L1 translation.
  (P) Reading aloud / cued oral recall.

- Written form
  (R) Say these written words.
  (P) Word or sentence dictation.

- Word parts
  (R) Break the word into parts.
  (P) What do you call someone who paints houses?

- Form and meaning
  (R) Translate these words into L1.
  (P) Translate these words into L2.

- Concept and referents
  (R) Translate the underlined words into L1. 'It was a <u>hard</u> frost.'
  (P) Choose the words to translate this L1 word.

- Associations
  (R) Choose the words that you associate with this word.
  (P) Add to this list of associated words.

- Grammatical functions
  (R) Is this sentence correct?
  (P) Use this word in a sentence.

- Collocations
  (R) Is this sentence correct?
  (P) Produce collocations to go with this word.

- Constraints
  (R) Which of these words represent UK use?
  (P) What is the formal word for x?

Different types of tests that focus on the same aspect of knowledge correlate with each other to a reasonable degree, but there is still a substantial amount of difference. Paul, Stallman and O'Rourke (1990) compared three vocabulary test formats: multiple-choice, interview and Yes/No. They found reasonably high and significant correlations between the interview scores and the Yes/No and multiple-choice scores, ranging from .66 to .81. The correlations show that the three kinds of tests are doing a similar job but that there is enough unshared variance to see each of them as revealing some different aspects of vocabulary knowledge. Nist and Olejnik (1995) compared four different vocabulary tests of the same words: one requiring learners to write an illustrative sentence, another involving sentence completion, and others testing meanings and examples. The correlations between the tests were all less than .7, showing that it is likely that different aspects of vocabulary knowledge of the same words were being tested. This lack of high correlation indicates that we must look at item types carefully to see if they are measuring what we want to measure. One item type cannot replace another without changing what will be measured.

Interviews

Interviews are often used to test several aspects of a word in the same session. When this is done, a lot of care has to be taken in planning in order to be sure that the early parts of the interview do not provide answers for the later parts. An advantage of interviews is that they allow the researcher to explore an aspect of knowledge in depth by giving the learner repeated opportunities to answer, if necessary with some guidance. Nagy, Herman and Anderson (1985) describe their interview procedure in detail. Wesche and Paribakht (1996) have done considerable work on their interview based Vocabulary Knowledge Scale. In this, learners are given a word which they respond to using the following statements:

1. I haven't seen this word before.
2. I have seen this word before, but I don't know what it means.
3. I have seen this word before and I think it means . . . .
4. I know this word. It means . . . .
5. I can use this word in a sentence.

They are then questioned further on the word and their response is ranked on this scale.

1. The word is not familiar at all.
2. The word is familiar but its meaning is not known.
3. A correct synonym or translation is given.
4. The word is used with semantic appropriateness in a sentence.
5. The word is used with semantic appropriateness and grammatical accuracy in a sentence.

Both Nagy, Herman and Anderson's (1985) and Wesche and Paribakht's (1996) interview procedures mix aspects of knowing a word, in particular recognising its form, knowing its meaning and being able to use it in a sentence. These different aspects do not fit comfortably into one scale. It is possible to use a word in a sentence, for example, without fully comprehending its meaning.

Anglin's (1993: 112–113) exemplification of interviews about word meanings shows the different roles that interview tests and multiple-choice tests can play, particularly with items where there are literal meanings that are not the required answer.

I. OK. What does the word *twenty questions* mean?
C. It could mean like questions like things that are asked by people.
I. Mm-mmm.
C. *Twenty* might mean that you're asking them twenty questions.
I. OK. Can you tell me anything more about the word *twenty questions*?
C. *Twenty's* a number, and it's the amount of questions you can ask.
I. Can you use it in a sentence to show me you know what it means?
C. The teacher asked us twenty questions in the afternoon.
    (*Multiple-choice question answered correctly.*)
I. Have you ever played that game?
C. Ya, I just forgot about that.

In an interview, although learners might pursue a meaning that is on the wrong track, in a multiple-choice item they can choose the wanted answer even when one of the wrong choices is the wrong track they pursued in the interview.

I. What does the word *dust bowl* mean?
C. *Dust bowl?*
I. Mmm.
C. Well dust is, like, is like little dirt in the air that it'll, it'll collect on things.

I. Mmm.
C. Dust. And a bowl is like you eat your cereal out of it.
I. Mmm.
C. A dust bowl. Wouldn't be dust in a bowl I don't think.
I. Mmm.
C. So I don't know.
I. OK. Do you think you might be able to use it in a sentence to show me you know what it means?
C. No. These ones are getting tougher.
   (*Multiple-choice question answered correctly.*)

Interviews in general have the value of being a stringent unguided test of knowledge. A disadvantage is that learners' initial mind-sets might stop them from reaching the correct answer. In this study multiple-choice items seemed to be more sensitive than interviews in that learners gained higher scores.

Multiple-choice items allow a focus on particular meanings but provide answers and so there may be a doubt about whether the learners really knew the answer in that detail. However, by providing choices they allow the learners to consider responses that they knew but may not have considered in the interview.

There is considerable evidence that for young native speakers the concepts of some words develop over a considerable period of time. A striking example of this is words expressing family relationships like *brother* where children may take a long time to learn that adults as well as children can have brothers, and that if you are male and you have a brother then that relationship is reciprocal, that is you are also that person's brother (Clark, 1973). Another well researched area is that of prepositions. Young native speakers can take several years to get control of the range of meanings of words like *near*, *between*, and *next to* (Durkin, Crowther, Shire, Riem and Nash, 1985).

How can we measure words that learners don't know well?

Other ways of putting this question include 'How can we measure how strongly learners know a word?' and 'How can we make tests that give learners credit for partial knowledge?'

Three important distinctions affecting difficulty in learning a word are: reception/production, recognition/recall, and imprecise/precise. The receptive/productive distinction is well recognised in second language teaching and is sometimes called passive/active (Stoddard, 1929; Morgan and Oberdeck, 1930; Laufer, 1998). Receptive knowledge is that used in listening and reading, and involves going from the form of a word to its meaning, for example:

Translate the underlined word into your first language.
He is a <u>bold</u> writer. _____

Productive knowledge is that used in speaking and writing, and involves going from the meaning to the word form, for example:

Translate this word into English.
<u>gendarme</u> _____

Where the test item format is controlled for (Stoddard, 1929) receptive recall is easier than productive recall, irrespective of whether the tested items were learned receptively or productively.

A recognition vocabulary item format involves the use of choices.

<u>gendarme</u>   a. policeman
               b. path
               c. finger
               d. chair

A recall item requires the test-taker to provide the required form or meaning.

Translate this word into English.
<u>gendarme</u> _____

Recognition items are easier because even with partial knowledge a test-taker may be able to make the right choice. The recognition/recall distinction has been a matter of some debate in memory research (Baddeley, 1990: 271–275), but when the distractors are not very close in form or meaning to the target word, then recognition tests are easier than recall tests.

The imprecise/precise distinction relates to the degree of accuracy required in the answer. This can be reflected in the similarity of the choices provided, the degree of prompting and the degree of acceptance of an approximate answer. Items allowing for imprecise knowledge are easier because credit is given for partial knowledge.

In experimental research, it is very useful to test the same word in several different ways. In a study of vocabulary learning from oral retelling of a written text, Joe (1994, 1995) used three measures of vocabulary knowledge, each at a different level of difficulty. The measures were all receptive and consisted of: (1) an easy multiple-choice measure like Nagy, Herman and Anderson's (1985), (2) a more demanding multiple-choice measure and (3) an interview using an adaptation of the Vocabulary Knowledge Scale (Wesche and

Table 10.2. *Eight test formats classified according to three distinctions affecting difficulty*

Receptive	Recognition		Imprecise	Sensitive multiple-choice, for example,
				     fertilizer a. growing plants
				                  b. medicine
				                  c. history
				                  d. don't know

			Precise	Non-sensitive multiple-choice, for example,
				 There was no *response* a. movement
				                         b. answer
				                         c. sound
				                         d. sign

	Recall		Imprecise	Recalling a related meaning Does this word remind you of anything?
			Precise	Meaning recall
Productive	Recognition		Imprecise	Sensitive multiple-choice
			Precise	Non-sensitive multiple-choice
	Recall		Imprecise	Cued recall, for example, an *additional part* suppl___
			Precise	Form recall

Paribakht, 1996). By testing each target word with these three measures, Joe was able to give a strength of knowledge score for each word by giving one point for each of the two multiple-choice measures answered correctly and rating knowledge of items in the interview on a scale of one to six. Scores ranged from one to eight for each word. Joe could then relate strength of knowledge to the degree of generative use that the word received during the retelling activity. Use of an item is generative if its use differs in some way from the input on which it is based. She found that words that had been used more generatively during the retelling intervention were more strongly known than words that were less generatively used. This finding would not have been possible without using a range of vocabulary measures of differing difficulty.

McKeown, Beck, Omanson and Pople's (1985) study with first language learners shows the importance of using various measures of vocabulary knowledge to pick up the effects of different types of vocabulary learning. McKeown *et al.* compared three learning conditions: traditional (involving the learning of form–meaning connections), rich (involving learning the meanings, sentence completion, context generation, comparing and contrasting words) and extended/rich (involving rich instruction plus learners bringing evidence of having seen, heard or used the word outside class). All three treatment groups performed equally well on a multiple-choice vocabulary test. A fluency of lexical access test measured how quickly learners decided whether a word matched a given meaning. Learners with extended/rich instruction performed at significantly faster speeds than learners in the other two treatments. On an interview test involving the interpretation of a context containing the target word, the extended/rich and rich groups equally outperformed the traditional group. If only one measure of vocabulary knowledge had been used, important differences in the effects of the treatments might not have been revealed.

How can we measure how well learners actually use words?

Most of the tests we have looked at so far in this chapter have involved testing vocabulary that learners consciously and deliberately retrieve. They could be described as tests of declarative knowledge, that is, knowledge that learners can talk about (*declare*) and describe. Ultimately, what we should be most interested in is procedural knowledge: learners' ability to use words receptively and productively when their focus is on the message that they are receiving or conveying.

Vocabulary learning is not a goal in itself; it is done to help learners listen, speak, read or write more effectively. When testing vocabulary, it is important to distinguish between how well a word is known and how well a word is used. By doing this, it is possible to investigate learners with listening, speaking, reading or writing problems and see if lack of vocabulary knowledge is a source of these problems. For example, a learner may score poorly on a reading comprehension test. There are many causes that could contribute to this. By testing the learner's vocabulary size or knowledge of the particular words in the reading text, it is possible to begin to see if lack of vocabulary knowledge is playing a part in the poor reading performance. If it is found that the learner does not know a lot of the vocabulary in the text or has a small vocabulary size, then an important cause has been found. If the learner seems to know most of the vocabulary, then that does not exclude vocabulary knowledge as a factor, but it excludes some aspects of vocabulary knowledge.

The Lexical Frequency Profile (LFP) (Laufer and Nation, 1995) is an attempt to measure the amount of vocabulary from different frequency levels used by learners in their composition writing. It is important in applying this measure that learners write the compositions as they would normally, without giving more than usual attention to vocabulary choice. The measure is normally applied using a computer program called *VocabProfile* which compares words in a text with word lists that accompany the program. When the learners' texts are typed into the computer, spelling errors need to be corrected, wrongly used lexical words should be omitted, and proper nouns should also be omitted. A learner's lexical frequency profile is the percentage of word types at the high-frequency (2,000 word family) level, the *University Word List* (Xue and Nation, 1964) level, and not in those levels, totalling 100%. The LFP has been shown to be a reliable and valid measure (Laufer and Nation, 1995) which can measure change in language proficiency (Laufer, 1994). It has been used in studies of vocabulary size and growth (Laufer, 1998). The LFP does not show how well particular words are known, but indicates what use learners are making of words at a particular frequency level. This is useful for diagnostic purposes to see if the vocabulary shown to be known on tests like the *Vocabulary Levels Test* is actually being used in meaning-focused performance.

How can we measure total vocabulary size?

The vocabulary size of native speakers of English is of interest to language teachers because it provides one kind of goal for learners of

English as a second or foreign language. It is a particularly compelling goal when second language learners are in the same English speaking educational system as native speakers. There has been a recent revival of interest in the vocabulary size of native speakers of English largely as a result of interest in how children's vocabularies grow and the role of direct teaching and incidental learning in this growth.

There are two major methods of measuring vocabulary size. One is based on sampling from a dictionary and the other is based on a corpus or a frequency list derived from a corpus. The dictionary-based method involves choosing a dictionary that is large enough to contain all the words that learners might know. A representative sample of words is taken from the dictionary and the learners are tested on those words. The proportion of words known in the sample is then converted to the proportion likely to be known in the whole dictionary. So, if the sample consisted of one in every 100 words in the dictionary, learners' scores on the test based on the sample would be multiplied by 100 to get the total vocabulary size. Historically, this method has been the most popular way of measuring the vocabulary size of native speakers. Goulden, Nation and Read (1990) and D'Anna, Zechmeister and Hall (1991) are examples of this method.

The corpus-based method can be applied in two ways. One way is to collect a corpus of language used by a person or group of people and see how many words it consists of. This will not give a measure of total vocabulary size because any corpus is likely to represent only part of a language user's vocabulary. Estimates of Shakespeare's vocabulary (based on his plays and poems) and Schonell, Meddleton and Shaw's (1956) study are of this type. Nagy and Anderson's (1984) study is like these in that it was based on a frequency list derived from a corpus of texts used in schools in the United States (Carroll, Davies and Richman, 1971). None of these corpus-based studies involved testing. It is however possible to sample from frequency counts based on a corpus and to make a test. Typically, the sampling involves arranging the vocabulary into frequency based groups – the most frequent 1,000 words, the 2nd 1,000 most frequent words, and so on – and sampling from each frequency group. Meara and Jones' (1990) *Eurocentres Vocabulary Size Test 10KA* is of this type. Because ordering words according to frequency is very unreliable for the low-frequency words of the language, this kind of vocabulary test has only been used with learners who have a small vocabulary size, namely non-native speakers of English.

Miller and Wakefield (1993: 167) note that trying to answer the question 'How many words does a person know?' is much more difficult than asking it. Early dictionary-based studies of vocabulary size

(Seashore and Eckerson, 1940, and related studies by Smith, 1941; Templin, 1957; Diller, 1978) suffered from serious methodological flaws. Thorndike (1924) had been aware of these problems and had suggested solutions, but his paper was published in a collection that was not readily accessible and thus remained unknown to generations of researchers in this area who committed the errors that he warned against. Lorge and Chall (1963) and Nation (1993c) review the situation. These flaws related to the basic questions in measuring vocabulary size.

• What is counted as a word?
• How do we choose what words to test?
• How do we measure if learners know a word?

Although there is now an awareness of the issues related to the three questions, there is by no means a consensus on how they are best answered. However, recent studies of vocabulary size usually deal explicitly with the issues and generally make it clear how they have answered the questions. Let us now look at each of the three questions to get a feeling for what is involved.

What is counted as a word? This basic question relates to the even more fundamental question 'What is involved in knowing a word?' which we looked at in chapter 2. Does knowing a word include knowing its closely related, derived and inflected forms? Does knowing *agree* involve knowing *agrees, agreeing, agreed*? Does it also include *agreement, disagree, agreeable*? Do we count the word type (*agree* and *agrees* are counted as different words)? Do we count the lemma (*agree* and *agrees* are counted as one word but *agreement* is a different word)? Do we count the word family (*agrees, agreeing, agreed, agreement, disagree* are counted as the same word)? For good reasons, most counts aimed at learners of English use some form of word family. What is included in a word family needs to be clearly and explicitly described. Some counts unwisely rely on dictionary makers' division of words into dictionary entries. More consistent, well justified criteria are needed.

Another important issue in what is counted as a word is what is considered to be a word and what is not. For example, are proper nouns like *Jane* and *Jim* included or excluded? Are alternative spellings *(labor/labour)* counted? Are foreign words *(perestroika)* counted? Once again decisions need to be made and criteria described and justified. These decisions have a direct effect on the results of any counting.

How do we choose the words to test? This is a sampling problem and has been the major source of weakness in studies of vocabulary size based on dictionaries (Nation, 1993c; Lorge and Chall, 1963; Thorndike, 1924). In essence, the source of the problem is this. In a dictionary, high-frequency words have more entries per word and each entry takes more space than the entries for low-frequency words. If a spaced sampling method is used to choose words (the first word on every tenth page, for example), then there will be more high-frequency words in the sample than there should be. If the sample contains too many high-frequency words, then learners' vocabulary size will be overestimated because high-frequency words are more likely to be known than low-frequency words. This sampling problem has occurred in many studies (Seashore and Eckerson, 1940; Diller, 1978). Nation (1993c) describes procedures to avoid this problem.

How do we measure if learners know a word? Tests of vocabulary differ greatly in the amount of knowledge of each word that they require. Some formats, like translation tests, require strong knowledge of the words while others, like multiple-choice tests with distractors not closely related in meaning, give credit for partial knowledge. The difficulty of the test format can have a strong influence on the number of words that learners get correct and thus influence the measurement of their vocabulary size. The test format used needs to be clearly described and justified according to the construct of vocabulary knowledge that the researcher is interested in.

Dictionary-based studies of the vocabulary size of native speakers

Recent estimates of young adult university graduates (Goulden, Nation and Read, 1990; D'Anna, Zechmeister and Hall, 1991) indicate that native speakers have a smaller vocabulary size than earlier estimates showed (Seashore and Eckerson, 1940; Diller, 1978). Seashore and Eckerson's study, for example, estimated that, on average, college students knew over 58,000 basic words and over 155,000 basic and derived words. The Goulden *et al.* and D'Anna *et al.* studies suggest basic word vocabularies of less than 20,000 words.

In a very carefully designed study that took account of the methodological issues involved in measuring vocabulary size, Anglin (1993) investigated the vocabulary size of six-, eight- and ten-year-old native speakers of English. Anglin distinguished word types in *Webster's Third New International Dictionary* according to their morphological characteristics and looked at the following categories: root words (*happy*, *define*), inflected words (*running*, *sourer*), derived words (*happiness, redefine*), literal compounds (*birthday, live-born*) whose meanings can be interpreted from their parts and idioms (*dead heat, red herring*) whose meanings cannot be correctly constructed from their parts. The derived words were distinguished from root words using the criterion of whether the words were 'psychologically basic' or not. Psychologically basic words were those for which there are separate entries in long-term memory (*ibid.*: 25) and which could not be decoded through morphological problem solving. In most but not all cases, the root of a derived word seems to have been a free form. The distinction between psychologically basic words and words which were potentially knowable through morphological problem solving was very important in Anglin's study because he wanted to distinguish vocabulary growth through learning new words from vocabulary growth through mastering the morphological systems of English.

Anglin found that six-year-olds knew about 3,000 root words, eight-year-olds about 4,500 root words and ten-year-olds about 7,500 root words. These figures agree with recent conservative estimates of native speakers' vocabulary size. What was more striking, however, was the growth in knowledge of derived words with six-year-olds knowing just over 2,000 derived words, eight-year-olds about 5,500, and ten-year-olds about 16,000. Clearly there is enormous growth in the ability to understand derived words between the ages of eight and ten years old.

Anglin tried to untangle words which were known by having been previously met and words which were known by the learners using morphological problem solving. Here is an example of morphological problem solving (*ibid.*: 97). The learner starts by saying the word is unknown and then decodes it by unpacking its morphology.

I. What does the word *unbribable* mean?
C. Never heard of that word.
I. OK. Do you think you might be able to use it in a sentence to show me you know what it means?
C. The boy was unbribable.
I. OK. When you say 'the boy was unbribable,' what do you mean by the word *unbribable*?
C. That you can't bribe him with anything.
I. And when you say you can't bribe him with anything, what does it mean to bribe?
C. Um . . . sort of like talking him into something by using things.
I. OK. Can you give me an example?
C. Um . . . I might talk you into giving me a phone number by giving you a piece of gum.

Anglin classified the interviews in his experiment according to whether the learners overtly used morphological analysis procedures to successfully arrive at the meanings of words. This estimation is equivocal as Anglin points out because learners may not have displayed morphological analysis procedures even though they were using them, or may have displayed such procedures as a kind of informed hindsight even though they originally learned the particular derivational word as an unanalysed item. Nonetheless, Anglin's approach is important, because studies like Goulden, Nation and Read (1990) tacitly assume that words classified as derived (involving derivational affixes) will be learned as members of a word family centred around a root word. For many derived words this may not be so. They may be learned as unanalysed psychologically basic words. Sinclair's (1991) idiom principle suggests that different forms behave in different ways, certainly in terms of collocation and as a result possibly in terms of their meaning. We can look at words with derivational affixes as members of a word family closely related to the root word, and we can look at words with derivational affixes as independent words which differ in many respects from other words which have a formal morphological link with them. It is not difficult to find examples in Anglin's items to support both viewpoints. *Treelet* (a small tree) shares many of the features of its root *tree* including part of speech, overlapping meaning (*tree* is the superordinate of the hyponym *treelet*), and possibly similar collocates. *Soaking* (very wet) as an adjective in 'I'm absolutely soaking' differs in important ways from its root word *soak*: it is a different part of speech, it has different collocates, it requires some grammatical gymnastics to relate its meaning to *soak* (something is soaking wet because it has been soaked with water) and it is likely to be represented by words not related to the translation of *soak* in the learner's first language.

Given these cautions, Anglin attempted to calculate how many psychologically basic words native speaking children who are six, eight and ten years old know. This will be a higher figure than the number of root words and idioms they know because it includes derived words and literal compounds which did not show evidence of morphological problem solving in his research.

In Table 10.3, 'Words showing no evidence of morphological problem solving' includes root words and some derived words. 'Total words of all types' includes all root words, inflected words, literal compounds and idioms. For psychologically basic words these represent learning rates for native speakers between one and a half and six years old of 3.26 words per day, between six and eight years old of

Table 10.3. *Estimated vocabulary size of children at three grade levels for root words and psychologically basic words (from Anglin, 1993)*

Types of words	6-year-olds	8-year-olds	10-year-olds
Root words	3,092	4,582	7,532
Words showing no evidence of morphological problem solving	6,173	11,094	19,830
Total words of all types	10,398	19,412	39,994

6.63 words per day, and between eight and ten years old of 12.13 words per day.

Corpus-based studies of native speakers

Corpus-based studies draw on language in use. If the corpus is large enough, the resulting word list will probably provide a good representation of the high-frequency words of the language but it is likely to not include many of the low-frequency words. This is not a major issue if the aim is not to measure total vocabulary size but knowledge of high- and medium-frequency vocabulary. It is also not a major issue if the test is to be used with non-native speakers of limited proficiency. Let us look first at studies that did not attempt to measure native speakers' vocabulary size but looked at how much vocabulary might be needed or met in spoken and written language use.

Schonell, Meddleton and Shaw (1956) carried out a frequency count of the oral vocabulary of the Australian worker. The data was collected from unrehearsed conversations by surreptitious recording of speech in public places, recording conversations at work, and through interviews, and totalled 512,647 running words. The count excluded profanity, blasphemy and proper nouns (*ibid.*: 44). No indication is given of how many items were of those types. Table 10.4 details the number of items in the count.

The most frequent 1,007 word families (head words) included 5,916 types, and covered 94% of the tokens. 755 of the most frequent 1,007 word families appeared in the most frequent 1,000 words of the *General Service List* (West, 1953). About a third of the remaining 245 words appeared in West's second 1,000. This lack of a complete overlap is not surprising. The *GSL* is based on a count of written English while Schonell *et al.* counted spoken English. The Schonell

Table 10.4. *Words and number of occurrences in the Schonell* et al.
count

Items	Number of occurrences	Comments
Tokens	512,647	*to* + infinitive counted as one item.
Types	12,611	Homonyms were distinguished.
Lemmas	6,616	Includes comparative and superlative; homonyms were distinguished.
Word families	4,539	Includes inflections, derivatives and compound words.

count has a deliberately restricted focus on the informal, colloquial language of unskilled and semi-skilled workers. As such it has its own special vocabulary, relating to speech (*hurray, Mum*), work (*boss*) and Australia (*bloke, creek, pub*).

There are now several frequency counts of a wide variety of written English. The one million running word corpora modelled on the *Brown* corpus (Kučera and Francis, 1967) each typically contain 40,000–50,000 word types. The *American Heritage Word Frequency Book* of Carroll, Davies and Richman (1971) is a count of a 5,088,721 running word corpus of a wide variety of texts used in a range of subjects in US schools. It contains a maximum of 86,741 word types but this included capitalised words as different types. Nagy and Anderson (1984), using a detailed study of a sample from this list, set out to calculate the number of words in printed school English. They did this in a two step procedure. First, they took a representative 7,260 word type sample from Carroll *et al.*'s corpus and carefully classified the word types in the sample into word families. Second, they used the results of this analysis to predict the number of word families in the *whole* population of printed school English, not just that included in the *American Heritage* count. Nagy and Anderson did not claim that this is the number of words that native speakers at school will know, but it is the number of words that they could meet. They carefully distinguished derived forms of words that were very closely related in meaning to the base word from derived forms that were best treated as different words because they were not clearly related in meaning to the base word. Nagy and Anderson calculated that printed school English contains 88,533 distinct word families. These word families contain members that are all closely related in meaning. In addition, there are around 90,000 proper names. In chapter 8 (see

p. 266), the typical membership of a word family from Nagy and Anderson's study was shown. The size of word families (on average almost five closely related members) stresses the importance of word building knowledge in dealing with words. Nagy and Anderson (*ibid*.: 317–319) noted that their estimate of the number of words in printed school English fits reasonably well with calculations of entries in *Webster's Third New International Dictionary* (Gove, 1963). They also estimated that about half the words in printed school English would occur roughly once in a billion words of text. Many of these words are useful however. Their low-frequency may reflect their technical nature and therefore limited range.

The receptive and productive vocabulary size of non-native speakers

Laufer (1998) compared the amount of passive and active vocabulary in 16-year-old and 17-year-old learners using three quite different types of tests. Passive vocabulary was measured by using the levels test (Nation, 1983 and 1990). Active vocabulary was measured by using the *Productive Levels Test* (Laufer and Nation, 1999) and the Lexical Frequency Profile (Laufer and Nation, 1995). Because Laufer used very different test formats, she was comparing more than active and passive knowledge and thus was careful in her report to mark this by using the terms *passive*, *controlled active* and *free active*. Her study showed passive vocabulary being larger than controlled active vocabulary and the size difference between them increasing with age. There were significant correlations of .67 for the 16-year-olds and .78 for the 17-year-olds between passive and controlled active vocabulary size.

In a later study, Laufer (1998) used the same three measures to look at ESL and EFL learners. Once again she found significant and substantial correlations between receptive and productive vocabulary size (.72 for ESL and .89 for EFL learners).

Waring (1997a) used the same levels tests (passive and controlled active) that Laufer used but, because he was using Japanese translation for the meaning, Waring was able to add a 1,000 word level section below the usual 2,000 word starting level. Waring found that learners always scored higher on the receptive test than on the controlled productive test, with the difference in receptive and productive scores increasing at the lower-frequency levels of the tests. That is, as learners' vocabulary increases, their receptive vocabulary becomes progressively larger than their productive vocabulary. Learners with larger vocabulary sizes and learners with low vocabulary sizes did not differ greatly from each other in the relative proportion of receptive and productive vocabulary.

The following conclusions can be drawn from these three studies.

- Learners' receptive vocabulary size is greater than their productive vocabulary size.
- The ratio of receptive vocabulary to productive is not constant.
- As learners' vocabulary increases the proportion of receptive vocabulary becomes greater. That is, the gap between receptive and productive vocabulary becomes greater at the lower-frequency levels.
- A large proportion of the high-frequency vocabulary is known both receptively and productively.
- Increases in vocabulary size as measured by direct measures of vocabulary (decontextualised vocabulary tests) are not necessarily reflected in an increase in vocabulary in use (proportion of low-frequency words used in writing a composition).

These findings indicate that although the various kinds of vocabulary knowledge are clearly related to each other, they develop in different ways. This probably reinforces the idea that a balanced language course has to provide for learning across the four strands – meaning-focused input (listening and reading), language-focused learning (the direct study and teaching of vocabulary), meaning-focused output (speaking and writing) and fluency development – so that there is a wide range of varied opportunities for vocabulary development.

Laufer's (1998) study suggests that vocabulary growth may proceed in different ways for ESL and EFL learners. Laufer found that intermediate and advanced EFL learners' active (productive) vocabulary size was closer to their passive (receptive) vocabulary size than was the case with ESL learners. It seemed that the form-focused instruction (direct teaching and direct learning) typical of many EFL courses may account for these learners' close passive/active scores. ESL learners however had large passive vocabularies which could be accounted for by the large amount of input they get. This passive knowledge does not seem to transfer readily to active use.

Umbel, Pearson, Fernandez and Oller (1992) examined Spanish-English bilinguals' receptive vocabulary knowledge in both languages. They found that learners who spoke both English and Spanish in the home scored more highly than those who spoke Spanish only in the home. It seems that learning two languages at once does not harm receptive language development in the first language, and it helps gain higher performance in the majority language (*ibid*.: 1012). Umbel *et al.* also found that while there was a large overlap of knowledge of words from the two languages referring to the same thing in both languages, there was still a significant difference in items known only in one language. To truly estimate a learner's vocabulary size these non-overlapping words would have to be added together.

Choosing a test item type

The choice of a particular type of item should depend upon the following criteria.

1. Is the knowledge required to answer the item correctly similar to the knowledge that you want to test? If the test is an achievement test, then it should reflect the knowledge taught in the course. Thus, word building items would not be suitable if the course has not focused on word building at all. Similarly, asking learners to make sentences using words is not suitable if the aim of the course is to develop reading vocabulary.
2. Is it easy to make enough items to test all the vocabulary you want to test? If the teacher is spending hours on a test that learners will complete in a short time, something is wrong. For this reason, traditional multiple-choice items are often unsuitable.
3. Will the items be easy to mark? If the teacher plans the layout of the test carefully with marking in mind, a great deal of time can be saved. For example, if a matching lexical cloze test is used, typing it double-spaced will make it easy to make a marking key with holes cut in it to fit over the answer sheets. Similarly, if the place for the learners to write their answers is clearly indicated, marking becomes easier.
4. Will answering the item provide useful repetition of the vocabulary and perhaps even extend learners' knowledge? It is not usually a good idea for a test item to be an exact repetition of what occurred in the course. Using language is a creative activity which involves understanding and using words in new contexts. Unless learners can do this we cannot be sure if useful learning has occurred. When testing knowledge of prefixes, for example, it is a good idea to test the prefixes in unknown words which are made of known parts. Then learners cannot rely solely on memory but have to use their analysis skills. When getting learners to do a matching lexical cloze, the passage should be one learners have not seen before, even though it is made up of known vocabulary and constructions.

If teachers use such tests skilfully and often, they can have a significant effect on vocabulary learning.

Types of tests

We have looked at different types of test items. Now we must look at different types of tests. Language tests can be used for a variety of purposes:

- to find out where learners are experiencing difficulty so that something can be done about it (diagnostic tests)
- to see whether a recently studied group of words has been learned (short-term achievement tests)
- to see whether a course has been successful in teaching particular words (long-term achievement tests)
- to see how much vocabulary learners know (proficiency tests)

When making these tests, the major difference between the types is how the vocabulary is selected to go into the tests. When using them, the major difference should be how the results are used.

How can we test to see where learners need help?

A diagnostic test is used so that a teacher or learners can decide what course of action to take. It is important for a teacher to know whether learners have enough vocabulary to do particular tasks. For example, if learners know the 500-word vocabulary of level 2 of the Longman Structural Readers, they will be able to read all the books at that level and at lower levels. If learners know the vocabulary of the *General Service List* (West, 1953), then they can read the enormous amount of material written using that vocabulary. They are also ready to study the words in the *Academic Word List* (see appendix 1) which builds on the *General Service List* for learners who want to do university study.

The *Vocabulary Levels Test* is a diagnostic test. When using the test, the teacher is not particularly interested in the learners' total score on the test, but is interested in whether the learner knows enough of the high-frequency words. If the learner has a good score at this level and will do academic study in English, then the next point of interest is the learner's score on the *Academic Word List* section. As we have seen earlier in this book, teachers need to deal with high- and low-frequency words in quite different ways. It is thus very important to know where learners are in their vocabulary knowledge so that an appropriate vocabulary learning programme can be designed.

Usually it is not possible to test all the words within a particular group. A vocabulary test with 100 items is very long. When we make a test we have to be very careful selecting so that the items we choose are good representatives of our total list of words. For example, if we wish to make a test of the words in the *General Service List* (*GSL*), we have to choose between 60 and 100 words which will be used to represent the 2,000 head words in the list. To do this we must first exclude all the words that we cannot easily test, for example, *a, the, of, be*. In fact, the test will be easier to make if we decide to test only nouns, verbs, adjectives and adverbs but decisions like this depend on the type of test item we use. If the learners can use translation we may be able to test words that we could not test with a monolingual test. If we use pictures instead of synonyms or definitions, then the words we can test will be an even smaller group and our list of test items will not be a good representation of the total list because it will consist mainly of concrete nouns. As a result, our test will not be a good one.

Second, we must find a good way of choosing the test items from the words left. The best way is to number the words and then to choose every tenth word – if this will give us enough words for the test.

One test (Barnard, 1961) of the *GSL* included almost every testable word in the list. The only exclusions were a few words which were needed to make simple contexts for the tested words. The following items are taken from the test. The learners had to translate the underlined word into their first language.

I cannot say much about his <u>character</u>.   ____
Her <u>idea</u> is a very good one.   ____
I want to hear only the <u>facts</u>.   ____

The test was divided into several parts and different learners sat different parts. The aim of the test was to discover which words in the *GSL* were and were not known. The test was used in India (Barnard, 1961) and Indonesia (Quinn, 1968). Barnard found that entrants to university knew 1,500 of the words in the *GSL*. Quinn found that a similar Indonesian group knew 1,000.

There is a need for diagnostic tests of the major vocabulary learning strategies: guessing from context, using word parts, direct learning and dictionary use. Diagnostic tests need to be designed so that it is easy to interpret their results and to relate this interpretation to action.

How can we test whether a small group of words in a course has been learned?

Short-term achievement tests comprise words that learners have been studying recently, usually within the last week or two. The words that go into such a test therefore come from the course material. The results of a short-term achievement test do not tell you how many words learners know in the language, or what vocabulary they should be working on; the results tell the teacher and learners how successful their recent study has been. Short-term achievement tests need to be easy to make (because they might not be used again), easy to mark (because the learners need to know quickly how well they have done) and fair (they should relate to what was studied in a predictable way, and should not expect too much for a short learning time). Here is a sample of a test that meets most of these criteria.

The learners know that each week they will be tested on twenty words. They can choose ten of these themselves that they have worked on in the preceding week. They write these words one under the other on a sheet of paper with their name on the top. Each learner hands their piece of paper to the teacher the day before the test. The teacher looks at each list of words and writes a letter next to each word. If the teacher writes *S* next to a word, the learner has to write a sentence using that word. If the teacher writes *C*, the learner has to write three collocates for the word. If the teacher writes *M*, the learner has to give the meaning of the word. If the teacher writes *F*, the learner has to write other members of the word family. Thus the learners individually choose words to be tested on but they do not know how the teacher will test each word. The other ten words in the test are provided by the teacher and are the same for everyone in the class.

Other useful item types for short-term tests include translation, matching completion in sentence contexts and true/false items.

The washback effect of such tests can be very strong. Moir (1996) found that many learners studied for the weekly vocabulary test in ways that they knew were not useful for them in the long term. Short-term achievement tests are often used to encourage learning.

How can we test whether the total vocabulary of the course has been learned?

A short-term achievement test can test most of the words that have been studied in the preceding week. A long-term achievement test has to be based on a sample of the words that have been studied. Such a test is usually given at the end of a course, but in long courses, there may be a mid-course test. When choosing the words to go into a long-term achievement test, the teacher needs to consider what the results of the test will be used for. Most commonly, the results are used to evaluate the students' learning and to help give them a grade for their work on the course. The results may also be used to evaluate the course to see how well it has done what it set out to do.

The words selected to go into a long-term vocabulary achievement test should come from the words covered in the course and should

Table 10.5. *Testing declarative and procedural knowledge of the important vocabulary learning strategies*

Strategy	Testing declarative knowledge (what learners can do)	Testing procedural knowledge (what learners actually do)
Guessing from context	*Sub-skills* • Test recognition of part of speech • Test use of 'What does what?' • Test application of conjunction relationships • Test word analysis skills *Integration* • Get the learner to think aloud while guessing	• Use sensitive multiple-choice items to test incidental learning from guessing from context.
Direct vocabulary learning	*Sub-skills* • Test steps of keyword technique • Test knowledge of direct learning principles *Integration* • Observe the learner doing direct vocabulary learning and question the learner or get the learner to think aloud	• Set the learner a direct vocabulary learning task and measure the speed and amount of learning. • Get the learner to retrospect.
Using word parts	*Sub-skills* • Test knowledge of frequent word parts • Test word analysis skills • Test re-wording skills (redefine the word using the meaning of the parts)	• Set a piece of learning as a part of a larger task. • Measure the learning. Get the learner to retrospect.

Integration
- Get the learner to think aloud while learning analysable complex words

Dictionary use

Sub-skills
- Test knowledge of types of information available in a dictionary
- Test knowledge of a search procedure

Integration
- Test speed and accuracy at finding certain pieces of information in a dictionary

- Observe dictionary use during a reading comprehension task.
- Determine the success of the dictionary use. Get the learner to retrospect.

represent those words in a reasonable way. For example, a certain number of words could be chosen from each week of lessons or each unit of work. The way the words are tested should reflect the goals of the course and the way the words were taught. If the course aimed largely at expanding reading vocabulary, then written receptive test items using sentence contexts may be the most appropriate and fair.

Achievement tests may also aim to test how well learners can use the vocabulary they have learned. This could involve vocabulary testing combined with reading and listening tests, for example, where vocabulary in the reading and listening texts is tested along with comprehension of those texts.

How can we measure how well learners have control of the important vocabulary learning strategies?

Just as we can distinguish between declarative and procedural knowledge of vocabulary – what the learner knows compared with what the learner can do – it is also possible to distinguish between declarative and procedural knowledge of vocabulary learning strategies. These strategies include guessing from context, direct learning of vocabulary, mnemonic techniques including the use of word parts, and dictionary use. The declarative/procedural distinction is particularly important for vocabulary learning strategies because teachers tend to spend insufficient time on helping learners become fluent and comfortable with the strategies. As a result, the strategies may be known, but not used. Learners may need to change their knowledge, attitudes and awareness in order to feel responsible for their own learning. When they adopt a deliberate vocabulary learning strategy, they may be changing their knowledge, attitudes and awareness to do this.

It is possible to measure declarative knowledge of a strategy by directly testing explicit knowledge of the sub-skills of the strategy. For example, with guessing from context, learners can be tested on their skill at working out the part of speech of an unknown word in context, doing the 'What does what' (see p. 258) activity on the unknown word, determining the conjunction relationships between the clause containing the unknown word and adjoining clauses, and breaking the word into its component affixes and stem.

To measure procedural knowledge, it is necessary to look at the result of strategy use, usually while the learners' attention is directed towards some other goal such as comprehension of a text or doing a piece of writing. Table 10.5 looks at possibilities for testing declarative and procedural knowledge of vocabulary learning strategies. Tests need to be developed in all these areas.

This chapter began by asking the question 'What kind of vocabulary test is the best?' In order to answer this question, the test maker has to consider the purpose of the test, the kind of knowledge it will try to measure and the conditions under which it will be used. After considering these factors the test maker should be able to make a sensible choice from the range of vocabulary test formats and at least come close to making the best test.

11 Designing the vocabulary component of a language course

This chapter draws together many of the ideas discussed in other chapters by looking at the points to consider when doing curriculum design on the vocabulary component of a language course. It also describes important vocabulary principles by seeing how learners can be encouraged to take control of their vocabulary learning. This chapter follows a traditional model of curriculum design shown in Figure 11.1 (Nation, 2000b).

Goals

In general, the goals of the vocabulary component of a course will be to increase learners' usable vocabulary size and to help learners gain effective control of a range of vocabulary learning and coping strategies. 'Usable' vocabulary size implies that learners need to not only increase the vocabulary they know but also develop the fluency and skill with which they can use that vocabulary in the relevant language skills of listening, speaking, reading and writing. Similarly, 'effective control' of strategies implies that learners need to not only learn appropriate strategies but be confident and fluent in their use.

In order to set specific goals, it is essential to know if learners need to focus on high-frequency, academic, technical or low-frequency words. This is best decided on by diagnostic testing using the *Vocabulary Levels Test* or another, similar test. Knowing which of these four types of vocabulary to focus on is essential knowledge for course design because high-frequency vocabulary and low-frequency vocabulary need to be dealt with by the teacher in quite different ways.

O'Dell (1997) reviews major movements in syllabus design and particularly the role given to vocabulary. She notes the early lack of attention to vocabulary and the recent increasing attention, largely as a result of the *COBUILD* project. There are however important

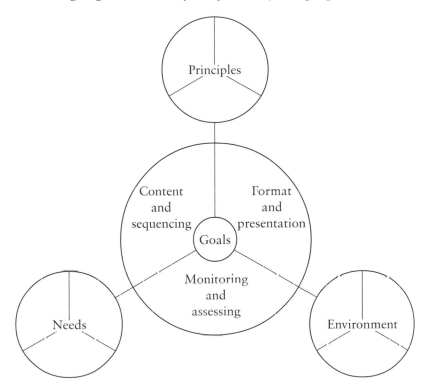

Figure 11.1 A model of the parts of the course design process

earlier examples of lexically-based syllabuses, most notably West's pioneering *New Method Readers* (1960a), the various graded readers' series which are in effect reading courses, and Helen Barnard's (1972) *Advanced English Vocabulary* which was very popular in the United States. These all give a central role to vocabulary in syllabus design.

Needs analysis

The quickest and most direct way to determine where learners are in their vocabulary development is to directly test their vocabulary knowledge. Tests like the *Vocabulary Levels Test* and the *Eurocentres Vocabulary Size Test* (Meara and Jones, 1987) can quickly indicate whether learners have sufficient control of the essential high-frequency words or not. Interpretation of the *Vocabulary Levels Test* also requires knowledge of learners' language use goals, particularly

Table 11.1. *Vocabulary needs analysis*

Type of need	Needs analysis tool
Lacks • What vocabulary do they know? • What strategies can they use?	• Vocabulary knowledge: a vocabulary size test • Vocabulary use: Lexical Frequency Profile, levels dictation • Strategy knowledge: knowledge test • Strategy use: observation of performance
Necessities • What vocabulary do they need? • What strategies do they need?	• Interview or questionnaire to determine language use goals • Refer to studies of vocabulary size and coverage
Wants • What vocabulary do they want to learn?	• Use class discussion, an interview or questionnaire to determine areas of interest

whether they intend to use English for academic study or not. Direct tests of vocabulary size however do not show whether learners are able to make use of the vocabulary they know; and they do not measure learners' control of essential vocabulary learning strategies like guessing from context, dictionary use and direct vocabulary learning. If the teacher feels the need for more detailed knowledge of learners' skill in using vocabulary, it will be necessary to look at things like the Lexical Frequency Profile of their writing (Laufer and Nation, 1995), their skill at reading a series of texts graded according to vocabulary level, their performance on the graded dictation test (appendix 5), or their skill in communicative speaking tasks, such as role playing relevant speaking tasks like talking to the doctor.

Table 11.1 looks at various types of needs and the ways that these needs can be investigated. Several needs analysis tools are listed in the table because good needs analysis covers a range of types of need (lacks, necessities, wants) and uses a range of quite different tools to get a clearer picture of what is needed.

Similarly, essential strategies can be assessed by questioning learners on their knowledge of the strategy, and by observing them using the strategy.

Published studies of the vocabulary size needed to perform certain tasks, such as reading academic texts (Sutarsyah, Nation and Kennedy, 1994) and taking part in conversation (West, 1956) are a useful source of information about how much and what kind of vocabulary learners may need. In order to choose the relevant studies to look at, it may be necessary to question learners on their future plans. Learners may have specialist areas of interest that they wish to pursue. These may include sport, cultural activities, reading interests or social activities. Discovering these through class discussion, questionnaires or interviews can help determine vocabulary needs.

Needs analysis should result in:

- an indication of which type of vocabulary (high-frequency, academic, technical, low-frequency) needs to be focused on
- an indication of how much of this type of vocabulary needs to be learned
- an indication of which strategies need attention
- an indication of any specialised areas of vocabulary that need attention
- knowledge of learners' present areas of strength in vocabulary knowledge and use, and their control of strategies

Environment analysis

Environment analysis involves discovering features of teachers, learners and the teaching/learning situation which may help or hinder learning. For example, if teachers are well informed about teaching and learning vocabulary, the course designer may not need to provide a lot of detail about the course. If learners are highly motivated and see the relevance of vocabulary learning, then ambitious learning goals could be set. If learners are not highly motivated, then regular vocabulary tests, discussion of vocabulary learning goals and reward activities may be needed.

Time is often a critical factor in courses; it may be short with much learning to be done. This may mean an emphasis on the direct learning and teaching of vocabulary, or if time is very short, an emphasis on strategies rather than particular words. Learners may favour certain styles of learning. Tinkham (1989) found that Japanese learners tended to have well developed rote learning skills, and he suggested that these should be put to good use rather than being neglected in favour of more communicative learning. The result of environment analysis should be a short list of factors that will have a strong effect on the design of the

Table 11.2. *Some environment factors and their effects on vocabulary course design*

Environment factor	The effect on the course
Learners	
• The learners share the same L1	• Use translation to define words and to test vocabulary knowledge
• The learners will do homework	• Set graded reading and direct vocabulary learning tasks
Teachers	
• The teachers do not have much time for marking	• Use vocabulary exercises with answer keys
Situation	
• L1 and L2 share cognate vocabulary	• Introduce cognate forms early in the course to get quick vocabulary growth
• Computers are available	• Use CALL activities

course. Each factor needs to be accompanied by a short description of how it will affect the course. Table 11.2 presents some examples.

Principles of vocabulary teaching

The vocabulary component of a language course should be guided by a set of well justified principles. These principles should have a major influence on: content and sequencing (what vocabulary is focused on and how it is divided into stages); format and presentation (how the vocabulary is taught and learned); monitoring and assessment (how learning is measured). Table 11.3 lists these principles and expresses them as directives. The principles focus on vocabulary teaching on the assumption that learners can be taught and can teach themselves.

It is worth noting that there are principles that some teachers and course designers follow that go against research findings. These include: 'All vocabulary learning should occur in context,' 'The first language should not be used as a means of presenting the meaning of a word,' 'Vocabulary should be presented in lexical sets,' 'Monolingual dictionaries are preferable to bilingual dictionaries,' 'Most attention should be paid to the first presentation of a word,' and 'Vocabulary learning does not benefit from being planned, but can be determined by the occurrence of words in texts, tasks and themes.' Course designers who follow these principles should read the relevant research and reconsider their position.

Table 11.3. *Principles of vocabulary teaching*

Content and sequencing
- Use frequency and range of occurrence as ways of deciding what vocabulary to learn and the order in which to learn it.
- Give adequate training in essential vocabulary learning strategies.
- Give attention to each vocabulary item according to the learning burden of that item.
- Provide opportunities to learn the various aspects of what is involved in knowing a word.
- Avoid interference by presenting vocabulary in normal use rather than in groupings of synonyms, opposites, free associates or lexical sets.
- Deal with high-frequency vocabulary by focusing on the words themselves, and deal with low-frequency vocabulary by focusing on the control of strategies.

Format and presentation
- Make sure that high-frequency target vocabulary occurs in all the four strands of meaning focused input, language-focused learning, meaning-focused output, and fluency development.
- Provide opportunity for spaced, repeated, generative retrieval of words to ensure cumulative growth.
- Use depth-of-processing activities.

Monitoring and assessment
- Test learners to see what vocabulary they need to focus on.
- Use monitoring and assessment to keep learners motivated.
- Encourage and help learners to reflect on their learning.

Content and sequencing

The principles of content choice and sequencing and the directives listed with them in Table 11.3 should guide what vocabulary is focused on at any particular stage of a course, how it is focused on (words or strategies) and how it is ordered. There are adequate word lists available to act as a basis for choosing the high-frequency and academic words to focus on. Although these lists should be used flexibly, careful thought needs to be given (and preferably research done) before making substantial changes to them. A substantial change means changing more than 5% of their content.

Within the high-frequency, academic, technical and low-frequency levels, there are sub-levels that should be considered. For example, the most common 60 words (Sublist 1) of the *Academic Word List* (Coxhead, 1998) cover 3.6% of the running words in an academic text. The fourth most common 60 words (Sublist 4) cover only 0.9%

of the running words. Clearly, it is sensible to give most attention to Sublist 1 and where possible to deal with these words before moving on to other academic words. Similarly, the 2,000 high-frequency words (West, 1953) can be divided into the most frequent 1,000 words which cover over 75% of the running words in an academic text, and the second 1,000 most frequent words which cover 5% to 6% of the running words.

One of the most important decisions concerned with content and sequencing is deciding on the 'unit of analysis' (Long and Crookes, 1992) or 'unit of progression' (Nation, 2000b). The unit of progression is what marks progress through a course. In a grammatically based course the unit of progression is generally grammatical constructions; each lesson deals with a new construction. In a functionally based course the unit of progression is language functions; each lesson deals with new functions. The unit of progression need not be a language component. Long and Crookes's (1992) advocacy of a task based syllabus sees integrated language tasks as units of progression, with progress through the course being marked by the increasing coverage of a range of tasks. The course designer needs to decide what unit of language (words, grammar items, functions, discourse types), ideas (topics, themes) or area of language use (situations, tasks) will be used to decide what goes into each lesson or unit, and how the lessons or units will be sequenced.

If vocabulary is used as the unit of progression, then each unit of the course systematically introduces new vocabulary according to principles such as frequency and range of occurrence. Some courses, like Michael West's *New Method Readers* (1960a), Helen Barnard's *Advanced English Vocabulary* (1972) and David and Jane Willis's *COBUILD English Course* (1988) have done this. Such courses generally combine a 'series' and a 'field' approach to selection and sequencing. In a series approach, the items in a course are ordered according to a principle such as frequency of occurrence, complexity or communicative need. In a field approach, a group of items is chosen and the course covers them in any order that is convenient, eventually checking that all the items in the field are adequately covered. Courses which use vocabulary as the unit of progression tend to break vocabulary lists into manageable fields, each of a few hundred words, according to frequency, which are then covered in an opportunistic way. Graded reader schemes are a very clear example of this approach to sequencing. For example, the excellent Oxford 'Bookworms' series has six levels, ranging from a vocabulary of 400 headwords at stage one to a vocabulary of 2,500 at stage six.

Sinclair and Renouf (1988) present the arguments for a lexical syllabus, surprisingly with little reference to West (1953) whose ideas are remarkably similar. Sinclair and Renouf see a lexical syllabus as describing the content and sequencing aspect of course design and being neutral regarding the methodology by which the course will be taught and how it will be assessed. They make the following points.

1. The most important criterion for deciding if and when an item should be included in a syllabus is frequency (range is not mentioned), not just frequency of word forms but also the frequency of the various meanings of those forms and their related inflected forms. Corpus-based research is the most important procedure underlying the specification of the content and sequencing of a syllabus.
2. Because the majority of the most frequent forms are function words, in the early stages of a course it is necessary to bring in lower-frequency words.
3. Care should be taken in introducing lexical sets because this goes against the criterion of frequent use. West (1951) presents similar and more elaborate arguments in his discussion of what he calls 'catenizing'. Further arguments against the presentation of lexical sets as a way of introducing vocabulary can be found in the research of Higa (1963), Tinkham (1993 and 1997) and Waring (1997b) which show the difficulty caused by learning related items together.
4. High-frequency words have many meanings but usually a few are much more frequent than the rest. It is therefore useful not only to have information about the frequency of word forms, but also to have information about the frequency of their meanings and uses.

Even where vocabulary is not the unit of progression, there needs to be selection and sequencing of vocabulary in some principled way. An important consideration in sequencing the introduction of vocabulary is the avoidance of interference. In general, courses which rely on units of progression like themes or normal language use in texts will easily avoid such interference. Where vocabulary is grouped according to paradigmatic mental associations as in situations or functions, interference will be a problem.

Like advocates of other units of progression, Sinclair and Renouf (1988) consider that if vocabulary is the unit of progression, then the appropriate grammar will automatically be met in an appropriate proportion (*ibid.*: 155). That is, it is not really necessary to check the occurrence of other language and content features. Long and Crookes (1992) make similar statements about the use of tasks as the unit of progression: if the tasks are properly chosen then there will be, as a direct result, a suitable representation of vocabulary, grammatical features and functions. A more cautious course designer however may wish to check on the representation and occurrences of high-frequency words in courses which are not lexically-based, and a list of high-frequency words is a very useful starting point. Computer programs are now available for quickly doing this (Nation and Heatley, 1996).

The outcome of the content and sequencing stage of course design is an ordered list of items that will form part of the learning goals of the course.

Format and presentation

This is the most visible aspect of course design and involves the general approach to vocabulary teaching, the selection of the teaching and learning techniques, and their arrangement into a lesson plan.

One of the basic ideas in this book is that there is a place for both direct and indirect vocabulary learning. Opportunities for indirect vocabulary learning should occupy much more time in a language learning course than direct vocabulary learning activities. This is in fact just another way of saying that contact with language in use should be given more time than decontextualised activities. The range of contextualised activities covers the range of the uses of language; as long as suitable conditions for language learning apply, then indirect vocabulary learning can take place.

As far as high-frequency vocabulary is concerned, the most important principle in handling format and presentation is ensuring that the vocabulary occurs across the four strands of meaning-focused input, language-focused learning, meaning-focused output and fluency development. This not only ensures repetition, but provides opportunities for different conditions of learning to occur which will eventually result in a good depth of knowledge for each high-frequency word. Approximately 25% of the learning time, inside and outside class, should be given to each of the four strands.

Learning through meaning-focused input and output requires around 98% coverage of the running words in the language comprehended or produced (Hu and Nation, in press). Carver (1994) argues that for native speakers this should be around 99%. This means that in meaning-focused language use, learners should know most of the language they need for a particular task, but a small percentage (1–5%) should be unfamiliar so that there is an opportunity for these items to be learned. If more than 5% of the running words are unknown, then it is likely that there is no longer meaning-focused learning because so much attention has to be given to language features. This is why simplified material is so important in language curriculum design. Without it, meaning-focused input and output will not operate successfully.

Table 11.4 lists the four strands, the general conditions which support learning in each strand, special vocabulary requirements, and the activities that put the conditions and requirements into practice. More information on each of the strands can be found in the relevant chapters of this book: chapter 4 describes learning from input with a focus on spoken input and learning through spoken meaning-focused output; chapters 7 and 8 describe the development of vocabulary strategies that are an important part of language-focused learning.

As a part of format and presentation, a teacher should evaluate the quality of the teaching and learning techniques used to ensure that conditions like repetition, retrieval, generation and thoughtful processing occur. If they do not occur, then the techniques should be adapted or replaced. For the teaching and learning of vocabulary strategies, it is fruitful to design mini-syllabuses that cover all the important aspects of a particular strategy and provide plenty of repetition and practice to ensure that learners have a good chance of gaining fluent control of the strategy. Using a variety of techniques is one way of keeping learners' interest. The outcome of the format and presentation stage of course design is a format for a lesson and an organised, balanced set of teaching and learning procedures.

Monitoring and assessment

A well designed course monitors learners' progress and the quality of their learning. It is extremely important that at the beginning of a course the teacher and the learners know what vocabulary level they should be focusing on. This is particularly vital for teachers because the way in which they deal with high-frequency words is quite different from the way that they deal with low-frequency words.

It is also useful to test learners' control of the various vocabulary learning strategies. These can be assessed in two complementary ways. One way is to see how well learners understand the strategies, the steps involved in applying them and the knowledge required at each step. Another way is to see how well learners apply the strategies under conditions of normal use. It may also be useful to look at learners' attitudes to each strategy – whether they value it, see its usefulness and are willing to apply it. Some studies (Moir, 1996) have shown that even though learners understand some strategies, they feel that they are not particularly useful for them.

Table 11.4. *The four strands and their application with a focus on vocabulary*

Strand	General conditions	Vocabulary requirements	Activities and techniques
Meaning-focused input	• Focus on the message • Some unfamiliar items • Understanding • Noticing	• 95%+ coverage (preferably 98%) • Skill at guessing from context • Opportunity to negotiate • Incidental defining and attention drawing	• Reading graded readers • Listening to stories • Communication activities
Language-focused learning	• Focus on language items	• Skill in vocabulary learning strategies • Appropriate teacher focus on high-frequency words, and strategies for low-frequency words	• Direct teaching of vocabulary • Direct learning • Intensive reading • Training in vocabulary strategies
Meaning-focused output	• Focus on the message • Some unfamiliar items • Understanding • Noticing	• 95%+ coverage (preferably 98%) • Encouragement to use unfamiliar items • Supportive input	• Communication activities with written input • Prepared writing • Linked skills
Fluency development	• Focus on the message • Little or no unfamiliar language • Pressure to perform faster	• 99%+ coverage • Repetition	• Reading easy graded readers • Repeated reading • Speed reading • Listening to easy input • 4/3/2 • Rehearsed tasks • 10 minute writing • Linked skills

Assessment can be used to look at progress, and it can also be used to encourage learners. Regular short-term achievement tests can help learners focus on vocabulary learning. These need to be carefully monitored to make sure the learners are not just going through the motions to satisfy the teacher.

Table 11.5 outlines the main options available for assessing learners' vocabulary knowledge within a course. In the table, placement tests have not been distinguished as a different type of test as their job can be performed by diagnostic or proficiency tests. Chapter 10 looks at vocabulary testing in more detail.

Evaluation

Evaluation tries to determine how good a course is. 'Good' can be defined from various viewpoints: good according to the students, good according to a teacher, good according to the curriculum designer, good according to an outside expert, good according to the business manager of a language programme and so on. Each of these people will be interested in different things and will look at different aspects of the course. The business manager will want to see if the course made a profit and if the learners were satisfied enough to recommend the course to others. The learners will think a course is good if they enjoyed the classes and felt they made relevant progress. Evaluation is thus a very broad topic and could involve looking at any or all parts of the curriculum design process and asking such questions as:

- Were the goals reached?
- Did the course take account of the important environment factors?
- Were the learners' needs met?
  and many others.

Table 11.6 presents an evaluation schedule that could be used to see if the vocabulary component of a course was getting informed attention.

A useful form of ongoing evaluation that can reshape a course is the careful observation of learning activities. There are four important questions that teachers can ask when doing this that we looked at in chapter 3 on conditions for vocabulary learning.

- What are the goals of the activity?
- What psychological conditions are needed to reach that goal?
- What are the signs that the conditions are occurring?
- What are the design features of the activity that make the conditions likely to occur?

Table 11.5. *Options for the assessment of vocabulary in a course*

Type of assessment	Aims of assessment	Available tests, test formats (length of the test)	How often and when administered	Content of the test
Diagnostic	• To determine the appropriate vocabulary level to work on • To place students in an appropriate group	• Vocabulary Levels Test (20–30 minutes)	• Once at the beginning of the course	• Vocabulary sampled from frequency levels
Short-term achievement	• To monitor progress • To motivate learners • To guide changes to the course	• A wide variety of easily prepared formats testing a range of aspects of vocabulary knowledge (10 minutes)	• Every week or fortnight throughout the course	• Vocabulary chosen from course materials or by learners
Long-term achievement	• To determine how well and how much vocabulary has been learned in the course • To help plan the next course	• Multiple-choice • Matching • Yes/No (30–40 minutes)	• Twice: at the beginning and at the end	• Vocabulary chosen from course materials
Proficiency	• To determine vocabulary size • To place students in an appropriate group	• Eurocentres Vocabulary Size Test (30–40 minutes)	• Once (or twice): at the end (and beginning)	• Vocabulary sampled from a dictionary or a frequency count

Table 11.6. *Evaluating the vocabulary component of a language programme*

What to look for	How to look for it	How to include it
Does the teacher know what the learners' vocabulary level and needs are?	• Ask the teacher	• Use the levels test • Interview the learners
Is the programme focusing appropriately on the most suitable level of vocabulary?	• Look at what vocabulary or strategies are being taught	• Decide whether the focus is high-frequency, academic, or low-frequency vocabulary
Is the vocabulary helpfully sequenced?	• Check that opposites, near synonyms or lexical sets are not being presented in the same lesson	• Use texts and normal use to sequence the vocabulary
Are the skills activities designed to help vocabulary learning?	• Look at the written input to the activities • Ask the teacher	• Include and monitor wanted vocabulary in the written input
Is there a suitable proportion of opportunities to develop fluency with known vocabulary?	• Look at the amount of graded reading, listening to stories, free writing and message based speaking	• Use techniques that develop 'well-beaten paths' and 'rich maps'
Does the presentation of vocabulary help learning?	• Look for deliberate repetition and spacing • Rate the activities for depth of processing	• Develop teaching and revision cycles • Choose a few deep processing techniques to use often
Are the learners excited about their progress?	• Watch the learners doing tasks • Ask the learners	• Set goals • Give feedback on progress • Keep records

Curriculum design can be seen as a continuing process, with adaptations and improvements being made even while the course is being taught. Good curriculum design means maintaining a balance between the various parts of the curriculum design process, so that important sources of input to the design are not ignored. The use of the eight part model – goals, needs, environment, principles, content and sequencing, format and presentation, monitoring and assessment, and evaluation – is an attempt to keep that balance by clearly distinguishing the parts to consider.

Let us now, using the curriculum design model, look at how learners can be encouraged to take responsibility for their own vocabulary learning.

Autonomy and vocabulary learning

Autonomous learners take control and responsibility for their own learning. This does not necessarily mean that they study alone. It is possible to be an autonomous learner in a strongly teacher-led class – by deciding what should be given the greatest attention and effort, what should be looked at again later, how the material presented should be mentally processed and how interaction with the teacher and others in the class should be carried out. No matter what the teacher does or what the course book presents, ultimately it is the learner who does the learning. The more learners are aware of how learning is best carried out, the better learning is likely to be. Here we will look at the kind of knowledge that a vocabulary learner needs to become autonomous, how that knowledge can be gained, and how autonomy can be fostered and hindered. It is useful to think of autonomy as relying on three factors: attitude, awareness, and capability.

1. *Attitude* is the need for the learner to want to take control and responsibility for learning. This is one of the hardest aspects of autonomy to develop and yet it is the most crucial. Moir (1996) found in her study that although most vocabulary learners knew what they should do and knew that what they were doing was not efficient, they were reluctant to make the needed changes. Immediate pressures, the influence of past behaviour and the effect of teacher demands easily overrode the wish to take control of their own learning.
2. *Awareness* is the need for the learner to be conscious of what approaches are being taken, to reflect on their effects and to consider other approaches. Some writers on autonomy consider that all autonomous learning must involve metacognitive

awareness (there is no autonomy without metacognition). In the development of autonomy, reflection is a very powerful tool and this alone may be sufficient to justify seeing metacognitive awareness as an important aspect of autonomy.

3. *Capability* is the need for the learner to possess the skills and knowledge to be autonomous in a particular area of study.

The remainder of this section discusses the knowledge and skills needed to be an autonomous vocabulary learner. The discussion is organised into eight principles of vocabulary learning, for example, the important principle that learners should direct their attention to the high-frequency words of the language. The reason for using such principles as the basis for a discussion of autonomy is that principles provide an opportunity for dialogue about learning, for personal reflection, and for the systematic coverage of a field of knowledge. These eight principles are grouped according to the major parts of the syllabus design process, namely: goals, content and sequencing, format and presentation, monitoring and assessment.

Although a list of principles is provided, to truly encourage autonomy, learners will later need to reflect on these principles on the basis of experience and to confirm, reject, modify or add to them. A similar list of principles can be found in Graves (1987).

The goals of vocabulary learning

Principle 1: Learners should know what vocabulary to learn, what to learn about it, how to learn it, how to put it to use and how to see how well it has been learned and used.

Because this principle represents the goals of vocabulary learning, it is in essence a summary of most of the other vocabulary learning principles. It subsumes content and sequencing, format and presentation, and monitoring and assessment.

Principle 2: Learners should continue to increase their vocabulary size and enrich the words they already know.

Whereas Principle 1 focuses on the nature of vocabulary learning, Principle 2 focuses on the results.

What should be learned and in what order?

Principle 3: Learners should use word frequency and personal need to determine what vocabulary should be learned.

This principle means that learners should be learning high-frequency words before low-frequency words, except where personal need and interest give importance to what otherwise would be low-frequency words. A learner with academic goals should be focusing on words in the *Academic Word List* (see appendix 1) after the general service high-frequency words are known.

Information about word frequency is not as accessible as it should be. The second edition of the *COBUILD Dictionary* (Sinclair, 1996) tags the higher-frequency words of English. It uses a useful system of five frequency bands which allows learners to distinguish high-frequency words from those of moderate and low-frequency. Unfortunately, the selection of words is suspect; the second highest band contains many very strange items (*Lithuanian, Byelorussian, Yemeni*) indicating that perhaps frequency alone and not frequency combined with range was used to select the words, or that an arbitrary decision was made regarding some kinds of proper nouns. Nevertheless, the idea of indicating frequency in learners' dictionaries is an excellent idea and a major step forward. The *Longman Dictionary of Contemporary English* also marks the high-frequency words in speaking and writing.

With a little practice and feedback it may be possible for learners to develop a feeling for what is high-frequency and what is low-frequency. This may be easier for speakers of other European languages to do for English vocabulary than for, say, speakers of Asian languages. Eaton's (1940) comparison of English, French, German and Spanish word frequency lists showed very close correspondences between the frequency levels of words referring to similar concepts in the four languages. The major problem in developing an intuitive feel for word frequency comes with synonyms like *start, begin, commence*. Generally, however, in English there is a tendency for shorter words to be more frequent than longer words, and for words of Anglo-Saxon origin to be more frequent than the morphologically more complex words from French, Latin or Greek. This area of developing learners' intuitions about word frequency is unresearched. However, for the 2,000 high-frequency words and the *Academic Word List*, teachers can usefully provide lists for learners to use as checklists that they can refer to as a frequency guide.

Hirsh and Nation (1992: 695) found that the more times a word occurred in one novel, the more likely it was to be found in other novels. If learners notice words recurring in their reading, this should suggest to them that the word is worth learning.

There are now computer programs which quickly turn a text into a word frequency list. Learners can get quite excited about such a list when they see the very high coverage of the text provided by a small number of high-frequency words, and the large number of low-frequency words needed to cover even a small proportion of the text.

This visual demonstration can be a useful way of underlining the importance of the high-frequency/low-frequency distinction.

McKenzie (1990) suggests that learners should focus on words they have met before but only partially understand. This ensures that the words are not in fact low-frequency but are words that have been repeated and are likely to be met again. Carroll and Mordaunt (1991: 24) suggest that the words chosen for study should not only be partially known but also ones learners can think of themselves using soon. McKenzie, and Carroll and Mordaunt, drawing on Pauk (1984), call these words 'frontier words' because they are on the boundary or frontier of the learner's present vocabulary knowledge.

Principle 4: Learners should be aware of what is involved in knowing a word and should be able to find that information about particular words.

Knowing a word involves knowing a wide range of features. At its most basic this involves being familiar with the written and spoken forms of the word and being able to associate a meaning with those forms. While this kind of knowledge is critically important, it is only a part of what is involved in knowing a word. Other kinds of knowledge include: being able to use it grammatically correctly in a sentence with suitable collocations, being able to interpret and create other members of its word family by using inflectional and derivational affixes, being aware of restrictions on the use of the word for cultural, geographical, stylistic or register reasons, and being aware of the range of meanings and associations the word has. For some words, much of this knowledge will be highly predictable from knowledge of the learners' first language and their knowledge of the subsystems of English. For other words, there will be a lot of new learning.

Learners need to be aware of the different things there are to know about a word. This awareness needs to be based on some organised system so that learners know what to look for and can easily check for gaps in their knowledge. One system is to use the categories shown in Table 2.1 (see p. 27) on what is involved in knowing a word. This table uses a simple three-part division with each succeeding part being more elaborate. It can be used as a means of recording information about words. The 'word spider' (McComish, 1990) uses similar divisions.

Learners can be alerted to the importance of this range of information about words by feedback on errors they make in vocabulary use, by reporting to others on new words they have met (Mhone, 1988) and by comparing information on L2 words with the corresponding L1 words. In order to gather this information for themselves, learners need to become skilful and critical in their dictionary use and need to be able to gather information from seeing words in context. This use

of context to gain information on grammar, collocation and derivatives can make use of computer-based concordance searches (McKay,
1980; Descamps, 1992; Stevens, 1991). Developing skill in gathering
this kind of information can begin as a cooperative activity in groups;
the group discussion and analysis can act as a consciousness-raising
activity (Ellis, 1992) encouraging reflection and metacognitive awareness of what is involved in knowing a word.

Principle 5: Learners should be familiar with the generalisable language systems that lie behind vocabulary use.

In spite of the irregularity of many aspects of language use, there are
regular patterns that can be used to help comprehend and produce language. These patterns exist at all levels – orthographic, phonological,
morphological, collocational, grammatical and discourse. Because
knowledge of these patterns allows learners to comprehend and
produce language that they have not met in that exact form before,
these patterns are much more important than the exceptions and
deserve more attention from the teacher and learner. Here are some
examples of patterns that affect vocabulary use.

- Spelling: the rule governing free and checked vowels affects a lot of
  English spelling including the doubling of consonants and the use of
  final silent *e*. The rule can be exemplified through the written
  vowel *i*. The free pronunciation of *i* is /ai/, the checked pronunciation is /i/. The free pronunciation usually occurs in the following
  pattern (c = consonant, v = vowel):

    *i*cv   (the vowel may be final silent *e*)   *dine, dining*

  The checked pronunciation usually occurs in the following patterns:

    *i*c   (where c is the final letter in a word)   *din*
    *i*ccv   *dinner, spinning*

  Note that when *-ing* is added to *spin*, the *n* is doubled so that *i*
  can keep its checked pronunciation.
      The rule governing free and checked vowels only applies to
  stressed syllables. Not only *i*, but also *a*, *e*, *o* and *u* have free and
  checked pronunciations and follow the same rule.

- Pronunciation: there is a grammar of sounds which describes the
  order and sounds that can occur in consonant clusters in English.
  For example, /spr/ is a permitted initial cluster, while /srp/ is not.

- Word building: there is a small group of very frequent, regular
  affixes which can be used to create new words (Bauer and Nation,

1993). These include: *-able, -er, -ish, -less, -ly, -ness, -th, -y, non-, un-*.

- *Collocation*: Sinclair's (1991) corpus-based studies of collocation show that there are general descriptions that can be used to characterise the collocates of a particular word. For example, *set about* typically refers to 'a subsidiary aim within a grander design. "We set about x in order, ultimately, to achieve Y."' (*ibid*.: 76)

In some cases, learners can gain information about these patterns through reading descriptions of them, for example, in grammar books written for learners of English. In other cases, they will need to rely on explanation from the teacher. The most important requirements are an awareness that there are patterns and an interest in looking for them. Awareness and interest can often be stimulated by activities which use data in the form of examples that have to be classified or analysed. Many of the consciousness-raising activities described by Ellis (1992) are like this. Learners also need to know which books containing descriptions of English are the most useful and accessible for them, and need to gain skill and confidence in using them. When learners meet a new word, they should reflect on the ways in which it is similar to the words they already know. This reflection need not be restricted to the second language but should also involve comparison with the first language. Many learners expect that English courses will teach them grammar and other descriptive aspects of the language and they feel somewhat cheated if a course does not do this. This perceived need can be usefully satisfied by encouraging learners to discover the frequent regular patterns that lie behind language use.

Learning procedures

Principle 6: Learners should know how to make the most effective use of direct, decontextualised learning procedures.

There has been a very large amount of research on the effectiveness of direct, decontextualised learning of vocabulary even though many teachers and writers about language learning have negative attitudes towards it. If it is the only kind of vocabulary learning undertaken it is insufficient, but when it is used along with message-focused incidental learning it can be extremely effective. There are several sub-principles that can guide this kind of learning.

1. Retrieve rather than recognise.
2. Use appropriately sized groups of cards.
3. Space the repetitions.
4. Repeat the words aloud or to yourself.

5. Process the words thoughtfully.
6. Avoid interference.
7. Avoid a serial learning effect.
8. Use context where this helps.

Because there are a number of sub-principles, it is worth giving plenty of time to developing an understanding of them and observing them in action. This can be done in several ways.

• Learners trial a principle and report on it to the class.
• Learners observe others learning, comment on what they see and interview the learners.
• Learners organise simple experiments with one group applying a principle and the other group deliberately not applying it. For example, one group can learn unrelated words while another learns closely related words. Or one group learns with cards and the other learns from a printed list.
• Learners report on successful and unsuccessful learning.
• Learners are tested on their understanding and application of the principles.

Learners may be aware of principles and yet not apply them. Counselling and class discussion needs to examine the causes of this and see what can be done.

Principle 7: Vocabulary learning needs to operate across the four strands of meaning-focused input, language-focused learning, meaning-focused output and fluency development.

There is a feeling among some teachers that focusing on vocabulary and grammar out of context is detrimental to learning. The research evidence does not support this view which suggests that there is only one way to do things. It is much more effective to see the many approaches to learning as complementary, each bringing different strengths that together can provide balanced support for learning.

One way of dividing up the approaches is to distinguish them on the basis of the conditions for learning that they set up. Table 11.7 outlines these approaches.

In terms of vocabulary learning, a balanced vocabulary course has a roughly equal proportion of time given to each of these four strands. This can be expressed as four sub-principles.

1. Learners need to have the opportunity to meet and learn vocabulary incidentally through meaning-focused listening and through extensive reading of material at a suitable level of difficulty.

Table 11.7. *The four strands of a language course*

Strand	Conditions for learning	Example activities
Meaning-focused input	• Focus on the message • Include a small number of unfamiliar items • Draw attention to the new items	• Extensive graded reading • Listening to stories • Working with familiar content
Language-focused learning	• Focus on language features (vocabulary, structures . . .) • Do deliberate repeated retrieval of the items	• Learning from word cards • Grammar exercises • Read difficult text
Meaning-focused output	• Focus on the message • Include a small number of new items	• Communication activities • Research and write
Fluency development	• Focus on the message • Work with completely familiar material • Work at a higher than normal speed • Do a large quantity of language use	• Repeated reading • Repeated speaking on familiar topics • Graded reading

This means that autonomous learners need to know ways to obtain comprehensible input: interacting with learners at a level roughly similar to theirs, interacting with native speakers who are sensitive to their level of knowledge of the language, preparing for communicative activity before it occurs, and choosing reading and listening material that suits their level of knowledge.

2. Learners need to be able to effectively choose and learn vocabulary using word cards and other decontextualised ways of learning.

   Here decontextualised means that vocabulary learning is not occurring in normal language use, but is taking place through words being deliberately focused on as part of the language system. The focus is directed towards their spelling, pronunciation, grammar, meaning, use, and the linguistic rules that lie behind those parts of the language systems.

3. Learners need to be encouraged – and have the opportunity – to use vocabulary in speaking and writing where their major focus is on communicating messages.

   Having to produce vocabulary to achieve communicative goals helps learners stretch their knowledge of words and become aware of gaps in their knowledge. It helps them gain control of the aspects of productive knowledge that differ from those required for receptive use. Autonomous learners need to be brave enough to seek out opportunities for speaking and writing, and need to know how to use those situations to set up conditions that can lead to successful learning.

4. Learners need to have the chance to use known vocabulary both receptively and productively under conditions that help them increase the fluency with which they can access and use that vocabulary.

   Learners not only need to know vocabulary, they need to be able to use it fluently. Decontextualised learning can rapidly increase vocabulary size, but message-focused language use, with very easy language and easy communicative demands, is needed to achieve fluency. In addition, there needs to be some pressure on the learners or some encouragement to perform at a faster than normal speed.

   It is not difficult for learners to arrange their own fluency activities. In reading, learners can work through a speed reading course which has strict vocabulary control, read graded readers at a level below their normal comfort level of reading and reread the same material several times. While doing this learners need to be aware that their goal is to increase speed. They should also reflect on how the language unit that they give attention to changes as fluency develops: from having to become fluent at decoding individual letters (particularly if the English writing system differs from that of the first language) they next move to the speedy recognition of words and then to the anticipation of phrases.

Learners can take control of the development of their writing fluency by writing on very easy topics, by writing on closely related topics, and by writing on the same topic several times. They can also write on topics that they have already read about and discussed, and on topics that relate closely to their own training and experience.

Learners can assume control of their listening and speaking fluency development by: setting up repeated opportunities to do the same kind of speaking; getting a teacher or friend to give them repeated practice with important words, phrases and sentences (numbers, dates, greetings and polite phrases, descriptions of yourself, your job, your recent experiences, your country, etc.), and by rehearsal just before speaking. It is usually not too difficult to anticipate the things that learners will need to talk about most often, and with the help of a teacher or friend these can be written out, checked for correctness, and then memorised and rehearsed to a high degree of fluency. The items in Crabbe and Nation's (1991) survival syllabus provide a useful starting point.

It is not easy to arrive at a suitable balance; learners need to make sure that the vocabulary that has been deliberately studied is also used for meaningful communication wherever possible and is brought to a suitable level of fluency. Similarly, vocabulary development through extensive reading needs to be stabilised and enriched through the deliberate study of words, affixes and lexical sets.

Checking learning

Principle 8: Learners should be aware of, and excited by, their progress in vocabulary learning.

It is often difficult for learners to realise that they are making progress in their learning. Learning a language is a long-term task which is often marked by frustration and disappointment when successful communication does not occur. Learners need to find ways of monitoring their progress and should use these when they feel the need for encouragement. There are several ways in which learners can keep track of their vocabulary learning.

1. A record of how many words have been learned should be kept; there are several ways of doing this. One method is to keep a record of the packs of vocabulary cards that have been used for

direct study. If the words already learned are kept in packs of 50, this becomes an easy task. Looking back over these familiar words can give a feeling of achievement. Another way to keep a record of quantity is to look through a dictionary and see how many words per page are known. If a frequency graded list is available, this can be used as a self-administered test to chart progress.

2. A feeling of progress may be encouraged by keeping a record of how quickly learning can occur. For example, after making a pack of 50 vocabulary cards to study, learners could record how much time and how many repetitions are needed to learn 80% or more of the words in the pack. The results will be surprising.

3. It is useful to make a list of situations and topics where the second language is used, and to tick these off as a certain degree of success is achieved. Table 11.8 contains a sample list.

   Using such a list makes learning more goal directed and breaks down a big task into smaller short-term goals.

   The list can also be used as a record of fluency development. An item can be ticked off when the vocabulary and phrases are known, and ticked off again when knowledge of these words and phrases has reached a high degree of fluency. For example, when buying stamps at a post office it is possible to know all the necessary numbers and words although further learning may be needed to quickly understand the numbers when the clerk tells the learner how much the stamps cost or asks unexpected questions. This can be practised and success noted.

4. Learners should record examples of their language use at regular intervals. These examples may be audio or video tapes, examples of written work, or texts read and understood. Looking back over earlier performance can provide reassurance that progress has been made. If a course book is used, then going back over very early lessons that once were difficult can give a feeling of progress. A further way of charting progress is to ask a native speaker friend to monitor progress by evaluating language use at regular intervals.

The principles outlined here focus on vocabulary, but learners should be encouraged to reflect on these principles which clearly apply to other kinds of learning. Taking personal control of learning is a challenge. It is a challenge for the learner to gain the attitude, awareness and capability required for control. It is also a challenge for the teacher, who needs to help foster these three requirements while stepping back from control.

Table 11.8. *A checklist of common situations*

1. Giving information about yourself and your family
- name
- address
- phone
- partner and family
- length of residence
- origin
- job
- age

2. Asking others for similar information

3. Meeting people
- greetings
- talking about the weather
- inviting for a meal, etc.
- telling the time and day
- saying what you like
- saying you are sorry
- joining a club

4. Going shopping
- finding goods
- asking for a quantity
- understanding prices

5. Using important services
- post office
- bank
- public telephone
- police
- garage

6. Asking how to get to places

7. Telling others directions
- directions
- distance and time
- using public transport

8. Taking care of your health
- contacting a doctor
- reporting illness
- describing previous illness and medical conditions
- calling emergency services

Table 11.8 (*cont.*)

9. Describing your home, town and country
- house/flat and furniture
- features of the town
- features of your country

10. Asking others for similar information

11. Describing your job

12. Asking others about their job
- the work they do
- place
- conditions
- travelling to work

13. Finding out how to get a job
- kind of job
- where to look
- what to do

14. Finding food and drink
- getting attention
- using a menu
- ordering a meal
- offering food
- praising the food
- finding a toilet
- giving thanks

15. Taking part in sport and entertainment
- saying when you are free
- buying tickets
- say what you like and do not like doing

16. Special needs

Appendixes

1. Headwords of the *Academic Word List*

This appendix contains the headwords of the families in the *Academic Word List*. The number beside each word indicates the sublist in which it appears. For example, *abandon* and its family members are in Sublist 8 of the *Academic Word List*. Sublist 1 contains the most frequent words, and Sublist 10 the least frequent. The list comes from Coxhead (1998).

abandon	8	amend	5	automate	8
abstract	6	analogy	9	available	1
academy	5	analyse	1	aware	5
access	4	annual	4	behalf	9
accommodate	9	anticipate	9	benefit	1
accompany	8	apparent	4	bias	8
accumulate	8	append	8	bond	6
accurate	6	appreciate	8	brief	6
achieve	2	approach	1	bulk	9
acknowledge	6	appropriate	2	capable	6
acquire	2	approximate	4	capacity	5
adapt	7	arbitrary	8	category	2
adequate	4	area	1	cease	9
adjacent	10	aspect	2	challenge	5
adjust	5	assemble	10	channel	7
administrate	2	assess	1	chapter	2
adult	7	assign	6	chart	8
advocate	7	assist	2	chemical	7
affect	2	assume	1	circumstance	3
aggregate	6	assure	9	cite	6
aid	7	attach	6	civil	4
albeit	10	attain	9	clarify	8
allocate	6	attitude	4	classic	7
alter	5	attribute	4	clause	5
alternative	3	author	6	code	4
ambiguous	8	authority	1	coherent	9

407

coincide	9	contrast	4	distort	9
collapse	10	contribute	3	distribute	1
colleague	10	controversy	9	diverse	6
commence	9	convene	3	document	3
comment	3	converse	9	domain	6
commission	2	convert	7	domestic	4
commit	4	convince	10	dominate	3
commodity	8	cooperate	6	draft	5
communicate	4	coordinate	3	drama	8
community	2	core	3	duration	9
compatible	9	corporate	3	dynamic	7
compensate	3	correspond	3	economy	1
compile	10	couple	7	edit	6
complement	8	create	1	element	2
complex	2	credit	2	eliminate	7
component	3	criteria	3	emerge	4
compound	5	crucial	8	emphasis	3
comprehensive	7	culture	2	empirical	7
comprise	7	currency	8	enable	5
compute	2	cycle	4	encounter	10
conceive	10	data	1	energy	5
concentrate	4	debate	4	enforce	5
concept	1	decade	7	enhance	6
conclude	2	decline	5	enormous	10
concurrent	9	deduce	3	ensure	3
conduct	2	define	1	entity	5
confer	4	definite	7	environment	1
confine	9	demonstrate	3	equate	2
confirm	7	denote	8	equip	7
conflict	5	deny	7	equivalent	5
conform	8	depress	10	erode	9
consent	3	derive	1	error	4
consequent	2	design	2	establish	1
considerable	3	despite	4	estate	6
consist	1	detect	8	estimate	1
constant	3	deviate	8	ethic	9
constitute	1	device	9	ethnic	4
constrain	3	devote	9	evaluate	2
construct	2	differentiate	7	eventual	8
consult	5	dimension	4	evident	1
consume	2	diminish	9	evolve	5
contact	5	discrete	5	exceed	6
contemporary	8	discriminate	6	exclude	3
context	1	displace	8	exhibit	8
contract	1	display	6	expand	5
contradict	8	dispose	7	expert	6
contrary	7	distinct	2	explicit	6

exploit	8	impact	2	isolate	7
export	1	implement	4	issue	1
expose	5	implicate	4	item	2
external	5	implicit	8	job	4
extract	7	imply	3	journal	2
facilitate	5	impose	4	justify	3
factor	1	incentive	6	label	4
feature	2	incidence	6	labour	1
federal	6	incline	10	layer	3
fee	6	income	1	lecture	6
file	7	incorporate	6	legal	1
final	2	index	6	legislate	1
finance	1	indicate	1	levy	10
finite	7	individual	1	liberal	5
flexible	6	induce	8	licence	5
fluctuate	8	inevitable	8	likewise	10
focus	2	infer	7	link	3
format	9	infrastructure	8	locate	3
formula	1	inherent	9	logic	5
forthcoming	10	inhibit	6	maintain	2
foundation	7	initial	3	major	1
found	9	initiate	6	manipulate	8
framework	3	injure	2	manual	9
function	1	innovate	7	margin	5
fund	3	input	6	mature	9
fundamental	5	insert	7	maximise	3
furthermore	6	insight	9	mechanism	4
gender	6	inspect	8	media	7
generate	5	instance	3	mediate	9
generation	5	institute	2	medical	5
globe	7	instruct	6	medium	9
goal	4	integral	9	mental	5
grade	7	integrate	4	method	1
grant	4	integrity	10	migrate	6
guarantee	7	intelligence	6	military	9
guideline	8	intense	8	minimal	9
hence	4	interact	3	minimise	8
hierarchy	7	intermediate	9	minimum	6
highlight	8	internal	4	ministry	6
hypothesis	4	interpret	1	minor	3
identical	7	interval	6	mode	7
identify	1	intervene	7	modify	5
ideology	7	intrinsic	10	monitor	5
ignorance	6	invest	2	motive	6
illustrate	3	investigate	4	mutual	9
image	5	invoke	10	negate	3
immigrate	3	involve	1	network	5

neutral	6	precede	6	rely	3
nevertheless	6	precise	5	remove	3
nonetheless	10	predict	4	require	1
norm	9	predominant	8	research	1
normal	2	preliminary	9	reside	2
notion	5	presume	6	resolve	4
notwithstanding	10	previous	2	resource	2
nuclear	8	primary	2	respond	1
objective	5	prime	5	restore	8
obtain	2	principal	4	restrain	9
obvious	4	principle	1	restrict	2
occupy	4	prior	4	retain	4
occur	1	priority	7	reveal	6
odd	10	proceed	1	revenue	5
offset	8	process	1	reverse	7
ongoing	10	professional	4	revise	8
option	4	prohibit	7	revolution	9
orient	5	project	4	rigid	9
outcome	3	promote	4	role	1
output	4	proportion	3	route	9
overall	4	prospect	8	scenario	9
overlap	9	protocol	9	schedule	8
overseas	6	psychology	5	scheme	3
panel	10	publication	7	scope	6
paradigm	7	publish	3	section	1
paragraph	8	purchase	2	sector	1
parallel	4	pursue	5	secure	2
parameter	4	qualitative	9	seek	2
participate	2	quote	7	select	2
partner	3	radical	8	sequence	3
passive	9	random	8	series	4
perceive	2	range	2	sex	3
percent	1	ratio	5	shift	3
period	1	rational	6	significant	1
persist	10	react	3	similar	1
perspective	5	recover	6	simulate	7
phase	4	refine	9	site	2
phenomenon	7	regime	4	so-called	10
philosophy	3	region	2	sole	7
physical	3	register	3	somewhat	7
plus	8	regulate	2	source	1
policy	1	reinforce	8	specific	1
portion	9	reject	5	specify	3
pose	10	relax	9	sphere	9
positive	2	release	7	stable	5
potential	2	relevant	2	statistic	4
practitioner	8	reluctance	10	status	4

straightforward	10	team	9	undergo	10
strategy	2	technical	3	underlie	6
stress	4	technique	3	undertake	4
structure	1	technology	3	uniform	8
style	5	temporary	9	unify	9
submit	7	tense	8	unique	7
subordinate	9	terminate	8	utilise	6
subsequent	4	text	2	valid	3
subsidy	6	theme	8	vary	1
substitute	5	theory	1	vehicle	8
successor	7	thereby	8	version	5
sufficient	3	thesis	7	via	8
sum	4	topic	7	violate	9
summary	4	trace	6	virtual	8
supplement	9	tradition	2	visible	7
survey	2	transfer	2	vision	9
survive	7	transform	6	visual	8
suspend	9	transit	5	volume	3
sustain	5	transmit	7	voluntary	7
symbol	5	transport	6	welfare	5
tape	6	trend	5	whereas	5
target	5	trigger	9	whereby	10
task	3	ultimate	7	widespread	8

2. 1,000 word level tests

A description of the making of these two tests can be found in Nation (1993a).

VOCABULARY TEST: 1,000 WORD LEVEL TEST A
Write T if a sentence is true. Write N if it is not true. Write X if you do not understand the sentence. The first one has been answered for you.

We cut time into minutes, hours and days.   T

This one is little.   ____

You can find these everywhere.   ____

Some children call their mother Mama.   ____

Show me the way to do it means 'show me how to do it'.   ____

This country is part of the world.   ____

This can keep people away from your house.   ____

When something falls, it goes up.   ____

Most children go to school at night.   ____

It is easy for children to remain still.   ____

One person can carry this.   ____

A scene is a part of a play.   ____

People often think of their home, when they are away from it.   ____

There is a mountain in every city.   ____

Each month has the same number of days.   ____

A chief is the youngest person in a group.   ____

Black is a colour. ____

You can use a pen to make marks on paper. ____

A family always has at least two people. ____

You can go by road from London to New York. ____

Silver costs a lot of money. ____

This is a hill. ____

This young person is a girl. ____

We can be sure that one day we will die. ____

A society is made of people living together. ____

An example can help you understand. ____

Some books have pictures in them. ____

When some people attack other people, they try to hurt them. ____

When something is ancient, it is very big. ____

Big ships can sail up a stream. ____

It is good to keep a promise. ____

People often dream when they are sleeping. ____

This is a date – 10 o'clock. ____

When something is impossible, it is easy to do it. ____

Milk is blue. ____

A square has five sides. ____

Boats are made to travel on land. ____

Cars cannot pass each other on a wide road. ____

When you look at something closely, you can see the details. ____

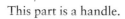

This part is a handle. ____

VOCABULARY TEST: 1,000 WORD LEVEL TEST B

Write T if a sentence is true. Write N if it is not true. Write X if you do not understand the sentence. The first one has been answered for you.

We can stop time.   N

Two of these are little.    ___

You must look, when you want to find the way.   ___

When someone asks 'What are you called?', you should say your name. ___

There are many ways to get money.   ___

All the world is under water.   ___

When you keep asking, you ask once.   ___

Sometimes people die when they fall off a building.   ___

Day follows night and night follows day.   ___

Remain here means 'stay'.   ___

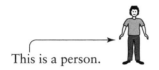

This is a person.   ___

When there is a change of scene, we see a different place.   ___

Often means 'many times'.   ___

This is a mountain.   ___

Each month has a different name.   ___

People follow the orders of a chief.   ___

Green is a colour.   ___

Dirty hands cannot leave marks on glass.   ___

You need at least five people to make a group.   ___

Cars move on a road.   _____

You can eat silver.   _____

You can see more when you are on a hill.   _____

Your child will be a girl or a boy.   _____

When you are sure, you know you are right.   _____

Each society has the same rules.   _____

Three examples of food are: shops, homes, and markets.   _____

This is a picture.   _____

It is good to attack people.   _____

Rome is an ancient city.   _____

A stream is a small river.   _____

When you promise something, you say you will really do it.   _____

Dreams are about things that really happened.   _____

When we give a date, we say the day, the month and the year.   _____

It is impossible to live for a long time without water.   _____

Very young children drink milk.   _____

This is a square.   _____

This is a boat.   _____

It is a short way from one side to the other side of a wide river.   _____

A detail is a small piece of information.   _____

A handle is part of our body.   _____

3. A Vocabulary Levels Test: Test B

The original Vocabulary Levels Test was made by Paul Nation and is described in Nation (1983 and 1990). The following test is one of a pair of equivalent forms and is a major improvement on the original test, which it replaces. This test was made by Norbert Schmitt, Diane Schmitt and C. Clapham: an equivalent form of this test can be found in Schmitt, Schmitt and Clapham (in press). Test A can be found in Schmitt (2000).

This is a vocabulary test. You must choose the right word to go with each meaning. Write the number of that word next to its meaning. Here is an example.

1 business
2 clock   _____ part of a house
3 horse   _____ animal with four legs
4 pencil   _____ something used for writing
5 shoe
6 wall

You answer it in the following way.

1 business
2 clock   __6__ part of a house
3 horse   __3__ animal with four legs
4 pencil   __4__ something used for writing
5 shoe
6 wall

Some words are in the test to make it more difficult. You do not have to find a meaning for these words. In the example above, these words are *business, clock, shoe*

Try to do every part of the test.

THE 2,000 WORD LEVEL

1 copy
2 event   _____ end or highest point
3 motor   _____ this moves a car
4 pity   _____ thing made to be like another
5 profit
6 tip

1 accident
2 debt
3 fortune
4 pride
5 roar
6 thread

_____ loud deep sound
_____ something you must pay
_____ having a high opinion of yourself

1 birth
2 dust
3 operation
4 row
5 sport
6 victory

_____ game
_____ winning
_____ being born

1 clerk
2 frame
3 noise
4 respect
5 theatre
6 wine

_____ a drink
_____ office worker
_____ unwanted sound

1 dozen
2 empire
3 gift
4 opportunity
5 relief
6 tax

_____ chance
_____ twelve
_____ money paid to the government

1 admire
2 complain
3 fix
4 hire
5 introduce
6 stretch

_____ make wider or longer
_____ bring in for the first time
_____ have a high opinion of someone

1 arrange
2 develop
3 lean
4 owe
5 prefer
6 seize

_____ grow
_____ put in order
_____ like more than something else

1 blame
2 elect
3 jump
4 manufacture
5 melt
6 threaten

_____ make
_____ choose by voting
_____ become like water

1 brave
2 electric   _____ commonly done
3 firm   _____ wanting food
4 hungry   _____ having no fear
5 local
6 usual

1 bitter
2 independent   _____ beautiful
3 lovely   _____ small
4 merry   _____ liked by many people
5 popular
6 slight

THE 3,000 WORD LEVEL

1 bull
2 champion   _____ formal and serious manner
3 dignity   _____ winner of a sporting event
4 hell   _____ building where valuable objects are
5 museum   shown
6 solution

1 blanket
2 contest   _____ holiday
3 generation   _____ good quality
4 merit   _____ wool covering used on beds
5 plot
6 vacation

1 apartment
2 candle   _____ a place to live
3 draft   _____ chance of something happening
4 horror   _____ first rough form of something written
5 prospect
6 timber

1 administration
2 angel   _____ group of animals
3 frost   _____ spirit who serves God
4 herd   _____ managing business and affairs
5 fort
6 pond

1 atmosphere
2 counsel   _____ advice
3 factor   _____ a place covered with grass
4 hen   _____ female chicken
5 lawn
6 muscle

1 abandon
2 dwell   _____ live in a place
3 oblige   _____ follow in order to catch
4 pursue   _____ leave something permanently
5 quote
6 resolve

1 assemble
2 attach   _____ look closely
3 peer   _____ stop doing something
4 quit   _____ cry out loudly in fear
5 scream
6 toss

1 drift
2 endure   _____ suffer patiently
3 grasp   _____ join wool threads together
4 knit   _____ hold firmly with your hands
5 register
6 tumble

1 brilliant
2 distinct   _____ thin
3 magic   _____ steady
4 naked   _____ without clothes
5 slender
6 stable

1 aware
2 blank   _____ usual
3 desperate   _____ best or most important
4 normal   _____ knowing what is happening
5 striking
6 supreme

THE 5,000 WORD LEVEL

1 analysis
2 curb   _____ eagerness
3 gravel   _____ loan to buy a house
4 mortgage   _____ small stones mixed with sand
5 scar
6 zeal

1 concrete
2 era   _____ circular shape
3 fibre   _____ top of a mountain
4 loop   _____ a long period of time
5 plank
6 summit

1 circus
2 jungle
3 nomination
4 sermon
5 stool
6 trumpet

_____ musical instrument
_____ seat without a back or arms
_____ speech given by a priest in a church

1 artillery
2 creed
3 hydrogen
4 maple
5 pork
6 streak

_____ a kind of tree
_____ system of belief
_____ large gun on wheels

1 chart
2 forge
3 mansion
4 outfit
5 sample
6 volunteer

_____ map
_____ large beautiful house
_____ place where metals are made and shaped

1 contemplate
2 extract
3 gamble
4 launch
5 provoke
6 revive

_____ think about deeply
_____ bring back to health
_____ make someone angry

1 demonstrate
2 embarrass
3 heave
4 obscure
5 relax
6 shatter

_____ have a rest
_____ break suddenly into small pieces
_____ make someone feel shy or nervous

1 correspond
2 embroider
3 lurk
4 penetrate
5 prescribe
6 resent

_____ exchange letters
_____ hide and wait for someone
_____ feel angry about something

1 decent
2 frail
3 harsh
4 incredible
5 municipal
6 specific

_____ weak
_____ concerning a city
_____ difficult to believe

1 adequate
2 internal   _____ enough
3 mature   _____ fully grown
4 profound   _____ alone away from other things
5 solitary
6 tragic

ACADEMIC VOCABULARY

1 area
2 contract   _____ written agreement
3 definition   _____ way of doing something
4 evidence   _____ reason for believing something is or is
5 method   not true
6 role

1 construction
2 feature   _____ safety
3 impact   _____ noticeable part of something
4 institute   _____ organization which has a special purpose
5 region
6 security

1 debate
2 exposure   _____ plan
3 integration   _____ choice
4 option   _____ joining something into a whole
5 scheme
6 stability

1 access
2 gender   _____ male or female
3 implementation _____ study of the mind
4 license   _____ entrance or way in
5 orientation
6 psychology

1 accumulation
2 edition   _____ collecting things over time
3 guarantee   _____ promise to repair a broken product
4 media   _____ feeling a strong reason or need to do
5 motivation   something
6 phenomenon

1 adult
2 exploitation   _____ end
3 infrastructure   _____ machine used to move people or goods
4 schedule   _____ list of things to do at certain times
5 termination
6 vehicle

1 alter
2 coincide   _____ change
3 deny   _____ say something is not true
4 devote   _____ describe clearly and exactly
5 release
6 specify

1 convert
2 design   _____ keep out
3 exclude   _____ stay alive
4 facilitate   _____ change from one thing into another
5 indicate
6 survive

1 bond
2 channel   _____ make smaller
3 estimate   _____ guess the number or size of something
4 identify   _____ recognizing and naming a person or thing
5 mediate
6 minimize

1 explicit
2 final   _____ last
3 negative   _____ stiff
4 professional   _____ meaning 'no' or 'not'
5 rigid
6 sole

1 analogous
2 objective   _____ happening after
3 potential   _____ most important
4 predominant   _____ not influenced by personal opinions
5 reluctant
6 subsequent

1 abstract
2 adjacent   _____ next to
3 controversial   _____ added to
4 global   _____ concerning the whole world
5 neutral
6 supplementary

THE 10,000 WORD LEVEL

1 alabaster
2 chandelier   _____ small barrel
3 dogma   _____ soft white stone
4 keg   _____ tool for shaping wood
5 rasp
6 tentacle

1 apparition
2 botany   _____ ghost
3 expulsion   _____ study of plants
4 insolence   _____ small pool of water
5 leash
6 puddle

1 arsenal
2 barracks   _____ happiness
3 deacon   _____ difficult situation
4 felicity   _____ minister in a church
5 predicament
6 spore

1 alcove
2 impetus   _____ priest
3 maggot   _____ release from prison early
4 parole   _____ medicine to put on wounds
5 salve
6 vicar

1 alkali
2 banter   _____ light joking talk
3 coop   _____ a rank of British nobility
4 mosaic   _____ picture made of small pieces of glass or
5 stealth   stone
6 viscount

1 dissipate
2 flaunt   _____ steal
3 impede   _____ scatter or vanish
4 loot   _____ twist the body about uncomfortably
5 squirm
6 vie

1 contaminate
2 cringe   _____ write carelessly
3 immerse   _____ move back because of fear
4 peek   _____ put something under water
5 relay
6 scrawl

1 blurt
2 dabble   _____ walk in a proud way
3 dent   _____ kill by squeezing someone's throat
4 pacify   _____ say suddenly without thinking
5 strangle
6 swagger

1 illicit
2 lewd   _____ immense
3 mammoth   _____ against the law
4 slick   _____ wanting revenge
5 temporal
6 vindictive

1 indolent
2 nocturnal   _____ lazy
3 obsolete   _____ no longer used
4 torrid   _____ clever and tricky
5 translucent
6 wily

4. Productive Levels Test: Version C

The Productive Levels Test is based on the old Vocabulary Levels Test (see appendix 3) and tests exactly the same vocabulary, but productively rather than receptively. An account of the making and validation of this test and an equivalent form can be found in Laufer and Nation (1999).

THE 2,000 WORD LEVEL
Complete the underlined words. The first one has been done for you.

He was riding a bic<u>ycle</u>.

1. I'm glad we had this opp_____ to talk.

2. There are a doz_____ eggs in the basket.

3. Every working person must pay income t_____.

4. The pirates buried the trea_____ on a desert island.

5. Her beauty and cha_____ had a powerful effect on men.

6. La_____ of rain led to a shortage of water in the city.

7. He takes cr_____ and sugar in his coffee.

8. The rich man died and left all his we_____ to his son.

9. Pup_____ must hand in their papers by the end of the week.

10. This sweater is too tight. It needs to be stret____.

11. Ann intro_____ her boyfriend to her mother.

12. Teenagers often adm_____ and worship pop singers.

13. If you blow up that balloon any more it will bur_____.

14. In order to be accepted into the university, he had to impr_____ his grades.

15. The telegram was deli_____ two hours after it had been sent.

16. The differences were so sl_____ that they went unnoticed.

17. The dress you're wearing is lov_____.

18. He wasn't very popu_____ when he was a teenager, but he has many friends now.

THE 3,000 WORD LEVEL

1. He has a successful car____ as a lawyer.

2. The thieves threw ac_____ in his face and made him blind.

3. To improve the country's economy, the government decided on economic ref_____.

4. She wore a beautiful green go_____ to the ball.

5. The government tried to protect the country's industry by reducing the imp_____ of cheap goods.

6. The children's pranks were funny at first, but finally got on the parents' ner_____.

7. The lawyer gave some wise coun_____ to his client.

8. Many people in England mow the la_____ of their houses on Sunday morning.

9. The farmer sells the eggs that his he_____ lay.

10. Sudden noises at night sca_____ me a lot.

11. France was proc_____ a republic in the 18th century.

12. Many people are inj_____ in road accidents every year.

13. Suddenly he was thru_____ into the dark room.

14. He perc_____ a light at the end of the tunnel.

15. Children are not independent. They are att_____ to their parents.

16. She showed off her sle_____ figure in a long narrow dress.

17. She has been changing partners often because she cannot have a sta_____ relationship with one person.

18. You must wear a bathing suit on a public beach. You're not allowed to walk na_____.

THE 5,000 WORD LEVEL

1. Soldiers usually swear an oa_____ of loyalty to their country.

2. The voter placed the ball_____ in the box.

3. They keep their valuables in a vau_____ at the bank.

4. A bird perched at the window led_____.

5. The kitten is playing with a ball of ya_____.

6. The thieves have forced an ent_____ to the building.

7. The small hill was really a burial mou_____.

8. We decided to celebrate New Year's E_____ together.

9. The soldier was asked to choose between infantry and cav_____.

10. This is a complex problem which is difficult to compr_____.

11. The angry crowd sho_____ the prisoner as he was leaving the court.

12. Don't pay attention to this rude remark. Just ign_____ it.

13. The management held a secret meeting. The issues discussed were not disc_____ to the workers.

14. We could hear the sergeant bel_____ commands to the troops.

15. The boss got angry with the secretary and it took a lot of tact to soo_____ him.

16. We do not have adeq_____ information to make a decision.

17. She is not a child, but a mat_____ woman. She can make her own decisions.

18. The prisoner was put in soli_____ confinement.

THE UNIVERSITY WORD LIST LEVEL

1. There has been a recent tr_____ among prosperous families towards a smaller number of children.

2. The ar_____ of his office is 25 square meters.

3. Phil_____ examines the meaning of life.

4. According to the communist doc_____, workers should rule the world.

5. Spending many years together deepened their inti_____.

6. He usually read the sport sec_____ of the newspaper first.

7. Because of the doctors' strike the cli_____ is closed today.

8. There are several misprints on each page of this te_____.

9. The suspect had both opportunity and mot_____ to commit the murder.

10. They insp_____ all products before sending them out to stores.

11. A considerable amount of evidence was accum_____ during the investigation.

12. The victim's shirt was satu_____ with blood.

13. He is irresponsible. You cannot re_____ on him for help.

14. It's impossible to eva_____ these results without knowing about the research methods that were used.

15. He finally att_____ a position of power in the company.

16. The story tells us about a crime and subs_____ punishment.

17. In a hom_____ class all students are of a similar proficiency.

18. The urge to survive is inh_____ in all creatures.

THE 10,000 WORD LEVEL

1. The baby is wet. Her dia_____ needs changing.

2. The prisoner was released on par_____.

3. Second year University students in the U.S. are called soph_____.

4. Her favorite flowers were or_____.

5. The insect causes damage to plants by its toxic sec_____.

6. The evac_____ of the building saved many lives.

7. For many people, wealth is a prospect of unimaginable felic_____.

8. She found herself in a pred_____ without any hope for a solution.

9. The deac_____ helped with the care of the poor of the parish.

10. The hurricane whi_____ along the coast.

11. Some coal was still smoul_____ among the ashes.

12. The dead bodies were muti_____ beyond recognition.

13. She was sitting on a balcony and bas_____ in the sun.

14. For years waves of invaders pill_____ towns along the coast.

15. The rescue attempt could not proceed quickly. It was imp_____ by bad weather.

16. I wouldn't hire him. He is unmotivated and indo_____.

17. Computers have made typewriters old-fashioned and obs_____.

18. Watch out for his wil_____tricks.

5. Vocabulary Levels Dictation Test

An account of the making and validation of equivalent forms of this test can be found in Fountain and Nation (2000). The test is read to the learners as dictation. It is read once only, and the teacher should pause where there is a vertical stroke. Only the italicised words are marked but the learners do not know this. Minor mis-spellings are accepted.

Introduction

The *demand* for *food* / *becomes more important* / as the *number* of *people* in the *world* / *continues* to *increase*. /

Paragraph 1:

The *duty* to *care* / for the *members* of a *society* / *lies* with those who *control* it, / but *sometimes governments* / *refuse* to *deal* with this *problem* / in a *wise way*, / and *fail* to *provide enough* to *eat*. / When this *occurs* many *ordinary* people *suffer*. /

Paragraph 2:

Often their *economic situation* / does not *permit* them to *create* / a *system* of *regular supply*. / When food is *scarce*, / the *pattern* of *distribution* / is *generally* not *uniform*. / In some *areas production* / is *sufficient* to *satisfy* the needs of the *population*. / In others *pockets* of *poverty exist*. /

Paragraph 3:

Using as their *basis* the *research* of *experts* / to discover the *factors* / in the *previous failures* to *prevent starving*, / those in *positions* of *leadership* / should *institute reforms*. / Unless *ancient traditions* of *administration* are *overthrown* / the *existence* of the coming *generations* of *mankind* / will be *threatened*. /

Paragraph 4:

Though it is *reasonable* to *presume* that a *reduction* of *consumption* / could be *recommended* in *regions* of *prosperity*, / if this was *enforced* it would meet *opposition* / with thousands *rebelling* / in their *determination* to *maintain* their *independence* / from those *politicians dictating* to them. / The *selection* of a *differently devised procedure* / would be *essential*. /

6. Function words

This is a list of the function words of English. Note that numbers are also included. Other lists may differ as there is not complete agreement on which words are function words.

Most of the words occur in the most frequent 2,000 words of English; words in **bold** appear in the *Academic Word List* (Coxhead, 1998); words in *italics* are not in the General Service List (West, 1953) or the *Academic Word List*.

Adverbial particles

again ago almost already also always anywhere back else even ever everywhere far **hence** here *hither* how however near nearby nearly never not now nowhere often only quite rather sometimes somewhere soon still then thence there therefore *thither* thus today tomorrow too underneath very when *whence* where *whither* why yes yesterday yet

Auxiliary verbs (including contractions)

am are aren't be been being can can't could couldn't did didn't do does doesn't doing done don't get gets getting got had hadn't has hasn't have haven't having he'd he'll he's I'd I'll I'm is I've isn't it's may might must mustn't ought oughtn't shall shan't she'd she'll she's should shouldn't that's they'd they'll they're was wasn't we'd we'll were we're weren't we've will won't would wouldn't you'd you'll you're you've

Prepositions/conjunctions (one category since there is some overlap)

about above after along although among and around as at before below beneath beside between beyond but by down during except for from if in into near nor of off on or out over round since so than that though through till to towards under unless until up **whereas** while with within without

Determiners/pronouns (omitting archaic thou, thee, etc.)

a all an another any anybody anything both each either enough every everybody everyone everything few fewer he her hers herself him himself his I it its itself less many me mine more most much my myself neither no nobody none no-one nothing other others our ours ourselves she some somebody someone something such that the their theirs them themselves these they this those us we what which who whom whose you your yours yourself yourselves

Numbers

billion billionth eight eighteen eighteenth eighth eightieth eighty eleven eleventh fifteen fifteenth fifth fiftieth fifty first five fortieth forty four fourteen fourteenth fourth hundred hundredth last million million next nine nineteen nineteenth ninetieth ninety ninth once one second seven seventeen seventeenth seventh seventieth seventy six sixteen sixteenth sixth sixtieth sixty ten tenth third thirteen thirteenth thirtieth thirty thousand thousandth three *thrice* twelfth twelve twentieth twenty twice two

Total = 320 word types

References

A larger list of vocabulary references can be found at
http://www.vuw.ac.nz/lals/staff/paul_nation/vocrefs.htm

Ahmed, M. O. (1989) 'Vocabulary learning strategies', in P. Meara (ed.), *Beyond Words* (3–14), London: BAAL/CILT.

Aisenstadt, E. (1981) 'Restricted collocations in English lexicology and lexicography', *ITL: Review of Applied Linguistics*, 53, 53–61.

Aitchison, J. (1994) *Words in the Mind* (2nd edn.), Oxford: Blackwell.

Ames, W. S. (1966) 'The development of a classification scheme of contextual aids', *Reading Research Quarterly*, 2, 57–82.

Anderson, J. I. (1980) 'The lexical difficulties of English medical discourse for Egyptian students', *English for Specific Purposes, Oregon State University*, 37, 4.

Anderson, J. P. and Jordan, A. M. (1928) 'Learning and retention of Latin words and phrases', *Journal of Educational Psychology*, 19, 485–496.

Anderson, R. C. and Freebody, P. (1983) 'Reading comprehension and the assessment and acquisition of word knowledge', *Advances in Reading/Language Research*, 2, 231–256.

Anderson, R. C. and Nagy, W. E. (1992) 'The vocabulary conundrum', *American Educator*, 16, 14–18; 44–47.

Anderson, R. C. and Ortony, A. (1975) 'On putting apples into bottles – a problem of polysemy', *Cognitive Psychology*, 7, 167–180.

Anderson, R. C. and Shifrin, Z. (1980) 'The meaning of words in context', in Spiro *et al.*, 330–348.

Anderson, R. C., Stevens, K. C., Shifrin, Z. and Osborn, J. (1978) 'Instantiation of word meanings in children', *Journal of Reading Behaviour*, 10, 149–157.

Anglin, J. M. (1993) 'Vocabulary development: a morphological analysis', *Monographs of the Society for Research in Child Development, Serial no. 238*, 58, 10.

Ard, J. (1982) 'The use of bilingual dictionaries by EFL students while writing', *ITL: Review of Applied Linguistics*, 58, 1–27.

Arden-Close, C. (1993) 'NNS readers' strategies for inferring the meanings of unknown words', *Reading in a Foreign Language*, 9, 867–893.

Arevart and Nation, I. S. P. (1991) 'Fluency improvement in a second language', *RELC Journal*, 22, 84–94.

Arnaud, P. J. L. (1984) 'A practical comparison of five types of vocabulary tests and an investigation into the nature of L2 lexical competence'. Paper presented at 7th World Congress of Applied Linguistics, Brussels, 1–21.

Arnaud, P. J. L. (1992) 'Objective lexical and grammatical characteristics of L2 written compositions and the validity of separate-component tests', in P. J. L. Arnaud and H. Béjoint (eds.) *Vocabulary and Applied Linguistics* (133–145), London: Macmillan.

Arnaud, P. J. L. and Béjoint, H. (eds.), (1992) *Vocabulary and Applied Linguistics*, London: Macmillan.

Artley, A. S. (1943) 'Teaching word-meaning through context', *Elementary English Review*, 20, 68–74.

Astika, Gusti Gede (1993) 'Analytical assessment of foreign students' writing', *RELC Journal*, 24, 61–72.

Atkins, B. T. S. and Varantola, K. (1997) 'Monitoring dictionary use', *International Journal of Lexicography*, 10, 1–45.

Atkinson, R. C. (1972) 'Optimizing the learning of a second-language vocabulary', *Journal of Experimental Psychology*, 96, 124–129.

Avila, E. and Sadoski, M. (1996) 'Exploring new applications of the keyword method to acquire English vocabulary', *Language Learning*, 46, 379–395.

Baddeley, A. (1990) *Human Memory*, London: Lawrence Erlbaum Associates.

Bahrick, H. P. (1984) 'Semantic memory content in permastore: fifty years of memory for Spanish learned in school', *Journal of Experimental Psychology: General*, 113, 1–37.

Bahrick, H. P. and Phelps, E. (1987) 'Retention of Spanish vocabulary over 8 years', *Journal of Experimental Psychology: Learning, Memory and Cognition*, 13, 344–349.

Bamford, J. (1984) 'Extensive reading by means of graded readers', *Reading in a Foreign Language*, 2, 218–260.

Barber, C. L. (1962) 'Some measurable characteristics of modern scientific prose', in *Contributions to English Syntax and Philology* (21–43), Goteburg: Acta Universitatis Gothoburgensis.

Barnard, H. (1961) 'A test of P.U.C. students' vocabulary in Chotanagpur', *Bulletin of the Central Institute of English*, 1, 90–100.

Barnard, H. (1972) *Advanced English Vocabulary*, Massachusetts: Newbury House.

Bauer, L. (1980) 'Review of *The Longman Dictionary of Contemporary English*', *RELC Journal*, 11, 104–109.

Bauer, L. (1981) 'Review of *Chambers Universal Dictionary*', *RELC Journal*, 12, 100–103.

Bauer, L. and Nation, I. S. P. (1993) 'Word families', *International Journal of Lexicography*, 6, 253–279.

Bawcom, L. (1995) 'Designing an advanced speaking course', *English Teaching Forum*, 33, 41–43.

Baxter, J. (1980) 'The dictionary and vocabulary behaviour: a single word or a handful?', *TESOL Quarterly*, 14, 325–336.

Bear, R. M. and Odbert, H. S. (1941) 'Insight of older pupils into their knowledge of word meanings', *School Review*, 49, 754–760.

Beaton, A., Gruneberg, M., and Ellis, N. (1995) 'Retention of foreign vocabulary using the keyword method: a ten-year follow-up', *Second Language Research*, **11**, 112–120.

Beck, I. L., McKeown, M. G. and McCaslin, E. S. (1983) 'Vocabulary: all contexts are not created equal', *Elementary School Journal*, **83**, 177–181.

Beck, I. L., McKeown, M. G. and Omanson, R. C. (1987) 'The effects and uses of diverse vocabulary instructional techniques', in McKeown and Curtis, 147–163.

Bečka, J. V. (1972) 'The lexical composition of specialized texts and its quantitative aspect', *Prague Studies in Mathematical Linguistics*, **4**, 47–64.

Becker, W. C., Dixon, R. and Anderson-Inman, L. (1980) *Morphographic and root word analysis of 26,000 high-frequency words*, University of Oregon, Follow Through Project; Eugene, Oregon: College of Education.

Béjoint, H. (1981) 'The foreign student's use of monolingual English dictionaries: a study of language needs and reference skills', *Applied Linguistics*, **2**, 207–222.

Benson, M. (1995) 'Review of *Longman Language Activator*', *System*, **23**, 253–255.

Benson, M. and Benson, E. (1988) 'Trying out a new dictionary', *TESOL Quarterly*, **22**, 2, 340–345.

Bensoussan, M. and Laufer, B. (1984) 'Lexical guessing in context in EFL reading comprehension', *Journal of Research in Reading*, **7**, 15–32.

Bensoussan, M., Sim, D. and Weiss, R. (1984) 'The effect of dictionary usage on EFL test performance compared with student and teacher attitudes and expectations', *Reading in a Foreign Language*, **2**, 262–276.

Bernbrock, C. (1980) 'Stemgo: a word-stems game', *English Teaching Forum*, **18**, 45–46.

Bhatia, V. K. (1983) 'Simplification v. easification – the case of legal texts', *Applied Linguistics*, **4**, 42–54.

Bierwisch, M. and Schreuder, R. (1992) 'From context to lexical item', *Cognition*, **41**, 23–60.

Bird, N. (1987) 'Words, lemmas and frequency lists: old problems and new challenges' (Parts 1 & 2), *Al-manakh*, **6**, 42–50.

Bird, N. (1990) *A First Handbook of the Roots of English*, Hong Kong: Lapine Education and Language Services Ltd.

Bird, S. A. and Jacobs, G. M. (1999) 'An examination of the keyword method: How effective is it for native speakers of Chinese?', *Asian Journal of English Language Teaching*, **9**, 75–97.

Blachowicz, C. L. Z. (1987) 'Vocabulary instruction: What goes on in the classroom?', *The Reading Teacher*, **41**, 132–137.

Blake, M. E. and Majors, P. L. (1995) 'Recycled words: holistic instruction for LEP students', *Journal of Adolescent and Adult Literacy*, **39**, 132–137.

Bloom, K. C. and Shuell, T. J. (1981) 'Effects of massed and distributed practice on the learning and retention of second-language vocabulary', *Journal of Educational Research*, **74**, 245–248.

Bock, C. (1948) 'Prefixes and suffixes', *Classical Journal*, **44**, 132–133.

Bogaards, P. (1996) 'Dictionaries for learners of English', *International Journal of Lexicography*, 9, 277–320.

Bonk, W. (unpublished article) 'L2 lexical knowledge and listening comprehension'.

Bradley, L. and Huxford, L. (1994) 'Organising sound and letter patterns for spelling', in Brown and Ellis, 425–439.

Bramki, D. and Williams, R. C. (1984) 'Lexical familiarization in economics text, and its pedagogic implications in reading comprehension', *Reading in a Foreign Language*, 2, 169–181.

Brett, A., Rothlein, L. and Hurley, M. (1996) 'Vocabulary acquisition from listening to stories and explanations of target words', *The Elementary School Journal*, 96, 415–422.

Brown, D. and Barnard, H. (1975) 'Dictation as a learning experience', *RELC Journal*, 6, 42–62.

Brown, D. F. (1974) 'Advanced vocabulary teaching: the problem of collocation', *RELC Journal*, 5, 1–11.

Brown, G. D. A. and Ellis, N. C. (1994) *Handbook of Spelling*, Chichester: John Wiley and Sons.

Brown, J. D. (1997) 'An EFL readability index', *University of Hawaii Working Papers in ESL*, 15, 85–119.

Brown, R. and McNeill, D. (1966) 'The "Tip of the Tongue" phenomenon', *Journal of Verbal Learning and Verbal Behaviour*, 5, 325–337.

Brown, T. S. and Perry, F. L. (1991) 'A comparison of three learning strategies for ESL vocabulary acquisition', *TESOL Quarterly*, 25, 655–670.

Bruton, A. and Samuda, V. (1981) 'Guessing words', *Modern English Teacher*, 8, 18–21.

Buikema, J. L. and Graves, M. F. (1993) 'Teaching students to use context cues to infer word meanings', *Journal of Reading*, 36, 450–457.

Burling, R. (1983) 'A proposal for computer-assisted instruction in vocabulary', *System*, 11, 181–170.

Burroughs, R. S. (1982) 'Vocabulary study and context, or how I learned to stop worrying about word lists', *English Journal*, 71, 53–55.

Cairns, H. S., Cowart, W. and Jablon, A. D. (1981) 'Effects of prior context upon the integration of lexical information during sentence processing', *Journal of Verbal Learning and Verbal Behavior*, 20, 445–453.

Campion, M. E. and Elley, W. B. (1971) *An academic vocabulary list*, Wellington: NZCER.

Canale, M. and Swain, M. (1980) 'Theoretical bases of communicative approaches to second language teaching and testing', *Applied Linguistics*, 1, 1–47.

Carnine, D., Kameenui, E. J. and Coyle, G. (1984) 'Utilization of contextual information in determining the meaning of unfamiliar words', *Reading Research Quarterly*, 19, 188–204.

Carrell, P. (1987) 'Readability in ESL', *Reading in a Foreign Language*, 4, 21–40.

Carroll, J. B. (1940) 'Knowledge of English roots and affixes as related to vocabulary and Latin study', *Journal of Educational Research*, 34, 102–111.

Carroll, J. B. (1963) 'Research on teaching foreign languages', in N. L. Gage (ed.), *Handbook of Research on Teaching* (1060–1100), Chicago: Rand McNally.

Carroll, J. B., Davies, P. and Richman, B. (1971) *The American Heritage Word Frequency Book*, New York: Houghton Mifflin, Boston American Heritage.

Carroll, M. C. and Mordaunt, O. G. (1991) 'The frontier method of vocabulary practice', *TESOL Journal*, 1, 23–26.

Carter, R. (1982) 'A note on core vocabulary', *Nottingham Linguistic Circular*, 11, 39–51.

Carter, R. and McCarthy, M. (eds.), (1988) *Vocabulary and Language Teaching*, London: Longman.

Carton, A. S. (1971) 'Inferencing: a process in using and learning language', in P. Pimsleur and T. Quinn (eds.), *The Psychology of Second Language Learning* (45–58), Cambridge: Cambridge University Press.

Carver, R. P. (1994) 'Percentage of unknown vocabulary words in text as a function of the relative difficulty of the text: implications for instruction', *Journal of Reading Behavior*, 26, 413–437.

Cassidy, F. G. (1972) 'Toward more objective labeling in dictionaries', in J. E. Alatis (ed.), *Studies in Honor of Albert H. Marckwardt* (49–56), Washington: TESOL.

Chall, J. S. (1958) *Readability: an appraisal of research and application*, Ohio: Ohio State Bureau of Education Research Monographs.

Chall, J. S. (1987) 'Two vocabularies for reading: recognition and meaning', in McKeown and Curtis, 7–17.

Channell, J. (1981) 'Applying semantic theory to vocabulary teaching', *ELT Journal*, 35, 115–122.

Chaudron, C. (1982) 'Vocabulary elaboration in teachers' speech to L2 learners', *Studies in Second Language Acquisition*, 4, 170–180.

Cheung Him (1996) 'Nonword span as a unique predictor of second-language vocabulary learning', *Developmental Psychology*, 32, 867–873.

Chihara, T., Oller, J., Weaver, K. and Chavez-Oller, M. A. (1977) 'Are cloze items sensitive to discourse constraints?', *Language Learning*, 27, 63–73.

Chun, D. M. and Plass, J. L. (1996) 'Effects of multimedia annotations on vocabulary acquisition', *Modern Language Journal*, 80, 183–198.

Clark, E. V. (1973) 'What's in a word? On the child's acquisition of semantics in his L1', in T. E. Moore (ed.) *Cognitive Development and the Acquisition of Language,* New York: Academic Press.

Clarke, D. F. and Nation, I. S. P. (1980) 'Guessing the meanings of words from context: strategy and techniques', *System*, 8, 211–220.

Cobb, T. (1997) 'Is there any measurable learning from hands-on concordancing?', *System*, 25, 301–315.

Cohen, A. D., Glasman, H., Rosenbaum-Cohen, P. R., Ferrara, J. and Fine, J. (1988) 'Reading English for specialised purposes: discourse analysis and the use of student informants', in P. Carrell, J. Devine and D. E. Eskey (eds.), *Interactive Approaches to Second Language Reading* (152–167), Cambridge: Cambridge University Press.

Cook, J. M., Heim, A. W. and Watts, K. P. (1963) 'The word-in-context: a new type of verbal reasoning test', *British Journal of Psychology*, 54, 227–237.

Corson, D. J. (1985) *The Lexical Bar*, Oxford: Pergamon Press.

Corson, D. J. (1995) *Using English Words*, Dordrecht: Kluwer Academic Publishers.

Corson, D. J. (1997) 'The learning and use of academic English words', *Language Learning*, 47, 671–718.

Cowan, J. R. (1974) 'Lexical and syntactic research for the design of EFL reading materials', *TESOL Quarterly*, 8, 389–400.

Coxhead, A. (1998) *An Academic Word List*, Occasional Publication Number 18, LALS, Victoria University of Wellington, New Zealand.

Coxhead, A. (2000) 'A new *Academic Word List*', *TESOL Quarterly*, 34, 2, 213–238.

Crabbe, D. and Nation, P. (1991) 'A survival language learning syllabus for foreign travel', *System*, 19, 191–201.

Craik, F. I. M. and Lockhart, R. S. (1972) 'Levels of processing: a framework for memory research', *Journal of Verbal Learning and Verbal Behavior*, 11, 671–684.

Craik, F. I. M. and Tulving, E. (1975) 'Depth of processing and the retention of words in episodic memory', *Journal of Experimental Psychology*, 104, 268–294.

Cripwell, K. and Foley, J. (1984) 'The grading of extensive readers', *World Language English*, 3, 168–173.

Crothers, E. and Suppes, P. (1967) *Experiments in Second-Language Learning*, New York: Academic Press.

Crow, J. T. (1986) 'Receptive vocabulary acquisition for reading comprehension', *Modern Language Journal*, 70, 242–250.

Cruse, D. A. (1986) *Lexical Semantics*, Cambridge: Cambridge University Press.

Cumming, G., Cropp, S. and Sussex, R. (1994) 'On-line lexical resources for language learners: assessment of some approaches to word definition', *System*, 22, 369–377.

Cummins, J. (1986) 'Language proficiency and language achievement', in J. Cummins and M. Swain (eds.), *Bilingualism in Education* (138–161), London: Longman.

Cunningham, J. W. and Moore, D. W. (1993) 'The contribution of understanding academic vocabulary to answering comprehension questions', *Journal of Reading Behavior*, 25, 171–180.

Cziko, G. A. (1978) 'Differences in first- and second-language reading: the use of syntactic, semantic and discourse constraints', *Canadian Modern Language Review*, 34, 473–489.

D'Anna, C. A., Zechmeister, E. B. and Hall, J. W. (1991) 'Toward a meaningful definition of vocabulary size', *Journal of Reading Behavior: A Journal of Literacy*, 23, 109–122.

Daneman, M. and Green, I. (1986) 'Individual differences in comprehending and producing words in context', *Journal of Memory and Language*, 25, 1–18.

Daulton, F. E. (1998) 'Japanese loanword cognates and the acquisition of English vocabulary', *The Language Teacher*, 22, 17–25.

Davis, J. N. (1989) 'Facilitating effects of marginal glosses on foreign language reading', *Modern Language Journal*, 73, 41–48.

Day, R. R. and Bamford, J. (1998) *Extensive Reading in the Second Language Classroom*, Cambridge: Cambridge University Press.

Day, R. R., Omura, C. and Hiramatsu, M. (1991) 'Incidental EFL vocabulary learning and reading', *Reading in a Foreign Language*, 7, 541–551.

de Bot, K. (1992) 'A bilingual production model: Levelt's speaking model adapted', *Applied Linguistics*, 13, 3–24.

de Bot, K., Paribakht, T. and Wesche, M. (1997) 'Towards a lexical processing model for the study of second language vocabulary acquisition: evidence from ESL reading', *Studies in Second Language Acquisition*, 19, 309–329.

Deese, J. (1965) *The Structure of Associations in Language and Thought*, Baltimore: The Johns Hopkins Press.

DeKeyser, R. M. and Sokalski, K. J. (1996) 'The differential roles of comprehension and production practice, *Language Learning*, 46, 613–642.

Dempster, F. N. (1987) 'Effects of variable encoding and spaced presentation on vocabulary learning', *Journal of Educational Psychology*, 79, 162–170.

Deno, S. L. (1968) 'Effects of words and pictures as stimuli in learning language equivalents', *Journal of Educational Psychology*, 59, 202–206.

Derewianka, B. (1990) *Exploring How Texts Work*, New South Wales: Primary English Teaching Association.

Descamps, J-L. (1992) 'Towards classroom concordancing', in Arnaud and Béjoint, 167–181.

Desrochers, A., Gelinas, C. and Wieland, L. D. (1989) 'An application of the mnemonic keyword method to the acquisition of German nouns and their grammatical gender', *Journal of Educational Psychology*, 81, 25–32.

Desrochers, A., Wieland, L. D. and Coté, M. (1991) 'Instructional effects in the use of the mnemonic keyword method for learning German nouns and their grammatical gender', *Applied Cognitive Psychology*, 5, 19–36.

Diack, H. (1975) *Test Your Own Wordpower*, St Albans: Paladin.

Diller, K. C. (1978) *The Language Teaching Controversy* (chapter 12), Rowley, Massachusetts: Newbury House.

Dolch, E. W. (1951) 'The use of vocabulary lists in predicting readability and in developing reading materials', *Elementary English*, 28, 142–9, 177.

Dowhower, S. L. (1989) 'Repeated reading: research into practice', *The Reading Teacher*, 42, 502–507.

Dresher, R. (1934) 'Training in mathematics vocabulary', *Educational Research Bulletin*, 13, 201–204.

Duin, A. H. and Graves, M. F. (1987) 'Intensive vocabulary instruction as a prewriting technique', *Reading Research Quarterly*, 22, 311–330.

Dunbar, S. (1992) 'Developing vocabulary by integrating language and content', *TESL Canada Journal*, 9, 73–79.

Dunmore, D. (1989) 'Using contextual clues to infer word meaning: an evaluation of current exercise types', *Reading in a Foreign Language*, 6, 337–347.

Dupuy, B. and Krashen, S. D. (1993) 'Incidental vocabulary acquisition in French as a foreign language', *Applied Language Learning*, 4, 1&2, 55–63.

Durkin, K., Crowther, R., Shire, B., Riem, R. and Nash, P. (1985) 'Polysemy in mathematical and musical education', *Applied Linguistics*, 6, 147–161.

Eaton, H. S. (1940) *An English-French-German-Spanish Word Frequency Dictionary*, New York: Dover Publications.

Eller, R. G., Pappas, C. C. and Brown, E. (1988) 'The lexical development of kindergarteners: learning from written context', *Journal of Reading Behavior*, **20**, 5–24.

Elley, W. B. (1969) 'The assessment of readability by noun frequency counts', *Reading Research Quarterly*, **4**, 411–427.

Elley, W. B. (1989) 'Vocabulary acquisition from listening to stories', *Reading Research Quarterly*, **24**, 174–187.

Elley, W. B. (1991) 'Acquiring literacy in a second language: the effect of book-based programs', *Language Learning*, **41**, 375–411.

Elley, W. B. and Mangubhai, F. (1981) *The Impact of a Book Flood in Fiji Primary Schools*, Wellington: New Zealand Council for Educational Research.

Ellis, N. C. (1994) 'Vocabulary acquisition: the implicit ins and outs of explicit cognitive mediation', in N. C. Ellis (ed.), *Implicit and Explicit Learning of Languages* (211–282), London. Academic Press.

Ellis, N. C. (1995) 'Vocabulary acquisition: psychological perspectives and pedagogical implications', *The Language Teacher*, **19**, 12–16.

Ellis, N. C. (1997) 'Vocabulary acquisition, word structure, collocation, word-class, and meaning', in Schmitt and McCarthy, 122–139.

Ellis, N. C. (2001) 'Memory for language', in P. Robinson (ed.), *Cognition and Second Language Instruction*, Cambridge: Cambridge University Press.

Ellis, N. C. and Beaton, A. (1993) 'Factors affecting foreign language vocabulary: imagery keyword mediators and phonological short-term memory', *Quarterly Journal of Experimental Psychology*, **46A**, 533–558.

Ellis, N. C. and Laporte, N. (in press) 'Contexts of acquisition: effects of formal instruction and naturalistic exposure on SLA, in A. de Groot and J. Kroll (eds.), *Tutorials in Bilingualism: Psycholinguistic Perspectives*. Hillsdale New Jersey: Lawrence Erlbaum.

Ellis, N. C. and Schmidt, R. (1997) 'Morphology and longer distance dependencies: Laboratory research illuminating the A in SLA', *Studies in Second Language Acquisition*, **19**, 145–171.

Ellis, N. C. and Sinclair, S. G. (1996) 'Working memory in the acquisition of vocabulary and syntax: putting language in good order', *Quarterly Journal of Experimental Psychology*, **49A**, 234–250.

Ellis, R. (1990) *Instructed Second Language Acquisition*, Basil Blackwell: Oxford.

Ellis, R. (1991) 'The interaction hypothesis: a critical evaluation', in E. Sadtono (ed.), *Language Acquisition and the Second/Foreign Language Classroom*, (179–211), RELC Anthology: Series 28.

Ellis, R. (1992) 'Grammar teaching – practice or consciousness-raising', in R. Ellis, *Second Language Acquisition and Second Language Pedagogy*, Clevedon, Avon: Multilingual Matters.

Ellis, R. (1994) 'Factors in the incidental acquisition of second language vocabulary from oral input: a review essay', *Applied Language Learning*, **5**, 1–32.

Ellis, R. (1995) 'Modified oral input and the acquisition of word meanings', *Applied Linguistics*, **16**, 409–441.

Ellis, R. and He, X. (1999) 'The roles of modified input and output in the incidental acquisition of word meanings', *Studies in Second Language Acquisition*, **21**, 285–301.

Ellis, R. and Heimbach, R. (1997) 'Bugs and birds: children's acquisition of second language vocabulary through interaction', *System*, **25**, 247–259.

Ellis, R., Tanaka, Y. and Yamazaki, A. (1994) 'Classroom interaction, comprehension and the acquisition of L2 word meanings', *Language Learning*, **44**, 449–491.

Elshout-Mohr, M. and van Daalen-Kapteijns, M. (1987) 'Cognitive processes in learning word meanings', in McKeown and Curtis, 53–71.

Engber, C. A. (1995) 'The relationship of lexical proficiency to the quality of ESL compositions', *Journal of Second Language Writing*, **4**, 139–155.

Fairclough, N. (1989) *Language and Power*, London: Longman.

Farid, A. (1985) *A Vocabulary Workbook*, Englewood Cliffs: Prentice Hall Inc.

Farrell, P. (1990) *Vocabulary in ESP: a lexical analysis of the English of electronics and a study of semi-technical vocabulary*, CLCS Occasional Paper 25, Dublin: Trinity College.

Feeny, T. P. (1976) 'Vocabulary teaching as a means of vocabulary expansion', *Foreign Language Annals*, **9**, 485–486.

Feifel, H. and Lorge, I. (1950) 'Qualitative differences in the vocabulary responses of children', *Journal of Educational Psychology*, **41**, 1–18.

Fernando, C. (1996) *Idioms and Idiomaticity*, Oxford: Oxford University Press.

Firth, J. R. (1957) *Papers in Linguistics 1934–1951*, London: Oxford University Press.

Flick, W. C. and Anderson, J. I. (1980) 'Rhetorical difficulty in scientific English: a study in reading comprehension', *TESOL Quarterly*, **14**, 345–351.

Flood, W. E. and West, M. P. (1950) 'A limited vocabulary for scientific and technical ideas', *ELT Journal*, **4**, 104–108; **5**, 128–137.

Flowerdew, J. (1992) 'Definitions in science lectures', *Applied Linguistics*, **13**, 202–221.

Fountain, R. L. (1979) 'Word making and word taking: a game to motivate language learning', *RELC Journal: Guidelines*, **1**, 76–80.

Fountain, R. L. and Nation, I. S. P. (2000) 'A vocabulary-based graded dictation test', *RELC Journal*.

Fox, J. (1984) 'Computer-assisted vocabulary learning', *ELT Journal*, **38**, 27–33.

Francis, G. (1994) 'Labelling discourse: an aspect of nominal-group lexical cohesion', in M. Coulthard (ed.), *Advances in Written Text Analysis*, (83–101), London: Routledge.

Francis, W. N. and Kučera, H. (1982) *Frequency Analysis of English Usage*, Boston: Houghton Mifflin Company.

Fraser, C. A. (1999) 'Lexical processing strategy use and vocabulary learning through reading', *Studies in Second Language Acquisition*, **21**, 225–241.

Fuentes, E. J. (1976) 'An investigation into the use of imagery and generativity in learning a foreign language vocabulary', *Dissertation Abstracts International*, **37**, 2694A.

Fukkink, R. G. and de Glopper, K. (1998) 'Effects of instruction in deriving word meaning from context: a meta-analysis', *Review of Educational Research*, **68**, 450–469.

Gass, S. M. (1988) 'Second language vocabulary acquisition', *Annual Review of Applied Linguistics*, **9**, 92–106.

Gass, S. M. and Madden, C. G. (eds.), (1985) *Input in Second Language Acquisition*, Rowley, Massachusetts: Newbury House.

Gathercole, S. E. and Baddeley, A. D. (1989) 'Evaluation of the role of phonological STM in the development of vocabulary in children: a longitudinal study', *Journal of Memory and Language*, **28**, 200–213.

Gathercole, S. E. and Baddeley, A. D. (1993) *Working Memory and Language*, Hove, New Jersey: Lawrence Erlbaum.

Gershman, S. J. (1970) 'Foreign language vocabulary learning under seven conditions', *Dissertation Abstracts International*, **31**, 3690B.

Ghadessy, M. (1979) 'Frequency counts, word lists, and materials preparation: a new approach', *English Teaching Forum*, **17**, 24–27.

Gibbons, H. (1940) 'The ability of college freshmen to construct the meaning of a strange word from the context in which it appears', *Journal of Experimental Education*, **9**, 29–33.

Gibbons, P. (1998) 'The centrality of talk', *Challenge in challenge*, QATESOL Occasional Papers **2**, 33–52.

Gibson, R. E. (1975) 'The strip story: a catalyst for communication', *TESOL Quarterly*, **9**, 149–154.

Gipe, J. P. and Arnold, R. D. (1979) 'Teaching vocabulary through familiar associations and contexts', *Journal of Reading Behavior*, **11**, 282–285.

Godman, A. and Payne, E. M. F. (1981) 'A taxonomic approach to the lexis of science', in *English for Academic and Technical Purposes: Studies in Honor of Louis Trimble* (23–39), Rowley, Massachusetts: Newbury House.

Goodman, K. S. and Bird, L. B. (1984) 'On the wording of texts: a study on intra-text word frequency', *Research in the Teaching of English*, **18**, 119–145.

Goodrich, H. C. (1977) 'Distractor efficiency in foreign language testing', *TESOL Quarterly*, **11**, 69–78.

Goulden, R., Nation, P. and Read, J. (1990) 'How large can a receptive vocabulary be?', *Applied Linguistics*, **11**, 341–363.

Gove, P. B. (ed.), (1963) *Webster's Third New International Dictionary*, Massachusetts: G. & C. Merriam Co.

Gradman, H. and Hanania, E. (1991) 'Language learning background factors and ESL proficiency', *Modern Language Journal*, **75**, 39–5.

Graves, M. F. (1986) 'Vocabulary learning and instruction', *Review of Research in Education*, **13**, 49–89.

Graves, M. F. (1987) 'The roles of instruction in fostering vocabulary development', in McKeown and Curtis, 165–184.

Green, J. M. and Oxford, R. (1995) 'A closer look at learning strategies, L2 proficiency and gender', *TESOL Quarterly*, **29**, 261–297.

Griffin, G. F. (1992) *Aspects of the psychology of second language vocabulary list learning*, unpublished Ph.D. thesis, Dept of Psychology, University of Warwick.

Griffin, G. F. and Harley, T. A. (1996) 'List learning of second language vocabulary', *Applied Psycholinguistics*, 17, 443–460.

Grinstead, W. J. (1915) 'An experiment in the learning of foreign words', *Journal of Educational Psychology*, 6, 242–245.

Grinstead, W. J. (1924) 'On the sources of the English vocabulary', *Teachers College Record*, 26, 32–46.

Gruneberg, M. M. (1992) 'The practical application of memory aids', in M. Gruneberg and P. Morris (eds.), *Aspects of Memory* Vol. 1, (2nd edn.), (168–195), London: Routledge.

Gruneberg, M. M. and Jacobs, G. C. (1991) 'In defence of Linkword', *Language Learning Journal*, 3, 25–29.

Gruneberg, M. M. and Pascoe, K. (1996) 'The effectiveness of the keyword method for receptive and productive foreign vocabulary learning in the elderly', *Contemporary Educational Psychology*, 21, 102–109.

Gruneberg, M. M. and Sykes, R. (1991) 'Individual differences and attitudes to the keyword method of foreign language learning', *Language Learning Journal*, 4, 60–62.

Gu Yongqi and Johnson, R. K. (1996) 'Vocabulary learning strategies and language learning outcomes', *Language Learning*, 46, 643–679.

Haastrup, K. (1985) 'Lexical inferencing – a study of procedures in reception', *Scandinavian Working Papers on Bilingualism*, 5, 63–87.

Haastrup, K. (1987) 'Using thinking aloud and retrospection to uncover learners' lexical inferencing procedures', in C. Faerch and G. Kasper (eds.), *Introspection in Second Language Research* (197–212), Clevedon: Multilingual Matters.

Haastrup, K. (1989) *Lexical inferencing procedures, Part 1 and Part 2*, Copenhagen: Handelshojskolen i Kobenhavn.

Hafiz, F. M. and Tudor, I. (1989) 'Extensive reading and the development of language skills', *ELT Journal*, 43, 4–13.

Hafiz, F. M. and Tudor, I. (1990) 'Graded readers as an input medium in L2 learning', *System*, 18, 31–42.

Hafner, L. E. (1965) 'A one-month experiment in teaching context aids in fifth grade', *Journal of Educational Research*, 58, 472–474.

Hafner, L. E. (1967) 'Using context to determine meanings in high school and college', *Journal of Reading*, 10, 491–498.

Halff, H. M., Ortony, A. and Anderson, R. C. (1976) 'A context-sensitive representation of word meanings', *Memory and Cognition*, 4, 378–383.

Hall, J. W. (1988) 'On the utility of the keyword mnemonic for vocabulary learning', *Journal of Educational Psychology*, 80, 554–562.

Hall, S. J. (1991) *The effect of split information tasks on the acquisition of mathematics vocabulary*, unpublished M.A. thesis, Victoria University of Wellington, New Zealand.

Hall, S. J. (1992) 'Using split information tasks to learn Mathematics vocabulary', *Guidelines*, 14, 72–77.

Halliday, M. A. K. (1994) *An Introduction to Functional Grammar*, London: Edward Arnold.

Halliday, M. A. K. and Hasan, R. (1976) *Cohesion in English*, London: Longman.

Hammerly, H. (1982) 'Contrastive phonology and error analysis', *IRAL*, **20**, 17–32.

Harley, B. and King, M. L. (1989) 'Verb lexis in the written compositions of young L2 learners', *Studies in Second Language Acquisition*, **11**, 415–436.

Harrington, M. (1994) 'CompLex: a tool for the development of L2 vocabulary knowledge', *Journal of Artificial Intelligence in Education*, **5**, 481–499.

Harris, D. P. (1970) 'Report on an experimental group administered memory span test', *TESOL Quarterly*, **4**, 203–213.

Hartmann, R. R. K. (1981) 'Style values: linguistic approaches and lexicographical practice', *Applied Linguistics*, **2**, 263–273.

Hartmann, R. R. K. (1982) 'Reviews of Chambers dictionaries', *System*, **10**, 85–86.

Hartmann, R. R. K. (1992) 'Lexicography, with particular reference to English learners' dictionaries', *Language Teaching*, **25**, 151–159.

Harvey, K. and Yuill, D. (1997) 'A study of the use of a monolingual pedagogical dictionary by learners of English engaged in writing', *Applied Linguistics*, **18**, 253–278.

Harwood, F. W. and Wright, A. M. (1956) 'Statistical study of English word formation', *Language*, **32**, 260–273.

Haynes, M. (1993) 'Patterns and perils of guessing in second language reading', in Huckin, Haynes and Coady, 46–64.

Haynes, M. and Baker, I. (1993) 'American and Chinese readers learning from lexical familiarization in English text', in Huckin, Haynes and Coady, 130–152.

Henning, G. (1991) 'A study of the effects of contextualization and familiarization on responses to the TOEFL vocabulary test items', *TOEFL Research Report, 35*. Princeton, New Jersey: Educational Testing Service.

Herbst, T. (1996) 'On the way to the perfect learners' dictionary: a first comparison of OALD5, LDOCE3, COBUILD2, and CIDE', *International Journal of Lexicography*, **9**, 321–357.

Herman, P. A., Anderson, R. C., Pearson, P. D. and Nagy, W. E. (1987) 'Incidental acquisition of word meaning from expositions with varied text features', *Reading Research Quarterly*, **22**, 263–284.

Higa, M. (1963) 'Interference effects of intralist word relationships in verbal learning', *Journal of Verbal Learning and Verbal Behavior*, **2**, 170–175.

Higa, M. (1965) 'The psycholinguistic concept of "difficulty" and the teaching of foreign language vocabulary', *Language Learning*, **15**, 167–179.

Higgins, J. J. (1966) 'Hard facts', *ELT Journal*, **21**, 55–60.

Hill, D. R. (1997) 'Survey review: graded readers', *ELT Journal*, **51**, 57–81.

Hill, D. R. and Thomas, H. R. (1988a) 'Survey review: graded readers (Part 1)', *ELT Journal*, **42**, 44–52.

Hill, D. R. and Thomas, H. R. (1988b) 'Survey review: graded readers (Part 2)', *ELT Journal*, **42**, 124–136.

Hill, D. R. and Thomas, H. R. (1989) 'Seven series of graded readers', *ELT Journal*, **43**, 221–231.

Hill, L. A. (1969) 'Delayed copying', *ELT Journal*, **23**, 238–239.

Hindmarsh, R. (1980) *Cambridge English Lexicon*, Cambridge: Cambridge University Press.

Hirsh, D. (1992) *The vocabulary demands and vocabulary learning opportunities in short novels*, unpublished M.A. thesis, Victoria University of Wellington.

Hirsh, D. and Nation, P. (1992) 'What vocabulary size is needed to read unsimplified texts for pleasure?', *Reading in a Foreign Language*, **8**, 689–696.

Hoey, M. (1983) *On the Surface of Discourse*, London: Allen and Unwin.

Hoey, M. (1991) *Patterns of Lexis in Text*, Oxford: Oxford University Press.

Holley, F. M. (1973) 'A study of vocabulary learning in context: the effect of new-word density in German reading materials', *Foreign Language Annals*, **6**, 339–347.

Holley, F. M. and King, J. K. (1971) 'Vocabulary glosses in foreign language reading materials', *Language Learning*, **21**, 213–219.

Homburg, T. J. and Spaan, M. C. (1982) 'ESL reading proficiency assessment: testing strategies', in M. Hines and W. Rutherford (eds.), *On TESOL '81* (25–33), Washington: TESOL.

Honeyfield, J. (1977) 'Word frequency and the importance of context in vocabulary learning', *RELC Journal*, **8**, 35–42.

Horst, M., Cobb, T. and Meara, P. (1998) 'Beyond a Clockwork Orange: acquiring second language vocabulary through reading', *Reading in a Foreign Language*, **11**, 207–223.

Hu, M. and Nation, I. S. P. (in press) 'Vocabulary density and reading comprehension', *Reading in a Foreign Language*.

Huang Xiao-hua and van Naerssen, M. (1987) 'Learning strategies for oral communication', *Applied Linguistics*, **8**, 287–307.

Hubbard, P., Coady, J., Graney, J., Mokhtari, K. and Magoto, J. (1986) 'Report on a pilot study of the relationship of high-frequency vocabulary knowledge and reading proficiency in ESL readers', *Ohio University Papers in Linguistics and Language Teaching*, **8**, 48–57.

Huckin, T. and Bloch, J. (1993) 'Strategies for inferring word meanings: a cognitive model', in Huckin, Haynes and Coady, 153–178.

Huckin, T., Haynes, M. and Coady, J. (eds.), (1993) *Second Language Reading and Vocabulary*, Norwood, New Jersey: Ablex.

Hulme, C., Maughan, S. and Brown, G. D. A. (1991) 'Memory for familiar and unfamiliar words: evidence for a long-term memory contribution to short-term memory span', *Journal of Memory and Language*, **30**, 685–701.

Hulstijn, J. H. (1988) 'Experiments with semi-artificial input in second language acquisition research', in B. Hammarberg (ed.) *Language Learning and Learner Language*, Papers from a Conference held in Stockholm and Åbo 17–18 October 1988, Scandinavian Working Papers on Bilingualism issued by the Centre for Research on Bilingualism, University of Stockholm, 8, 28–40.

Hulstijn, J. H. (1992) 'Retention of inferred and given word meanings: experiments in incidental vocabulary learning', in Arnaud and Béjoint, 113–125.

Hulstijn, J. H. (1993) 'When do foreign-language readers look up the meaning of unfamiliar words? The influence of task and learner variables', *Modern Language Journal*, **77**, 139–147.

Hulstijn, J. H. (2001) 'Intentional and incidental second-language vocabulary learning: a reappraisal of elaboration, rehearsal and automaticity', in P. Robinson (ed.), *Cognition and Second Language Instruction*. Cambridge: Cambridge University Press.

Hulstijn, J. H., Hollander, M. and Greidanus, T. (1996) 'Incidental vocabulary learning by advanced foreign language students: the influence of marginal glosses, dictionary use, and reoccurrence of unknown words', *Modern Language Journal*, **80**, 327–339.

Hwang Kyongho (1989) *Reading newspapers for the improvement of vocabulary and reading skills*, unpublished MA thesis, Victoria University of Wellington.

Hwang K. and Nation, P. (1989) 'Reducing the vocabulary load and encouraging vocabulary learning through reading newspapers', *Reading in a Foreign Language*, **6**, 323–335.

Ilson, R. (1962) 'The dicto-comp: a specialized technique for controlling speech and writing in language learning', *Language Learning*, **12**, 299–301.

Ilson, R. (1983) 'Etymological information: can it help our students?', *ELT Journal*, **37**, 76–82.

Ivanič, R. (1991) 'Nouns in search of a context: a study of nouns with both open- and closed-system characteristics', *IRAL*, **29**, 93–114.

Jacobs, G. M., Dufon, P. and Fong Cheng Hong (1994) 'L1 and L2 vocabulary glosses in L2 reading passages: their effectiveness for increasing comprehension and vocabulary knowledge', *Journal of Research in Reading*, **17**, 19–28.

Jacobs, H. L., Zingraf, S. A., Wormuth, D. R., Hartfiel, V. F. and Hughey, J. B. (1981) *Testing ESL Composition: a practical approach*, Rowley, Massachusetts: Newbury House.

Jacoby, L. L., Craik, F. J. M. and Begg, J. (1979) 'Effects of decision difficulty on recognition and recall', *Journal of Verbal Learning and Verbal Behavior*, **18**, 585–600.

James, M. (1996) *Improving second language reading comprehension: a computer-assisted vocabulary development approach*, unpublished Ph.D. thesis, University of Hawaii.

Jenkins, J. R. and Dixon, R. (1983) 'Vocabulary learning', *Contemporary Educational Psychology*, **8**, 237–260.

Jenkins, J. R., Matlock, B. and Slocum, T. A. (1989) 'Two approaches to vocabulary instruction: the teaching of individual word meanings and practice in deriving word meanings from context', *Reading Research Quarterly*, **24**, 215–235.

Jenkins, J. R., Stein, M. L. and Wysocki, K. (1984) 'Learning vocabulary through reading', *American Educational Research Journal*, **21**, 767–787.

Jenkins, S. (1993) *The vocabulary burden of controlled and uncontrolled reading materials used with beginning ESL readers*, unpublished MA thesis, Victoria University of Wellington.

Joe, A. (1994) *Generative use and vocabulary learning*, unpublished MA thesis, Victoria University of Wellington.

Joe, A. (1995) 'Text-based tasks and incidental vocabulary learning', *Second Language Research*, **11**, 149–158.

Joe, A. (1998) 'What effects do text-based tasks promoting generation have on incidental vocabulary acquisition?', *Applied Linguistics*, **19**, 357–377.

Johansson, S. and Hofland, K. (1989) *Frequency Analysis of English Vocabulary and Grammar*, Vols. 1 & 2, Oxford: Clarendon Press.

Johns, T. and Davies, F. (1983) 'Text as a vehicle for information: the classroom use of written texts in teaching reading in a foreign language', *Reading in a Foreign Language*, **1**, 1–19.

Johnson, P. (1982) 'Effects on reading comprehension of building background knowledge', *TESOL Quarterly*, **16**, 503–516.

Jordan, R. R. (1990) 'Pyramid discussions', *ELT Journal*, **44**, 46–54.

Judd, E. L. (1978) 'Vocabulary teaching and TESOL: a need for re-evaluation of existing assumptions', *TESOL Quarterly*, **12**, 71–76.

Kachroo, J. N. (1962) 'Report on an investigation into the teaching of vocabulary in the first year of English', *Bulletin of the Central Institute of English*, **2**, 67–72.

Kellerman, E. (1985) 'If at first you do succeed . . .', in S. M. Gass and C. G. Madden (eds.) (345–353).

Kellogg, G. S. and Howe, M. J. A. (1971) 'Using words and pictures in foreign language learning', *Alberta Journal of Educational Research*, **17**, 89–94.

Kelly, P. (1990) 'Guessing: no substitute for systematic learning of lexis', *System*, **18**, 199–208.

Kennedy, G. (1987) 'Expressing temporal frequency in academic English', *TESOL Quarterly*, **21**, 69–86.

Kennedy, G. (1990) 'Collocations: Where grammar and vocabulary teaching meet', in S. Anivan (ed.), *Language Teaching Methodology for the Nineties* (215–229), Singapore: RELC.

Kennedy, G. (1992) 'Preferred ways of putting things with implications for language teaching', in J. Svartvik (ed.), *Directions in Corpus Linguistics* (335–373), Trends in Linguistics: Studies and Monographs 65, Berlin: Mouton de Gruyter.

Kennedy, G. (1998) *An Introduction to Corpus Linguistics*, London: Longman.

Kennedy, G. (ed.), (1997) *Dictionary of New Zealand Sign Language*, Auckland: Auckland University Press.

Kilgarriff, A. (1997) 'Putting frequencies in the dictionary', *International Journal of Lexicography*, **10**, 135–155.

Kjellmer, G. (1982) 'Some problems relating to the study of collocations in the Brown corpus', in S. Johansson (ed.), *Computer Corpora in English Language Research* (25–33), Bergen: Norwegian Computing Centre for the Humanities.

Kjellmer, G. (1984) 'Some thoughts on collocational distinctiveness', in J. Aarts and W. Meijs (eds.), *Corpus Linguistics: Recent Developments in the Use of Computer Corpora in English Language Research* (163–171), Amsterdam: Rodopi.

Klare, G. R. (1963) *The Measurement of Readability*, Ames, Iowa: Iowa State University Press.

Knight, S. M. (1994) 'Dictionary use while reading: The effects on comprehension and vocabulary acquisition for students of different verbal abilities', *Modern Language Journal*, **78**, 285–299.

Knight, T. (1996) 'Learning vocabulary through shared tasks', *The Language Teacher*, **20**, 24–29.

Kopstein, F. F. and Roshal, S. M. (1954) 'Learning foreign vocabulary from pictures vs. words', *American Psychologist*, **9**, 407–408.

Kramsch, C. J. (1979) 'Word watching: learning vocabulary becomes a hobby', *Foreign Language Annals*, **12**, 153–158.

Kučera, H. and Francis, W. N. (1967) *A computational analysis of present-day American English*, Providence, Rhode Island: Brown University Press.

Kuhn, M. R. and Stahl, S. A. (1998) 'Teaching children to learn word meanings from context', *Journal of Literacy Research,* **30**, 119–138.

Kundu, M. (1988) 'Riddles in the ESL/EFL classroom: teaching vocabulary and structure', *Modern English Teacher*, **15**, 22–24.

Lado, R. (1965) 'Memory span as a factor in second language learning', *IRAL*, **3**, 123–129.

Lado, R., Baldwin, B. and Lobo, F. (1967) *Massive vocabulary expansion in a foreign language beyond the basic course: the effects of stimuli, timing and order of presentation*, 5–1095, Washington, DC: US Department of Health, Education and Welfare.

Lakoff, G. and Johnson, M. (1980) *Metaphors We Live By*, Chicago: University of Chicago Press.

Lameta-Tufuga, E. U. (1994) *Using the Samoan language for academic learning tasks*, unpublished MA thesis, Victoria University of Wellington.

Landauer, T. K. and Bjork, R. A. (1978) 'Optimum rehearsal patterns and name learning', in M. M. Gruneberg, P. E. Morris and R. N. Sykes (eds.), *Practical Aspects of Memory* (625–632), London: Academic Press.

Larson, D. N. and Smelley, W. A. (1972) 'Practising vocabulary', in *Becoming bilingual: a guide to language learning*, chapter 18, Practical Anthropology, Box 1041, New Canaan, Connecticut, 06840.

Laufer, B. (1988) 'The concept of "synforms" (similar lexical forms) in vocabulary acquisition', *Language and Education*, **2**, 113–132.

Laufer, B. (1989a) 'A factor of difficulty in vocabulary learning: deceptive transparency', *AILA Review*, **6**, 10–20.

Laufer, B. (1989b) 'What percentage of text-lexis is essential for comprehension?', in C. Lauren and M. Nordman (eds.), *Special Language: From Humans Thinking to Thinking Machines*, Clevedon: Multilingual Matters.

Laufer, B. (1991) 'Some properties of the foreign language learner's lexicon as evidenced by lexical confusions', *IRAL*, **29**, 317–330.

Laufer, B. (1992a) 'Corpus-based versus lexicographer examples in comprehension and production of new words', *EURALEX '92 – Proceedings*, 71–76.

Laufer, B. (1992b) 'How much lexis is necessary for reading comprehension?', in Arnaud and Béjoint, 126–132.

Laufer, B. (1992c) 'Reading in a foreign language: how does L2 lexical knowledge interact with the reader's general academic ability?', *Journal of Research in Reading*, **15**, 95–103.

Laufer, B. (1993) 'The effect of dictionary definitions and examples on the use and comprehension of new L2 words', *Cahiers de Lexicologie*, **63**, 131–142.

Laufer, B. (1994) 'The lexical profile of second language writing: does it change over time?', *RELC Journal*, 25, 21–33.

Laufer, B. (1995) 'Beyond 2000: a measure of productive lexicon in a second language', in L. Eubank, L. Selinker and M. Sharwood-Smith (eds.), *The Current State of Interlanguage* (265–272), Amsterdam: John Benjamins.

Laufer, B. (1998) 'The development of passive and active vocabulary: same or different?', *Applied Linguistics*, 19, 255–271.

Laufer, B. and Hadar, L. (1997) 'Assessing the effectiveness of monolingual, bilingual and "bilingualised" dictionaries in the comprehension and production of new words', *Modern Language Journal*, 81, 189–196.

Laufer, B. and Hill, M. (2000) 'What lexical information do L2 learners select in a CALL dictionary and how does it affect retention?', *Language Learning and Technology*, 3, 2, 58–76.

Laufer, B. and Hulstijn, J. (in press) 'Incidental vocabulary acquisition in a second language: the effect of task-induced involvement load', *Applied Linguistics*.

Laufer, B. and Kimmel, M. (1997) 'Bilingualised dictionaries: How learners really use them', *System*, 25, 361–369.

Laufer, B. and Nation, P. (1995) 'Vocabulary size and use: lexical richness in L2 written production', *Applied Linguistics*, 16, 307–322.

Laufer, B. and Nation, P. (1999) 'A vocabulary size test of controlled productive ability', *Language Testing*, 16, 36–55.

Laufer, B. and Osimo, H. (1991) 'Facilitating long-term retention of vocabulary: the second-hand cloze', *System*, 19, 217–224.

Laufer, B. and Paribakht, T. S. (1998) 'The relationship between passive and active vocabularies: effects of language learning context', *Language Learning*, 48, 365–391.

Laufer, B. and Shmueli, K. (1997) 'Memorizing new words: Does teaching have anything to do with it?', *RELC Journal*, 28, 89–108.

Laufer, B. and Sim, D. D. (1985a) 'Measuring and explaining the reading threshold needed for English for academic purposes texts', *Foreign Language Annals*, 18, 405–411.

Laufer, B. and Sim, D. D. (1985b) 'Taking the easy way out: non-use and misuse of clues in EFL reading', *English Teaching Forum*, 23, 7–10, 20.

Lawson, M. J. and Hogben, D. (1996) 'The vocabulary-learning strategies of foreign-language students', *Language Learning*, 46, 101–135.

Leki, I. and Carson, J. G. (1994) 'Students' perceptions of EAP writing instruction and writing needs across the disciplines', *TESOL Quarterly*, 28, 81–101.

Levelt, W. J. M. (1989) *Speaking: From Intention to Articulation*, Massachusetts: MIT Press.

Levelt, W. J. M. (1992) 'Accessing words in speech production: Stages, processes and representations', *Cognition*, 42, 1–22.

Levenston, E. A. (1990) *The acquisition of polysemic words with both literal and metaphorical meaning,* paper delivered at AILA, Thessalonika.

Levin, J. R., Levin, M. E., Glasman, L. D. and Nordwall, M. B. (1992) 'Mnemonic vocabulary instruction: additional effectiveness evidence', *Contemporary Educational Psychology*, 17, 156–174.

Levin, J. R., McCormick, C. B., Miller, G. E., Berry, J. K. and Pressley, M. (1982) 'Mnemonic versus nonmnemonic vocabulary-learning strategies for children', *American Educational Research Journal*, 19, 121–136.

Leys, M., Fielding, L., Herman, P. and Pearson, P. D. (1983) 'Does cloze measure intersentence comprehension? A modified replication of Shanahan, Kamil, and Tobin', in J. A. Niles and L. A. Harris (eds.), *Searches for meaning in reading/language processing and instruction, 32nd Yearbook of National Reading Conference* (111–114), Rochester, New York.

Li Xiaolong (1988) 'Effects of contextual cues on inferring and remembering meanings', *Applied Linguistics*, 9, 402–413.

Linnarud, M. (1986) *Lexis in composition*, Lund: Lund Studies in English, 74.

Liu Na and Nation, I. S. P. (1985) 'Factors affecting guessing vocabulary in context', *RELC Journal*, 16, 33–42.

Long, M. (1988) 'Instructed interlanguage development', in L. M. Beebe, (ed.), *Issues in Second Language Acquisition* (115–141), New York: Newbury House.

Long, M. and Crookes, G. (1992) 'Three approaches to task-based syllabus design', *TESOL Quarterly*, 26, 27–56.

Long, M. and Ross, S. (1993) 'Modifications that preserve language and content', in M. L. Tickoo (ed.), *Simplification: Theory and Application* (193–203), RELC Anthology Series No 31.

Longman Structural Readers Handbook (1976) (2nd edn.), London: Longman.

Lorge, I. and Chall, J. (1963) 'Estimating the size of vocabularies of children and adults: an analysis of methodological issues', *Journal of Experimental Education*, 32, 147–157.

Loschky, L. and Bley-Vroman, R. (1993) 'Grammar and task-based methodology', in S. Gass and G. Crookes (eds.), *Tasks and Language Learning* (122–167), Clevedon, Avon: Multilingual Matters.

Luppescu, S. and Day, R. R. (1993) 'Reading, dictionaries and vocabulary learning', *Language Learning*, 43, 263–287.

Lynn, R. W. (1973) 'Preparing word lists: a suggested method', *RELC Journal*, 4, 25–32.

MacFarquhar, P. D. and Richards, J. C. (1983) 'On dictionaries and definitions', *RELC Journal*, 14, 111–124.

Manzo, A. V. (1970) 'CAT – a game for extending vocabulary and knowledge of allusions', *Journal of Reading*, 13, 367–369.

Marco, M. J. L. (1998) 'Procedural vocabulary as a device to organise meaning and discourse', *Australian Review of Applied Linguistics*, 21, 57–70.

Marslen-Wilson, W., Tyler, L., Waksler, R. and Older, L. (1994) 'Morphology and meaning in the English mental lexicon', *Psychological Review*, 101, 3–33.

Martin, A. V. (1976) 'Teaching academic vocabulary to foreign graduate students', *TESOL Quarterly*, 10, 91–97.

Maurice, K. (1983) 'The fluency workshop', *TESOL Newsletter*, 8, 83.

McCarthy, M. (1991) *Discourse Analysis for Language Teachers* (64–87), Cambridge: Cambridge University Press.

McCarthy, M. and Carter, R. (1994) *Language as Discourse* (104–117), London: Longman.

McComish, J. (1990) 'The word spider: a technique for academic vocabulary learning in curriculum areas', *Guidelines*, **12**, 26–36.

McDaniel, M. A. and Pressley, M. (1984) 'Putting the keyword method in context', *Journal of Educational Psychology*, **76**, 598–609.

McDaniel, M. A. and Pressley, M. (1989) 'Keyword and context instruction of new vocabulary meanings: effects on text comprehension and memory', *Journal of Educational Psychology*, **81**, 204–213.

McGivern, J. E. and Levin, J. R. (1983) 'The keyword method and children's vocabulary learning: an interaction with vocabulary knowledge', *Contemporary Educational Psychology*, **8**, 46–54.

McKay, S. L. (1980) 'Developing vocabulary materials with a computer corpus', *RELC Journal*, **11**, 77–87.

McKenzie, M. (1990) 'Letting lexis come from the learner: a word in the hand is worth two in the bush', *English Teaching Forum*, **28**, 13–16.

McKeown, M. G. (1985) 'The acquisition of word meaning from context by children of high and low ability', *Reading Research Quarterly*, **20**, 482–496.

McKeown, M. G. (1993) 'Creating effective definitions for young word learners', *Reading Research Quarterly*, **28**, 17–31.

McKeown, M. G., Beck, I. L., Omanson, R. G. and Pople, M. T. (1985) 'Some effects of the nature and frequency of vocabulary instruction on the knowledge and use of words', *Reading Research Quarterly*, **20**, 522–535.

McKeown, M. G. and Curtis, M. E. (eds.), (1987) *The Nature of Vocabulary Acquisition*, Mahwah, New Jersey: Lawrence Erlbaum Associates.

McLaughlin, B. (1990) 'Restructuring', *Applied Linguistics*, **11**, 113–128.

McWilliam, N. (1998) *What's in a Word? Vocabulary Development in Multilingual Classrooms*, Stoke on Trent: Trentham Books.

Meara, P. (1989) 'Word power and how to assess it', *SELF*, **1**, 20–24.

Meara, P. (1990a) 'A note on passive vocabulary', *Second Language Research*, **6**, 150–154.

Meara, P. (1990b) 'Some notes on the Eurocentres vocabulary tests', *AFinLA Yearbook 1990*, **48**, 103–113.

Meara, P. (1991) *Scoring a YES/NO vocabulary test*, unpublished paper, http://www.swan.ac.uk/cals/

Meara, P. and Buxton, B. (1987) 'An alternative to multiple choice vocabulary tests', *Language Testing*, **4**, 142–151.

Meara, P. and Jones, G. (1987) 'Tests of vocabulary size in English as a foreign language', *Polyglot*, **8**, *Fiche* 1.

Meara, P. and Jones, G. (1990) *Eurocentres Vocabulary Size Test 10KA*, Zurich: Eurocentres.

Meara, P., Lightbown, P. and Halter, R. H. (1997) 'Classrooms as lexical environments', *Language Teaching Research*, **1**, 28–47.

Melka Teichroew, F. J. (1982) 'Receptive vs. productive vocabulary: a survey', *Interlanguage Studies Bulletin* (Utrecht), **6**, 5–33.

Memory, D. M. (1990) 'Teaching technical vocabulary: before, during, or after the reading assignment?', *Journal of Reading Behavior*, **22**, 39–53.

Meyer, P. G. (1990) *Non-technical vocabulary in technical language*, paper delivered at AILA congress in Thessalonika.

Mezynski, K. (1983) 'Issues concerning the acquisition of knowledge: effects of vocabulary training on reading comprehension', *Review of Educational Research*, 53, 253–279.

Mhone, Y. W. (1988) '". . . It's My Word, Teacher!"', *English Teaching Forum*, 26, 48–51.

Miller, G. A. (1956) 'The magical number seven, plus or minus two: some limits on our capacity for processing information', *Psychological Review*, 63, 81–97.

Miller, G. A. (1999) 'On knowing a word', *Annual Review of Psychology*, 50, 1–19.

Miller, G. A. and Fellbaum, C. (1991) 'Semantic networks in English', *Cognition*, 41, 197–229.

Miller, G. A. and Gildea, P. M. (1987) 'How children learn words', *Scientific American*, 257, 86–91.

Miller, G. A. and Wakefield, P. C. (1993) 'Commentary on Anglin's analysis of vocabulary growth', in Anglin, 167–175.

Mishima, T. (1967) 'An experiment comparing five modalities of conveying meaning for the teaching of foreign language vocabulary', *Dissertation Abstracts*, 27, 3030 3031A.

Moir, J. (1996) *Task awareness and learning effectiveness: a case study of ten learners' perceptions of a vocabulary learning task*, unpublished MA paper, LALS, Victoria University of Wellington.

Mondria, J-A. and Mondria-de Vries, S. (1994) 'Efficiently memorizing words with the help of word cards and "hand computer": theory and applications', *System*, 22, 47–57.

Mondria, J-A. and Wit-de Boer, M. (1991) 'The effects of contextual richness on the guessability and the retention of words in a foreign language', *Applied Linguistics*, 12, 249–267.

Moore, J. C. and Surber, J. R. (1992) 'Effects of context and keyword methods on second language vocabulary acquisition', *Contemporary Educational Psychology*, 17, 286–292.

Morgan, B. Q. and Oberdeck, L. M. (1930) 'Active and passive vocabulary', in E. W. Bagster-Collins (ed.), *Studies in Modern Language Teaching*, 16, 213–221, New York.

Morgan, C. L. and Bailey, W. L. (1943) 'The effect of context on learning a vocabulary', *Journal of Educational Psychology*, 34, 561–565.

Morgan, C. L. and Foltz, M. C. (1944) 'The effect of context on learning a French vocabulary', *Journal of Educational Research*, 38, 213–216.

Morrison, L. (1996) 'Talking about words: a study of French as a second language learners' lexical inferencing procedures', *Canadian Modern Language Journal*, 53, 41–75.

Moseley, D. (1994) 'From theory to practice: errors and trials', in Brown and Ellis, 459–479.

Murphey, T. (1992) 'The discourse of pop songs', *TESOL Quarterly*, 26, 770–774.

Myles, F., Hooper, J. and Mitchell, R. (1998) 'Rote or rule? Exploring the role of formulaic language in classroom foreign language learning', *Language Learning*, 48, 323–363.

Myong H. K. (1995) 'Glossing in incidental and intentional learning of foreign language vocabulary and reading', *University of Hawaii Working Papers in ESL*, **13**, 49–94.

Nagy, W. E. (1997) 'On the role of context in first- and second-language learning', in Schmitt and McCarthy, 64–83.

Nagy, W. E. and Anderson, R. C. (1984) 'How many words are there in printed school English?', *Reading Research Quarterly*, **19**, 304–330.

Nagy, W. E., Anderson, R. C. and Herman, P. A. (1987) 'Learning word meanings from context during normal reading', *American Educational Research Journal*, **24**, 237–270.

Nagy, W. E., Anderson, R. C., Schommer, M., Scott, J. A. and Stallman, A. (1989) 'Morphological families in the internal lexicon', *Reading Research Quarterly*, **24**, 263–282.

Nagy, W. E., Diakidoy, I. N. and Anderson, R. C. (1993) 'The acquisition of morphology: learning the contribution of suffixes to the meanings of derivatives', *Journal of Reading Behavior*, **25**, 155–169.

Nagy, W. E., Herman, P. and Anderson, R. C. (1985) 'Learning words from context', *Reading Research Quarterly*, **20**, 233–253.

Nation, I. S. P. (1977) 'The combining arrangement: some techniques', *Modern Language Journal*, **61**, 89–94.

Nation, I. S. P. (1978a) '"What is it?": a multipurpose language teaching technique', *English Teaching Forum*, **16**, 20–23, 32.

Nation, I. S. P. (1978b) 'Translation and the teaching of meaning: some techniques', *ELT Journal*, **32**, 171–175.

Nation, I. S. P. (1979) 'The curse of the comprehension question: some alternatives', *Guidelines: RELC Journal Supplement*, **2**, 85–103.

Nation, I. S. P. (1982) 'Beginning to learn foreign vocabulary: a review of the research', *RELC Journal*, **13**, 14–36.

Nation, I. S. P. (1983) 'Testing and teaching vocabulary', *Guidelines*, **5**, 12–25.

Nation, I. S. P. (1984) 'Understanding paragraphs', *Language Learning and Communication*, **3**, 61–68.

Nation, I. S. P. (1989) 'Dictionaries and language learning', in M. L. Tickoo (ed.), *Learners' Dictionaries: State of the Art* (65–71), RELC Anthology Series, 23, SEAMEO Singapore: Regional Language Centre.

Nation, I. S. P. (1990) *Teaching and Learning Vocabulary*, Massachusetts: Newbury House.

Nation, I. S. P. (1991a) 'Dictation, dicto-comp and related techniques', *English Teaching Forum*, **29**, 12–14.

Nation, I. S. P. (1991b) 'Managing group discussion: problem-solving tasks', *Guidelines*, **13**, 1–10.

Nation, I. S. P. (1993a) 'Measuring readiness for simplified material: a test of the first 1,000 words of English' in M. L. Tickoo (ed.), *Simplification: Theory and Application* (193–203), RELC Anthology Series, 31.

Nation, I. S. P. (1993b) 'Predicting the content of texts', *The TESOLANZ Journal*, **1**, 37–46.

Nation, I. S. P. (1993c) 'Using dictionaries to estimate vocabulary size: essential, but rarely followed, procedures', *Language Testing*, **10**, 27–40.

Nation, I. S. P. (1994) 'Morphology and language learning', in R. E. Asher (ed.),

The Encyclopaedia of Language and Linguistics (2582–2585), Pergamon Press: Oxford.

Nation, I. S. P. (1997) 'The language learning benefits of extensive reading', *The Language Teacher*, 21, 5, 13–16.

Nation, I. S. P. (2000a) 'Learning vocabulary in lexical sets: dangers and guidelines', *TESOL Journal*, 9, 2, 6–10.

Nation, I. S. P. (2000b) 'Designing and improving a language course', *English Teaching Forum*, 38, 4, 2–11.

Nation, I. S. P. (ed.), (1994) *New Ways in Teaching Vocabulary*, Alexandria, Virginia: TESOL.

Nation, I. S. P. and Coady, J. (1988) 'Vocabulary and reading', in Carter and McCarthy, 97–110.

Nation, I. S. P. and Heatley, A. (1996) *VocabProfile, Word, and Range: programs for processing text*, LALS, Victoria University of Wellington, New Zealand.

Nation, I. S. P. and Hwang K. (1995) 'Where would general service vocabulary stop and special purposes vocabulary begin?', *System*, 23, 35–41.

Nation, P. and Wang, K. (1999) 'Graded readers and vocabulary', *Reading in a Foreign Language*, 12, 355–380.

Nattinger, J. and DeCarrico, J. (1989) *Lexical phrases, speech acts and teaching conversation*, unpublished manuscript.

Nesi, H. and Meara, P. (1994) 'Patterns of misinterpretation in the productive use of EFL dictionary definitions', *System*, 22, 1–15.

Neubach, A. and Cohen, A. (1988) 'Processing strategies and problems encountered in the use of dictionaries', *Dictionaries: Journal of the Dictionary Society of North America*, 10, 1–19.

Neuman, S. B. and Koskinen, P. (1992) 'Captioned television as comprehensible input: Effects of incidental word learning from context for language minority students', *Reading Research Quarterly*, 27, 95–106.

Newton, J. (1993) *The relationship between pedagogic tasks, interaction and language learning*, unpublished Ph.D. thesis, Victoria University of Wellington.

Newton, J. (1995) 'Task-based interaction and incidental vocabulary learning: a case study', *Second Language Research*, 11, 159–177.

Newton, J. (forthcoming) 'The influence of task type on qualitative differences in negotiation of meaning in native non-native interaction', in J. Deen and L. Holliday (eds.), *Interaction and Negotiation of Meaning in a Second Language*.

Newton, J. and Kennedy, G. (1996) 'Effects of communication tasks on the grammatical relations marked by second language learners', *System*, 24, 309–322.

Nist, S. L. and Olejnik, S. (1995) 'The role of context and dictionary definitions on varying levels of word knowledge', *Reading Research Quarterly*, 30, 172–193.

Nurweni, A. and Read, J. (1999) 'The English vocabulary knowledge of Indonesian university students', *English for Specific Purposes*, 18, 161–175.

O'Dell, F. (1997) 'Incorporating vocabulary into the syllabus', in Schmitt and McCarthy, 258–278.

Ostyn, P. and Godin, P. (1985) 'RALEX: an alternative approach to language teaching', *Modern Language Journal*, 69, 346–355.

Ott, C. E., Butler, D. C., Blake, R. S. and Ball, J. P. (1973) 'The effect of interactive-image elaboration on the acquisition of foreign language vocabulary', *Language Learning*, 23, 197–206.

Oxford, R. (1990) *Language Learning Strategies: What every Teacher should Know*, New York: Newbury House/Harper and Row.

Oxford, R. and Crookall, D. (1990) 'Vocabulary learning: a critical analysis of techniques', *TESL Canada Journal*, 7, 9–30.

Paivio, A. and Desrochers, A. (1981) 'Mnemonic techniques in second-language learning', *Journal of Educational Psychology*, 73, 780–795.

Palincsar, A. S. and Brown, A. L. (1986) 'Interactive teaching to promote independent learning from text', *The Reading Teacher*, 40, 771–777.

Palmberg, R. (1988a) 'Computer games and foreign-language learning', *ELT Journal*, 42, 247–251.

Palmberg, R. (1988b) 'On lexical inferencing and language distance', *Journal of Pragmatics*, 12, 207–214.

Palmer, D. M. (1982) 'Information transfer for listening and reading', *English Teaching Forum*, 20, 29–33.

Palmer, H. E. (1921) *The Principles of Language Study*, London: George G. Harrap & Co.

Palmer, H. E. (1933) *Second Interim Report on English Collocations*, Tokyo: Kaitakusha.

Pany, D. and Jenkins, J. R. (1978) 'Learning word meanings: a comparison of instructional procedures', *Learning Disability Quarterly*, 1, 21–32.

Pany, D., Jenkins, J. R. and Schreck, J. (1982) 'Vocabulary instruction: effects on word knowledge and reading comprehension', *Learning Disability Quarterly*, 5, 202–215.

Papagno, C., Valentine, T. and Baddeley, A. (1991) 'Phonological short-term memory and foreign-language vocabulary learning', *Journal of Memory and Language*, 30, 331–347.

Paribakht, T. S. and Wesche, M. B. (1993) 'Reading comprehension and second language development in a comprehension-based ESL programme', *TESL Canada Journal*, 11, 9–27.

Paribakht, T. S. and Wesche, M. B. (1996) 'Enhancing vocabulary acquisition through reading: a hierarchy of text-related exercise types', *The Canadian Modern Language Review*, 52, 155–178.

Parker, K. and Chaudron, C. (1987) 'The effects of linguistic simplifications and elaborative modifications on L2 comprehension', *University of Hawaii Working Papers in ESL*, 6, 107–133.

Parkin, M. (1990) *Macroeconomics*, Massachusetts: Addison-Wesley.

Parry, K. (1991) 'Building a vocabulary through academic reading', *TESOL Quarterly*, 25, 629–653.

Pauk, W. (1984) *How to Study in College*, Boston: Houghton Mifflin.

Paul, P. V., Stallman, A. C. and O'Rourke, J. P. (1990) 'Using three test formats to assess good and poor readers' word knowledge', *Technical Report No. 509 of the Center for the Study of Reading*, University of Illinois at Urbana-Champaign.

Pawley, A. and Syder, F. H. (1983) 'Two puzzles for linguistic theory: nativelike selection and nativelike fluency', in J. C. Richards and R. W. Schmidt (eds.), *Language and Communication* (191–225), London: Longman.

Penno, J. F., Wilkinson, I. A. G. and Moore, D. W. (forthcoming) *Vocabulary acquisition from teacher explanation and repeated listening to stories: Do they overcome the Matthew effect?*

Pickard, N. (1996) 'Out of class language learning strategies', *ELT Journal*, 50, 150–159.

Pickering, M. (1982) 'Context-free and context-dependent vocabulary learning: an experiment', *System*, 10, 79–83.

Pienemann, M. (1985) 'Learnability and syllabus construction', in K. Hyltenstam and M. Pienemann (eds.), *Modelling and Assessing Second Language Development* (23–75), Clevedon, Avon: Multilingual Matters.

Pierson, H. (1989) 'Using etymology in the classroom', *ELT Journal*, 43, 57–63.

Pimsleur, P. (1967) 'A memory schedule', *Modern Language Journal*, 51, 73–75.

Pitts, M., White, H. and Krashen, S. (1989) 'Acquiring second language vocabulary through reading: a replication of the Clockwork Orange study using second language acquirers', *Reading in a Foreign Language*, 5, 271–275.

Porte, G. (1988) 'Poor language learners and their strategies for dealing with new vocabulary', *ELT Journal*, 42, 167–172.

Praninskas, J. (1972) *American University Word List*, London: Longman.

Pressley, M., Levin, J. R., Hall, J., Miller, G. and Berry, J. K. (1980) 'The keyword method and foreign word acquisition', *Journal of Experimental Psychology: Human Learning and Memory*, 5, 22–29.

Pressley, M., Levin, J. R., Kuiper, N., Bryant, S. and Michener, S. (1982) 'Mnemonic versus nonmnemonic vocabulary-learning strategies: additional comparisons', *Journal of Educational Psychology*, 74, 693–707.

Pressley, M., Levin, J. R. and McCormick, C. B. (1980) 'Young children's learning of foreign language vocabulary: a sentence variation of the keyword method', *Contemporary Educational Psychology*, 5, 22–29.

Pressley, M., Levin, J. R. and Miller, G. E. (1981) 'The keyword method and children's learning of foreign vocabulary with abstract meanings', *Canadian Journal of Psychology*, 35, 283–287.

Pressley, M., Levin, J. R. and Miller, G. E. (1982) 'The keyword method compared to alternative vocabulary learning strategies', *Contemporary Educational Psychology*, 7, 50–60.

Pressley, M., Samuel, J., Hershey, M., Bishop, S. and Dickinson, D. (1981) 'Use of a mnemonic technique to teach young children foreign language vocabulary', *Contemporary Educational Psychology*, 6, 110–116.

Prince, P. (1996) 'Second language vocabulary learning: the role of context versus translations as a function of proficiency', *Modern Language Journal*, 80, 478–493.

Quinn, G. (1968) *The English vocabulary of some Indonesian university entrants*, Salatiga: IKIP Kristen Satya Watjana.

Rankin, E. F. and Overholser, B. M. (1969) 'Reaction of intermediate grade children to contextual clues', *Journal of Reading Behavior*, 1, 50–73.

Rasinski, T. V. (1989) 'Fluency for everyone: incorporating fluency instruction in the classroom', *The Reading Teacher*, 42, 690–693.

Read, J. (1988) 'Measuring the vocabulary knowledge of second language learners', *RELC Journal*, **19**, 12–25.

Read, J. (1995) 'Refining the word associates format as a measure of depth of vocabulary knowledge', *New Zealand Studies in Applied Linguistics*, **1**, 1–17.

Read, J. (2000) *Assessing Vocabulary*, Cambridge: Cambridge University Press.

Renouf, A. and Sinclair, J. (1991) 'Collocational frameworks in English', in K. Aijmer and B. Altenberg (eds.), *English Corpus Linguistics* (128–143), Harlow: Longman.

Richards, B. J. and Malvern, D. D. (1997) *Quantifying lexical diversity in the study of language development*, University of Reading: The New Bulmershe Papers.

Richards, J. C. and Taylor, A. (1992) 'Defining strategies in folk definitions', *Working Papers of the Department of English, City Polytechnic of Hong Kong*, **4**, 1–8.

Richardson, M. (1990) 'Vocabulary learning hypercard stack', *Macademia*, December 1990, 9.

Robb, T. N. and Susser, B. (1989) 'Extensive reading vs skill building in an EFL context', *Reading in a Foreign Language*, **5**, 239–251.

Roberts, A. H. (1965) *A Statistical Linguistic Analysis of American English*, Janua Linguarum, Series Practica 8, The Hague: Mouton & Co.

Robinson, P. J. (1989) 'A rich view of lexical competence', *ELT Journal*, **43**, 274–282.

Rodgers, T. S. (1969) 'On measuring vocabulary difficulty: an analysis of item variables in learning Russian–English vocabulary pairs', *IRAL*, **7**, 327–343.

Royer, J. M. (1973) 'Memory effects for test-like events during acquisition of foreign language vocabulary', *Psychological Reports*, **32**, 195–198.

Rudzka, B., Channell, J., Putseys, Y. and Ostyn, P. (1981) *The Words You Need*, London: Macmillan.

Ruhl, C. (1989) *On Monosemy: a Study in Linguistic Semantics*, Albany: State University of New York Press.

Rye, J. (1985) 'Are cloze items sensitive to constraints across sentences? A review', *Journal of Research in Reading (UKRA)*, **8**, 94–105.

Saemen, R. A. (1970) *Effects of commonly known meanings on determining obscure meanings of multiple-meaning words in context*, Washington, DC: Office of Education (DHEW).

Salager, F. (1983) 'The lexis of fundamental medical English: classificatory framework and rhetorical function (a statistical approach)', *Reading in a Foreign Language*, **1**, 54–64.

Salager, F. (1984) 'The English of medical literature research project', *English for Specific Purposes, Oregon State University*, **87**, 5–7.

Sanaoui, R. (1995) 'Adult learners' approaches to learning vocabulary in second languages', *Modern Language Journal*, **79**, 15–28.

Sanaoui, R. (1996) 'Processes of vocabulary instruction in 10 French as a second language classrooms', *The Canadian Modern Language Review*, **52**, 179–199.

Santos, T. (1988) 'Professors' reactions to the academic writing of nonnative-speaking students', *TESOL Quarterly*, **22**, 69–90.

Saragi, T., Nation, I. S. P. and Meister, G. F. (1978) 'Vocabulary learning and reading', *System*, **6**, 72–78.

Schatz, E. K. and Baldwin, R. S. (1986) 'Context clues are unreliable predictors of word meaning', *Reading Research Quarterly*, **21**, 439–453.

Schmidt, R. W. (1990) 'The role of consciousness in second language learning', *Applied Linguistics*, **11**, 129–158.

Schmidt, R. W. (1992) 'Psychological mechanisms underlying second language fluency', *Studies in Second Language Acquisition*, **14**, 357–385.

Schmidt, R. W. and Frota, S. (1986) 'Developing basic conversational ability in a second language: a case study of an adult learner of Portuguese', in R. Day (ed.), *Talking to Learn: Conversation in Second Language Acquisition*, Rowley, Massachusetts: Newbury House.

Schmitt, N. (2000) *Vocabulary in Language Teaching*, Cambridge: Cambridge University Press.

Schmitt, N. (1997) 'Vocabulary learning strategies', in Schmitt and McCarthy, 199–227.

Schmitt, N. and McCarthy, M. (eds.), (1997) *Vocabulary: Description, Acquisition and Pedagogy*, Cambridge: Cambridge University Press.

Schmitt, N. and Meara, P. (1997) 'Researching vocabulary through a word knowledge framework: word associations and verbal suffixes', *Studies in Second Language Acquisition*, **19**, 17–36.

Schmitt, N. and Schmitt, D. (1995) 'Vocabulary notebooks: theoretical underpinnings and practical suggestions', *ELT Journal*, **49**, 133–143.

Schmitt, N., Schmitt, D. and Clapham, C. (in press) 'Developing and exploring the behaviour of two new versions of the *Vocabulary Levels Test*', *Language Testing*.

Scholes, Robert J. (1966) 'Phonotactic Grammaticality', *Janua Linguarum, Series Minor 50*, The Hague: Mouton & Co.

Scholfield, P. J. (1981) 'Writing, vocabulary errors and the dictionary', *Guidelines*, **6**, 31–40.

Scholfield, P. J. (1982a) 'The role of bilingual dictionaries in ESL/EFL: a positive view', *Guidelines*, **4**, 84–98.

Scholfield, P. J. (1982b) 'Using the English dictionary for comprehension', *TESOL Quarterly*, **16**, 185–194.

Scholfield, P. J. (1997) 'Vocabulary reference works in foreign language learning', in Schmitt and McCarthy, 279–302.

Scholfield, P. J. and Gitsaki, C. (1996) 'What is the advantage of private instruction? The example of English vocabulary learning in Greece', *System*, **24**, 117–127.

Schonell, F. J., Meddleton, I. G. and Shaw, B. A. (1956) *A study of the oral vocabulary of adults*, Brisbane: University of Queensland Press.

Schreuder, R. and Weltens, B. (eds.), (1993) *The Bilingual Lexicon*, Amsterdam: John Benjamins Publishing Company.

Scott, J. A. and Nagy, W. E. (1997) 'Understanding the definitions of verbs', *Reading Research Quarterly*, **32**, 184–200.

Seashore, R. H. and Eckerson, L. D. (1940) 'The measurement of individual differences in general English vocabularies', *Journal of Educational Psychology*, **31**, 14–38.

Seibert, L. C. (1927) 'An experiment in learning French vocabulary', *Journal of Educational Psychology*, **18**, 294–309.

Seibert, L. C. (1930) 'An experiment on the relative efficiency of studying French vocabulary in associated pairs versus studying French vocabulary in context', *Journal of Educational Psychology*, **21**, 297–314.

Seibert, L. C. (1945) 'A study of the practice of guessing word meanings from a context', *Modern Language Journal*, **29**, 296–323.

Sen, A. L. (1983) 'Teaching vocabulary through riddles', *English Teaching Forum*, **21**, 12–17.

Service, E. (1992) 'Phonology, working memory, and foreign language learning', *The Quarterly Journal of Experimental Psychology*, **45A**, 21–50.

Shefelbine, J. L. (1990) 'Student factors related to variability in learning word meanings from context', *Journal of Reading Behavior*, **22**, 71–97.

Shu, H., Anderson, R. C. and Zhang, Z. (1995) 'Incidental learning of word meanings while reading: a Chinese and American cross-cultural study', *Reading Research Quarterly*, **30**, 76–95.

Simcock, M. (1993) 'Developing productive vocabulary using the "Ask and Answer" technique', *Guidelines*, **15**, 1–7.

Simensen, A. M. (1987) 'Adapted readers: how are they adapted?', *Reading in a Foreign Language*, **4**, 41–57.

Sinclair, J. M. (1987) 'Collocation: a progress report', in R. Steele and T. Threadgold (eds.), *Language Topics: Essays in Honour of Michael Halliday Vol. II* (319–331), John Benjamins, Amsterdam.

Sinclair, J. M. (1991) *Corpus, Concordance, Collocation*, Oxford: Oxford University Press.

Sinclair, J. M. (ed. in chief), (1995) *Collins COBUILD Dictionary* (2nd edn.). London: HarperCollins.

Sinclair, J. M. and Renouf, A. (1988) 'A lexical syllabus for language learning', in Carter and McCarthy, 140–160.

Smith, M. K. (1941) 'Measurement of the size of general English vocabulary through the elementary grades and high school', *Genetic Psychology Monographs*, **24**, 311–345.

Sokmen, A. J. (1992) 'Students as vocabulary generators', *TESOL Journal*, **1**, 16–18.

Spinelli, E. and Siskin, H. J. (1992) 'Selecting, presenting and practicing vocabulary in a culturally-authentic context', *Foreign Language Annals*, **25**, 305–315.

Spiro, R. C., Bruce, B. C. and Brewer, W. F. (eds.), (1980) *Theoretical Issues in Reading Comprehension*, New Jersey: Erlbaum.

Stahl, S. A. (1990) 'Beyond the instrumentalist hypothesis: some relationships between word meanings and comprehension', *Technical report no. 505 of the Center for the Study of Reading*, University of Illinois at Urbana-Champaign.

Stahl, S. A. and Clark, C. H. (1987) 'The effects of participatory expectations in classroom discussion on the learning of science vocabulary', *American Educational Research Journal*, 24, 541–545.

Stahl, S. A. and Fairbanks, M. M. (1986) 'The effects of vocabulary instruction: a model-based meta-analysis', *Review of Educational Research*, 56, 72–110.

Stahl, S. A. and Vancil, S. J. (1986) 'Discussion is what makes semantic maps work in vocabulary instruction', *The Reading Teacher*, 40, 62–67.

Stahl, S. A., Jacobson, M. G., Davis, C. E. and Davis, R. L. (1989) 'Prior knowledge and difficult vocabulary in the comprehension of unfamiliar text', *Reading Research Quarterly*, 24, 27–43.

Stauffer, R. G. (1942) 'A study of prefixes in the Thorndike list to establish a list of prefixes that should be taught in the elementary school', *Journal of Educational Research*, 35, 453–458.

Stein, G. (1988) 'ELT dictionaries, the teacher and the student', *JALT Journal*, 11, 36–45.

Stenstrom, A. (1990). 'Lexical items peculiar to spoken discourse', in J. Svartvik (ed.), 'The London-Lund Corpus of Spoken English: Description and Research', *Lund Studies in English* 82 (137–175), Lund: Lund University Press.

Sternberg, R. J. and Powell, J. S. (1983) 'Comprehending verbal comprehension', *American Psychologist*, 38, 878–893.

Stevens, V. (1991) 'Classroom concordancing: vocabulary materials derived from relevant, authentic text', *English for Specific Purposes*, 10, 35–46.

Stieglitz, E. L. (1983) 'A practical approach to vocabulary reinforcement', *ELT Journal*, 37, 71–75.

Stieglitz, E. L. and Stieglitz, V. S. (1981) 'SAVOR the word to reinforce vocabulary in the content areas', *Journal of Reading*, 25, 46–51.

Stoddard, G. D. (1929) 'An experiment in verbal learning', *Journal of Educational Psychology*, 20, 452–457.

Strevens, P. (1973) 'Technical, technological, and scientific English', *ELT Journal*, 27, 223–234.

Stubbs, M. (1995) 'Collocations and semantic profiles', *Functions of Language*, 2, 1, 23–55.

Summers, D. (1995) *Longman Dictionary of Contemporary English* (3rd edn.), Harlow: Longman.

Sutarsyah, C., Nation, P. and Kennedy, G. (1994) 'How useful is EAP vocabulary for ESP? A corpus-based study', *RELC Journal*, 25, 34–50.

Swain, M. (1985) 'Communicative competence: some roles of comprehensible input and comprehensible output in its development', in Gass and Madden, 235–253.

Swan, M. (1997) 'The influence of the mother tongue on second language vocabulary acquisition and use', in Schmitt and McCarthy, 156–180.

Swanborn, M. and de Glopper, K. (1999) 'Incidental word learning while reading: a meta-analysis', *Review of Educational Research*, 69, 261–285.

Swenson, E. and West, M. P. (1934) 'On the counting of new words in textbooks for teaching foreign languages', *Bulletin of the Department of Educational Research, University of Toronto*, 1.

Templin, M. (1957) 'Certain language skills in children: their development and inter-relationships', Institute of Child Welfare, monograph series no. 26, Minnesota: University of Minnesota Press.

Terrell, P., Schnorr, V., Morris, W. and Breitsprecher, R. (1991) *Collins German Dictionary*, Collins.

Thomas, H. C. R. and Hill, D. R. (1993) 'Seventeen series of graded readers', *ELT Journal*, **47**, 250–267.

Thomas, M. H. and Dieter, J. N. (1987) 'The positive effects of writing practice on integration of foreign words in memory', *Journal of Educational Psychology*, **79**, 249–253.

Thompson, G. (1987) 'Using bilingual dictionaries', *ELT Journal*, **41**, 282–286.

Thompson, G. and Ye Yiyun (1991) 'Evaluation in the reporting verbs used in academic papers', *Applied Linguistics*, **12**, 365–382.

Thorndike, E. L. (1908) 'Memory for paired associates', *Psychological Review*, **15**, 122–138.

Thorndike, E. L. (1924) 'The vocabularies of school pupils', in J. Carelton Bell (ed.), *Contributions to Education* (69–76), New York: World Book Co.

Thorndike, E. L. (1932) *Teacher's Word Book of 20,000 Words*, Columbia University: Teachers College.

Thorndike, E. L. (1941) *The teaching of English suffixes*, Columbia University: Teachers College.

Thorndike, E. L. and Lorge, I. (1944) *The Teacher's Word Book of 30,000 Words*, Columbia University: Teachers College.

Thurstun, J. and Candlin, C. N. (1998) 'Concordancing and the teaching of the vocabulary of academic English', *English For Specific Purposes*, **17**, 267–280.

Tickoo, M. L. (1987) 'New dictionaries and the ESL teacher', *Guidelines*, **9**, 57–67.

Tinkham, T. (1989) 'Rote learning, attitudes, and abilities: a comparison of Japanese and American students', *TESOL Quarterly*, **23**, 695–698.

Tinkham, T. (1993) 'The effect of semantic clustering on the learning of second language vocabulary', *System*, **21**, 371–380.

Tinkham, T. (1997) 'The effects of semantic and thematic clustering on the learning of second language vocabulary', *Second Language Research*, **13**, 138–163.

Tomaszczyk, J. (1979) 'Dictionaries: users and uses', *Glottodidactica*, **12**, 103–119.

Towell, R., Hawkins, R. and Bazergui, N. (1996) 'The development of fluency in advanced learners of French', *Applied Linguistics*, **17**, 84–119.

Treiman, R. (1994) 'Sources of information used by beginning spellers', in Brown and Ellis (eds.), 75–91.

Trimble, L. (1985) *English for Science and Technology: a Discourse Approach*, Cambridge: Cambridge University Press.

Tsang Wai-king (1996) 'Comparing the effects of reading and writing on writing performance', *Applied Linguistics*, **17**, 210–233.

Tudor, I. and Hafiz, F. (1989) 'Extensive reading as a means of input to L2 learning', *Journal of Research in Reading*, **12**, 164–178.

Tuinman, J. J. and Brady, M. E. (1974) 'How does vocabulary account for variance on reading comprehension tests? A preliminary instructional analysis', in P. Nacke (ed.), *Interaction: reading and practice for college-adult reading* (176–184), Clemson, South Carolina: National Reading Conference.

Turner, G. (1983) 'Teaching French vocabulary: a training study', *Educational Review*, 35, 81–88.

Tweissi, A. I. (1998) 'The effects of the amount and type of simplification on foreign language reading comprehension', *Reading in a Foreign Language*, 11, 191–206.

Tyler, A. and Nagy, W. (1989) 'The acquisition of English derivational morphology', *Journal of Memory and Language*, 28, 649–667.

Umbel, V. M., Pearson, B. Z., Fernandez, M. C. and Oller, D. K. (1992) 'Measuring bilingual children's receptive vocabularies', *Child Development*, 63, 1012–1020.

Ur, P. (1981) *Discussions that Work*, Cambridge: Cambridge University Press.

van Bussel, F. J. J. (1994) 'Design rules for computer-aided learning of vocabulary items in a second language', *Computers in Human Behavior*, 10, 63–76.

van Daalen Kapteijns, M. M. and Elshout Mohr, M. (1981) 'The acquisition of word meanings as a cognitive learning process', *Journal of Verbal Learning and Verbal Behavior*, 20, 386–399.

van Elsen, E., van Deun, K. and Decoo, W. (1991) 'Wordchip: the application of external versatility to an English lexical CALL program', *System*, 19, 401–417.

van Parreren, C. F. and Schouten-van Parreren, M. (1981) 'Contextual guessing: a trainable reader strategy', *System*, 9, 235–241.

Visser, A. (1989) 'Learning core meanings', *Guidelines*, 11, 10–17.

Walker, L. J. (1983) 'Word identification strategies in reading a foreign language', *Foreign Language Annals*, 16, 293–299.

Wang, A. Y. and Thomas, M. H. (1992) 'The effect of imagery-based mnemonics on the long-term retention of Chinese characters', *Language Learning*, 42, 359–376.

Wang, A. Y. and Thomas, M. H. (1995) 'Effect of keywords on long-term retention: help or hindrance?', *Journal of Educational Psychology*, 87, 468–475.

Wang, A. Y., Thomas, M. H., Inzana, C. M. and Primicerio, L. J. (1993) 'Long-term retention under conditions of intentional learning and the keyword mnemonic', *Bulletin of the Psychonomic Society*, 31, 545–547.

Ward, J. (1999) 'How large a vocabulary do EAP Engineering students need?', *Reading in a Foreign Language*, 12, 309–323.

Waring, R. (1997a) 'A comparison of the receptive and productive vocabulary sizes of some second language learners', *Immaculata (Notre Dame Seishin University, Okayama)*, 1, 53–68.

Waring, R. (1997b) 'The negative effects of learning words in semantic sets: a replication', *System*, 25, 261–274.

Watanabe, Y. (1997) 'Input, intake and retention: effects of increased processing on incidental learning of foreign vocabulary', *Studies in Second Language Acquisition*, 19, 287–307.

Watts, S. M. (1995) 'Vocabulary instruction during reading lessons in six class-rooms', *Journal of Reading Behavior*, **27**, 399–424.

Webb, W. B. (1962) 'The effects of prolonged learning on learning', *Journal of Verbal Learning and Verbal Behavior*, **1**, 173–182.

Webber, N. E. (1978) 'Pictures and words as stimuli in learning foreign language responses', *The Journal of Psychology*, **98**, 57–63.

Wesche, M. and Paribakht, T. S. (1996) 'Assessing second language vocabulary knowledge: depth versus breadth', *Canadian Modern Language Review*, **53**, 13–40.

West, M. (1935) *The New Method English Dictionary*, London: Longman, Green & Co.

West, M. (1938) 'The present position in vocabulary selection for foreign language teaching', *Modern Language Journal*, **21**, 433–437.

West, M. (1951) 'Catenizing', *ELT Journal*, **5**, 147–151.

West, M. (1953a) *A General Service List of English Words*, London: Longman, Green & Co.

West, M. (1953b) 'The technique of reading aloud to a class', *ELT Journal*, **8**, 21–24.

West, M. (1955) *Learning to Read a Foreign Language* (2nd edn.), London: Longman.

West, M. (1956) 'A plateau vocabulary for speech', *Language Learning*, **7**, 1–7.

West, M. (1960a) *New Method Readers*, London: Longman, Green and Co.

West, M. (1960b) *Teaching English in Difficult Circumstances*, London: Longman.

White, T. G., Power, M. A. and White, S. (1989) 'Morphological analysis: Implications for teaching and understanding vocabulary growth', *Reading Research Quarterly*, **24**, 283–304.

Widdowson, H. G. (1976) 'The authenticity of language data', in J. F. Fanselow and R. H. Crymes (eds.), *On TESOL '76*, Washington: TESOL.

Williams, R. (1985) 'Teaching vocabulary recognition strategies in ESP reading', *ESP Journal*, **4**, 121–131.

Willis, J. and Willis, D. (1988) *Collins COBUILD English Course*, London: Collins.

Winn, S. (1996) 'Vocabulary revitalized', *TESOL Journal*, **5**, 40.

Winter, E. O. (1977) 'A clause-relational approach to English texts: a study of some predictive lexical items in written discourse', *Instructional Science*, **6**, 1–92.

Winter, E. O. (1978) 'A look at the role of certain words in information structure', in K. P. Jones and V. Horsnell (eds.), *Informatics* 3 (85–97), London: Aslib.

Wittrock, M. C. (1974) 'Learning as a generative process', *Educational Psychologist*, **11**, 87–95.

Wittrock, M. C. (1991) 'Generative teaching of comprehension', *Elementary School Journal*, **92**, 169–184.

Wittrock, M. C., Marks, C. and Doctorow, M. (1975) 'Reading as a generative process', *Journal of Educational Psychology*, **67**, 484–489.

Wixson, K. K. (1986) 'Vocabulary instruction and children's comprehension of basal stories', *Reading Research Quarterly*, **21**, 317–329.

Wodinsky, M. and Nation, P. (1988) 'Learning from graded readers', *Reading in a Foreign Language*, 5, 155–161.

Woodeson, E. (1982) 'Communicative crosswords', *Modern English Teacher*, 10, 29–30.

Woodward, T. (1985) 'From vocabulary review to classroom dictionary', *Modern English Teacher*, 12, 29.

Woodward, T. (1988) 'Vocabulary posters', *Modern English Teacher*, 15, 31–32.

Worthington, D. and Nation, P. (1996) 'Using texts to sequence the introduction of new vocabulary in an EAP course', *RELC Journal*, 27, 1–11.

Xue Guoyi and Nation, I. S. P. (1984) 'A university word list', *Language Learning and Communication*, 3, 215–229.

Yang, H. (1986) 'A new technique for identifying scientific/technical terms and describing science texts', *Literary and Linguistic Computing*, 1, 93–103.

Yano, Y., Long, M. H., and Ross, S. (1994) 'The effects of simplified and elaborated texts on foreign language comprehension', *Language Learning*, 44, 189–219.

Yavuz, H. (1963) 'The retention of incidentally learned connotative responses', *Journal of Psychology*, 55, 409–418.

Yavuz, H. and Bousfield, W. A. (1969) 'Recall of connotative meaning', *Psychological Reports*, 5, 319–320.

Zechmeister, E. B., Chronis, A. M., Cull, W. L., D'Anna, C. A. and Healy, N. A. (1995) 'Growth of a functionally important lexicon', *Journal of Reading Behavior*, 27, 201–212.

Subject index

In this index *t* following a page reference refers to tables and *f* to figures

Author index

van Elsen, E. 108
van Daalen-Kapteijns, M. 83–4, 238, 247–8
van Parreren, C. 247, 257
Vancil, S. 65, 69, 129
Varantola, K. 282, 294
Visser, A. 102, 204

W
Wakefield, P. 363
Waksler, R. 269, 321
Walker, L. 247
Wang, A. 43, 310, 313
Wang, K. 68, 163–71, 238
Ward, J. 192
Waring, R. 32, 92, 103, 303, 306, 370, 387
Watanabe, Y. 93–4, 175–7, 253, 353
Watts, K. 234
Watts, S. 74
Weaver, K. 245
Webb, W. 298
Webber, N. 304
Weiss, R. 284
Wesche, M. 37, 149, 158–9, 357, 359
West, M. 7, 11, 15, 24, 116, 152, 163, 167, 179, 187–8,, 200, 230, 340–1, 368, 373, 381, 383, 386–7
White, H. 155, 237
White, S. 264
White, T. 264
Widdowson, H. 173

Wieland, L. 313
Wilkinson, I. 118–9
Williams, R. 85–91, 171, 217, 253
Willis, J. 386
Willis, D. 386
Winn, S. 103
Winter, E. 207, 211, 213
Wit-de-Boer, M. 253
Wittrock, M. 69, 246
Wixson, K. 157
Wodinsky, M. 165, 168–9, 339
Woodeson, E. 125
Woodward, T. 105, 107
Wormuth, D. 177, 180
Worthington, D. 193
Wright, A. 264, 267–8
Wysocki, K. 237

X
Xue, G. 12, 48, 179, 188, 193, 362

Y
Yamazaki, A. 64–5, 68, 123
Yang, H. 187, 199
Yano, Y. 173–4
Yavuz, H. 55
Ye, Y. 210
Yuill, D. , 184, 282

Z
Zechmeister, E. 9, 95, 363, 365
Zhang, Z. 236
Zingraf, S. 177, 180